THE JUDEO-CHRISTIAN VISION
AND THE MODERN CORPORATION

The Judeo-Christian Vision and the Modern Corporation

EDITED BY

Oliver F. Williams, C.S.C.

AND

John W. Houck

UNIVERSITY OF NOTRE DAME PRESS
NOTRE DAME & LONDON

Copyright © 1982
University of Notre Dame Press
Notre Dame, Indiana 46556

Library of Congress Cataloging in Publication Data

Main entry under title:

The Judeo-Christian vision and the modern corporation.

Includes index.
1. Corporations—Religious aspects—Judaism—Addresses, essays,
lectures.   2. Corporations—Religious aspects—Christianity—Addresses,
essays, lectures.   3. Corporations—Moral and ethical aspects—
Addresses, essays, lectures.   4. Industry—Social aspects—Addresses,
essays, lectures.   5. Business ethics—Addresses, essays, lectures.
6. Christianity—Addresses, essays, lectures.   7. Judaism—Addresses,
essays, lectures.   I. Williams, Oliver F.   II. Houck, John W.
HF5387.J8   261.8'5   81-40448
ISBN 0-268-01200-8   AACR2
ISBN 0-268-01201-6 (pbk.)

Manufactured in the United States of America

Contents

Preface

Except for matters of defense, the modern business corporation is as powerful and as influential as a nation-state. The corporation ranges across the country and around the world; in Peter Drucker's phrase, it does more than market products, it markets a culture. There can be no doubt that the corporation does more than draw resources from all parts of the globe, employ tens of millions, utilize talent and technology, or produce material wealth of both necessities and luxuries. In large measure, the corporation forms the vision and attitudes about the good life of those within its orbit.

Historically, Jews and Christians have had a vision of what constitutes the good life: love of God and service to others. This vision informs their view of the sort of person one ought to become and shapes their understanding of the attitudes or virtues that constitute a Judeo-Christian character. Such believers would go further and claim that their religious view of the good life is more comprehensive, more satisfying and more "true" than any other.

Does all this lead to a fundamental impasse between religion and business? If *not* a fundamental impasse, then can theologians present the religious tradition in a way that is faithful to the past and yet speaks to business people in the present? Similarly, can the professional, especially the corporate executive, find ways to bring the Judeo-Christian tradition into complex decision-making? There can be no doubt that there is great interest in these questions, in both the business and the religious communities. Certainly there was wide coverage in the national media about the Notre Dame conference where these essays were presented. The *New York Times* reported: ". . . there would be no facile resolution to the conflict between the values of a just society and the sharply opposing values of successful corporations." *The Washington Star, The National Catholic Reporter,* and *The Arizona Republic* emphasized the inevitable tension between religion and business regarding basic values and personal fulfillment. *The Los Angeles Times* discussed the importance of the tension ". . . particularly in the light of the development of capitalism into a system of mega-corporations

which exercise profound power and influence throughout the world."
The challenge of answering these questions is the subject of the essays
in this volume.

These twelve essays are part of an on-going project of interdis-
ciplinary cooperation between business and the humanities at the University of Notre Dame. Authors include economists, theologians,
philosophers, corporate executives and business scholars. Ten of the
essays were originally presented at the conference in April, 1980,
convened by Father Oliver F. Williams, C.S.C., and Professor John
Houck under the sponsorship of the University of Notre Dame's Joint
Committee on Business, Theology and Philosophy. The conference
entitled "The Judeo-Christian Vision and the Business Corporation,"
brought together some one hundred business leaders and academics
for three days of intense and fruitful discussion. Two of the essays,
authored by Christopher Stone and Kirk O. Hanson, were presented at
other times and are included in the volume because of their particular
relevance to the theme.

The University of Notre Dame Joint Committee on Business,
Theology and Philosophy was founded in 1976 by Leo V. Ryan, C.S.V.,
then Dean of the College of Business Administration, and David B.
Burrell, C.S.C., then chairperson of the Department of Theology.
Members of the committee have included: Kenneth E. Goodpaster,
Department of Philosophy; John A. Ruhe, Department of Manage-
ment; Michael Heppen, C.S.C., University Administration; Leon Mer-
tensotto, C.S.C., Department of Theology and David C. Leege, Di-
rector of the Center for the Study of Man in Contemporary Society.
Representatives from the business community include John Connor,
Vice Chairman, A. G. Becker & Co., Chicago; John Pimenta, Chairman, Multinational Corporate Development, Inc., Chicago; and David
Major, Executive Vice President, South Bend-Mishawaka Area
Chamber of Commerce. The purpose of the Joint Committee is to
build bridges between business, business studies and the humanities.
The resulting interchange has provided for cross-disciplinary cur-
riculum development, research guidance and faculty-business dialogue.

We are indebted to the members of the Joint Committee for their
generous sharing of ideas and continuous support over the years. We
want to acknowledge the special leadership of Dr. John A. Ruhe, now
of Saint Mary's College, Notre Dame, Indiana, who was for many years
the chairperson of the Joint Committee; and Dr. Kenneth E. Goodpaster, now of the Graduate School of Business Administration, Harvard
University, who with John Ruhe, convened the very helpful confer-

ence, "Policies and Persons: Dilemmas in Corporate Decision-Making," in 1978. We are also indebted to Brother Leo V. Ryan, C.S.V., who, with Dr. Ruhe and Dr. Goodpaster, was instrumental in obtaining funding to support our work.

We are most grateful for financial assistance provided by the Metropolitan Life Insurance Company, the Vilter Foundation, the Indiana Committee for the Humanities, the University of Notre Dame Center for Pastoral and Social Ministry, and the Dean's Fund, College of Business Administration, University of Notre Dame.

One of us, Oliver Williams, had the good fortune to spend the 1980-81 academic year at the Graduate School of Business of Stanford University. Kirk Hanson of the Stanford University faculty was an insightful partner in dialogue on many of the issues discussed in these pages, as well as a good friend. Also Lee Bach, Joel Demski, Alain Enthoven, William Beaver and Jeffrey Pfeffer of Stanford University provided much light on important aspects of the business world considered here.

The support of our colleagues at the University of Notre Dame Press, E. Ann Rice and John E. Ehmann, made our task much lighter. Finally, our thanks to Mary Dooley Houck, Katharine Terry Dooley, Katherine Breidenthal Grossman, Janice Coffield, and Georgeanna Caldwell for their editorial contributions.

Father Theodore M. Hesburgh, C.S.C., wrote in his introduction to *Full Value* (our earlier work): "The debate about values gives us our best hope for mastering and transcending the change and turmoil of our times." This volume is dedicated to the men and women of goodwill and competence who will pursue this debate.

> Oliver F. Williams, C.S.C.
> John W. Houck
> University of Notre Dame
> Notre Dame, Indiana   1982

Introduction

Oliver F. Williams, C.S.C.

> . . . while the law permits the Americans to do what they please,
> religion prevents them from conceiving, and forbids them to
> commit, what is rash or unjust.
>   . . . I do not know whether all Americans have a sincere faith
> in their religion — for who can search the human heart? — but I am
> certain that they hold it to be indispensable to the maintenance of
> republican institutions. This opinion is not peculiar to a class of
> citizens or to a party, but it belongs to the whole nation and to
> every rank of society.[1]

Although the above report was made some 150 years ago by the young
French lawyer, Alexis de Tocqueville, in his classic *Democracy in
America,* there is little reason to suspect that religion does not continue
to play a significant role in individual lives today. A 1981 Gallup Poll
reported that "two out of three Americans believe religion is relevant to
modern society."[2] (Twenty percent expressed no opinion, and only 15
percent said religion was "largely old-fashioned and out of date.")
What does religion have to say to the modern business corporation?
More specifically, what guidance for corporate life can one find in the
Hebrew and Christian Scriptures and the communities founded in
their names? It is these questions that provide the focus for the twelve
essays that follow.

Machiavelli would see no problem but simply a misunderstanding.
From his perspective there is a clear difference between public and
private moral standards, and to attempt to bring personal moral values
into corporate decisions would be sheer folly. Yet perhaps he saw the
magnitude of the problem. R. H. Tawney, in his world-famous *Religion
and the Rise of Capitalism,* in criticizing church leadership of the past,
may have something to say to our times.

> Granted that I should love my neighbor as myself, the questions
> which, under modern conditions of large-scale organization,

1

remain for solution are: Who precisely *is* my neighbor? and, How exactly am I to make my love for him effective in practice? . . . traditional social doctrines had no specific to offer, and were merely repeated, when, in order to be effective, they should have been thought out again from the beginning and formulated in new and living terms.[3]

Not only must religion think through its basic message to modern corporations and communicate it in terms that are likely to be heard and understood, but corporations too must be open to fresh perspectives. Although all major social institutions are losing the confidence of the American public, that is little comfort to perceptive business executives aware that the legitimacy of large corporations is being increasingly called into question. A 1978 Harris Poll, reported in *Fortune* magazine, found that only 22 percent of those interviewed expressed "a great deal of confidence" in major companies; a similar poll in 1976 had revealed that 55 percent had such confidence—two years had seen a startling decline. A national survey by Yankelovich, Skelly, and White found that in 1968 70 percent of the respondents agreed with the statement: "Business tries to strike a fair balance between profits and the interests of the public." In 1977, nine years later, only 15 percent of the respondents agreed with the same statement![4] There is a growing conviction that some corporations, by virtue of their size, wield an enormous amount of power in social, political, and economic arenas. Where they perceive power, people begin to have expectations as to how it ought to be used, and they seek to make their expectations heard. This is especially true when things are thought to be going poorly—in the area of economics or of social values (ethics).

The Problem

Executives today are living "between the times"—that is, they are caught between the time when there was a strong social consensus that the market mechanism was the best way to control business activity, and some possible future time when society has a clear consensus about just how business institutions ought to advance human welfare. We are now searching for a new consensus: economic language, which has in the past often provided the sole rationale for corporate decisions, no longer, in itself, strikes a note of legitimacy for the American public. While corporate critics speak in ethical language employing terms such as fairness, justice, rights, and so on, corporate leadership often responds solely in economic language of profit and loss. Such discussion generates much heat but little light, and the disputing parties pass like ships in the night.

The upshot of this lack of consensus on values is that business executives are often caught in the middle. One senior-level executive confided that his high-school- and college-age children seemed to be almost embarrassed that their father was a corporate leader. Needless to say, he was unsettled over their response to his work. This particular executive had just been involved in a decision to close a steel plant. While closing a plant has never been an easy matter, the outcry from the community far exceeded what the company might have expected fifteen to twenty years ago. Corporation critics argued that in considering such a move the company ought to take into account moral values and society's best interests, and not simply focus single-mindedly on its own economic welfare. Yet it was not so long ago that the market mechanism and its economic language were generally accepted as *the* key to relating managerial obligations to human welfare. What has happened to make the arguments of the critics of this company seem legitimate to so many thoughtful persons? How has the social environment changed?

How does one judge whether the plant closing was good for society? The economic arguments of the company were stated in terms of efficiency, productivity, profit and loss; there is a clear and "fair" procedure for assessing these values, and it seemed at one time to have a popular consensus. The company critics, rather than judging the closing "good" because it followed a "fair" procedure, focused exclusively on the harm the closing would cause in the immediate community. It was not "fair" because a number of the constituencies (stakeholders) of the company would suffer undue harm. While corporate leadership explained their rationale for closing the plant in terms that made sense to stockholders, their arguments had little plausibility to the other stakeholders. Employees, local communities, and institutions such as hospitals, schools, and so on, would be affected. *This is not to argue that management can never close a plant,* but rather that such decisions must be considered from many perspectives, and, finally, defended in the language that the various stakeholders are speaking.[5] Today people are much more aware of the total cost of economic decisions and their import for the social and political values of a community. In order for a society to function, there must be cooperation, and it depends upon a common agreement among the people as to how the benefits and burdens of the community's institutions will be shared. The outcry over the plant closing may be one of a number of signs that large corporations have to learn some new thinking and some new language.

In the plant-closing example, company critics were led by a coalition of religious leaders, and their language and thought patterns were founded on Hebrew and Christian Scriptures and on religious convictions of what constitutes the common good and the proper role of economic activity. Why does this language seem to resonate with so many today, and what is its vision of society? This book hopes to begin to answer these important questions.

To be sure, the social environment of business institutions includes much more than religious influences. Historian Thomas C. Cochran provides what he takes to be an abbreviated list of the significant elements of the social and physical environment of business: "family life, education, religion, law, politics, conditions of employment, and the general social structure."[6] He also notes that the social mechanism of change is not simply a one-way process, but a dynamic one. In this volume we hope to bring into relief one dimension of the social environment—the religious dimension—and to explore the various ways in which the Judeo-Christian vision claims to influence business.

A Retrieval of Religious Insight

The fundamental theme of this book is the retrieval of the ancient religious insight for our time, and especially for the corporate world. This is not simply a call from the churches and synagogues and their theologians; it is a move that has received encouragement from a number of scholars. Irving Kristol, a professor at New York University and a member of the *Wall Street Journal*'s Board of Contributors, has suggested a searching inquiry into the religious heritage in order to re-create a public consensus on the legitimacy of business institutions. Kristol calls for a fresh examination of some basic assumptions:

> . . . the idea of progress in the modern era has always signified that the quality of life would inevitably be improved by material enrichment. To doubt this is to doubt the political metaphysics of modernity and to start the long trek back to pre-modern political philosophy—Plato, Aristotle, Thomas Aquinas, Hooker, Calvin, etc. It seems to me that this trip is quite necessary. Perhaps then we shall discover some of those elements that are most desperately needed by the spiritually impoverished civilization that we

have constructed on what once seemed to be sturdy bourgeois foundations.[7]

A key ailment of the times, writes Kristol, derives from the fact that "the institutions of our society have lost their vital connection with the values which are supposed to govern the private lives of our citizenry."[8] His point is that we as a people need to have a clearer vision of what constitutes a good and virtuous life, *and* to shape our institutions accordingly. Religious and philosophic thinkers, in his view, give us one way to retrieve such a vision.

The Bible and the Benedictine Monks

The Judeo-Christian tradition views work as essential and of value, and yet also as drudgery. Genesis 2:15 relates that God intended humankind "to cultivate and take care of" the world, and that work is essential to human fulfillment. Genesis 3:17-19 goes on to portray work as a burden and a tribulation, and blames this aspect of work on sin, humankind's turning away from God and his plan. Matthew 25:14-30, the parable of the talents, teaches that work and creativity are serious responsibilities that ought not be avoided. The theme of the parable is that persons are gifted by God and that full use of their talents is the appropriate and loving response.

Lewis Mumford has suggested that the Benedictine monasteries of the sixth century were the founders of capitalism.[9] For monks work was an essential dimension; it was their conviction that through their life together, consisting of work, prayer, and recreation, they grew closer to God. In order to have ample time for prayer, meditation, and so on, labor-saving devices were developed. Tasks were standardized so that they might be interchanged among the brothers. As a result of their thrifty living, they were able to save money, and they used this accrued wealth to build better equipment—hence they were called the "first capitalists."

Arnold Toynbee draws a significant parallel between monasticism and capitalism when he points to the inner-directed motivation of a monk.

> The Benedictine Rule achieved what has never been achieved by the Gracchan agrarian laws or the Imperial alimenta, because it worked, not, as state action works, from above downwards, but from below upwards, by evoking the individual's initiative through enlisting his religious enthusiasm.[10]

The positive attitude of the monks toward work had an influence throughout the Middle Ages.[11] One could find dignity and self-respect in labor or craftmanship: "To labor is to pray."

Thomas Aquinas

Thomas Aquinas (1225-1274), perhaps the best-known medieval religious scholar, brought together much of the biblical teaching and writings of the Fathers and other commentators in a grand synthesis with Aristotelian philosophy. Society during Aquinas's time was primarily based on an agricultural economy and was poor by any contemporary standards. The differences between the haves and have-nots (the feudal lords and the serfs) were large, and upward mobility was unknown. It was a static society where lords, peasants, craftsmen, and merchants were each thought to have a "right" to whatever it took to perform their particular function in society. Members of society understood themselves in terms of the analogy of the human body, each class having a particular role to perform in the grand scheme of things, in accordance with the divine plan. While the manor might obtain goods from traders and guilds, the scale of commerce was miniscule compared to that of later centuries.

The Church taught that all should have sufficient means for their particular state in life; accruing wealth beyond this level was sinful, the sin of avarice. In the medieval world commerce was suspect, and although it was tolerated, it could never be acknowledged as a good. The fear was that trade and commerce would accent and strengthen the acquisitive traits of one's character.[12] In the words of R. H. Tawney, the attitude of medieval thinkers toward the acquisitive appetites "was that of one who holds a wolf by the ears."[13] Extended reflections on just prices, usury, and trade occupied theologians as they sought to provide guidance to preserve the traditional standards of personal morality. It is worth noting that the point of their work was not so much to change social structures, for their perspective on society was the prevailing static view. Their work was an effort to formulate a code of ethics that would provide practical guidance for living a life of Christian virtue.

To be sure, Kristol's advice quoted above to return to the philosophy of Aquinas is not commending the specific teaching of Aquinas on price and usury, or applying the view of a static society to corporations today; these medieval reflections only make sense in their own context and have little meaning in the twentieth century.[14] Because of advances in technology, and in the social and human sciences, humankind has discovered how to increase productivity and accrue wealth. In our time there is a growing realization that, with appropriate advances, no one has to be poor in the future. Rather, Kristol is concerned that we find a way to establish some congruence between the "principles that organize public life" and "those that shape private lives."[15] Tawney points out that the compartmentalizing of the various dimensions of life into an absolute dichotomy was totally foreign to medieval thought. He notes that in nineteenth-century England there was a common acceptance of this total separation; people came to believe that "Trade is one thing, religion is another," yet the strict division between private and public morality was something new.[16]

Because this sort of separation between private and public life would have been totally alien to Aquinas and the tradition of Aristotle, they might have something to say to our times. A retrieval of Aquinas offers us a social philosophy that points to one way of healing the breach between outer and inner life. While a number of the essays that follow will suggest some of the practical implications for today of this perspective, it may be helpful here to provide a brief summary of its salient features.

For Aquinas, the basis of moral goodness is God's *wisdom,* that is, the wisdom of God intends that creatures be in a proper relationship to each other and to him.[17] Thus moral goodness is constituted by being in harmony with God's plan of creation. Creation is taken to be that act of God which gives finite beings an existence apart from him. All things have a "nature," an essence, and various actions are required to bring that nature to perfection. For example, an acorn requires sun, water, soil, and so on, if it is finally to become what it is destined to be—an oak tree. Knowing the End (the oak tree), one can determine the Means (sun, water, soil, and so on) to bring it to perfection. The centerpiece of Aquinas's reflection on the person is his understanding of the End of human life: "Man's ultimate happiness consists solely in the contemplation of God. . ."[18] His thinking is marked by a teleological cast, that is, first one determines the End of human life (enjoying the presence of God), and then one ascertains the Means to attain it.

The Means to attain the vision of God—which can only be fully attained in the next life—include a supernatural gift of grace which enables one to become the sort of person who might enjoy this vision. Becoming this sort of person entails the slow process of appropriating the virtues; Aquinas's program combines the virtues enjoined by the Bible—faith, hope, and charity—with Aristotle's four cardinal virtues —wisdom, justice, temperance, and fortitude. Part of being oriented properly to God is the appropriate orientation toward the natural good. For Aquinas, then, ethics (moral theology) is the means by which one brings into actuality the sort of person one potentially is, a person capable of and suited for union with God.

Creation, as an act of God, mirrors his eternal law; this "eternal law," insofar as it is implanted in creation, is called "natural law." This natural law is discerned by human intelligence as people in community seek to determine the right things to do and to be. For the Thomist-Aristotelian synthesis, a society ordered by law and custom discerned by right reason is a society in accordance with the divine plan. A law is taken to be just if it responds to the demands of reality, if it is arrived at by right reason reflecting on the many aspects of the situation. The context for this reflection is the End of humankind, and the role that society has in shaping persons for that end; the forming of virtuous persons is all-pervasive. In this account, the human will is not the source of the rightness of a law, but rather the human intelligence, for it is this faculty that reads the "imperatives of nature" implanted by God in creation. To be sure, God has not so specified things that there is only *one* concrete action, or *one* type of government, and so on, to meet the demands of reality. Rather natural law is a generalized pattern of action which may be concretized by persons in a variety of "just" ways. To be free means to be able to work out the concrete demands of reality for oneself; it does not mean to be purely spontaneous, as some utilitarians might suggest.[19] The Introductions to Parts II and IV of the book further elaborate the discussion of natural law.

All of creation has its own "natures," its own ends—and hence its own autonomy—and yet ultimately all is oriented toward the creator. The human intellect has the task of discovering what it takes to bring the various "natures" to perfection. For example, one might argue that humankind has recently discovered how to produce wealth, a relatively new skill in the history of the human race. But in the Thomistic vision this new skill cannot be allowed to dominate, for it must be subordinated to the end of life on this earth, *the formation of virtuous persons.* Economic activity is only a means, and it must be guided by reference to the moral ends. This is the heart of the teaching of Thomas Aquinas, and it continues to form the basis of Church documents. Some 700 years later, the Second Vatican Council decree, "The Church in the Modern World," restates the point clearly: ". . . economic activity is to be carried out according to its own methods and laws but within the limits of morality, so that God's plan for mankind can be realized."[20]

The Protestant Ethic and the Spirit of Capitalism

Sociologist Daniel Bell, following a theme similar to that of Joseph Schumpeter, develops the point that there is a crisis of legitimacy in business institutions that ultimately stems from a loss of religious values.[21] For Bell, the social system only made sense when work derived meaning and value from the Protestant ethic. In his judgment the Protestant ethic is no longer a significant influence in the culture, and hence the rational technocratic system so essential to capitalism is slowly being undermined. Some discussion of the Protestant ethic will illuminate what many take to be a crucial influence on the course of capitalism.

The rapid economic growth that marks what is known as capitalism was not to come for some eleven centuries after Benedict and five centuries after Aquinas. In the early twentieth century Max Weber advanced the thesis that two key doctrines of the Protestant Reformers provided the force that enabled modern capitalism to come into being: Martin Luther's doctrine of vocation (*Beruf*), and John Calvin's teaching on predestination. What made capitalism unique, according to Weber, was the pursuit of profit by means of systematic and rational behavior.[22] He cited rational bookkeeping as a key characteristic of this entity called capitalism. Why was it that capitalism was able to marshal such enormous amounts of human energy for the cause of economic growth? Why was it that characteristic pre-Reformation Christian attitudes which extolled the virtue of poverty, encouraged withdrawal from the world, and honored the intellectual life over commerce were suddenly transformed into attitudes which fostered the development of business — attitudes of austerity, industry, thrift, frugality, and so on. The answer to these questions, according to Weber, lies in the theological teachings of Luther and Calvin, and the way in which these teachings were passed along to the people by Reformed pastors. It is worth noting that R. H. Tawney and other scholars modified Weber's theory. For example, Tawney includes the influence of the bankers of Venice and Florence, and hence of *Catholic* ideas, in the ethos that spawned capitalism.[23] In any event, it is instructive to consider the original Weberian thesis.

Luther brought a fresh perspective to the notion of Christian vocation.[24] He taught that one's occupation in the world was not to be taken lightly, for doing the task well was the way to serve God and to give thanks for divine justification. This conviction provided motivation for high performance in one's station in life, whether it be as a

scholar, craftsperson, or laborer. Yet Weber argues that the life pattern
of systematic and rational activity that characterized capitalism was not
sufficiently explained by Luther's doctrine of calling or vocation. He
also examined Calvin's doctrine of predestination. In Calvin's theology, God elects some to be saved and others to be damned, and one is
powerless to affect the outcome of God's sovereign will. In the face of
the great uncertainty over salvation, there were many in these communities who suffered great anxiety. Weber suggests that one look to
the advice given by Reformed pastors who were ministering to this
salvation-anxiety problem in order to find the significant motive power
for economic growth.[25]

In order to calm consciences, the pastors were saying that there
were *signs* of election, and that these signs were material success in one's
business. While one could not *attain* salvation by prudent management
of a business enterprise, one could have some assurance that salvation
was in line for him if material prosperity prevailed. Thus everyone
struggled to ensure that businesses were profitable, and this produced
the driven quality in the "Protestant ethic." Although the pastors
encouraged people to live frugally, to be austere, they were also
counseling industriousness and persistance. This combination of advice enabled people to overcome their anxiety and also to accrue
wealth. Since Calvinism taught that wealth would be an obstacle to
holiness in that it led to pride and sensuality, this posed a problem. It
was not long, therefore, before a new teaching emerged to account
for the new condition. The doctrine of stewardship was developed;
it taught that wealth was a trust and was to be used for the common
good.

The crucial point in Weber's analysis is that making profit became
a value in its own right. Since anxiety over possible damnation is calmed
if one is materially successful, it "made sense" to be almost single-
mindedly focused on material success. Thus the Protestant ethic
changed history, for heretofore ethical values had always discouraged
such a single-minded quest for profits. Weber goes on to show how the
Protestant ethic eventually lost its religious roots and yet still maintained its vitality with a secular vision. Benjamin Franklin epitomizes
this secular vision. Reading Franklin's works, one is struck by the fact
that all the values of the spirit of Christian asceticism are present,
although the religious basis of these values has died. What remains is
what Weber calls a "fundamental element of the spirit of modern
capitalism: Rational conduct on the basis of the idea of calling."[26]
Weber quotes Franklin:

Remember, that money is of the prolific, generating nature. Money can beget money, and its offspring can beget more, and so on. Five shillings turned is six, turned again it is seven and threepence, and so on, till it becomes a hundred pounds. The more there is of it, the more it produces every turning, so that the profits rise quicker and quicker. He that kills a breeding-sow, destroys all her offering to the thousandth generation. He that murders a crown, destroys all that it might have produced, even scores of pounds.[27]

The writings of Benjamin Franklin exhort the reader to the practice of austerity, honesty, frugality, thrift, industry, and so on—all the virtues of the Puritan ethic—not for the sake of the signs of salvation, but rather in order to accrue wealth and to live as a moral athlete—the best way to live.

Adam Smith

Any account of the formation of modern capitalism would be incomplete without the mention of the moral philosopher and political economist Adam Smith (1723-1790). In 1776 Smith published *An Inquiry into the Nature and Causes of the Wealth of Nations,* and even today this work is often cited as the bible of capitalism and free enterprise.[28] Smith writes about the economy and business of his own time, and focuses on the principles that are operative. He could have posed other interesting questions: Why are some nations godly righteous? Or, why are some nations humanly good? He chose rather to explore why England, France, and Poland were noticeably wealthier than their neighbors: "Why are some nations wealthier?"

Smith's approach was decidedly empirical, and he set forth principles that he found to be operative in sound business and economics. Certain nations were wealthier precisely because of the "division of labor" and the free competitive market. He demonstrates the effectiveness of the division of labor by his famous example of the making of pins:

One man draws out the wire, another straightens it, a third cuts it, a fourth points it, a fifth grinds it at the top for receiving the head.
. . . ten persons . . . could make among them upwards to forty-eight thousand pins a day. But if they had all wrought separately and independently, and without any of them having been educated to this particular business, they certainly could

not each of them have made twenty, perhaps not one pin in a day.[29]

Reflecting on the commerce of his time, Smith concludes that goods will be produced more efficiently and cheaply for all if each person strives to maximize his or her self-interest in the market place. Producing attractive goods at competitive prices will be in the self-interest of the producer and in the best interest of the public. Smith speaks of "an invisible hand" which guides self-interested behavior to be of benefit to the whole society. His hope was that if governments would understand the real source of the wealth of nations, they would forgo all tariffs and other measures which provide protection to the producers and advocate a free market.

For Smith, wealth is not determined by how much precious metals a nation possesses; he argued against this mercantilist view of wealth in favor of determining the nation's wealth in terms of its productivity, "the value of the annual produce of its land and labour."[30] Significantly, Smith does not see accruing wealth as an end in itself. Rather, increased productivity (wealth) is sought because it not only brings a better life to more people, but also enhances the nation by fostering the growth of desirable character traits.

> We are more industrious than our forefathers; because in the present times the funds destined for the maintenance of industry, are much greater in proportion to those which are likely to be employed in the maintenance of idleness, than they were two or three centuries ago. Our ancestors were idle for want of a sufficient encouragement to industry. It is better, says the proverb, to play for nothing, than to work for nothing. In mercantile and manufacturing towns, where the inferior ranks of people are chiefly maintained by the employment of capital, they are in general industrious, sober, and thriving; as in many English and most Dutch towns. In those towns which are principally supported by the constant or occasional residence of a court, and in which the inferior ranks of people are chiefly maintained by the spending of revenues, they are in general idle, dissolute, and poor.[31]

Whether in fact all of the key assumptions of Adam Smith's analysis are still prevalent in our time is a matter to be considered in Part Three. The central point to be made in this brief discussion is that for Smith profit was pursued in the light of a higher cultural vision that took moral virtue for granted.

Religion in American Business Life

Tawney pointed out that what differentiates modern from medieval economic ideas is the modern assumption that economic criteria are the sole authoritative standard.[32] The single criterion of economic expediency, how to provide the greatest possible amount of material goods, replaces medieval natural law and its concern for providing guidance for a society of virtuous persons. Part One of this volume offers an implicit challenge to the notion that indeed economic criteria offer the *sole* standard. We must recognize, however, that the churches have much less to say today than in the medieval world. In the face of this massive cultural shift, what guidance has been provided by the church leaders of the United States? In order to understand the present state of the discussion between religious values and business, a brief historical sketch should be helpful.

When it comes to considering the influence of religion on business life in the United States, we are, for the most part, speaking of Protestant denominations. Although today about 25 percent of Americans are Catholics, this sizable percentage represents a relatively recent phenomenon. In colonial America, Catholics were a distinct minority. A 1708 Maryland census reported 2,974 Catholics in a population of 33,833 persons. Pennsylvania in 1757 recorded 1,365 Catholics out of some 200,000 persons. As the population of the United States was approaching 4,000,000 in 1785, only 25,000 Catholics were recorded.[33] The nineteenth-century influx of Catholic immigrants from Europe achieved economic success only relatively recently. The same can be said for the Jewish people. The mass immigration of Jews did not take place until the twentieth century, and although their early positive influence was far greater than their numbers, they did not have a substantial role in shaping colonial America.

The medieval ideal was surely not dead in the New World—at least not in the Massachusetts of the 1600s. The Puritan colony was governed with an overarching religious principle which claimed authority over the economy.[34] For example, prices and wages were fixed by leaders of the colony to reflect what they took to be a "fair" standard. The clergy, who were often the political leaders as well, wielded power over all dimensions of community life. The doctrine of the "calling" was elaborated by Cotton Mather, a famous Puritan cleric, in his work *Two Brief Discourses, One Directing a Christian in His General Calling; Another Directing Him in His Personal Calling,* published in 1701. Mather teaches that a Christian has two callings, one "to serve the Lord Jesus Christ," and the other, to pursue a particular vocation in which, in some fashion, one serves fellow community members. To portray the challenge of living a Christian life, Mather uses the image of a person rowing a boat toward heaven: each of the two oars (callings) must be given its proper attention in order to reach the shore. Thus one's worldly calling is essential to the attainment of eternal life, and business is actually taken to be God's work. Scholars have noted that this way of framing the doctrine of the calling contained within itself the seeds of its own destruction. Since their daily work was a religious task, merchants took their businesses with dead seriousness; they became so successful that they soon asserted their independence from clerical interference![35]

Indeed just how independent economics was becoming in eighteenth-century America is illustrated by the writings of Reverend Joseph Morgan; Morgan taught the famous "hidden hand" doctrine almost forty years before Adam Smith. In his *Nature of Riches*, published in 1732, Morgan says:

> A rich man is a slave to others, while he thinks others are Slaves to him. He is a great Friend to the Publick, while he aims at nothing but serving himself. God will have us live by helping one another and since Love will not do it, Covetousness will.[36]

Taken to its extreme, this position signals the abandonment of the medieval ideal and the acknowledgment that indeed business and religion are two discrete, impenetrable worlds.

Yet the struggle to keep one unified vision of life in which economics was subordinated to religion continued into the nineteenth century. There was a pervasive belief that economic success was intimately related to moral virtue. The comment of a Massachusetts Quaker merchant about settlements in Ohio was typical for the period: "With a population governed by such habits [industry, temperance, morality, and love of gain] the state must necessarily advance in improvement at a rapid rate."[37] There was also a continuous concern that acquisitive attitudes had overtaken the merchant class; sermons and clerical writings of the time stressed the need to bring Christian values to business practice. The Reverend Theodore Parker sums up the tenor of the times: "If religion is good for anything, it is as a rule of conduct for daily life, in the business of the individual and the business of the nation."[38]

The Protestant churches of the mid-nineteenth century became more and more identified with the wealthy and the powerful classes, and had little attraction for the workingman. There was a prevailing opinion that hard work, moral character, and perseverance would bring the good life (material success) to all who would try it. The spirit of the times is perhaps best captured by the novels of Horatio Alger, a popular writer who began his career as a Unitarian minister in Massachusetts. Alger's stories tell of poor boys rising to financial success through honesty, frugality, and persistence; these "rags to riches" stories were used as models by many of the clerics writing and speaking to their people.[39] Henry F. May, in *Protestant Churches and Industrial America,* notes that in 1876 Protestantism was almost totally identified with the status quo, and was the source of little prophetic insight for business and political life. Prominent clerics, more often than not, opposed unions in favor of setting wages by the "natural law" of supply and demand.[40]

There was a dramatic shift in the posture of the churches as sensitive pastors saw their people locked in violent labor conflict. The railroad strike of 1877, the strikes of 1886 culminating in the Haymarket bomb explosion in Chicago, and the series of conflicts over Carnegie Steel Corporation's threat to reduce wages all conspired to reorient the thinking of religious leaders to the plight of the worker. The turn of the century saw a new focus by leading theologians on the social teachings of Jesus. Congregationalist Pastor Washington Gladden in *Applied Christianity* (1886) and *Church and Modern Life* (1908) and Baptist Walter Rauschenbusch in *Christianity and the Social Crisis* (1910) and *A Theology of the Social Gospel* (1917) set the new agenda for the Protestant world. Catholic scholars such as Bishop Francis Haas and Monsignor John A. Ryan made great contributions in defense of the American Labor movement. Ryan's *A Living Wage* (1906) and *Distributive Justice* (1916) were especially influential.[41]

Walter Rauschenbusch tells a story which illustrates the new consciousness of *social* sin which theologians were advocating. There was a farmer who belonged to a small religious community known for its strict observance and pietistic spirit. One day this farmer was caught shipping milk that was polluted. Upon being confronted with the violation, "he swore a worldly oath" in anger. The church censored the sinful farmer: "But, mark well, not for introducing cow-dung into the intestines of babies, but for expressing his belief in the damnation of the wicked in a non-theological way."[42] Rauschenbush's point was that the churches often focus on minor sins and totally overlook major wrongs committed in the world of work. Changing history, making the world a better place, ought to be part of the Christian vocation.

While the influence of the social-gospel movement was never pervasive, it did spark a general interest in reform of the marketplace and a concern for the problems of the poor. The Federal Council of

Churches in America, formed in 1908, was an ecumenical group of thirty denominations that came to be the social conscience of Protestant America. While the horrors of World War I destroyed the easy optimism of the Progressive movement and drew attention to the ever-present evil dimension of humankind, the call for social reform was not to be forgotten. Adequate working conditions, child-labor laws, a living wage, and a host of other social issues were championed by the churches. In 1948 the World Council of Churches was formed to strengthen Christian influence throughout the globe. Although initially it was composed of some 152 member churches from Western Europe and North America, today the council is dominated by Third World Members. At present there are some 295 Protestant and Eastern Orthodox member churches from 100 countries. Periodical Assemblies are held and position papers are issued; a 135-member Central Committee representing worldwide churches makes decisions when assemblies are not in session.

In 1950 the National Council of Churches was formed by twelve interdenominational agencies. Today its membership includes Methodists, Episcopalians, Baptists, Presbyterians, Lutherans, and Quakers, as well as the Greek, Syrian, Serbian, Ukrainian, Russian, and Armenian Orthodox communions. The 266-member governing board of the council takes positions on social issues and offers guidance to church members (some 40,000,000 in all) in the United States. Part Two of this volume includes a summary of the statements on business and the modern corporation from the World and National Councils of Churches. Part Three considers the implications of these statements for practice in the marketplace, and also probes whether they reflect an adequate understanding of economics.

As mentioned earlier, until recently Catholics were not especially influential in shaping America. Their major contribution has been their role in the labor movement and their activities in behalf of social justice for the worker. Since the Catholic contribution is discussed in the Introduction to Part Two of the book, only some brief historical notes are included here. In 1920 the Bishops of the United States organized the Social Action Department of the National Catholic Welfare Conference under the leadership of Monsignor John A. Ryan. The conference was to be a vehicle for making pronouncements in the name of all the U.S. bishops on matters of concern. Usually it met once a year and considered a number of issues. In 1920, the Administrative Committee of the Conference approved a major statement on social issues drafted by the talented moralist John A. Ryan. *Social Reconstruction: A General Review of the Problems and Survey of Remedies* provided a general framework for considering social concerns in a moral perspective, and made suggestions on issues such as unemployment and health insurance, minimum-wage laws, child-labor laws, the rights of labor to organize, public housing, and so on. From our perspective today, the document is rather moderate in tone, and many of its recommendations have been implemented in law. The significant point, however, is that the program was highly controversial when first released, and it was even taken to be subversive in some quarters. The president of the National Association of Manufacturers wrote a strong letter of protest to Cardinal Gibbons in response to the statement:

> It is pretty generally assumed that the Roman Catholic Church of the United States is, and always has been, unalterable in its antagonism to all forms of Socialism. It is our belief that a careful reading of this pamphlet will lead you to the conclusion we have reached, namely, that it involves what may prove to be a covert effort to disseminate partisan, pro-labor union, socialistic propaganda under the official insignia of the Roman Catholic Church in America.[43]

The Conference document prevailed, however, and today its major proposals are taken for granted as the minimum requirements of justice in a democratic society. In 1966, the National Catholic Welfare Conference was reorganized and named the United States Catholic Conference — an administrative arm of the National Conference of Catholic Bishops. The key function of the Conference remains: to develop and promulgate guidance on social and economic questions of the day. That this task is a complex one involving much more than goodwill and religious concern is the burden of the essays that follow.

Conclusion

What becomes clear from this brief summary is that churches have had a fairly constant record of challenging capitalism to be more humane and just. From the religious perspective, profit is not an evil in itself, but simply an index of success — a report card, if you will. But profit was to be sought in the context of the higher religious and cultural values — love of God (Benedictine monks), a sign of salvation (Calvinists and Puritans, etc.), the virtuous life (Thomas Aquinas, Benjamin Franklin), and so on. Religious persons strive to provide some coherence and direction to the business enterprise, and to set some limits to the acquisitive appetites. On the other hand, the challenge for religious critics is to understand the economic system, its strengths and weaknesses, as well as those of alternative systems.

It is well to remember, however, Max Weber's ominous warning. Weber feared that once people abandoned the interplay between religious and business values, civilization would be on the decline. In the closing pages of *The Protestant Ethic and the Spirit of Capitalism,* Weber expressed his fears:

> Where the fulfillment of the calling cannot be directly related to the highest spiritual and cultural values, or when, on the other hand, it need not be felt simply as economic compulsion, the individual generally abandons the attempt to justify it at all. In the field of its highest development, in the United States, the pursuit of wealth, stripped of its religious and ethical meaning, tends to become associated with purely mundane passions, which often actually give it the character of sport.
>
> . . . For of the last stage of this cultural development, it might well be truly said: "Specialists without spirit, sensualists without heart; this nullity imagines that it has attained a level of civilization never before achieved."[44]

There are some signs that Weber's warning is being heeded. For example, some corporations clearly see the need for business values to be operative in the larger context of social values. A recent statement by a senior corporate executive articulates this vision:

> The basic goal of private enterprise remains what it has always been—to produce needed goods and services, earn a fair return on investment, and succeed as an economic institution. But the new dimension that must be observed—a new "bottom line" for business, really—is social approval. Without it, economic victory would be Pyrrhic indeed.
>
> . . . A successful business organization must possess a moral sense as well as an economic sense.[45]

But what constitutes "social approval" and a "moral sense" today? This volume lays a foundation and offers some answers to these questions. The purpose of Part One is to delineate some of the inner workings of the modern corporate world. In Chapters 1 and 2 two business scholars provide an overview of today's corporation, the context for the essays which follow. The religious world is the subject of Part Two; it includes chapters by leading thinkers in the Protestant, Catholic, and Jewish communities. It assumes that persons steeped in a religious tradition have been shaped by religious symbols, a set of stories, and a sense of reality which have been nurtured in their churches or synagogues, and in their families, and that this formation shapes their perspective on the corporate world.

The authors of the three essays of Part Three highlight some of the more controversial issues raised by the religious focus. What are the limits to a theological critique of capitalism? Is bigness bad? What changes in the economic system are appropriate in light of the poverty of the less developed countries? Part IV speaks to some of the practical questions. What do the changes in the role of women imply for corporate structures? What are the limits of law in guiding corporate behavior? What are the resources of the churches for the business executive? The final essay offers a systematic approach to ethical decision-making in business.

This volume stands as evidence that we are not yet ready to abandon "the highest spiritual and cultural values" in the pursuit of profit.

NOTES

1. Alexis de Tocqueville, *Democracy in America,* ed. Phillips Bradley (New York: Vintage Books, 1945), I, 316.

2. "Religion Held Relevant in Survey," *New York Times,* March 20, 1981, p. 11.

3. R. H. Tawney, *Religion and the Rise of Capitalism* (New York: New American Library, 1958), p. 156.

4. For an interpretation of this data, see Seymour Martin Lipset and William Schneider, "How's Business? What the Public Thinks," *Public Opinion,* July/August 1978, pp. 41–47.

5. For a discussion of how to apply a stakeholder management process, see James R. Emshoff and R. Edward Freeman, "Stakeholder Management: A Case Study of the U.S. Brewers and the Container Issue," *Applications of Management Science,* ed. R. Schultz (Greenwich, Conn.: JAI Press, 1980).

6. Thomas C. Cochran, *Business in American Life: A History* (New York: McGraw-Hill, 1972), p. 2.

7. Irving Kristol, *Two Cheers for Capitalism* (New York: Basic Books, 1978), pp. 269–70.

8. *Ibid.,* p. 266.

9. Lewis Mumford, *Techniques and Civilizations* (New York: Harcourt, Brace, 1934), p. 14.

10. Arnold J. Toynbee, *A Study of History* (London: Oxford University Press, 1947), p. 226.

11. Cf. Thomas Aquinas, *Summa Theologica,* II–II, 187, 3.

12. *Ibid.*, 77, 4.

13. Tawney, *Religion and the Rise of Capitalism,* p. 37.

14. For an analysis of the doctrine of usury in its historical context, see John T. Noonan, *The Scholastic Analysis of Usury* (Chicago: University of Chicago Press, 1957).

15. Kristol, *Two Cheers for Capitalism,* p. 267.

16. Tawney, *Religion and the Rise of Capitalism,* p. 4.

17. Aquinas, *De Veritate* 23, 6.

18. Aquinas, *Summa Contra Gentiles,* III, 37.

19. See Aquinas's Treatise on Law in *Summa Theologica,* I–II, 90–97.

20. "Pastoral Constitution on the Church in the Modern World," *The Documents of Vatican II,* ed. Walter M. Abbott, S.J. (New York: Guild Press, 1966), para. 64, p. 273.

21. Daniel Bell, *The Cultural Contradictions of Capitalism* (New York: Basic Books, 1976); Joseph A. Schumpeter, *Capitalism, Socialism, and Democracy,* 3d ed. (New York: Harper & Brothers, 1950).

22. Max Weber, *The Protestant Ethic and the Spirit of Capitalism,* trans. Talcott Parsons (New York: Charles Scribner's, 1958), pp. 15–31.

23. Tawney, *Religion and the Rise of Capitalism,* p. 76.

24. Weber, *Protestant Ethic,* pp. 84–86.

25. *Ibid.,* pp. 98–112, 229, nn. 47, 48.

26. *Ibid.,* p. 180.

27. *Ibid.,* p. 49.

28. Adam Smith, *The Wealth of Nations,* ed. Edwin Cannan (Chicago: University of Chicago Press, 1976).

29. *Ibid.,* p. 8.

30. *Ibid.,* p. 362.

31. *Ibid.,* pp. 356–57. See also Smith's chapter, "How the Commerce of the Towns Contributed to the Improvement of the Country," pp. 432–45. For a discussion of this theme, see Stephen Miller, "Adam Smith and the Commercial Republic," *The Public Interest,* Fall 1980, pp. 106–122.

32. Tawney, *Religion and the Rise of Capitalism,* p. 227.

33. The statistics on the Catholic population in America are from John Tracy Ellis, *American Catholicism,* 2d ed. (Chicago: University of Chicago Press, 1969), pp. 21, 82.

34. The discussion of the influence of Protestant denominations in United States follows closely the work of Thomas C. Cochran, *Business in American Life.* See also Marquis W. Childs and Douglas Cater, *Ethics in a Business Society* (New York: New American Library, 1954).

35. Cochran, *Business in American Life,* p. 37.

36. Quoted in *ibid.,* p. 38.

37. Quoted in *ibid.,* p. 106.

38. Quoted in *ibid.,* p. 109.

39. Horatio Alger, *Struggling Upward and Other Works* (New York: Crown Publishers, 1945).

40. Cf. Henry F. May, *Protestant Churches and Industrial America* (New York: Harper & Brothers, 1949).

41. Cf. George A. Kelly, *The Catholic Church and the American Poor* (New York: Alba House, 1976).

42. Walter Rauschenbusch, *A Theology for the Social Gospel* (New York: Abingdon Press, 1945), p. 35.

43. Quoted and discussed in Ellis, *American Catholicism,* p. 145.

44. Weber, *Protestant Ethic,* p. 182.

45. The quotation is from Thornton F. Bradshaw, formerly president of Atlantic Richfield Company. He later accepted the position of chairman of RCA Corporation. For the full text, see ARCO's 1980 corporate social report, *Participation III: Atlantic Richfield and Society,* pp. 2–4.

PART ONE

Understanding the Corporation

There is an old axiom in theological discourse which says "grace presupposes nature." If we enlarge our concept of nature to include more than trees, mountains, oceans, and the stars—that is, to include the works of human effort—this axiom is relevant to a volume on the interface between the world of religion and the world of business. It suggests a need for intellectual caution by religious thinkers when speaking out about anything as complex as modern business. The *theologizing* is bound to be better if there is a comprehensive understanding of what it is businessmen and women do.

For purposes of clarity, our focus in this volume will be on the larger units of business, and will not consider small businesses, such as neighborhood stores or family restaurants and farms. This exclusion, while necessary, does an injustice to the richness of our economic system by ignoring a major source of freedom and initiative in our society for many people without the inclination to join larger organizations. Smallness is still alive and reasonably healthy in our business world, and it is socially important. So much so that David Riesman wanted to add to the Bill of Rights the right to start a small business, which "sustains democracy by freeing people from the fear of offending a single regime which controls both the economy and the polity."[1]

The following table of nine corporations, 1980 results, is a good place to start our examination of the corporate world.

Businessmen and women are taught to "pay attention to the numbers." While 1980 was not the best year for economic activity,

Selected U.S. Corporations, 1980 Results

	Assets ($ bil.)	Employees (thousands)	Sales ($ bil.)	Net Income ($ mil.)	% of Profits on Sales
Top Three Oil Companies					
Exxon	56	176	103	5600	5.5
Mobil	33	212	59	3200	5.5
Texaco	26	67	51	2600	5.2
Three Large Manufacturing					
G.M.	34	746	58	762 loss	—
I.B.M.	27	341	26	3600	13.6
G.E.	18	402	25	1500	6.1
Three High Technology-Computer					
Texas Instruments	2.3	90	4	212	5.2
Hewlett Packard	2.3	57	3	269	8.7
Control Data	2.5	49	2.8	150	5.4

Source: "The Fortune Directory of the 500 Largest U.S. Industrial Corporations," *Fortune* magazine, May 4, 1981, pp. 324–43.

given sluggishness and inflation, it is apparent that the oil companies do control immense wealth in assets and profits. Their assets exceed those of many nations! Our large manufacturing firms have huge organizations of hundreds of thousands; three companies alone give employment to a million and a half men and women. By examining three innovative firms—Texas Instruments, Hewlett-Packard, and Control Data—we find three factors—wealth, huge organizations, and ideas—yet there is more to the complex story of what makes corporations tick. We must examine the values (or norms) held by the men and women who staff these organizational giants. It is the purpose of the papers by business scholars Edward Trubac and William Sexton to sketch out the key values of the business world. In later essays we shall examine the values highlighted by the Jewish and Christian religions today.

The 200-Year Growth in the Business Mentality

Is there such a thing as a business mentality? Our common experience tells us that there is, and that there are large cadres of men and women whose view of the world and sense of reality are nurtured in the business tradition. In contrast to other world views—such as the religious, humanistic, romantic, or scientific—the business mentality is relatively young, but it has had immense influence on our lives and our planet.

When Adam Smith published his *Wealth of Nations* in 1776, he was responding to a new social phenomenon: an unprecedented outpouring of wealth that was apparent even to the casual observer. Slowly at first, but widely spread over the countries of Europe, there was a dramatic surge of growth in new manufacturing, inventions, raw materials, and transportation. The Old Order of things, badly buffeted intellectually and politically by the Renaissance, by printing, and by the scientific and democratic revolutions, was experiencing what was later called the early period of the Industrial Revolution. To this day it is changing our wealth and, equally important, our potential for good or evil. Marx and Engels, writing some 75 years after Adam Smith in *The Communist Manifesto,* observed:

> The bourgeoisie (the new business class) during its rule of scarcely one hundred years, has created more massive and more colossal productive forces than have all preceding generations together. The subjection of nature's forces to man and machinery; the application of chemistry to industry and agriculture; (the development of) steam navigation, railways and electric telegraphs; the clearing of whole continents for cultivation; the canalization of rivers; and the conjuring of whole populations out of the ground (off the land?)—What earlier century had even a presentiment that such productive forces slumbered. . . ?[2]

Further, Marx and Engels, no friends of business, argued that such marvels as the pyramids, Roman aqueducts, and Gothic cathedrals were surpassed by the accomplishments of the business mentality which "show what man's activity can bring about."[3]

To be sure, there was a cultural and ethical component to this revolution. Where formerly the status of churchmen, noblemen, scholars, guildsmen, and the huge bottom of the social pyramid—peasants—held sway *and rigid,* now a new dynamic, revolutionary in nature, was operating. Village and town barter, because of transportation improvements, had to give way to national and worldwide markets. Regions and countries, again because of transportation, could specialize, and thereby become more efficient in producing wheat, cotton, coal, or a long list of manufactured goods. At the same time, factories grew larger as exploitable markets expanded from town or district to the nation and across the oceans. Of course, these changes were not without their costs—no radical change ever is. One cost was that both the religious and political orders had to accommodate to another way of determining the value of a person: what he or she could command in the market. "We all may be sons and daughters of God, and citizens of a political unit with certain rights and duties, but we also are sellers of skills in a floating market of worth-determination." Religious and political evaluation is joined by the methods of the market and economic analysis.

Marx and Engels described "exchange value" (still another variant for business mentality) as leaving "no other nexus between man and man than naked self-interest . . . It has drowned the most heavenly ecstasies of religious fervor, of chivalrous enthusiasm, of philistine sentimentalism, in the icy water of egotistical calculation."[4] (Today, we would talk in terms of rational calculations of cost and benefits by corporate executives.) There are no issues that divide the business world from that of religion and ethics more clearly than: What is the worth of a person? How far can we deviate from this business calculus? Practical answers to these questions are not easy. Religion, by its very nature, is a community of men and women who are making a dedicated search for the meaning of fidelity to God, and who take to heart Tobit's advice to his son: "Remember the Lord our God all your days, and refuse to sin or transgress his commandments (Tob. 4:5)." This sets forth a fundamental norm for all religious persons, and suggests that God's will may, or may not, be found in the business world, with its definitions of success and value.

To tell the complete story, there is skepticism from both sides— religion and business—which is illustrated by a joke frequently told by students here at Notre Dame:

Question: What is the difference between a theology professor and a business professor?

Answer: A theology professor knows the *value* of everything and the *cost* of nothing; a business professor knows the *costs* of everything and the *value* of nothing!

There is much truth in all this as to how these two traditions, theology and business, approach a problem. This very difference in approach is the source of the conflict reflected in the essays of this volume.

Joseph Schumpeter, the economic theorist and historian, saw the business mentality as contributing significantly to a new way of looking at the world and events in their development of what he calls a "rationalistic civilization." He observed that from its earliest times, business exalted the numbers from the balance sheets and operating statements. Unlike churchmen or noblemen, the business class knew very quickly whether they were having a good year, and how to plot a course for even a better one. The key was a simple intellectual tool, double-entry bookkeeping, which Schumpeter describes as

> . . . primarily a product of the evolution of economic rationality; by crystallizing and deferring numerically, it powerfully propels the logic of [business] enterprise. And thus defined and quantified for the economic sector, this type of logic or attitude or method then starts upon its conqueror's career subjugating— rationalizing—man's tools and philosophies, his medical practice, his picture of the cosmos, his outlook of life, everything, in fact, including his concepts of beauty and justice and his spiritual ambition.[5]

While most businessmen and women would demur that they get their cosmology from the Annual Statement, there is still validity in Schumpeter's judgment about the power of the business mentality. It does ignore questions of ultimates in human value and meaning, concentrating more on instrumental values and techniques in "how to get the job done." Through trial and error—including many bankruptcies—the business mind has distilled a list of norms for the careful measurement of human and, especially today, corporate enterprise. And while it cannot guarantee the good life, the economic record does point to success in guaranteeing the plentiful life.

For our first essay, Edward Trubac was asked to describe the contemporary stage of this rationality that operates within business organizations. Trubac's essay is descriptive in that it does not purport to suggest what the corporation *should* do, but rather presents an account of what in fact does take place in business corporations—what occupies the attention of executives and what motivates and inspires corporate activities. A fundamental observation is stated: "A corporation is an institution attempting to realize a multiplicity of goals with a *satisfactory* level of profits among the most important of these objectives." The burden of the essay is a discussion of the activities designed to achieve this central objective. The seeking of a "satisfactory level of profits" is the key agenda for business executives and involves such activities as: expanding market share; moving to a growing segment of the market or industry; promoting efficiency and thereby reducing costs; reducing risks through such policies as market research, risk-adjusted capital budgeting techniques, socialization of risk, and merger activity. Trubac also lists "being a good citizen" as the final activity which engages executives seeking a satisfactory level of profit. Under this category, he means to include everything which is "consistent with enhancing the long-term profit growth potential of the corporation." He notes that there are degrees of importance in the various actions which entail good citizenship, ranging from tasks essential to the survival of a firm—efficiently providing products, jobs, and economic growth—to the more comprehensive challenges posed by the problems of the broader society.

As to this last point, which anticipates the theme of Part Four, Corporations and Social Responsibility, it is well to remember that Trubac starts off with the proposition that in non-socialist countries, a corporation is "the large scale organization through which a modern society primarily accomplishes its economic purposes of production and distribution." This, of course, is an agency relationship, with society the principal. Clearly, Trubac is suggesting that in the nature of things the corporation (the agent) must serve the larger interests of society (the principal.) This is an important ethical insight which is often forgotten in business circles: corporations are created to serve the common good. Lately there has been considerable ferment about what the "common good" is, and corporations have come under criticism, even hostility, as to their role and contribution. It is argued that they can do a much better job in preserving the environment, product safety, hiring of minorities, serving communities, or expanding into less developed countries. And if they do not respond to this criticism, then higher legal standards should be imposed on them.

From Trubac's perspective, the answers to these understandable concerns will be "yes, but . . ." His hesitation stems from his belief that the social role of business remains primarily economic. What is most important is attention to the numbers, and any deviation, no matter how laudable, does indeed incur costs that have to be calculated before any competent moral and legal judgment can be made. This is the essence of the business mentality.

Large Organizations and Their Impact on Employees

If Edward Trubac sees corporations as economic entities with special norms stemming from the business mentality, William Sexton sees them as collectivities with critical, often negative, impacts on their huge armies of employees. For example, General Motors has 750,000 employees, and General Electric has 400,000. Can traditional economic factors of growth, richer markets, higher return on investment, and so forth, suffice as the major tools of analysis in such huge enterprises? Sexton, drawing from the humane tradition as well as from his consulting experience, says "no," and he goes further to point out that growth, much desired by an attention-to-the-numbers mentality, has a cost: bureaucracy with even greater division of labor and tasks. But Sexton is quite cautious in viewing this tendency toward growth and quantifiable results: business isn't the only group caught up in its web; he cites examples from not-for-profit hospitals to even church missionaries.

Concern about the effects of industrialization on millions of men and women goes back to the eighteenth century. Adam Smith believed the spurt in material output was caused by an organizational development, the division of labor, but he questioned the costs:

> In the progress of the division of labour, the employment of the far greater part of those who live by labour, that is, of the great body of the people, comes to be confined to a few very simple operations, frequently to one or two. But the understandings of the greater part of men are necessarily formed by their ordinary employments. The man whose whole life is spent in performing a few simple operations has no occasion to exert his understanding. . . He naturally loses, therefore, the habit of such exertion, and generally becomes as stupid and ignorant as it is possible for a human creature to become. The torpor of his mind renders him, not only incapable of relishing or bearing a part in any rational conversation, but of conceiving any generous, noble, or tender sentiment, and consequently of forming any just judgment concerning many even of the ordinary duties of private life. . . It corrupts even the activity of his body, and renders him incapable of exerting his strength with vigour and perseverance, in any other employment than that to which he has been bred.[6]

And as if this determination were not bad enough, he contrasted the worker in industrial society with his counterpart in nonindustrial societies, or, to use his term, barbarous societies:

> It is otherwise in the barbarous societies, as they are commonly called, of hunters, of shepherds, and even of husbandmen in that rude state of husbandry which precedes the improvement of manufactures, and the extension of foreign commerce. In such societies the varied occupations of every man oblige every man to exert his capacity, and to invent expedients for removing difficul-

ties which are continually occurring. Invention is kept alive, and the mind is not suffered to fall into that drowsy stupidity, which, in a civilized industrialized society, seems to benumb the understanding of almost all the inferior ranks of people.[7]

Later, Karl Marx, in *The Economic and Philosophical Manuscripts of 1844*,[8] saw that alienating (to use our contemporary term) conditions grew out of this new industrial order, which technically perfected the worker as producer but degraded the worker as human. Adopting the pessimism of Adam Smith, he wrote that the worker "does not affirm himself but denies himself . . . does not develop freely his physical and mental energy but mortifies his body and ruins his mind."[9] It is this issue that Sexton addresses when he describes the worklife of Jim Spencer on the assembly line:

> With an uninterrupted supply of cars, 50-60 cars move through the line in each hour. Within one minute, Jim must walk 20 feet to a conveyor belt, pick up a front seat weighing 30 pounds, carry it back . . . place the seat on the chasis, and put in four bolts using an air gun. . .

Sexton describes in Spencer's life and work some of the symptoms of Marx's theme of alienation: loss of pride and ambition, negative feelings about work, and resignation to a drab work existence.

This struggle to cope has for Jim Spencer, his co-workers, and his society, considerable costs in mental ill health, alcoholism, drug use, absenteeism, and physical sickness. The prestigious report, *Work in America,* points out that we assumed too long that there was no such thing as social-psychological pollution—that the effects of monotonous or meaningless jobs could be sloughed off as the workers went through the plant gates to home and community.[10]

In 1941, F. J. Roethlisberger, a leader in exploring industrial culture, wrote:

> Too frequently the human activities of industry are conceived of as essentially economic. An industrial organization is assumed to be composed of a number of individuals entering into relations of contract for the promotion of their own individual economic interests. It is not easy to explain why this conception which seems counter to every day experience, should be so firmly entrenched in the minds of men and why it should be so difficult to eradicate.[11]

It is precisely this point that separates the world view of the business mentality, described in Edward Trubac's essay, from William Sexton's contention that our corporations have to be perceived as psychological, social, and it is to be hoped, humane entities. The reconciliation of these two points of view will not be easy. Fortunately, in this age of inflation Sexton can chronicle enough examples of reform in quality of work life that are both humane *and* productive.

In his essay Sexton next shifts from the worker to that of the managerial ranks. He gives the story of Elizabeth Bradford, a member of a corporate bureaucracy at the level of lower middle management. He describes how she comes to her initial entry position in the personnel department with certain ethical aspirations: both to be competent and to be fair in the hiring of minorities. It is soon apparent that she is "sticking her nose in matters that should not concern her"; she is told that her initiatives are not appreciated. She is experiencing the bureaucratic process as described by Max Weber:

> The individual bureaucrat cannot squirm out of the apparatus in which [she] is harnessed. . . In the great majority of cases, [she] is a single cog in an ever-moving mechanism which prescribes to [her] an essentially fixed route of march. . .[12]

And while the blue-collar worker, Jim Spencer, is a victim of the tyranny of the machine, Elizabeth Bradford is likewise under a tyranny, in this case the large structures of our corporations. For Sexton, four profoundly important changes occur in this manager's life: first, her enthusiasm for "trying new things" in her job is dampened; second, ethical values, like working against job discrimination, are dropped; third, her conscience moves from being inner-directed to being company-directed; fourth, her career becomes obsessional. Finally, Sexton describes her at a meeting with her boss and her competitors, alert to every word and action that will help or hurt in the contest for promotion. He comments: "Of late, all of this has caused Beth to become more conservative in her decisions, less inclined to take risks and generally more reluctant to delegate."

For reasons that are not all that clear, Sexton appears more optimistic about improving the work life of Jim Spencer than he is about the moral nurturing of Elizabeth Bradford. It may be that since Jim Spencer's problem has a longer history, as witnessed to by both Adam Smith and Karl Marx, we have a better picture of the problem. The growth of managerial bureaucracy is more recent, and our techniques of analysis are still being developed.[13] It is this theme that the theological ethicist, James Gustafson, and the business consultant, Elmer Johnson, address in their dialogue in Part IV, on the resources of religion in forming *and informing* corporate men and women.

Religion can encourage an "inner liberation" which frees a person from the need to prove his or her merits to others and to institutions, and can bring about an "openness to be courageous, to take risks, to stand for what is right when consequences are painful." This is in sharp contrast to Sexton's story of Elizabeth Bradford, whose work life illustrates the erosion of moral commitment, vision, and courage. What should not be forgotten in Sexton's bleak assessment is the equally important fact that the corporation was adversely affected; it experienced the loss of a morally and professionally "effective person," to use the ideal model espoused by Gustafson and Johnson, and therefore its capacities to perceive the common good were lessened. The corporation must have men and women of strong moral conviction as well as managerial competence and personal ambition.

NOTES

1. David Riesman, "Capitalism, Socialism, and Democracy: A Symposium," *Commentary,* April, 1978, p. 67.

2. Karl Marx and Friedrich Engels, *The Communist Manifesto.* Available in many editions, see *Essential Works of Marxism,* ed. Arthur P. Mendel (New York: Bantam Edition, 1971), p. 17.

3. *Ibid.,* p. 16.

4. *Ibid.,* p. 15.

5. Joseph A. Schumpeter, *Capitalism, Socialism, and Democracy,* 3d ed. (New York: Harper & Brothers, 1950), p. 123.

6. Adam Smith, *The Wealth of Nations* (New York: Modern Library, 1937), p. 734.

7. *Ibid.,* p. 735.

8. Karl Marx, *Economic and Philosophic Manuscripts of 1844,* trans. Martin Milligan (Moscow: Foreign Languages Publishing House, 1961).

9. *Ibid.,* p. 72.

10. *Work in America* (Cambridge, Mass: MIT Press, 1973).

11. F. J. Roethlisberger, *Management and Morale* (Cambridge, Mass: Harvard University Press, 1941), p. 46.

12. Max Weber, *From Max Weber: Essays in Sociology,* trans. H. H. Gerth and C. Wright Mills (New York: Oxford Press, 1946), p. 228.

13. For a discussion of the historical development of bureaucratic structures in large organizations and their impact on both blue- and white-collar employees, see W. J. Heisler and John W. Houck (eds.), *A Matter of Dignity: Inquiries into the Humanization of Work* (Notre Dame, Ind.: University of Notre Dame Press, 1977).

1. Economic Guidelines for Corporate Decision-Making

Edward R. Trubac

While much has been written about the social, cultural, ethical, and political roles of the large business corporation, this paper will focus on the corporation as an economic institution. As such, it may simply be defined as the large-scale organization through which a modern society primarily accomplishes its economic purposes of production and distribution.

As a large-scale organization, it has very shallow roots in history, compared to such institutions as governments, military organizations, and universities. At best, it can trace its lineage a little farther back than a century. The first modern businesses, the first truly organized enterprises, were the large railroads, especially the transcontinental lines that spanned the country in the decades after the Civil War. The building of these railroads was a massive project that required tremendously large concentrations of capital; the business corporation emerged to supply this need.[1] Since then, its growth has been phenomenal. The combined sales of the 500 largest U.S. industrial companies have moved close to the $1.5 trillion mark. The billion dollar club—composed of companies reporting sales of more than $1 billion—has a membership of more than 280 companies. The more exclusive $5 billion club now totals almost 60 members.[2] The typical large corporation also engages in a variety of businesses. The modern firm that accounts for the vast bulk of the production of our Gross National Product and employs a significant proportion of those in the labor force is a product-diversified firm. To dramatize this point, General Electric owns over a hundred $100 million businesses.

The Role of Profits

Business corporations were initially organized as profit-seeking

33

institutions. Is this still the prime motivating force, or have some of the changes in society and in corporate structure during the past thirty to forty years relegated the profit goal to a secondary position? The issue has been and remains a controversial one. Two internal corporate developments are particularly relevant to this issue; interestingly enough, they each tend to pull in an opposite direction. One involves both the decentralizing of corporate operations and the emergence of the technology that made this decentralization possible. The other pertains to the increased separation of ownership and control, with control apparently firmly lodged in a group of professional managers and ownership remaining in a separate group of stockholders. The first has often been cited as a factor which has magnified the role of profits, while the second has been used to explain the growing importance of other corporate goals. While those are also unsettled areas, I believe the force of the following arguments makes it reasonable to view the corporation as an institution attempting to realize a multiplicity of goals with a *satisfactory* level of profits among the most important of these objectives.

Let us first discuss corporate decentralization, which was introduced as a way to make the rapidly growing corporation manageable. Decentralization is possible only if there is a genuine business entity with its own products and its own markets—that is, a unit which can truly show a profit and loss. Moreover, this financial information must be conveyed to top management which still makes the major entrepreneurial decisions of setting policy, allocating capital, and developing and placing key personnel.[3] In other words, decentralization will work only when the central corporate management has information and dependable knowledge regarding the company's businesses. Information and knowledge set the limits to decentralization, but these limits have been vastly expanded during the past decade with the improved capabilities of the computer and the rapid gains in information-processing technology. These changes have contributed to the image of large product-diversified firms absorbed in increasing profits, particularly short-term profits. This image portrays division managers as evaluated primarily on the basis of the profitability of the operations under their control. Since computer capabilities have reached the point where financial information can be quickly assembled and reported, the "financial performance" of divisional executives can be and is regularly monitored on a short-term basis by top management. Middle managers respond to this pressure by emphasizing the realization of short-term profits, even at the expense of greater profits in the future, let alone wider corporate goals.

A recent special issue of *Business Week* entitled, "The Reindustri-alization of America," underscored the current focus on short-term profits. While computer technology made it possible to monitor short-term profits in a multi-division business corporation, the "compensation" systems of many companies (e.g., bonuses tied to short-term profits), the financial requirements for investment projects (e.g., that the project must pay for itself within two or three years), and the criteria for management by objective goals and for performance appraisal, all point to an exceedingly short-term orientation.[4]

The literature discussing the effect of the separation of ownership and control is vast, but the main points can be easily summarized. One main line of reasoning claims that management, emancipated from control by owners, who are viewed as passive and interested only in dividends, formulates objectives and pursues managerial goals that may differ from those of the stockholders. Goals such as controlling the largest possible industrial empire, solving social problems, maximizing personal remuneration, and avoiding any risk taking are considered by some observers to have replaced the attainment of profits as a predominant goal.

Those expressing the conterargument, while acknowledging the existence of multiple corporate goals, believe that the case has been overstated. Stockholders have turned out to be far less passive than was earlier assumed. Two factors account for their more aggressive stance. First, an increasing proportion of stockholdings is in the hands of institutional investors. The institutional investor, like other stockholders, is interested primarily in profits. But unlike many small individual investors, however sophisticated, these institutions allocate staff and executive time to the observation and study of the policies and prospects of firms in which they have invested. Moreover, even if institutions refrain from exercising their control through voting power or support existing management as a matter of policy, their investment decisions will have an important influence on security prices and the availability of capital.[5] Second, the flurry of merger and acquisition activity during the past ten to fifteen years has given most large corporations a controlling interest in a number of diversified companies. Whatever the reason for the acquisition, one can be certain that the controlling firm is interested in the profit potential of the acquired company. For example, Reliance Electric was recently purchased by Exxon; one of the first orders of business was to align Reliance's fiscal year with that of Exxon's.

In summary, while the large business corporation pursues multiple goals, achieving a satisfactory level of profits continues to be one of the major objectives. Since few corporations would admit to having attained a satisfactory profit level, the objective is almost always operationally expressed in terms of improvement.

Corporate Decisions and Economic Concerns

What are the activities in which managers engage to better profit levels? Although the following list is by no means complete, it does identify the major economic concerns which occupy a good part of the time of the top management of large U.S. corporations:

1. Expand the product market share.
2. Consider the special case of advertising.
3. Shift from low- to high-growth segments of their industries, or move into new industries that are growing or are expected to grow at a rapid rate.
4. Attempt to reduce costs by promoting efficiencies.
5. Reduce risk.
6. Be a good citizen (the economic base of this guideline will be discussed later).

Each of these items will be discussed in turn.

Expand the market share. Apart from the prestige of being one of the largest firms in the industry, there are a number of economic reasons why corporations concentrate on expanding market share. One reason is that sales must be high enough to justify the large research expenditures, plant and capital-equipment requirements, distribution costs, etc., that are needed in some industries to achieve lower unit costs. In the jargon of the economist, economies of scale often require large organizations (the automobile industry is a classic example of economies of scale). But the demand for the product must be sufficient to validate the large organization; hence the need to expand market share. Obviously, the benefits of economies of scale are not limited to profit-seeking corporations. One local community, for example, might use several CAT scanners to do the same number of procedures that another system does with one placed in a single hospital. Because average unit costs of computerized tomography decline substantially with volume, the community that concentrates all the procedures at one hospital can have much lower unit costs.

A closely related but distinct reason for increasing market share applies especially to new products and new technologies and revolves around the theory of the learning curve. The theory says simply that manufacturing costs, for example, can be brought down by a fixed percentage, depending on the product, each time the *cumulative* volume of output and sales is doubled. This is not merely a matter of spreading overhead costs over a larger volume of sales, as we noted above. It primarily involves constantly forcing manufacturing costs down through design improvement of the product and the production process. The more that is produced, the more one learns about how to cut costs in making the product.[6] The best-known proponent of this approach to market share in this country is Texas Instruments, particularly with respect to its production and sales of pocket calculators and digital watches.

Another motive behind obtaining larger market share would be to simply secure market power. The extreme case here, of course, would be the acquisition of monopoly power in which the sales of one firm are identical with industrial sales. Unless regulated by the government, such a position would give the firm complete discretion to raise prices by restricting production. A similar result could be obtained by a small number of firms acting in collusion. The actions of the OPEC cartel, in raising crude oil prices more than tenfold since 1973, dramatically illustrate the exercise of this type of raw market power.

The above discussion attempts to make a critical distinction between *realizing* a *high* market share and *attempting* to secure a *higher* market share. The former would most likely be associated with high monopoly prices, while the latter would likely be consistent with lower prices in a competitive setting. One could argue, however, that lower prices are simply a transitional phase, a required stop in the inevitable drive toward the attainment of monopoly power; for example, firms could price at or below cost in order to eliminate competition, after which prices would be raised to enjoy monopoly profits. Despite legal strictures, this possibility certainly exists.

However, this practice does not seem to be the rule in high-technology, high-growth domestic markets. Texas Instruments has consistently generated high profits while, at the same time, lowering prices for pocket calculators. Besides, market power has become more difficult to obtain or sustain during the past decade in an environment characterized by rapid technology developments and intense international competition. No market ought to be considered in solely domestic terms until study justifies that conclusion. Schumpeter's "gale of competition" blows from all points on the compass, but particularly from Europe and Japan. To discuss the U.S. automobile market solely in terms of General Motors, Ford, Chrysler, and American Motors is to neglect the 25 percent of sales that reflect foreign production. Witness the extraordinary recent visit to Japan by the president of the United Auto Workers to try to persuade the Japanese to build their plants in the United States in order to save union jobs. Moreover, the recent efforts made by both the auto industry and the steel industry to enlist the government's help in protecting domestic producers against foreign imports hardly suggest the exercise of raw monopoly power.

Having identified the reasons *why* firms try to obtain a larger market share, the next step is to discuss *how* they go about attempting to do so. Most of the techniques can be subsumed under price reductions, quality improvements, or increased advertising.

We have already hinted at the price-reduction/quality-improvement approach used by Texas Instruments. Prices are reduced in order to obtain greater market share; the resulting gains in production yield the experience necessary to generate the product improvement and reductions in production costs which justify the lower price.[7] The Japanese leadership in the color TV industry is another interesting example of this price-reduction/quality-improvement approach. Net wages in Japan are nearly equal to those in U.S. industry. Yet by applying superb process engineering, the Japanese, during the past several years, have achieved both lower costs and higher reliability than their U.S. competitors. Sony, Matsushita, Hitachi, and Toshiba enjoy roughly a 75 percent world market share. When their higher market share and consequently lower-per-unit costs permitted the introduction of a one-year warranty (U.S. practice was 90 days), the warranty costs for one prominent U.S. firm allegedly rose from 2 percent to 9 percent of the sales, a reflection of the relatively poor quality of the U.S. product.[8] But in major home appliances, General Electric and Whirlpool have made the investments in efficient manufacturing process and scale necessary to block any Japanese advantage in both quality and price. In fact, TV and major appliances are a dramatic and instructive contrast. In one industry, imports have captured the major share of the U.S. market. In the other, a similar industry with respect to manufacturing and distribution, the U.S. manufacturers are pre-eminent.[9] However, no firm or country has a monopoly on technology gains, and U.S. TV manufacturers, for example, have managed to recapture some of their former market share.

The present auto industry is also a classic case of the price/quality mix as a determinant of market share. Reflecting the production of superior foreign-made cars that meet the demand for fuel efficiency, auto imports soared in February 1980 to 27 percent of the total sales, as large U.S.-made cars piled up in dealer showrooms. In fact, as a proportion of total U.S. sales, sales of *full-size* cars have fallen from 30 percent in 1977 to only 14 percent today. But U.S. producers are also at a disadvantage in making small cars. When the Motor and Equipment Manufacturers Association canvassed 10,000 American households in 1978 and 1979, it found that imports strongly outranked U.S. small cars in perceived fuel economy, engineering, and even durability. Chrysler's popular four-door Omni and Horizon subcompacts—both with front-wheel drive—are virtual copies of Volkswagen's five-year-old Rabbit.[10]

Consider the special case of advertising. Another approach commonly used in garnering a larger market share is advertising. One line of argument stresses that advertising raises prices to consumers and is instrumental in the establishment of monopoly power. A recent study of the soft-drink industry concluded that "consumer prices for soft drinks are substantially above the competitive level" and that "large scale advertising (25 percent of sales revenue) has once more taken its toll, converting what might have been a highly competitive American industry into a tightly oligopolistic one that serves the public poorly."[11] We are all too familiar with this type of consumer advertising, in which product differences are all too often a function of consumer perception than grounded in fact.

However, there is another line of reasoning that argues that advertising often results neither in higher prices nor increments in monopoly power. To the extent that advertising provides firms with the opportunity to make their product or service known to a wider market, we might well expect decreases in production costs per unit (economies of scale) which may, in some cases, exceed the additional expense of advertising and allow the product to be sold at a lower price.

George Stigler, in his pioneering article on "The Economics of Information," demonstrated that *price* advertising can be expected to decrease the price of products by providing consumers with better information. In the absence of price advertising, consumers must search about for the best price. Since in many cases, the cost of this consumer search will be high relative to the item purchased, the consumer will benefit from price advertising.[12] This position is supported by Lee Benham's study of the price differences for eye examinations and eyeglasses in states that permit advertising of these services and products and those that prohibit such advertising. Professor Benham found that consumers paid significantly less for these services and products in states where advertising was permitted. Differences in income and demographic characteristics were accounted for in his studies, so that the results indicate that advertising allows these firms to communicate with customers, to reach larger markets, and to offer lower prices because of the competition it fosters.[13]

What about false or misleading advertising? Although examples of such advertising are legion, recent empirical work argues that they often tend to be relatively short-lived in either duration or impact because consumers learn to judge their validity. Phillip Nelson, for example, makes a distinction between "search" and "experience" qualities of goods and services.[14] Search qualities are those that can be determined prior to the actual purchase of an item, (e.g., dress) while experience qualities can only be determined after the purchase (e.g., can of tuna). Advertising for search goods stresses high-information content about product or service features. This information then reduces the search process as does Stigler's price advertising. For search goods, the consumer can compare the advertising claims to the product features prior to actually making the purchase. If the firm has misrepresented the product, it may lose credibility with the consumer. The consumer, whose confidence in future advertising by the firm is shaken, can influence others in his sphere of influence.

With respect to experience goods, the consumer has much less power to control advertising through prepurchase comparisons than with search goods. If an advertiser makes claims about the contents of a can of tuna, the only way the consumer is able to validate those claims is by purchasing the can and consuming the tuna. This fact would seem to support widespread and continued misrepresentation of the product. However, sellers of this class of goods cannot continue in business without repeat sales. If products do not live up to advertising claims, consumers will change to an alternative product when making future purchases. The profitability of the firm depends primarily on repeat purchases, and repeat purchases will be an increasing function of the truthfulness of advertising.[15]

Needless to say, this approach to the issue of false and misleading advertising has its severe critics and the question remains a controversial one.

Seeking high market growth. As we noted earlier, large U.S. corporations attempt to shift from low- to high-growth segments of their industries, or move to new industries (through the acquisition of firms) that are growing or are expected to grow at a rapid rate. These decisions lean heavily on the notion of the market life of a product; this life is typically characterized by an early phase in which the growth of sales is slow while the market learns about the product, a second phase in which growth is extremely rapid, a third phase in which growth slows, and a fourth phase in which sales may actually decline. While firms are constantly looking for products that are in their early growth phases, the identification process is by no means precise and mistakes are often made.

An interesting example of a firm moving into high-growth sectors within the same industries in which it has been active for many years is PPG (formerly Pittsburgh Plate Glass). PPG still depends on glass production for more than one-third of its revenues with PPG active only in a limited number of markets. The transportation and construction industries account for 40 percent of PPG sales, mainly through the purchase of glass products. The dangers of such reliance are especially apparent with both the auto and housing markets depressed. For the long term, moreover, the two markets seem to offer dismal prospects for glassmakers. Since 1973, auto down-sizing already has reduced the amount of glass used in the average car by about 10 percent. In construction, ordinary flat glass, of which PPG is the leading U.S. producer, is synonymous with energy loss. Although an orderly retreat from those markets might seem prudent, PPG is launching an aggressive marketing and capital investment program that will maintain the company's existing dependence on the housing and auto sectors by expanding its position in a few strong niches of these otherwise weak markets. To counter its losses in the automotive sector, PPG is building a huge plant designed to almost double its total capacity in producing fiberglass-reinforced plastic (FRP). FRP is eagerly sought by the auto industry to reduce car weight by replacing steel parts. PPG's investments also are dedicated to increasing capacity to produce construction glasses that save energy, such as multiplane windows and reflective glasses.[16]

While the above example is an interesting case of a company finding a high-growth segment in new product development in existing markets, many corporations instead seek higher-growth markets by diversifying into other industries. We earlier noted that General Electric owns over 100, $100 million businesses. The U.S. economy is dominated by large diversified firms seeking higher returns by regularly scanning their portfolio of businesses, deciding where their funds should be allocated by acquisition, modernization, and expansion of productive capacity, new product development, etc. Du Pont has, for example, been a leading producer of fibers for years. There is still some room for innovation in the fibers business, but it is essentially a mature industry, at least in the advanced industrial countries. Du Pont's strategy, therefore, is to take some of the cash generated by the fibers business and invest it in businesses that have more potential for growth, such as plastics.[17] Even the steel industry, faced with long-term projections of very slow growth for its products, has diversified into such areas as insurance, savings and loan associations, oil equipment, and petrochemicals.

The development of industries that have strong growth possibilities has obvious effects in terms of gains in employment and income. Regional growth is, to a significant extent, dependent on the decisions made by corporations in deciding where to locate their plants, distribution centers, headquarters, etc. A recent article analyzing the New England computer industry offers a partial explanation for these location decisions in terms of the product life cycle described above. The main thrust of this argument is that innovation occurs mainly in the established centers of the industry, especially when new products require high-technology resources and specialized inputs from other industries in the centers. Production is on a small scale at first and tends to use, for example, skilled engineers and machinists. Mature, large-scale production, on the other hand, stresses mechanization and low-skill labor. Mature industries look for locations that have low labor costs and ready access to markets.

This process appears to be important for some facets of the computer industry. The New England region seems to be strongest in the new parts of the industry as well as in research and development. Thus, while some production processes in the computer industry are choosing locations outside the region, the more innovative segments remain in New England. The message that can be read from these trends is that New England should be concerned less with attracting industry into the region or preventing firms from leaving than with fostering an environment that will allow the continued health and development of innovative activities.[18]

But what about communities where there are no such special attractions and where long-established, no-growth industries have decided to close antiquated facilities employing thousands of people? One case in point is the recent attempt by U.S. Steel to close its two aged steel plants in Youngstown, Ohio, because they are no longer financially viable operations. These plants have experienced losses in the past and they are projected to generate losses into the foreseeable future. In issuing a temporary restraining order against the planned March-through-June 1980 phasedown-shutdown of the Youngstown plants, the U.S. district court judge stated that, "U.S. Steel cannot leave the Mahoning Valley in a complete state of waste."[19] The purpose of citing this example is not to argue for or against the position taken by U.S. Steel, but simply to point out that a corporate policy of pursuing the development of growth markets can be costly to regions that contain no-growth industries and to the people employed by these firms.

The pursuit of a growth strategy is not limited to profit-making firms; not-for-profit institutions also engage in this type of activity. As populations shifted to the suburbs, schools, hospitals, and other agencies followed. Concern has been expressed over the quantity and quality of those institutions that remained to serve the people still living in the inner city. Moreover, a recent attempt by the City of New York to close some of its municipal hospitals was attacked not only because health-care services for residents would be more difficult to obtain, but also because some of the hospitals were the major employers in particular sections of the city.

Promoting efficiencies. We would define efficiency as the attempt to economize on the use of resources in producing a product or services. The fewer the resources used, the lower the per-unit costs and the higher the per-unit profits, or the lower the prices in a highly competitive industry. For the most part, not-for-profit institutions also have incentives to operate efficiently, since reductions in costs per unit of service provided means that more services can be provided with a given budget. Our previous discussion touched on growth in market share as a vehicle for reductions in cost per unit. Here, we are simply talking about conscious attempts to eliminate waste and inefficiency for a given level of output. A wide variety of approaches might be used, including plant modernization, worker retraining, eliminating unnecessary jobs, or substituting materials. One obvious factor stimulating a massive efficiency effort by corporations has been the rapid rise in energy prices during the past several years. In response to these higher prices, many corporations have achieved reductions in energy costs per unit of output of 20 percent or more. Some eliminated obvious waste through simple conservation practices, whereas others installed more energy-efficient machinery. Still others altered their capital/labor ratios and substituted labor for capital whenever possible. In fact, it has been argued by some that, in the face of substantial increases in the labor force, rising energy prices have kept unemployment significantly lower than it would have been if energy prices had remained stable.

The airlines, for example, have attempted to cope with rising fuel prices by pulling out of small cities involving relatively short flights and using their planes instead for longer routes which use less fuel per mile traveled. Needless to say, they have also placed large orders for new, fuel-efficient planes. Another efficiency program that has received a great deal of publicity during the past three years is the one that was inaugurated at International Harvester by Archie McCardell, former president of Xerox, who was hired by International Harvester three years ago. A short time after he joined the company, he installed a widely publicized massive cost-cutting plan. He claims to have saved $460 million in a two-year period, in good part by eliminating 11,000 jobs. While he had added other positions in order to handle Harvester's 40 percent sales growth during the last three years, the net result has been that total employment has risen only from 93,000 to 97,660. In fact, the five-month-old strike at International Harvester has had much more to do with work rules and efficiency than with wages, with McCardell arguing that more employer discretion in mandating overtime work is needed if plant inefficiences are to be significantly reduced.[20]

We have already cited the advantages of promoting efficiency. In a competitive economy, lower-per-unit costs tend to result in lower prices paid by consumers for goods and services. In addition, resources are conserved rather than wasted, a goal espoused by both profit-seeking and not-for-profit corporations. On the other hand, efficiency programs may result in structural unemployment in which an individual who is laid off in a cost-cutting program has difficulty finding employment either because of age, or because he or she lacks the type of skills demanded in the marketplace. The Youngstown situation cited above illustrates this point. The domestic steel industry, faced with dismal growth prospects, has reduced its capacity during the past few years, with the cutbacks concentrated in its oldest, most inefficient plants. Those who are unemployed as a result will have difficulty finding other jobs in a low-growth area in which the steel industry has been a major employer.

Another concern is that a drive for efficiency may result in products that harm the environment or that are shoddy or unsafe. One could, of course, argue that decisions to produce these products do not result in true efficiency since costs are not reduced but are merely passed on to the public in the form of, for example, impure air or unsafe cars. The controversy surrounding the Ford Pinto is a clear illustration of the latter point. Apart from the issues of criminal negligence and conformance with federal standards, the fact remains that Ford's decisions, for cost reasons, not to reposition the gas tank did increase the possibility of an explosion upon collision.

Normally, one would expect product issues of environmental protection and safety to be handled through mandated costs imposed on corporations by government regulation. Catalytic converters on cars and precipitators on smokestacks of electric power plants are examples of approaches taken to attain cleaner air. We attempt to promote car safety, for example, by installing seat belts. All of the above examples involve costs incurred by the firm which are then passed on to the users of these commodities. The point is that manufacturing a product that pollutes the air because it is cheaper for the firm is not an example of efficiency. The costs remain, but they are borne by the general public. What is needed is a mechanism that makes the firm bear the initial costs of cleaning the air which would then be passed on in the form of higher prices to those who buy the product.

One could generalize and argue that competition or limited budgets tend to promote efficiencies, while their absence encourage inefficiencies. There has been widespread concern, for example, over the tremendous rise in health-care costs in the U.S. While there are several reasons for this phenomenon, it is easy to identify one of the major factors. Because most medical payments are made by third-party payees (e.g., Blue Cross) under insurance or government welfare plans, the cost of a specific course of treatment is frequently of only minor importance, if any, to the patient who receives it or his physician who selects it. With no incentive to look for cheaper alternatives, costs tend to increase at rapid rates.

Inefficiency is also encouraged in our treatment of regulated natural monopolies, such as electric utility companies. Although there is a need for regulation, the usual approaches taken have little to do with encouraging efficiency. States normally limit the profit rates that can be earned. This type of regulation makes sense if we assume that the firm is, in fact, minimizing costs. Yet, there are no real incentives to minimize costs under a profit-regulating mechanism. Even if profits are limited to a set rate, both costs and prices will be very different from what they are under competition. The profit rate is not a good test for social policy if the product market is not competitive, since low profits can be associated with unnecessarily high costs and will perhaps result in higher prices than those that would result from a competitive market.[21] As an example, consider the widespread controversy over the substantial increase in advertising expenditures by electric utility companies. This spending was designed to encourage the use of electricity by consumers in the face of an anticipated sluggish growth rate in consumption. These expenditures then became the basis for requesting higher prices from state commissions in order to maintain targeted profit rates.

Arguing in the same vein one can evaluate the efficiency of nationalized corporations in part by the extent to which they are sheltered from competition. If they are so sheltered, they tend to be less efficient. But there are obviously instances where the nationalized companies operate in (and are responsive to) an atmosphere of a high degree of international competition. Thus Volkswagen, although largely nationally owned, is an efficient producer of cars, while the French steel industry, subsidized by the government for years, is in the process of radically restructuring itself in order to become competitive in world markets. On the other hand, one could logically argue that U.S. private firms that sell the bulk of their products to the federal government on a cost-plus contract basis have fewer incentives to be efficient than Volkswagen, since the latter is involved in a very competitive world auto market. In his book, *The New Industrial State,* John Kenneth Galbraith touches on a related point when he states that

> Increasingly, it will be recognized that the mature corporation, as it develops, becomes part of the larger administrative complex associated with the state. In time, the line between the two will disappear. Men will look back in amusement at the pretense that once caused people to refer to General Dynamics and North American Aviation as private businesses.[22]

I share this amusement but I would still stress that from the viewpoint of efficiency, the critical distinction is not whether the firm is public or private, or whether it is a profit-seeking corporation or a not-for-profit institution, but rather whether it provides its products and services in a competitive market or has its costs subsidized by a third-party payee or through the government budget.

Reduce risk. Risk aversion has a positive value for managers as it has for most groups of society. Faced with choosing between projects with similar expected levels of profits but with different levels of risk (with the higher risk level associated with greater possibilities of both greater profits and greater losses), most businesses would choose the less risky alternative. In a real sense, there is a trade off between profit and risk, in which a firm might accept less profit from a project if it entailed less risk. How, then, do firms go about trying to reduce risk? A partial listing would include such approaches as market research, risk-adjusted capital budgeting techniques, socialization of risk, and merger activity. Each will be briefly discussed in turn.

(a) *Market research.* This activity ranges from informal conversations with suppliers to sophisticated analysis done by highly trained specialists. While the approaches vary, the objectives remain the same—to find out as much as possible about the markets in which the firm's products and services are sold in order to minimize the risk of incorrect judgments. While most mistakes about the customer markets result from little or no market research, those errors which have received the most publicity occurred despite huge expenditures for market research. They illustrate how difficult it is to make good judgments about risk aversion. Two examples that come to mind are the Edsel car produced by the Ford Motor Company and Corfam leather made by Du Pont in the mid-1960s. Both products did not meet market needs and resulted in company losses of hundreds of millions of dollars.

(b) *Risk and capital investment decisions.* There are a number of techniques, such as the net present value and internal rate of return methods, which have been developed to measure risk-adjusted rates of return on long-term capital investment. Perhaps the crudest but still popular approach to dealing with risk in investment decisions is setting an arbitrary span of time over which the investment generates cash proceeds equal in amount to the initial outlay for the investment. A serious shortcoming of this technique is that the payback period does not take into consideration any of the cash proceeds that are received after the payback date. Those managers who use it justify it on the basis of the substantial uncertainty inherent in forecasting future cash flows in their particular businesses. Because of this uncertainty, only the immediate and near-term cash flows can be considered with any degree of confidence, and therefore only investments that have a relatively short payback period should be undertaken. As an example of the problems that arise with this approach, business managers who invest in projects located in foreign countries that have a history of unstable governments and nationalization of externally owned firms will sometimes demand a sufficiently high rate of return to ensure that their ventures will be recouped within, say, three years. Such behavior throws them open to the criticism of exploiting the poor.[23]

(c) *Socialization of risk.* This term basically has to do with private firms sharing business risks with the government. Perhaps the best example is that of the U.S. government largely assuming the risks of new product development (mostly of defense items) under cost-plus contracts signed with private firms. The phenomenon, however, has been much more fully developed in Japan. In fact, a close observer of the Japanese economy has argued that socialization of risk has been one of the major factors accounting for the rapid growth rate in the Japanese economy during the post-World War II period.[24] The process works in the following fashion. For certain key sectors which have been targeted as growth industries—such as the auto, steel, and chemical sectors — there is an essential government guarantee against failure, financial stringency, or substantial lay-off of permanent workers. This guarantee against failure removes much of the uncertainty and risk associated with long-term capital investments in plant and equipment and has been a major item in promoting the growth of the latter. It would be very difficult for the Chrysler debacle to have been duplicated in Japan since their management team would have been replaced much earlier because of pressure exerted by the government. The basic policy stance is that workers should not be made to suffer for the mistakes of management; consequently, there would have been no substantial reduction in the labor force. Another example of socialization of risk is the fact that Japan prides itself on applying a "polluter pay principle" to compensate victims of environmental pollution, on the basis of what our common law calls strict liability. However, the firm's resulting liabilities are then financed by long-term government loans at preferentially low interest rates.[25]

(d) *Mergers and acquisitions.* There are at least two ways that mergers and acquisitions can reduce business risk. The first is by increasing market power at the expense of competition, either by the merging of two or more firms in the same industry or by one firm acquiring one or more firms in the same industry. Multifirm consolidations at the turn of the century permitted scores of firms to control more than half of their markets. While such combinations are now illegal, mergers among firms in related industries have continued. Walter Adams has pointed out that between 1956 and 1963, 20 major oil companies were involved in 226 mergers and thereby gained control over a variety of substitute fuels, such as coal and atomic energy. The oil companies also moved into allied businesses such as fertilizers, plastics, and chemicals.[26] Whatever the social impact of these mergers, they certainly reduced the risks stemming from potential competition and possible loss of markets.

Most of the recent mergers and acquisitions during the past twenty years, however, have been in unrelated industries. One reason for diversifications of this type was to reduce the risks inherent in business fluctuations. By acquiring unrelated industries, the hope was that sales declines in one business would be offset by increased sales in another business whose pattern of cyclical fluctuations may be different. A good example here would be the acquisition policies followed by the major copper companies. Copper sales and copper prices are extremely volatile and sensitive to the swings of the business cycle. Partially to reduce this cyclical risk, Kennecott Copper recently acquired Carborundum, a major manufacturer of abrasives, while Arco

Steel, which owns Anaconda Copper, has marked the latter's aluminum business for expansion in order to stabilize its profits.

"Be A Good Corporate Citizen." Since this paper deals only with the economic motivations of corporate managers, we will limit our discussion of this motivating factor to what has been called "enlightened self-interest," that is, a set of activities that are consistent with enhancing the long-term-profit growth potential of the corporation.

Obviously, this goal is more difficult to define than the other economic criteria discussed thus far. Increasing market share is a rather precise concept; acting in one's enlightened self-interest is a notion that contains far more ambiguity. One very interesting interpretation of this concept of "enlightened self-interest" was supplied by the Research and Policy Committee of the Committee for Economic Development (CED) in their June 1971 statement.[27] The Committee described public expectations of business with reference to three concentric circles of responsibilities. The inner circle included the fundamental responsibilities of efficiently providing products, jobs, and economic growth. The intermediate circle required an additional awareness of changes in social values and priorities, say, of environmental impacts, employee relations, greater desire by customers for more product information, and protection from injury. The outer circle encompassed the broader responsibilities of business to take an active part in improving the social environment, for example, by ameliorating poverty and urban blight—not necessarily because business has caused the problem, but because it possesses the resources and skills to make an improvement and because such improvements are in its "enlightened self-interest." In developing this last point, the CED argued that corporate grants to universities, for example, provide future trained personnel. Similarly, grants for health and cultural facilities can be justified as a way to attract skilled people to the community, and grants to improve ghetto housing and recreational facilities contribute to a safer and more acceptable environment for employees and business operations. Indeed, corporate interest as it is broadly defined in this way can support efforts by management to solve social problems, because "people who have a good environment, education and opportunity make better employees, customers and neighbors for businesses than those who are poor, ignorant and oppressed."[28]

A review of some recent statements made by top executives of large corporations regarding their perception of what constitutes "enlightened self-interest" supplemented by some personal discussions, has enabled me to develop a sample composite of their current interpretation of the 1971 CED statement. I do not know to what extent the views stated below reflect the feelings of a majority of business leaders.

First, the inner circle of efficiently providing products, jobs, and growth pertains to the basic nature of the business and would be defined in terms of immediate corporate self-interest. The second set of concerns—environmental impacts, employee relations, product information, and protection from injury—would also be considered by most corporate executives as obligations that emanate from the fundamental job of running the business. Whether mandated by government regulation or through voluntary programs, these activities, as indicated by their statements, are viewed as legitimate responsibilities of a profit-seeking corporation. The following quotation by Mr. James Ferguson, Chairman and Chief Executive of General Foods Corporation, is illustrative in this regard.

> There is clearly an "enlightened corporate self-interest" in being a fair employer, a reliable supplier, a law-abiding citizen, and a good neighbor. Regardless of how enlightened that self-interest may be, however, it's still self-interest. It is neither healthy nor wise to claim otherwise. We should not attempt to fool ourselves or the public on this point, nor should we adopt an attitude of moral superiority. If a company fails to act as a good citizen and a good neighbor, sooner or later there will be a reaction which will affect its ability to function effectively. No responsible manager can afford to overlook that fact.[29]

The murky sector is the outer circle, the area that encompasses such items as grants to universities, reducing poverty and blight, etc. While the CED clearly identified all the activities cited in this outer circle as consistent with "enlightened self-interest," I sensed only partial agreement about that among corporate executives. Certainly, there are rather clear cases of "enlightened self-interest" here. For example, the efforts of J. Irwin Miller, Chairman of the Board of Cummins Engine, in rejuvenating the town of Columbus, Indiana, have much to do with the need to attract top-flight managerial talent to the corporate headquarters of a large firm located in a small Midwest community. In a similar manner, grants given by national accounting firms to schools that supply a significant proportion of their managers clearly suggest a quid pro quo relationship. However, direct efforts to solve a broad spectrum of social problems in local communities are often perceived by business executives as public-service activities that are the primary responsibility of local and state governments. My limited sense of current corporate policy is that such activities should be encouraged to a point, but that they should not be carried beyond the capacity of the enterprise to fulfill the obligations cited in the two inner circles. There is, however, an increasingly prevalent point of view that corporate management should not ignore social problems once that point is reached. Instead, they should educate themselves about political, social, and economic reality and then put that knowledge to work through meaningful participation in the political process.[30]

Summary

This paper focused on the large business corporation as an economic institution. Although the corporation tries to meet a number of objectives, attaining a satisfactory level of profits is one of its primary goals. The major part of the paper was devoted to identifying and discussing those activities in which corporate managers engage in order to reach their profit goals. The nonexclusive list included (a) expanding market share; (b) shifting resources from low- to high-growth industries; (c) attempting to reduce costs by promoting efficiencies; (d) reducing risk; and (e) engaging in activities that make the firm a good corporate citizen.

In discussing the expansion of market share, we distinguished between *realizing* a *high* market share and *attempting* to secure a *higher* market share, with the former normally associated with rising monopoly prices and the latter consistent with competitive pricing. Despite the claims of those who identify size with monopoly power, we argued that the typical large business corporation finds itself in an environment characterized by rapid technology developments and intense domestic and international competition.

In discussing the corporate drive toward high market growth, reference was made to the ongoing process by which large U.S. corporations attempted to shift from low- to high-growth segments of their industries, or move into new industries (through the acquisition of firms) that are growing or are expected to grow at a rapid rate. In essence, the U.S. economy is dominated by large diversified firms seeking higher returns by regularly scanning their portfolios of businesses, and deciding where their funds should be allocated for such purposes as acquisition, modernization and expansion of productive capacity. As an illustration, General Electric owns over a hundred $100 million businesses. Corporate decisions in this area are closely linked to regional development with regional and/or community growth or decay dependent, to a significant extent, on the decisions made by corporations in deciding where to locate their plants, distribution centers, headquarters, etc. Criteria used by the computer industry in making these decisions were presented for illustrative purposes.

Improving efficiency is another approach used by firms to improve profits. It involves attempts to economize on the use of resources in producing a given product or service by such means as plant modernization, worker retraining, eliminating unnecessary jobs, or substituting materials. In discussing incentives to promote efficiency, the critical distinction is not whether the firm is public or private, or even whether it is a profit-seeking corporation or a not-for-profit institution, but rather whether it provides its products and services in competitive markets.

Most firms pursue the goal of risk aversion. Faced with choosing between profits with similar expected levels of profits but with different levels of risk, most businesses would choose the less risky alternative. A partial listing of some of the ways in which firms would attempt to reduce risk would include market research, risk-adjusted capital budgeting techniques, socialization of risk, and merger activity. For example, socialization of risk basically has to do with private firms sharing business risks with the government. One illustration would be that of the federal government largely assuming the risks of new product development under cost-plus contracts with private firms. Another example here would be that of the Chrysler loan guarantee.

In discussing the goal of being a good corporate citizen, the discussion was limited to what has been called enlightened self-interest, that is, a set of activities that are consistent with enhancing the long-term profit growth potential of the corporation. Besides the basic corporate functions of efficiently providing products, jobs, and growth, enlightened self-interest also encompassed concern over environmental impacts, employee relations, and product information and safety. The paper also discussed the admittedly murky area of corporate responsibilities in improving education, rejuvenating local communities, and reducing poverty. While there are some rather clear cases of enlightened self-interest in the promotion of these activities, direct efforts to solve a broad spectrum of social problems of local communities are often perceived as public-service activities that are the primary responsibility of local and state governments.

NOTES

1. Peter F. Drucker, *The Concept of the Corporation* (New York: Mentor, 1964), p. x.

2. "The Fortune Directory of the 500 Largest U.S. Industrial Corporations," *Fortune* Magazine, May 5, 1980, pp. 276-78.

3. Drucker, *Concept of the Corporation,* p. 239.

4. "The Reindustrialization of America," *Business Week,* June 30, 1980, p. 75.

5. William L. Baldwin, "The Motives of Managers, Environmental Restraints, and the Theory of Managerial Enterprise," *The Quarterly Journal of Economics,* 78 (May 1964): 252.

6. Phillip Kotler, *Principles of Marketing* (Englewood Cliffs, N.J.: Prentice-Hall, 1980), pp. 80-84.

7. "Texas Instruments Shows U.S. Business How to Survive in the 1980's," *Business Week,* September 18, 1978, pp. 68-69.

8. Joseph L. Bower, "The Business of Business is Serving Markets," *Papers and Proceedings, American Economic Review,* May 1978, p. 324.

9. *Ibid.,* p. 325.

10. "U.S. Autos Losing a Big Segment of the Market — Forever?," *Business Week,* March 24, 1980, p. 84.

11. James F. Mongoven, "Advertising as a Barrier to Entry: Structure and Performance in the Soft-Drink Industry," *Antitrust Law and Economic Review* 8, no. 1 (1976): 101.

12. George Stigler, "The Economics of Information," *Journal of Political Economy,* June 1961, pp. 213-25.

13. Lee Benham, "The Effect of Advertising on the Price of Eyeglasses," *Journal of Law and Economics,* (October 1972, pp. 337-52.

14. Phillip Nelson, "The Economic Consequences of Advertising," *The Journal of Business,* April 1975, pp. 213-41.

15. *Ibid.*

16. "PPG Industries: Still Relying on Glass — But Now in Growth Areas," *Business Week,* January 21, 1980, pp. 96-97.

17. Lee Smith, "Dow Vs. Dupont: Rival Formulas for Leadership," *Fortune* Magazine, September 10, 1979, p. 79.

18. John Heckman, "The Future of High Technology Industry in New England: A Case Study of Computers," *New England Economic Review,* January-February 1980, pp. 16-17.

19. *American Metal Market,* March 21, 1980, p. 13.

20. "International Harvester: When Cost-Cutting Threatens the Future," *Business Week,* February 11, 1980, p. 100.

21. Harvey Leibenstein, "X-Efficiency: From Concept to Theory," *Challenge,* September-October 1979, p. 21.

22. John Kenneth Galbraith, *The New Industrial State,* rev. ed. (New York: Mentor, 1971) pp. 377-78.

23. Samuel Webb, *Managerial Economics* (Boston: Houghton-Mifflin, 1976), p. 404.

24. Martin Bronfenbrenner, "On Japanese Economic Growth," *Federal Reserve Bank of San Francisco Economic Review,* Summer 1979, p. 8.

25. *Ibid.,* p. 9.

26. "Is John Sherman's Antitrust Obsolete?," *Business Week* March 23, 1974, p. 51.

27. Committee on Economic Development, *Social Responsibilities of Business Corporations* (New York: Committee for Economic Development, 1971), pp. 11-16, 26-29. The Committee for Economic Development, founded in 1942, is a nonprofit, nonpolitical, educational and research institution. The members of the Committee are heads of American business and educational institutions. Its primary goals are (a) objectively studying our economy and the machinery that makes it work, and (b) developing recommendations for public policy.

28. *Ibid.*

29. James L. Ferguson, "The Chief Executive's Responsibility for Corporate Public Service," *Sloan Management Review,* Fall 1978, p. 76.

30. *Ibid.,* p. 77.

2. The Human Ecology of Modern Corporations

William P. Sexton

For some time, the modern business corporation has been the target of a significant amount of criticism from social scientists, behavioral researchers, management consultants, theologians, and many others. Unquestionably, there is a good deal of justification for this criticism. However, certain of the charges relating to the modern corporation's creation of unhealthy and unwanted conditions for individuals and groups should be leveled not at business alone but at all organizations which have grown large. These potentially dehumanizing circumstances and the subtle seduction of professionals in large organizations are not a part of the stated goal of the enterprise *as much as they are a result of its size*. When a church, a hospital, a university, or a social agency grows large, the same unattractive characteristics generally ascribed to the business enterprise will emerge. The manner in which organizations experience conditions that are dysfunctional for human beings may be different, but that they will be encountered is not in doubt.

"We Need to Grow to Survive"

All organizations have a natural tendency to pursue growth in size.[1] Several reasons seem to account for this. The success of the enterprise is most often calculated with respect to some standard of base, often the previous year's performance. The marketing manager plans to add new products or services to the existing line. The religious community institutes a new apostolate. The hospital initiates a new specialized service. "Progress is our most important product." With progress comes size.

Some time ago, C. Northcote Parkinson shouted a warning: "As the work increases arithmetically, the number of those assigned to its performance increases geometrically."[2] Managers want to multiply subordinates, not rivals; and managers make work for each other. When new work is given to the already overworked manager, he or she will tend to request the assistance of subordinates rather than sharing the work with a colleague. Sharing the work leads to rivalry, whereas taking on subordinates gives the manager additional prestige and power. However, if new employees are hired, there will be a consequent increase in paper work, coordination, communication, and soon, specialization, which will lead to hiring of even more staff.

Effective management requires that objectives be quantified. This drive to quantify results has the effect of inducing administrators to see desired outcomes in material or observable terms. Here again, growth is the outcome. Ironically, this occurs in organizations that we might expect to have nonquantitative goals. Recently, in response to the question, "What events or conditions do you feel must occur over the next two years in order for your parish to be successful," a Third World missionary priest's recipe for success included: "75 active lay ministers, 50 pre-Cana discussion teams, 100 families having completed a sacraments preparation series, a lay ministers program, a parish council, and two facilities." It is no different when a business enterprise expands its market area. There may be higher visibility and more press coverage, but the inclination to growth will be the same.

Any organization which sees itself as having the potential to increase its influence, whether in a market, in a health-care community, or in response to the need for "corporate witness," will respond by mounting a strategy for growth. The marketing manager may envision greater leverage on suppliers and customers by having his or her company handle more products or larger volume. As the hospital's facilities and census counts increase, so will its power to obtain supplies, labor, power, and other cost savings through increased buying power.

This seemingly universal quest for growth is stimulated also by economic interests. Students in basic economics learn about economies of scale that can only be effected at relatively high levels of asset accumulation. The increased productivity and reduced unit costs made possible by specialization of labor and enlarged capacity are real inducements for growth. Diversification, which is made possible through the growth of the enterprise, provides the organization with a hedge in the event of failure in one of the areas of its operation, thereby enhancing stability.

Finally, society tends to protect the large organization.[3] When an organization has grown to such proportions as to employ a substantial part of the labor force of a community or a country, it may justifiably anticipate special privileges and even the direct assistance of society should its survival be threatened. While the Chrysler Corporation and the Penn-Central Railroad immediately come to mind, the same circumstances and actions have been duplicated with social agencies, diocesan charities, hospitals, and the like. There is a subtle danger in this process. Society preserves the large organization because it cannot accept the consequences if the organization ceases to exist. In this fashion, society implicitly supports bureaucratic growth within the organization, encouraging it to remain large.

Bureaucratic Values

Bureaucratic development is a function of size above all else. It can be predicted with confidence that as any organization grows larger, it will take on the character of a bureaucracy. The dominant values which underlie the bureaucratic organization are control, hierarchy, authoritative influence, and impersonal relationships. A large organization cannot survive if it fails to secure coordination among the various divisions and departments. As the organization grows, the complexity of relationships resulting from work specialization requires elaborate systems of control. The hierarchial form imposes a rational distribution of authority needed by managers to make proper decisions and to command action. People within the organization look to authority for the initiation of action. Implicitly, management comes to believe that personal motivation is less reliable in the achievement of organization goals than is submission to legitimate authority. In this setting, the functioning of the enterprise is enhanced if relationships between employees, and particularly between managers and subordinates, can be kept at an impersonal level. Consistency of action, legitimization of authority, and adherence to plans, policies, and procedures are thereby facilitated. Some of us may be repulsed by such values and by their implications for organization life. However, these factors account for the awesome growth of large corporations, universities, churches, and governments over the past fifty years.[4]

What, then, is our concern? Haven't these institutions served society well? It is argued that were it not for their size, the unprecedented progress and achievements which have been recorded in health care, transportation, education, communication, agriculture, the harnessing of resources, and in the provision of goods and services needed to support a modern society simply would not have occurred.

Our concern is for the human beings employed in these large organizations. Size naturally leads to a bureaucratization of activities, and creates conditions for those involved which are dysfunctional. There is no immunity in this progression of events. All large organizations, regardless of the character of their charter, will experience these unhealthy and unwanted human conditions.

The Worker: Jim Spencer

Social scientists for some time have reported that the work world places demands upon the individual which are at odds with psychological well-being. This thesis is powerfully stated by Dostoevski.

> To punish him atrociously, to crush him in such a manner that the most hardened criminal would tremble before such punishment—it would be necessary only to give his works the character of complete uselessness. . . Let him be constrained in his work as to pour water from one vessel to another and back again, then I am sure that at the end of a short period he would strangle himself or commit a thousand crimes punishable with death rather than live in such an abject condition or endure such treatment.[5]

The conventional work assignment forces the individual to concentrate on a process which involves little of the whole person. All that may be required is a set of physical motions mastered in a matter of minutes. There is little opportunity to engage the variety of skills and personal ingenuity possessed by the mature adult. The worker is induced to value precision, to adopt a short time span, and to adjust to external controls. Psychological success, by which personal growth and self-esteem are experienced, calls for a decidedly different setting. While some writers have played down dehumanizing conditions of work, most research into the work world of large corporations paints a picture of frustration, discontent, hostility, and degradation.

Jim Spencer is a seat mounter in a large auto assembly plant. Following high school, he attended a technical college, receiving a Millwright Certificate after two years of study. The economic situation did not favor his hopes of finding a position in maintenance or machine setup. After several months of search, Jim accepted his present job. That was four years ago. At the beginning, he had a good feeling when he paused to appreciate that he was an employee of one of the largest companies in the world.

There is a virtuosolike symmetry to the organization of the work which, for a period of time, seemed to distract Jim from the essential qualities of his assignment. With an uninterrupted supply of parts, fifty to sixty cars move through the line in each hour. Within one minute, Jim must walk twenty feet to a conveyor belt, pick up a front seat weighing thirty pounds, carry it back to his work station, place the seat on the chassis, and put in four bolts using an air gun to tighten them according to standard. From start to completion, the work cycle for the seat mounting job is 52 seconds. Sometimes the bolts fail to fit into the holes, the gun refuses to function, the seats do not fit properly over the holes, or the threads are stripped on the bolts. But the line does not stop.

Jim's initial feeling of pride in the company soon gave way to feelings of frustration as he found himself playing "catch-up" more and more. Finally, he simply rationalizes that it is not all that important if a mounting bolt is missing. The inspector will catch it, and if he does not, someone down the line will.

Jim car-pools to work with several friends who are in similar jobs on adjoining lines. The ride to work is typically quiet with an almost ominous atmosphere. The trip home is always a startling contrast, with much laughing, joking, and kidding. Jim's friends are very important to him, not only those in his car pool but the men and women who work the stations next to his own. Breaks and lunch are particularly enjoyable times, with work rarely being a topic of conversation. On the job, Jim and several of his friends on adjacent stations have arranged to spell each other from time to time. In this way, one of the group can enjoy a break of up to thirty minutes. The person who "covers" the extra position must work doubly hard, and there is a general uneasiness at the prospect of being discovered. Nonetheless, all have agreed that "doubling" provides them with variety and brings a sort of excitement to an otherwise boring day.

Entering the plant is like leaving this world for another. In the spring, when the world outside is fresh and colorful, the factory atmosphere of continuous noise, of stale lubricant-flavored air, of heat sometimes to 110 degrees, and of the unrelenting machine pacing, is particularly noticeable and debilitating. Jim's supervisor seems to appreciate how difficult and unpleasant all of this is for his employees. However, he has made it clear that the cars must be built and that no delays will be tolerated. With the exception of the two ten-minute breaks (in mid-morning and mid-afternoon), work rules absolutely forbid leaving the line. In addition, reasons given for missing work are checked very closely by the Benefits Department and the medical director.

In the last year or so, Jim's earlier aspirations and dreams for more responsible jobs in setup or maybe in tool making have been all but forgotten. His adverse reactions to the work are now more subdued, and, on the surface, it does not seem to bother him anymore. In a few words, Jim does not seem to care. He is earning well over $12.00 per hour and his benefit package affords him a feeling of security. Jim is married now, and with the birth of his first child imminent, he wants to "make the best" of the situation.

Lost in Work

Jim's experience is quite predictable in view of a series of recent studies into worker-organization orientation in highly structured, routinized jobs. In the initial period of employment on a repetitious, short work cycle and machine-paced job, adverse reactions to the task do not exert as great an influence on the person as does his readiness to accept legitimate authority and to identify with a positive image of the organization.[6] This sometimes powerful influence serves to support the individual in the perception that the assignment is necessary and important to the organization even though it isn't difficult or complex. The worker's identification with the organization may initially reduce his dissonant feelings toward an unchallenging task. It has been shown that these "compensatory" feelings may be sustained over a significant period, possibly one year. However, there is evidence that after this "honeymoon" period, as we saw in Jim's case, initial identification with the organization is not enough to offset the pressures created by the growing realization that one's skills are being underutilized and one's potential remains untapped.

It is at this point, then, that Jim's work group and his friends assume the influence which he had previously given to the company. When identification with the organization is insufficient to withstand the negative feelings emanating from the work, the individual often "compensates" by informally restructuring the job more to his liking. The group of workers contrives to establish conditions of work that supply each with the opportunity for greater freedom or challenge. "Doubling," as practiced in Jim's work group, is the most common form of restructuring otherwise repetitious and boring tasks. During this second phase of adjusting to underemployment, some workers also succeed in constructing more positive images of personal work roles through the development of meaningful and important relationships within the peer group. This "substitution" of positive feelings which comes from an expanded personal role and status within the informal group compensates for the adverse feelings created by the work, and may sustain the worker indefinitely. But, as in Jim's case, feelings of alienation will gradually displace the contentment achieved through work-group membership and informal job restructuring.

Plans for advancement to more meaningful and responsible work will require a painful reassessment, and downward adjustment of personal estimates of self-worth.[7] It is not difficult to understand that, in the face of what represents a profoundly humiliating personal defeat, some workers turn to alcohol and drugs. Or, the worker may find solace from disorientation by cultivating strong negative feelings for middle-class values such as upward mobility, success, and the role of work. Jim is now in the process of adjusting to the reality of his work life. He will soon conclude that there is little that he can do personally to affect important events in his life.[8] Work is a means of subsistence. Anything more is accidental (being in the right place at the right time) or political. Nonetheless, the strong pervasive pressures to advance socially will torment Jim more intensely as time passes and his soon-to-be born child grows to adulthood. While he may achieve a certain visible upward movement (through accumulating material possessions), he learns that the means for deriving personal prestige in this world of work are unavailable to most people, and his conviction that access is a result of birth and decidedly unequal opportunity is intensified.

Quality of Work Life (QWL)

Certainly the high personnel costs and lower productivity which generally result from these dehumanized conditions account for some of the growing interest of corporations in improving the quality of work life. But the quality-of-work-life movement of the last decade is creating conditions which respond to the worker's deeper needs, reinforce the employment of his unique skills, and encourage involvement in decisions which affect his work role. Whether this is a direct response to economic conditions, the logical next step in an evolutionary series of reform movements, or simply an idea whose time has come, the concern is intense and widespread.

When we speak of improving the quality of work life, we must include a wide range of elements. Eight conceptual categories can be distinguished:
1. Adequate and fair compensations
2. A safe and healthy environment

3. The development of human capacities
4. Growth and security of the worker
5. Social integration—a sense of community, interpersonal openness, freedom from prejudice
6. Constitutionalism—protection of human rights in the workplace
7. The total life space—balanced role of work in life
8. Social relevance—the worker's perception that the organization is socially responsible.[9]

Efforts to improve the quality of work life seek to enhance the degree to which members of a work organization are able to satisfy important personal needs through their experiences in the organization. The targets of these efforts are increased job satisfaction, decreased turnover and absenteeism, and increased productivity.

Some QWL programs have addressed the problem of waning job satisfaction directly. They do not necessarily represent active measures to rid the job of its repetition or of its machine pacing, but attempts to respond to the unique needs of the individual worker, and thus contribute favorably to his total life-space balance. This process requires the individual to assume control over the essential elements which affect the role that work plays in his life. The goal is to help the worker experience a suitable balance between his work role and the role he assumes within his family and his community and in his leisure-time activities.

Successful Experience in QWL

The four-day, forty-hour work week, flextime, and other alternative work schedules are growing fast in popularity. There is substantial evidence that a large majority of the labor force favors flexible work schedules or other forms of compressed work weeks. In a recent survey, it was found that in all programs involving some form of alternative work scheduling, job satisfaction increased, absenteeism declined, morale improved, and in one-half of the cases, productivity increased.[10] Similar results are being achieved with the introduction of more individualized compensation packages. Under a plan referred to as Cafeteria Benefits Program, employees receive the amount of money the organization allocates for their total pay package and spend it as they wish.[11] Some choose the broadest medical insurance coverage. Others may forgo vacation for more take-home pay. Older employees may wish to shift the compensation package toward retirement benefits. The TRW Corporation, one of an increasing number of firms adopting pay-package programs that incorporate some form of employee discretion or control, reports that over 80 percent of employees have changed their benefit packages. As in all such programs, higher satisfaction with pay and greater feelings of involvement and commitment to the organization are found.

Some observers may look at these programs and criticize the corporation even more intensely than before. They might argue that these are solely and totally cosmetic changes which temporarily placate workers. "The work itself won't have been changed." Jim Spencer may have more time with his family and may achieve a sense of choice (control) in respect to his time and economic payoffs, but when he enters the plant, he will still be mounting seats on a stream of cars rolling by at nearly 60 per hour. In response, management will point out that the change which is being demanded by academicians, social commentators, philosophers, and others will take a good deal of time. The programs mentioned here are first steps toward humanizing work.

The key feature in the successful QWL program is individual choice. Workers are not alike in their dominant needs and in their choices of action to fulfill them. In General Foods' Topeka Plant, skill-based pay plans have been introduced. This program, which is an outgrowth of early efforts to enhance job satisfaction, is focused on the individual worker and responds to challenges that the work itself remains oppressive. Pay is determined by skill level. All nonmanagement personnel begin with the same starting rate. After mastering five different jobs, they move to the next higher pay rate. They continue moving up until they have mastered all of the jobs in the plant. This requires approximately two years. At that time, they receive the top or plant rate. There are many benefits: the organization enjoys a highly flexible work force, and the worker obtains a broader perspective of the work, enhanced feelings of self-worth, and a sense of personal growth. There is job variety, increased worker participation, and an equitable linking of pay with performance. General Foods' Topeka Plant has improved the quality of the work life of its employees. Nonetheless, some will again complain that "the work itself has not been changed." Perhaps that is true, but the program is evidence that not *all* corporations are indifferent to the quality of the work life of their employees.

Another type of QWL program responds directly to the challenge of rebuilding jobs so that the worker may use his or her special skills, exercise judgment, and experience independence and control from within. U.S. corporations have taken the cue from their counterparts in Western Europe, and have shown progress in their efforts to enrich work. The general strategy is to "load" jobs with more of the core dimensions: the variety of skills required, the complete task as an identifiable piece of work, the significance of the job in the over-all organization, autonomy—personal responsibility and adequate feedback—continual realization of the worker's own effectiveness.[12] This strategy hopes to create feelings of meaningfulness, responsibility, and personal control for the worker, thereby increasing personal motivation, quality of work performance, satisfaction, and at the same time reducing employee turnover and absenteeism. Programs of job enrichment are being operated in every major industry in the United States. Successes have been recorded, along with some failures. There is strong momentum in the direction of a genuine humanization of work. AT&T, Motorola, Gaines, Non-Linear Systems, and TRW Systems are among the corporations showing progress.

More Advanced Experiments

One company, Non-Linear Systems, has totally reconstructed the work away from specialized, repetitive tasks and toward more complete, holistic units which are assigned to independent production groups of six or seven workers. Each unit, or team, is free to organize itself in the way it deems best so as to produce digital voltmeters and other electrical measuring instruments. Time clocks are no longer used. Departments assume more autonomy, and decision making is shared in a true sense. Production has jumped 30 percent; customer complaints (formerly a severe problem) have declined by 70 percent. While economic setbacks in the aerospace industry and poor financial planning have brought a halt to NLS's success story, the consequences for productivity are clear.

Over the past decade, Gaines (a pet-food manufacturer), in response to considerable experience with many of the symptoms of alienation in their plants, has embarked on a significant redesigning of work. The new job assignments include a set of functions which will require higher-order human abilities and responsibilities (planning, diagnosing problems, communications, etc.). The basic technology of new plants is designed to eliminate dull or routine jobs when possible. Clearly, these ambitious changes require a good deal of education and training on the part of worker and manager alike. The role of the manager has changed almost as dramatically as that of the worker. The manager must take on the role of resource person, liaison, supplier of knowledge, and dispenser of feedback. His supervisory and decision-making roles are basically shifted to self-managed work teams. A team is comprised of seven to fourteen members and a team leader. The team has jurisdiction over a natural set of highly interdependent tasks. Assignments of members to tasks are made by team consensus. The team is also given responsibility for coping with manufacturing problems, redistributing work to accommodate absences or leaves for members, selecting team members for plant-wide committees, screening and selecting team members, and counseling and assisting those encountering problems in their work.

Gaines's program of job enrichment is becoming more and more common today. As these programs are instituted and allowed to mature, it has become clear that the reassignment of heretofore managerial responsibilities and prerogatives to a team of workers is imperative. In virtually all of the companies cited above, management's efforts to upgrade the quality of work life have included the creation of work teams entrusted with significant responsibility.[13]

New Challenges for Management

Establishment of self-regulating teams of workers is dominant among the elements which account for QWL program success.[14] Autonomous work groups are both productive and humanly satisfying. These results have been achieved by: (a) the positive responses of workers to greater task variety, (b) increased autonomy and discretion, (c) genuine involvement in problem solving and decision making, (d) greater access to information and feedback, and (e) greater emphasis on interpersonal relations, group process, and a "holistic" notion of the work experience.

The Harwood Manufacturing[15] experience demonstrates the crucial role that the work group plays in effecting genuine improvements in the quality of work life. Certain group and organizational conditions have been found to be essential. First, standards favoring productivity and teamwork must be developed within the group. Second, an equalization of skills must be achieved among group members, and tasks must be rotated. Third, the incentive system must be tied to group outcomes. Finally, the group must experience a supportive management style that creates feelings of mutual trust. Those who participated at Harwood point to the program's success in developing a system of management approaching "System 4," discovered by the well-known organization expert, Rensis Likert.[16] Essentially, System 4 exists when there are high levels of mutual confidence and trust between manager and worker. Other factors include high levels of interaction and information sharing within and between all organization units, decision making which is done widely all throughout the organization in overlapping self-regulated groups, high aspirations for group productivity, and an unusually high level of psychological closeness between manager and worker. As we descend through Systems 3 and 2 to System 1, we encounter continually increasing repressive control, depersonalization, authoritarian styles, and negative motivations. The contrast between this system and traditional management is dramatic. Totally new demands are placed on managers, demands for which they may not be psychologically or professionally prepared. As Dick Norton, superintendent of General Motor's Fisher Body Plant No. 2, recently put it:

> Frankly, I've become frustrated and discouraged at times. This type of system is more demanding and time-consuming when compared to traditional management. I find myself in the role of a teacher, monitor, consultant, and source of feedback on the results of our actions. I often serve as a third party when other team members are in conflict.
>
> I view many employees as now more relaxed after work. Yet a complete trust of upper management has not yet been established. Also, a degree of permissiveness has crept into our business which must be systematically dealt with.[17]

The adjustment of the beliefs, attitudes, skills, and expectations of managers is probably the single most confounding obstacle in the path of efforts to humanize life in modern corporations.

The Manager: Elizabeth Bradford

If managers are to assume the changing roles required of them by new forms of organization, several obstacles inherent in the more traditional organization design must be overcome. Jim Spencer's work life is profoundly affected by the unplanned dysfunctional consequences of bureaucratization within the corporation. The most obvious of these is the fragmentation of work. The way in which he receives supervision is also affected by the impact bureaucratization can have on managers at all levels in the organization.

Elizabeth Bradford graduated from a prestigious midwestern college with a degree in business administration. After working several years in retailing, she accepted a position in the personnel office of a large corporation in the electronics industry. Beth's initial assignment involved continuous interviewing of prospective candidates for non-salaried job openings. At first, she was very thorough and attentive to each individual and was sensitive to the job-person fit from a human and social, as well as technical, point of view. She studied the jobs and their organizational settings in detail before any screening of candidates was begun. In less than one month, this practice was brought to a halt when Beth's supervisor informed her that her presence in the operating department was having a disruptive effect on line managers. The section and department chiefs did not trust her intentions, and after consultation, it was agreed that she should stay in the personnel office "where she belongs." It soon became apparent to Beth that "rocking the boat" could be costly to her hopes for promotion and advancement. Some five months later, when she was informed that no blacks were to be sent to the stock selecting department for jobs, she quietly complied. Beth rationalized that management must have seen an unhealthy racial situation developing in that part of the plant and was taking appropriate action to protect all involved.

Over the next eight-year period, Beth's performance, her loyalty to the company and, more particularly, to her immediate management did not go unnoticed. She was section chief in the cable-forming department for three years before moving to her present position as department chief, crossbar wiring. She is good to her employees and feels that her department is doing all that it can to provide continuous, safe work at a just wage. She has a reputation for getting the job done with no questions asked. Beth has begun to think of the company first and herself second. What's good for the company is good for her. At parties, should anyone bring up the matter of the class-action suit being brought against the company as a result of its hiring practices, Beth will argue as though it were she being attacked. Criticisms of the company are taken personally, for she now identifies completely with its mission, its work, and her role in which she takes pride.

There have been company policies and decisions made recently which Beth considers either unnecessary or unwise. She was initially prompted to object. However, on further reflection, she concluded that those above her possessed more information which gave them a broader view of the problems. And anyway, if she hopes to be chosen the next assistant superintendent, it is best not to create the impression that she is less than a team player. This promotion is extremely important to Beth; it is becoming an obsession. As she sits in manufacturing staff meetings, she is alert to the words and actions of fellow department chiefs. She has come to feel that, like it or not, she is in a contest. The winner will be the person demonstrating that she or he can meet the highest expectations and do so by expending the least resources. Of late, all of this has caused Beth to become more conservative in her decisions, less inclined to take risks, and generally more reluctant to delegate.

"To Get Along–Go Along"

Subtle forces are set into motion which serve to entice the manager to substitute the values, attitudes, and expectations of the organization or upper management for his or her own. So pervasive can our need for organizational affirmation become that, like Beth, we are willing to subordinate our independently based pictures of reality to the view supplied by the company, the school, the hospital, the church. Because of this readiness to reject personal experience and choices rather than risk being denied acceptance, those individuals whose personal futures are seen by them in terms of the organization are highly vulnerable to exploitation by its prevailing system of values and actions. When we take into account the character of a conventional hierarchial business organization, it is not difficult to understand the process by which this outcome is effected.[18] Problems are typically defined at one organization level and solved (actions carried out) at the next lower level. Those identifying the problem and charting courses of action have more power than those assigned to solve it. Lacking the broader perspective available at the higher level, the problem solver has little recourse but to carry out the task as it has been defined, often suppressing his or her own ideas. Therefore, the middle and lower manager is ultimately judged according to how well he or she follows the plans and methods given for solution of the problem.

An aura of paternalism may often attend this process of top-down determination of problems and solutions. The need for organizational affirmation keeps Beth Bradford from requesting information or explanations of broader perspectives. Instead, her boss offers assurances and encouragement that, had she "a better, more objective perspective of the organization, the wisdom of the chosen course of action would be clear." In such a setting, the incidence of transference among managers is quite natural. Transference occurs when people project upon the organization human qualities and then relate to them as if the organization did in fact possess these qualities.[19] The organization may become a surrogate father or mother for many, creating for them the same feelings of security and support they knew with their parents. There are social and psychological benefits to be drawn by the manager from this sort of institutional identification. However, the process exacts a price. The price is excessive loyalty and obedience.

There is a good deal of evidence that these qualities have natural roots within those who function in the bureaucratic mode. For many people, obedience is a deeply ingrained behavior trait. When complemented by fragmentation of functions, inaccessibility of information, a separation of decision maker and doer, and the vesting of interests in suborganization units, the readiness of a manager to obey is quite predictable. As Milgram demonstrated in his classic study, beyond a simple inability to muster the courage to resist authority, there is a tendency in each of us to derive the satisfaction of doing a job well from the act of pleasing the person holding authority over us.[20] The consequence is that in this setting, Beth Bradford comes to view herself as the instrument for carrying out another person's decisions, and she therefore no longer regards herself as responsible for her actions. She feels accountable to the authority directing her but feels no responsibility for the content of these actions.

Climbing the Corporate Ladder

The obsession that many managers have with climbing the corporate ladder makes them extremely poor candidates for their new roles in the "reformed" organization which we have been advocating. A preoccupation with successful career advancement leads a person to fear becoming a loser, left behind in the lower levels of the organization. The early signs of careerism can be seen in Beth Bradford's persistent analysis of her own actions and those of her peers so that she is satisfied that she remains the front-runner for promotion and advancement. The anxiety she feels has already been reflected in her defensive posture (marked by conservatism, less risk taking, and delegating).

Careerism results not only in anxiety but also in an underdeveloped heart.[21] Beth is moved to put aside idealistic, compassionate, and courageous impulses that might jeopardize her career. Careerism demands a detachment from social responsiveness, from her own feelings. In this way, she is protected from being too involved with the emotions of others. The manager is induced to form only limited personal relationships, defined in functional terms by the traditional organization form and thereby facilitating the detachment process. Such a manager plugs into but one small module of the other's personality.[22] To become more involved would require the development of the heart, and, as some managers have argued, you cannot let yourself act out your human feelings or you will back off from the hard decisions (matters of the head). There is evidence that in order to get to the top of the bureaucratized organization, those aspirants who value qualities of the head—such as taking the initiative, pride in performance, coolness under stress, creating something new—are more successful than those who value qualities of the heart—such as independence, loyalty, openness, honesty, compassion.[23] The new organization forms will require a dramatic rearrangement of these priorities. Qualities of the head will remain important but will be simply insufficient to fulfill the revised role of management.

Cause for Optimism

The bureaucratic organization is under fire. It would be naïve to predict that we will see the end of such pathological organizational forms in the eighties or even in the decade to follow. Nonetheless, the values which spawned these institutions are being challenged by society and by the management of modern corporations. Values are shifting toward "personalism," with a concomitant emphasis on the discovery of one's own identity not only as a member of society but also as a member of a work organization.[24] Business corporations are at the crossroads. Management has begun to realize that the development of one's self-concept must be continually reinforced in the organizational experience if employees are to participate fully, to realize their potential, and to truly identify with the organization.

There is no place for blind obedience and devotion to hierarchial authority in a management role which requires employee involvement and the genuine participation triggered by the introduction of job enrichment and autonomous group structures. As Dick Norton at General Motors has commented, "One has the feeling that we are running on blind faith in our people, and frankly, we are. We are trusting our people more, and job satisfaction has increased for everyone." Many companies across the country today are encouraging intensified involvement with employees. The new role of the manager is dominated not by decision making or exercises of authority, but rather by communications, support, and reinforcement. The latter cannot possibly be delivered with a hardened or underdeveloped heart. A detachment from social responsiveness, from feelings of shame and humiliation, and from human emotions is totally antagonistic to effective performance of this role.

As we look to the eighties, there is reason to be optimistic about the growing sensitivity of corporations to their organizations' instruments for gratifying workers' needs for self-expression and genuine personal involvement. These new organizational forms reinforce new values that are totally in conflict with those that support bureaucratic forms. The key to success will lie in the quality of our efforts to cause managers to reorient themselves to these new roles and to identify genuinely with the emerging values. Corporations will employ incentives to this end, but more are needed. By 1985, fully one-third of the labor force will have had some college education. Our schools of higher education must seek to inculcate a questioning attitude, one that is genuinely more participative—in which students are encouraged to get involved in the learning experience, to think independently, and to emphasize values of the heart as well as of the head. This training will arm the manager with a set of values that places priority not with the organization and its method of operation but with the person and human relationships. It is hoped that the manager will come to see the organization as nothing more than patterns of human relationships. In this way it will become possible for human beings to work at their newly designed tasks in the fullness of what it means to be human. Thereby, corporations will be providing society with work organizations which can be the cornerstones for a higher quality of life. Only then will corporate managers be leaders in society as well as in their companies.

NOTES

1. Theodore Caplow, "Organization Size," *Administrative Science Quarterly* 1 (1967): 236–51.

2. See C. Northcote Parkinson, *Parkinson's Law* (Boston: Houghton Mifflin, 1957).

3. Philip L. Hunsaker, "Organization Growth: Implications for Human Resources," *Personnel,* November-December 1979, p. 12.

4. S. N. Eisenstadt, "Bureaucracy, Bureaucratization and Debureaucratization," *Administrative Science Quarterly* 4 (1959–60): 305.

5. F. Dostoevski, *The House of the Dead* (New York: Dutton, 1911), p. 1.

6. William Sexton, "Temporal Influences on Employee-Institution Orientation," *Institute of Management Science Proceedings,* March 1980, p. 118.

7. W. J. Heisler and John W. Houck, *A Matter of Dignity* (Notre Dame: University of Notre Dame Press, 1977), p. 134.

8. Harold Wool, "What's Wrong With Work in America," *Monthly Labor Review* 96 (March 1973): 61.

9. Richard Walton, "Improving the Quality of Work Life," *Harvard Business Review*, May–June 1974, p. 12.

10. William H. Wagel, "Alternative Work Schedules: Current Trends," *Personnel*, January–February 1979, p. 28.

11. Edward E. Lawler, III, "New Approaches to Pay: Innovations in Work," *Personnel*, September–October 1976, p. 36.

12. J. Richard Hackman et al., "A New Strategy for Job Enrichment," *California Management Review* 17, no. 4 (Summer 1975): 57–71.

13. Thomas G. Cummings and Edmond Malloy, *Improving Productivity and the Quality of Work Life* (New York: Praeger Publishers, 1977), pp. 40–41.

14. Edward E. Lawler and Cortlandt Cammann, "What Makes a Work Group Successful," in *Perspectives on Behavior in Organizations* (New York: McGraw-Hill, 1977).

15. Rensis Likert, *The Human Organization* (New York: McGraw-Hill, 1967), p. 165.

16. *Ibid.*, p. 222.

17. *World of Work Report*, vol. 2, no. 7 (July 1977).

18. Samuel A. Culbert, "How the Organization Exploits Our Need for Acceptance," in *Organizational Reality*, ed. Peter Frost et al. (Santa Monica, Calif.: Goodyear Publishing Co., 1978), pp. 411–18.

19. Harry Levinson, "Reciprocation: The Relationship Between Man and Organization," *Administrative Science Quarterly* 9 (1965): 386–99.

20. Stanley Milgram, *Obedience to Authority* (New York: Harper & Row, 1974).

21. Michael Maccoby, *The Gamesman* (New York: Simon and Schuster, 1976), pp. 200–224.

22. For a discussion of Modular Man, see Alvin Toffler, *Future Shock* (New York: Random House, 1970), pp. 95–108.

23. Barry Z. Posner and J. Michael Munson, "The Importance of Values in Understanding Organization Behavior," *Human Resource Management*, Fall 1979, pp. 9–14.

24. Richard H. Viola, *Organizations in a Changing Society*, (Philadelphia: W. B. Saunders, 1977).

Patterns of Religious Authority in Business Matters: Protestant, Catholic, and Jewish

Part Two consists of three chapters by prominent scholars of religious thought. Chapter 3 is by a Protestant theologian, John C. Bennett; Chapter 4 is written by the Roman Catholic Jesuit, James V. Schall; Chapter 5 is authored by a scholar of Jewish thought, Burton Leiser. Each of the authors presents some of the highlights of his community's distinctive approach to business ethics. There was a time when there seemed to be clear lines of demarcation among the Protestant, Catholic, and Jewish approaches to moral matters. A joke that is often told in ecumenical gatherings captures the common understanding of religious authority. When asked to respond to a particular moral problem, the Catholic priest began his answer by saying: "The teaching of the Church is. . ." The Jewish rabbi said, "According to tradition, the teaching is. . ." The Protestant minister responded, "In my opinion, the biblical teaching is. . . ." While this little story obviously over-simplifies some complex matters, the three authors demonstrate in the essays that follow that the caricature continues to have a kernel of truth.

The Protestant Teaching

The first essay is by John C. Bennett, a leading authority on ethics in the Protestant churches. Bennett brings a unique wisdom to the question of the implications of the Protestant teaching for the behavior of corporations, for he was not only present at the various conferences or assemblies that formulated the major statements, but several times served as secretary of key sections. Significantly, he was secretary of the section that focused on the economic order at the 1937 Oxford Conference on Church, Community, and State. This meeting brought together some seven hundred persons appointed by Protestant and Eastern Orthodox churches and is generally thought to have been a landmark in social thinking. Not surprisingly, the tone of this document is decidedly negative toward capitalism.

This anti-capitalistic bias is understood in light of the fact that many Christians of the 1930s were socialists. Bennett himself was a member of Reinhold Niebuhr's group, the Fellowship of Socialist Christians, and in espousing socialism he was in the company of such distinguished theologians as Paul Tillich, Karl Barth, and Emil Brunner. In the days of the Great Depression, John Bennett believed socialism to be the answer. In speaking of the 1930s, Bennett says: "For me democratic socialism, inspired in part by the socialistic tendencies that I found in Christianity, was the goal."[1]

In his seventies, and after having taught many years and having served as president of New York City's prestigious Union Theological Seminary, John Bennett changed his mind, and became an advocate of democratic capitalism. "I am not returning to a belief that I held in the 1930's—a belief in a comprehensive system of socialism as a panacea, or almost a panacea. The total union of economic and political power could well be more oppressive than some degree of pluralism among private economic empires that coexist with a democratic state."[2]

As is clear in his essay, however, Bennett is far from satisfied with the status quo in corporate America. The church documents he cites all point toward a capitalism that is more accountable to the public for its use of power and resources. But Bennett notes that the experience of the churches does not lend credence to economist Milton Friedman's optimism that the free workings of the market place will in themselves realize most social values. Bennett reminds us that capitalism has been made more humane by democratic inspiration, and that before the Wagner Act of 1935 there was little "democratic capitalism" for many in the work force. In his earlier writings on this point, Bennett underscored the great struggles of labor against tyranny and violence in which the state and the police often supported the employers. He recalled the Steel Strike of 1919 when the workers fought for such basic freedoms as the right to organize into independent unions, and relief from the twelve-hour day and the seven-day week!

Bennett is careful to remind the business community that although church groups are critical of corporate behavior, especially in shareholder resolutions, this criticism derives from a fundamental acceptance of the corporation as a form of economic organization. This point is crucial, for many in the business world are convinced that religious groups sponsoring shareholder resolutions are intent on destroying the free-enterprise system in favor of some form of socialism.[3] The Interfaith Center on Corporate Responsibility, a coalition representing 17 Protestant denominations and 170 Roman Catholic orders and dioceses, has presented almost 500 shareholder resolutions with over 100 companies from 1970 to 1980. These resolutions were all aimed at correcting some perceived injustice or social injury involved with the policies and practices of a company.[4] The significant point, however, is that this coalition (ICCR) has a combined investment portfolio of over $6 billion. In this light, Bennett's point that the goal of ICCR is *responsible* corporate behavior, not the demise of the corporation, seems to be well taken!

In his opening comments at the conference when the essay was first presented, Bennett was quick to emphasize that there is no "Protestant position" on corporations. This points to a deeper issue regarding the Protestant understanding of the church as a moral teacher. Unlike the Roman Catholic church, the Protestant church has no doctrine of apostolic succession and hence makes no claim that its leaders ought to be the focal point of authentic teaching. The Catholic church sees the role of the bishops as one of discerning the truth in the community through dialogue and other measures; somewhat as a lens focuses light, church leaders are charged to bring the best insights of the community to bear on issues and problems. The resulting "church teaching" has the presumption of authenticity, and is not lightly disregarded.

To be sure, the Protestant conviction is that the role of the church is to bring the moral teachings of the Bible into dialogue with the problems of the contemporary world. While assemblies of church leaders and representatives of the churches do formulate positions, these teachings are "authoritative" only in that they are able to persuade by virtue of their intellectual and spiritual cogency. In some cases, authority is granted to church leaders by the constitution of a denomination, but for the most part the validity of moral teaching is not based on whether it is an official pronouncement. The compelling quality of the arguments involved is most often the *sole* criteria for authoritative teaching.

Bennett and the tradition he represents assume that church

positions formulated in assemblies are more likely to be free of group or individual bias, and hence more faithful to the Bible. Thus Bennett provides a helpful summary and background of some key statements by the World Council of Churches, the National Council of Churches, and other denominational bodies, In recent assemblies the World Council of Churches has been dominated by very poor Third World countries, and this may explain the biting criticism of capitalism.

The Catholic Teaching

The second article, by the scholar James V. Schall, presents the fundamentals of the Roman Catholic moral teachings on the business world. The Catholic approach takes its lead from the medieval theologians — in particular, from Thomas Aquinas and his appropriation of Aristotle, Augustine, and neo-Platonic themes. The basic Catholic vision sees all of creation as flowing from God and finally returning to God. There is the conviction that the created order is good and embodies God's intentions; thus all truth that humankind discovers by use of intellect and will is taken to be God's intention, God's way of guiding persons in their "return," a "natural law" of God implanted in creation. When Schall quotes Josef Pieper and comments that grace challenges the secular world to "its *own* proper ends, as well as to ends beyond itself, yet not at the cost of neglecting its own proper being," he captures the heart of the Catholic approach.

The traditional Catholic teaching on social justice is based on an understanding of natural rights that are arrived at on the basis of reason informed by faith. While the Protestant teaching in social justice does not differ in substantive conclusions, the *basis* of the Protestant teaching is biblical — the message of Jesus and the prophets. To be sure, the Catholic approach employs human reason in the light of biblical faith, but it emphasizes that the biblical message is not discontinuous with reason but rather adds depth and breadth to the fruit of human intelligence. While the Protestant leader, John Calvin, would agree that in principle the content of divine law is ascertainable by human reason, he is more inclined to emphasize the distortions of the intellect as a result of sin.

This Catholic confidence in human reason is exemplified in the way Thomas Aquinas appropriates the great philosophic work of Aristotle. Aristotle argued that by nature the person has a unique dignity over all other creatures because of reason and free will

(Nichomachean Ethics). He also contended that the family and the state are "natural" societies because by nature the person needs others to develop full potentialities *(Politics).* Aquinas took the work of Aristotle on the dignity and the social nature of the person and extended it in the light of biblical faith. The dignity of the person is broadened and deepened in the light of the teaching of Genesis that the person is created in the image and likeness of God, and the New Testament teaching that persons are adopted sons of God redeemed by Christ. The idea of the social nature of the person is expanded by focusing on how salvation comes to those joined together in a society founded by Christ.

In a similar manner the notions of justice of the classical period are baptized by the Catholic scholars. Plato taught that justice entailed giving every person his or her due with all the rights and responsibilities involved *(The Republic).* The Roman conception of justice stressed that all were equal before the law and that the role of the state is to protect the individual. Aquinas deepens these notions and focuses on the source of human rights and responsibilities—God's creative act in bringing the person into being. Because of the sacredness of human life, the dignity of the person is to be respected, both by society and by other individuals; the person, in turn, has obligations to society as well.

In contrast to the Protestant approach of going to Scripture directly for the moral will of God, Catholic thought on social justice has been characterized by the conviction that human reason can discern God's intentions, and that the "natural law" is in harmony with the scriptural data. As Father Schall notes, official pronouncements by the church were made in response to particular problems, and only gradually did a "social theory" of the Catholic church emerge. It was not until 1891 when Pope Leo XIII published the encyclical *Rerum novarum* that the social theory took distinctive shape. The encyclical was an attempt to meet the dehumanizing tendencies of the day, and, as Father Schall notes, it steered a "middle way" between laissez-faire capitalism and a totalitarian socialism.

While the liberal-democratic theory of laissez-faire capitalism asserts freedom to be *the* foundation of all rights, Catholic social theory sees freedom as only one right which is itself grounded in the more basic notion of human dignity. Marxism, with its interpretation of class conflict as *the* vehicle for social justice, was also criticized for its myopic vision. The 1931 encyclical *Quadragesimo anno* highlights three principles which have been dominant in all Catholic social theory: concern for the protection of the dignity of the person; subsidiarity—the concern that organizations be no larger than necessary; and pluralism—the concern for mediating structures (family, church, etc.) between the person and the state.

Catholic moral teaching is written with the sacrament of penance in mind, for the assumption is that all Catholics ought at least to take authentic teachings very seriously as a guide for life and as an aid in examining one's conscience for sins. One function of the sacrament of penance is to offer an opportunity to consider how one's life is to be formed by the moral teaching of the church. The church is understood as having been endowed by Christ with a special competence to interpret tradition, Scripture, and the natural law. To be sure, the primacy of the informed conscience as the final judge of moral matters is a doctrine as valid today as in ancient times.

Although the church has always formed the conscience of its members on the need to be compassionate and generous to the poor, the new and remarkable breakthrough in our time is that the church now teaches that social justice is at the heart of the gospels. Not only charity to the poor but endeavors to change social structures that impede a better life for poor persons are advanced as the norm. The document issued by the Roman Synod of Bishops of 1971 clearly highlights the new focus.

> Action on behalf of justice and participation in the transforma-
> tion of the world fully appear to us as a constitutive dimension of
> the preaching of the Gospel, or, in other words, of the Church's
> mission for the redemption of the human race and its liberation
> from every oppressive situation.[5]

In different eras different dimensions of the gospel message have received emphasis in church teaching. In the past the focus has been on such areas as sexual morality and loyalty to the church. A new arrival on center stage is the theme of social justice.

Scholars have noted that from the time of the Second Vatican Council and the encyclicals of Pope Paul VI there has been a shift in papal, conciliar, and episcopal documents from the language of natural law to a more biblically based language.[6] For example, the great symbols of Christian faith—creation, redemption, and the mutual love of Christians as expressed in the mystery of Christ's death and resurrection—are much more dominant in the Vatican II document, "The Church in the Modern World," than in Pope John XXIII's encyclical *Pacem in Terris*. One of the strengths of the focus on natural law in past church teaching is that the teaching had the possibility of being accepted by all persons regardless of religious persuasion. Magisterial teaching made no claim to being based exclusively on revelation, but rather was said to follow from the demands of nature itself. What became very clear at the Second Vatican Council is that in the midst of cultural, social, and intellectual pluralism the documents of the church must explicitly delineate and reflect on the religious symbols that were formerly only implicit in the natural-law-based documents of the past. Natural-law teaching only makes sense if one accepts certain presuppositions. A key statement of the Vatican II document, "The Church in the Modern World," signals a shift toward a more biblically based ethic: "The truth is that only in the mystery of the incarnate Word does the mystery of man take on light."[7] It is this judgment reflected in many of the documents of the Second Vatican Council that has had a profound effect on subsequent church statements—now there is an explicit Christian vision as the context for moral teaching of the church.

Often the church documents characterized by the natural-law approach, appealing to man's being to ground moral teaching, seemed to many to speak with an almost ahistorical certainty. Today there is a renewed understanding of the historical character of church teaching. This new perception of the church is referred to a number of times in the Vatican II decree "The Dogmatic Constitution on the Church," which uses the image the "People of God" or the "Pilgrim Church."[8] This image harkens back to the ancient Hebrews who were led out of bondage to the Promised Land; they were pilgrims on a journey, humbly following their Lord through all types of hardships. A servant people, they lived in faith and discerned God's will in their own circumstances. The church as "People of God" is groping for the truth, and from its fundamental biblical vision it searches with all the skills of our time—intellectual, moral, and spiritual—to formulate guidance for the Christian way of life. Church teachings in this perspective are more modest in tone and less specific in direction, yet remain faithful to the Scriptures.

Father Schall notes an important shift of focus in church teaching from a concern about internal social orders of countries to an international perspective on the question of poverty in the Third World. This change in emphasis began during the pontificate of John XXIII and continues to the present day under the leadership of Pope John Paul II. The poverty issue first began to loom large as bishops in Third World countries listened to the problems of their people and struggled to offer solutions. The Report of the 1968 Second General Conference of Latin American Bishops known as the Medellín Documents set the tone for many Roman documents that followed. In reflecting on poverty, the documents declare:

> . . . it will be necessary to reemphasize strongly that the example and teaching of Jesus, the anguished condition of millions of poor people in Latin America, the urgent exhortations of the Pope and of the Council, place before the Latin American Church a challenge and a mission that she cannot sidestep and to which she must respond with a speed and boldness adequate to the urgency of the times.
>
> The present situation, then, demands from bishops, priests, religious and laymen the spirit of poverty which, "breaking the bonds of the egotistical possession of temporal goods, stimulates the Christian to order organically the power and the finances in favor of the common good."[9]

The emphasis on poor people rather than on poverty is typical of the church's posture. Significantly, poverty does not simply mean lack of money, but perhaps more importantly, it means lack of power and all that power can bring—education, rights, justice, and so on. Traditionally, the church documents point to the "common good," a term which refers to all the cultural, social, political, religious, and economic benefits which will afford persons the opportunity of living a humane life.

As any student of Catholic social justice has discovered, the literature in this area is vast, and no one essay could encompass all the salient themes. Readers who care to explore this field in greater depth will find a comprehensive bibliography following this essay.

The Jewish Teaching

Burton Leiser presents an incisive essay outlining the Jewish approach to moral matters. Jewish moral reflection is based on a biblical text, yet Jewish scholars have always insisted on interpretation to specify and explicate the sense of the biblical reference. The basis of Jewish life is the Torah, the teaching of Moses as recorded in the Pentateuch and expounded in later writings. The Talmud, written down between A.D. 400 and 500 is an enormous work which interpreted the Scriptures for new situations in Jewish communities. In the Jewish world the talmudic literature and all subsequent moral literature serves a function somewhat analogous to the Code of Canon Law for Catholics. That is, it explicates and details the meaning of the Scriptures for a faithful life for a given era.

There is no central ecclesiastical body vested with authority for Jews. Synagogues are congregations that come together to study the law and to worship. The rabbi is the teacher of the law, and is not understood as having any other special ecclesiastical authority. In Jewish life ethics flows from a relationship with God, although ethics does not *require* religion for its justification. The "wisdom" and "understanding" of the law are quite apparent without benefit of revelation. This attitude is expressed clearly in the Book of Deuteronomy.

> See, as Yahweh my God has commanded me, I teach you the laws and customs that you are to observe in the land you are to enter and make your own. Keep them, observe them, and they will demonstrate to the peoples your wisdom and understanding. When they come to know of all these laws they will exclaim, "No other people is as wise and prudent as this great nation" (Deut. 4:5-6).

Leiser outlines some biblical and talmudic principles and then shows how they might be applied in the corporate world today. Such issues as deceptive advertising, false weights and measures, unfair competition, labor relations, excess profits, and preservation of the environment are considered in the light of biblical and talmudic literature. Leiser offers the tantalizing suggestion that excessive government regulation may have been avoided had corporations been sensitive to the wisdom of these ancient biblical rules.

A Final Note

Although there are diverse theories of the church operative in the Protestant, Catholic, and Jewish approaches to moral matters, on a practical level there is a common problem shared by all.[10] All believe that the church ought to be a community of moral formation, listening as well as shaping the moral outlook and consciences of its members. The common practical problem is how to be more effective in this task.

NOTES

1. John C. Bennett, *The Radical Imperative* (Philadelphia: Westminster Press, 1975), p. 142.

2. *Ibid.*, p. 156.

3. See Herman Nickel, "The Corporation Haters," *Fortune*, June 16, 1980, pp. 126-36.

4. For a discussion of the objectives of the Interfaith Center on Corporate Responsibility, see Timothy Smith, "The Ethical Responsibilities of Multinational Companies," *Corporations and Their Critics*, ed. David Vogel and Thornton Bradshaw (New York: McGraw-Hill, 1980), pp. 77-86.

5. "Justice in the World," *The Gospel of Peace and Justice: Catholic Social Teaching Since Pope John*, ed. Joseph Gremillion (Maryknoll, N.Y.: Orbis Books, 1976), p. 514.

6. This theme is developed in David Hollenbach, *Claims in Conflict: Retrieving and Renewing the Catholic Human Rights Tradition* (New York: Paulist Press, 1979). For an example, see Pope John Paul II's encyclical *Laborem Exercens* (On Human Labor) which focuses on the biblical vision of the person as co-creator.

7. "Pastoral Constitution on the Church in the Modern World," *The Documents of Vatican II*, ed. Walter M. Abbott, S.J. (New York: Guild Press, 1966), par. 22, p. 220.

8. "Dogmatic Constitution on the Church," *The Documents of Vatian II*, ed. Walter M. Abbott, S.J. (New York: Guild Press, 1966), pars. 6-9, pp. 18-26.

9. "Medellín Documents," *The Gospel of Peace and Justice: Catholic Social Teaching Since Pope John*, ed. Joseph Gremillion (Maryknoll, N.Y.: Orbis Books, 1976), p. 473.

10. For a discussion of the Hebrew-Christian moral tradition by a creative philosopher, see Alan Donagan, *The Theory of Morality* (Chicago: University of Chicago Press, 1977).

3. Protestantism and Corporations

John C. Bennett

Although Protestantism has articulated no clearly formulated or extensive teachings relevant to corporations as such, I shall discuss three aspects of Protestant teaching and of the policies of Protestant churches which directly or indirectly have significance for the behavior of corporations. The first is a body of ecumenical Protestant teaching about theological ethics and economic ethics which has important implications for the life and self-understanding of corporations. Out of this teaching criteria can be derived by which corporations may be judged. The second aspect of Protestant teaching and policies is the strong support given by many Protestant institutions to labor in its struggle to organize and to gain power for collective bargaining. This power of labor has done a great deal to change corporate behavior. In the third place I shall give attention to the recent tendencies in the churches to emphasize the social responsibility of corporations and to use their own power as investors to influence the policies and behavior of corporations. American churches have often sought to influence the conduct of American corporations abroad. In all of this activity the churches take for granted the corporation as a form of economic organization but seek to keep them under ethical criticism and, from time to time, to bring pressure on them to change.

Protestant Teaching: Ethical Criteria

When I speak of ecumenical Protestant thinking I refer especially to the ecumenical movement which functions mainly in the World Council of Churches. This is a movement of both Protestant and Eastern Orthodox churches. It has become very open to and cooperative with the Roman Catholic church. Protestantism has been dominant, however, and in the earlier stages it was American and European

Protestantism that provided most of the leadership. From the early 1960s to the present day the constituency of the World Council has become global with strong representation from the Third World. This has led to changes of emphasis on issues relating to corporate activity.

The Oxford Conference

The most influential work on economic ethics in the early days of the ecumenical movement was done by the Oxford Conference on Church, Community, and State in 1937. This preceded the formation of the World Council of Churches at the Amsterdam Assembly in 1948 but its thought had an important effect on the later thinking of the Council. If there is one important idea coming from the Oxford Conference, it is the idea that there is no one Christian economic system. There was strong opposition to communism as a political system, opposition to its atheism and to its totalitarianism, but there was no opposition to socialist systems as such.

This conference and the Amsterdam Assembly of the World Council of Churches in 1948 made very similar criticisms of capitalism. Oxford did not mention capitalism by name, but referred to "the assumptions and operation of the economic order of the industrialized world" and called attention to four conflicts between this order and Christian faith and ethics. The first was that this familiar combination of economic institutions tends to enhance acquisitiveness.[1] The Oxford report said that "when the necessary work of society is so organized as to make the acquisition of wealth the chief criterion of success, it encourages a feverish scramble for money, and a false respect for the victors in the struggle which is as fatal in its moral consequences as any other form of idolatry." The second criticism was that this economic order has led to shocking inequalities. There was no call for complete equality produced by regimentation, but it was said that the present inequalities deny human dignity and make impossible even the equality of opportunity in which many profess to believe. The third criticism was that this order has encouraged "irresponsible possession of economic power." It was recognized that the power of those who control corporations is "qualified at many points by trade unionism and by the law," but it was claimed that there remained a good deal of what was called economic "autocracy." The fourth criticism was that there is a very widespread "frustration of the sense of Christian vocation." It was said that most workers "are *directly* conscious of working for the profit of the employer (and for the sake of their wages) and only *indirectly* conscious of working for any public good."

Amsterdam Assembly

It is significant that eleven years later the first official Assembly of the World Council of Churches repeated the first two criticisms of what it then called "capitalism" and added two others: the development of a "practical form of materialism" which was implied also at Oxford, and the fact that "it has also kept the people of capitalist countries subject to a kind of fate which has taken the form of such social catastrophes as mass unemployment."

In what came to be a famous and much-criticized statement, the Amsterdam report rejected what it called the ideologies of both communism and laissez-faire capitalism and said that the Christian churches "should draw men away from the false assumption that these extremes are the only alternatives." The two ideologies were described in this way: "Communist ideology puts the emphasis upon economic justice, and promises that freedom will come automatically after the completion of the revolution. Capitalism puts the emphasis upon freedom, and promises that justice will follow as a by-product of free-enterprise." It was evident in 1948, more than thirty years after the revolution, that the promise in the communist ideology had not been fulfilled. This is still true another thirty years later, though some Communist countries have shown that the system can become more mellow and flexible. The charge that the capitalist promise had not been fulfilled needs to be accompanied by the recognition that capitalism in democratic countries has been greatly modified by the intervention of government and by labor unions—factors that free enterprise alone did not produce. I think that it would be an accurate generalization to say that all subsequent ecumenical Protestant and Catholic teaching recognized that the promise that justice would be a by-product of free enterprise alone (suggestive of the "trickle-down" theory) was not being fulfilled and that the economic developments in Third World countries were stark reminders of this fact.

I have said that this ecumenical teaching has not sought to identify the churches with any one system. Americans reading the materials may think that there was a tendency to be more critical of capitalism than of democratic socialism. I repeat that the Amsterdam report strongly criticized communism, which at that time was associated almost entirely with Stalinism. There were such theological criticisms as the following: a rejection of the "Communist promise of what amounts to a complete redemption of humanity in history" and "the demand of the party on its members for an exclusive and unqualified loyalty which belongs only to God and the coercive policies of communist dictatorship in controlling every aspect of life." There are implicit criticisms of a centralized socialistic system, criticisms that are suggestive of the Catholic emphasis on "subsidiarity." The following paragraph, which makes room for many forms of initiative in economic life was especially important:

> Coherent and purposeful ordering of society has now become a major necessity. Here governments have responsibilities which they must not shirk. But centers of initiative in economic life must be so encouraged as to avoid placing too great a burden upon centralized judgment and decision. To achieve religious, cultural, economic, social and other ends it is of vital importance that society should have a rich variety of smaller forms of community, in local government, within industrial organizations, including trade unions, through the development of public corporations and through voluntary associations. By such means it is possible to prevent an undue centralization of power in modern technically organized communities, and thus escape the perils of tyranny while avoiding the dangers of anarchy.[2]

We do not find in those words any celebration of the large private corporation! But they show an unwillingness to trust socialistic panaceas or what might be called 'statism," and they make room for private corporations so long as they are limited in their powers.

Evanston Assembly

The second Assembly of the World Council at Evanston in 1954 went much further in this same direction. For one thing it dropped the label, "capitalism," on the ground that it was too ambiguous to describe the economic system that Amsterdam had criticized under that name.[3] It called attention to the great diversities of economic organization that may be regarded as capitalistic. It said that "in some countries the 'welfare state' or the 'mixed economy' suggests a new pattern of economic life." It said that "the concrete issues in all countries concern the newly evolving forms of economic organization, and the relative roles of the state, organized groups and private enterprise." There is a warning "against the danger that the union of political and economic power may result in an all-controlling state," though there is no retreat from previous emphasis on the responsibility of the state "when necessary in the public interest" to intervene "to prevent any center of economic power" from becoming "stronger than itself," for the state alone has the power and authority under God to act as trustee for society as a whole.

In the Evanston report much is said about the changes in the direction of a more equal justice for which churches should witness and work, but at the same time there are also statements which give more credit than previous ecumenical documents to the achievements of private business. Two passages are of special interest: "Many socialists have come to appreciate the importance of the private sector of the economy and the necessity for the energetic, enterprising, and expert business man as well as being aware of the dangers of centralized government." "The churches have been properly critical of monopolistic practices, and of the effects of irresponsible business practices on people and society generally. But they also need to understand and lay stress on the contribution which the skilled executive has to make to society, irrespective of the form of ownership or organization. At its best the business system has provided incentives for the responsible initiative and hard work which produce economic progress, and has embodied the wisdom of decentralized decisions and widely distributed power." It is significant that the following sentence was added to keep the churches from embracing any one system: "These virtues are needed in any system."

I think that those passages make considerable room for the private corporation, though there is always an implicit demand for justice for the community as a whole. As the voices from the Third World came to be heard more and more with each successive World Council assembly, the emphasis shifted to international justice. These passages represent the most affirmative attitudes toward private corporations to be found in the official international ecumenical literature.

Nairobi Assembly

By the time of the Assembly in Nairobi in 1975 the ecumenical criticism of transnational corporations in response to the Third World experience was much emphasized. The Assembly called for study of transnational corporations: "We request the churches to coordinate efforts with the WCC—through its appropriate sub-units—in order to continue research and dialogue and to develop documentation on the role of transnational corporations." Another section of the Assembly gave expression to the widespread feeling that "transnational corporations, often in league with oppressive regimes, distort and exploit the economies of poor nations" and that "transnational corporations are a typical example of the ways in which capitalistic forces in the international and national spheres join to oppress the poor and keep them under domination."[4] The degree of hostility to transnational corporations is seen in the next sentence: "Measures to check the activities of transnational corporations are now under discussion, but because of the immense control they exercise over the channels of the 'free market' international economy, it is very difficult to envisage any effective measures which will eradicate their innate exploitative patterns." The use of "innate" is revealing.

There is a return here to the anti-capitalism that found a much more restrained expression at Oxford and Amsterdam. It may be said that this is due to the fact that the World Council has been taken over by the Third World and no longer reflects the older and more disciplined ethical thinking of the First World. That does not alter the fact that the problems of most of humanity have come to be better perceived. The First World theologians can be criticized for provincialism and complacency. Walter Rauschenbusch wrote in 1907: "Eminent theologians, like other eminent thinkers, live in the social environment of wealth and to that extent are slow to see."[5] This has never ceased to be their weakness, yet in part it has been overcome by ecumenical exposure in recent decades to the struggles of the majority of the human race who have been victims both of economic stagnation, for which their cultures have much responsibility, and exploitation by the stronger and richer nations.

Although in terms of viable policies for change, these expressions of resentment against transnational corporations as symbols of capitalistic power may be lacking, this resentment may stimulate more perceptive thinking by the churches of the First World countries about the conditions that make for greater economic justice. I wonder if the pilgrimage of the World Council in this context is different in any way from the experience of Roman Catholicism as it faces the same resentments. *Populorum Progressio*, Medellín, and Puebla trouble First World Catholics in much the same way as First World Protestants are troubled by the World Council of Churches.

Ecumenical Assemblies in the United States

I shall briefly examine some of the things that have been said in the United States on these same issues. One would expect that the whole atmosphere of thinking within the Protestant churches of this country would be entirely different from that of the World Council of Churches. But a study of the most representative American ecumenical statements shows that the differences are not as great as one would expect. I have before me three documents which were the result of years of cooperative thinking, first by the Federal Council of Churches and then by its successor in dealing with these public issues—The National Council of Churches. All three resulted from the continuous collaboration of a department which came to be called in the National Council: "the department on the Church and Economic Life." This brought together theologians, other clergy, economists, and representatives of corporate management, labor, and agriculture.

The first statement, which was adopted by the department and by the executive committee of the Federal Council of Churches in 1948, strikes me now as I re-read it as quite similar to the very critical attitude toward capitalistic institutions of Oxford and Amsterdam.[6] It is said with emphasis that existing economic systems are not ordained by God, that there "is no 'Christian' economic system that is suitable for all situations." It is said that "there is no Christian sanction for one-sided support of either economic individualism or economic collectivism." There is emphasis on equal opportunity, but it is also stated that this is not possible unless there is a minimum standard of living for all—for which society is responsible. There is great stress on the need for greater equality, though there is recognition that some inequalities can be justified for the sake of incentive and differences of function. The burden of proof is put on these inequalities, however. While it is affirmed that property is "a protection of individual freedom," there is ground for the widest possible distribution of property. It is seen that there are difficult moral dilemmas when we face both the obligation to preserve the health of economic institutions in our own country and the "responsibility to people in less favored lands." This last sentence is a preview of more to come!

The statement opposes ideologies "based on illusory hopes" and calls for the confronting of the world with the Gospel as a correction of these illusions. But emphasis is put on the idea that the Church should welcome "great movements of protest against inherited privileges and unjust structures in modern society." And it is said that the illusions that these movements often generate are partly the result of the fact that the Church has obscured the "radical ethical demands in its own teachings." This statement is similar to the international ecumenical statements in its demand that "the Church should keep under the strongest criticism those economic institutions which increase the self-interest of men and which develop a moral climate within which money is regarded as the chief good and in which success in acquiring it is most highly honored."

Although corporations are not mentioned, such words indicate the kind of criticism that might have been leveled against many of them if they had been. However, there is the following slight concession: "economic institutions should make constructive use of such motives as the desire for economic security, the desire to improve the economic condition of one's family, the desire for scope for one's capacities and for social approval." But it is also said that these motives should be kept in harmony both "with concern for the welfare of the community" and with the individual's sense of Christian vocation.

A second statement, adopted by the General Board of the National Council of Churches in 1954, also represented years of work and shows a considerable change, not unlike that in the Evanston report the same year.[7] One sees in it a greater concern about the Cold War and some hesitancy in offering too much criticism of our own society. There is a definite attack upon the idea that the "one sure road to economic justice is the socialization of the means of production." There is more concern about freedom and efficiency and a recognition of need to prevent the union of political and economic power. It is said that "there is no completely 'Christian economic system' suitable for all situations everywhere." Notice that the addition of the word "completely" makes the statement more guarded than the similar statement in the previous document. On specific issues this document often resembles the earlier one. There is the same emphasis on a minimum standard of living for all. Though there is less emphasis on equality the following statement is clear: "Great contrasts between rich and poor in our society tend to destroy fellowship, to undermine equality of opportunity, and to undercut the political institutions of a responsible society." The need for avoiding equality by regimentation is mentioned, as is the need for incentives for production and efficiency "provided when income varies with contribution," but then it is said that "Christian scrutiny—may well question any conventional appraisals of the value of a particular kind of contribution." There is a difference of emphasis, but there is also an attempt to preserve a balance that is influenced by the concerns expressed in the earlier document. I think that the main difference is that more is said about productivity and efficiency. It came to be seen more clearly that talking about justice cannot get us far if not enough is produced to go around.

A third corporate statement was prepared by the National Council of Churches' Department on the Church and Economic Life and adopted by the Council's General Board in 1966.[8] It was entitled "Christian Concern and Responsibility for Economic Life in a Rapidly Changing Technological Society." This statement does bring us into a quite different world. There was much more stress than in previous statements on the dominance of technology and its effect on culture. Issues of justice, on the feeling of helplessness that people often had in the presence of great aggregates of power, whether they were publicly or privately controlled, and on the quality of life were, however, addressed as well. Two sentences elicit this sense of new forms of power. "The explosive and impersonal forces of science and technology permeate every aspect of life, ranging far beyond the specific or private economic ends to which they are applied. Consequently decision-makers in the private sector must accept accountability for the impact of their decisions upon the whole society." "The role of government—local, state, and federal—in relation to the economic order has expanded and must expand to cope with the complexities of a technological age. This expansion of governmental powers, activities, and size requires increased sensitivity to the dangers inherent in concentrated power, and more responsible participation by citizens in public policy formation as well as in political parties."

Two words in these sentences have importance for this stage of thinking about economic ethics: "accountability" and "participation." It is not enough to depend on the subjective feeling of responsibility on the part of those who have power to make decisions. There must be new structures which hold them accountable. Both in the nation and on the international scene, the lack of structures of accountability has come to be increasingly felt. "Participation" both in the private and the public sectors and in political efforts to give society direction is affirmed in answer to the common feeling of helplessness in the presence of the great centers of private or public power. The statement emphasizes voluntary groups which can "provide a countervailing force against the depersonalizing tendencies of massive economic and political power centers." Checks and balances are called for in the economic as well as in the political order.

This statement also begins to show concern about the effect of human dominion over nature, over the environment. Here the rights of property need to be limited by our concern for future generations. Waste, "high-pressure consumption and built-in obsolescence" suggest a new dimension of ethical problems. These are seen in the context of "the pressure of an accelerating rate of population growth upon the world's resource base."

The concern about poverty has not diminished. The presence of the "involuntary poverty" of a fifth of the American people in the presence of great affluence remains a scandal. There is a reflection of Professor Galbraith's contrast between private wealth and public poverty and a call for improvement of public services for the sake of the wholeness of the community. It is said that "Christians are called to reinterpret the concept of social justice to include the overcoming of both private and public poverty." There are briefly stated concerns about the growing gap between rich and poor nations, and the responsibility of the industrially developed world for the development of nations now in poverty. Without spelling them out, the statement distinguished between different concepts of economic life and different views of basic human rights. Living with diversity in regard to the first should not lead us to be tolerant of threats to such basic human rights.

For various bureaucratic reasons that I do not need to discuss here the very carefully prepared statements on economic ethics were not implemented in the decade of the seventies by the National Council of Churches. This is regrettable, particularly in the face of the erosion of recent gains by inflation and unemployment. Spasmodic actions, such as Proposition 13, which have expressed middle-class frustrations and have tended to downgrade the contribution of government in the solution of economic problems have not been discussed thoroughly by Protestant ecumenical bodies. There have been both discussion and action about the racial aspect of many economic problems, and this has been to the good. There has also been some discussion and a great deal of official and unofficial action by many religious groups about the social responsibility of corporations. About this I shall have more to say later.

Church Support of the Labor Movement

A very significant aspect of the relationship between Protestant churches and corporations has been the official support by the churches of the labor movement during the period of its struggles for recognition and bargaining power. The strength of organized labor in recent decades has been an important check on corporate power. Especially since the Wagner Act in 1935 there has been a great improvement in the condition of American industrial workers in regard to wages, hours, and fringe benefits such as pensions and provisions for medical care. There still are some industries that are virtually unorganized—textiles, for example. The churches today are bringing pressure on the J. P. Stevens corporation because of its resistance to unionization. Problems such as the hazards to the health of workers that result from many processes in production are beginning to come to the fore.

The power of labor unions has created new problems for the community, for consumers, and sometimes for members of racial minorities who remain unorganized. Unions themselves are often undemocratic, and the rights of individual workers often need defense. However, there is great value in having two powers which check each other. Before the rise of labor unions corporations were apt to be either arbitrarily paternalistic, or little better than small fascist states that controlled workers by intimidation or violence—the violence of their own goons or of the police who were generally on the side of the employers. There have been remarkable changes for the better in these respects. Both unions and the law have been important protections for workers and even great strikes are not usually occasions for violent conflict.

I shall write only about the Protestant churches in this country and their relation to the struggles of labor for a share of the power. The constituency of the Protestant churches was not as much identified with labor as the membership of the Catholic church, yet by the 1920s the ecumenical institutions of Protestantism and the leaders of many denominations had come to be more and more advocates of labor's cause. The gulf between church leadership and the membership of many local middle-class white churches has often been considerable. In times of crisis this contrast between official teaching and local attitudes has often resulted in serious conflicts. Ministers have often been caught in the middle of conflicts and in many cases have lost their jobs. My impression today, however, is that Protestant churches are not as torn over such issues as was the case a few decades ago.

The Early History

The steel strike of 1919 was of great importance for the relationship between Protestantism and labor.[9] The strike was for union recognition and against the twelve-hour day and in many cases the seven-day week. It is difficult today to imagine the conditions of wage slavery that existed in this country as recently as 1919. The steel strike was one of the bitterest in our industrial history. Though in fact the workers lost the strike, it made such an impression on public opinion that as a result of initiatives of President Harding a few years later the twelve-hour day was abandoned by the industry. While the strike was on, the steel corporations claimed that they could not function effectively without the twelve-hour day. A short-lived ecumenical movement that was established at the end of World War I, the Interchurch World Movement, appointed a commission of inquiry headed by the very influential Methodist bishop, Francis J. McConnell. The report of the commission was in favor of the strikers and challenged the companies on the twelve-hour day with great persuasiveness. This report had enormous influence both on the churches and on public opinion. The steel companies had books written against the report. The Protestant constituency was much divided by this event, but the report and the discussion that it evoked demonstrated the close relation between Protestant teaching about social justice and the struggles of labor against industrial tyranny and unjust conditions that now seem remote from the practices of most large corporations. I remember the discussion of another steel strike by a department of the National Council of Churches in the 1950s when the most discussed issue was whether pensions should involve contributions from the employees or not—a far cry from the twelve-hour day!

In 1932 the Federal Council of Churches, which later became a unit in the National Council of Churches, adopted a new version of what had been called "The Social Creed of the Churches": the "Social Ideals of the Churches." Most of the items in it dealt with economic justice and social welfare. One of them was the following call for collective bargaining: "the right of employees and employers alike to organize for collective bargaining and social action; protection of both in the exercise of that right. . . ." In 1940 the Federal Council resolved to record its conviction "that not only has labor the right to organize but also that it is socially desirable that it do so because of the need for collective action in the maintenance of standards of living." Labor was urged to match its power with moral responsibility.

Department on the Church and Economic Life

"The Industrial Division," one of the departments of the Federal Council, was an advocate of the cause of labor in the 1920s and 1930s. In 1947 the Federal Council replaced this division by a "Department on the Church and Economic Life." Now the role of advocate no longer had a central place, though the rights of labor continued to be upheld. This department consisted of representatives of the main segments of the economy—labor, management, and agriculture—and it also included economists, representatives of the public, theologians, and church leaders. In 1950 it became an important part of the National

Council of Churches. Most of its members were lay men and women. I was a member of it for many years, and I think that it developed excellent processes for cooperative thinking on issues dividing the various groups represented. It reflected a stage in the development of the American economy in which the debate concerning the constructive role of labor unions had largely ceased, and corporations were accepted as a legitimate form of economic organization. There were conflicts between representatives of labor and management, especially as collective bargaining was punctuated by strikes, and they had different goals and ideological emphases when it came to national legislation, but it was now possible for their representatives to communicate with each other in the context of the Church. The three statements which I summarized in the first part of this chapter were the work of this department, and this meant that more than a mere majority of its members agreed to them. They were later adopted by the governing boards of the Federal and National Councils. I think, as I look back upon my own experience with the department, that the clergy, labor leaders, and economists usually had greater influence than the representatives of management, who were often more conservative. Yet the latter had real influence on the outcome.

Support of Major Denominations

I have been considering only the ecumenical organizations of Protestantism. I do not want to suggest that there has been the kind of support for labor that I have described in all regions, in relation to all types of industry, or in all denominations.[10] But I can point to strong support for labor by the representative bodies of major denominations. In mentioning a few of these I am not suggesting that there are not others that have also taken similar positions. The following denominations have had a long history of support of labor: The United Presbyterian Church, the United Methodist Church, the United Church of Christ and the denominations that formed it, the Episcopal Church, the National Baptist Convention, and the Christian Church (Disciples of Christ). I shall refer to two statements about the labor movements that can be duplicated from the history of other denominations.

The Lambeth Conference, which includes the bishops of the Anglican Communion from many countries, as early as 1920 strongly supported the labor movement. After denying that its interest in the labor movement was motivated by a desire to win labor for the

Anglican church, the conference said that "the purpose of the Labor Movement, at its best, is to secure fullness of life, the opportunity of a complete development of their manhood and womanhood for those who labor; it seeks to furnish a better world for people to live in." In 1922 in this country the bishops and the house of deputies at the General Convention of the Episcopal Church concurred in reaffirming those declarations of the Lambeth Conference. Those words now may seem safely general, but at the time they could only be used by people who favored labor in its early struggles to exist as a movement. In the Episcopal church, in spite of its generally privileged constituency, there have long been influential unofficial movements and periodicals that have supported labor not only in general terms but also in relation to particular industrial conflicts.

One of the most significant statements about the labor movement by any denomination was a report following considerable study that became an action of the General Assembly of the Presbyterian Church U.S.A. (Northern) in 1944. After a discussion of the responsibilities and contributions of labor unions, which expresses a very positive attitude toward them, the Assembly included the following very important paragraph about the question of the responsibility of Christians to join labor unions:

> We believe that the Christian Church must confront its members who are employees with their obligation to consider their relationship to a labor union in the light of the Christian principle of social responsibility. We believe that industrial relations generally stand a stronger possibility of improvement when management and labor are organized. The good that follows such organization works for the benefit of those who assume neither the obligations nor the responsibilities of union membership, which gives the labor movement social value and ethical validity.

That last sentence goes far beyond general statements in support of organized labor in raising a serious question about the ethical justification for Christians to remain outside unions that are available to them. Today the gains made by unions are taken for granted, and people forget what the condition of workers was before unions gained power. Workers are often tempted to cooperate with employers who now seek to dispense with unions, forgetting that the wages and working conditions that are enhancing their lives are in fact the result of union pressure and negotiation.

The Power of Churches as Investors

The present relations between Protestant churches and corporations are much influenced by the current emphasis on corporate social responsibility. As investors churches often bring pressure on the corporations in which they have stock to change their policies in the light of their responsibility for society as a whole. This often involves action to limit injury to society and to effect a positive change on specific issues such as the employment of minorities and women. The policies of American corporations abroad, especially with regard to the support that their presence in South Africa gives to apartheid, are the most common targets of criticism and pressure. Universities and foundations exert pressure as stockholders as well, but they are much less aggressive than the churches. This may be in part because they are more interested in preserving their neutrality in regard to public issues and because in the churches there are alert constituencies that keep pressing for more action.

It is significant that the churches seldom raise questions about the legitimacy of the private corporation as a form of economic organization as such. Their attention is focused on specific effects of corporate behavior. Ecumenical agencies have been set up to monitor the activities of corporations so that churches may have correct information as they seek to influence them.

One presupposition of this activity of churches is the complete rejection of the view that corporations have as their only responsibility the maximizing of profit for stockholders. As Milton Friedman expresses it, "A corporate executive is an employee of the owners of the business. He has direct responsibility to his employers. That responsibility is to conduct the business in accordance with their desires, which generally will be to make as much money as possible *while conforming to the basic rules of the society, both those embodied in law and those embodied in ethical custom.*"[11] The fact that he italicizes those words indicates that he neither wants corporations to violate well-established moral standards nor does he want them to give moral leadership directly in the improvement of society. From his point of view there is an implicit moral leadership in seeking to free the market from intervention by outside forces. In his view the freeing of the market is beneficent for society as a whole. The overexercising of the habit of self-seeking which this view involves has its own unfortunate by-products, and it is in conflict with the warning against acquisitiveness and the concern to encourage a sense of Christian vocation that were emphasized by the ecumenical teaching that I quoted in the first part of this chapter. Insofar as the churches have addressed themselves to this subject, they do not share Friedman's optimism that most social values will be realized as by-products of freedom and therefore need not be sought directly. Churches generally assume that the productive efficiency of corporations is combined with so much economic and political power that they need to be subject to social and political controls by other agencies that are directly responsible to the public and dedicated to the public welfare.

Another reason has been given for emphasizing the maximizing of profit or, more broadly, for considering the well-being of the corporation as the one sure responsibility of the corporation: the warning that particular groups in society may work through corporations to promote their own nostrums or dubious goals for education, foreign policy, or the economic order itself. This warning against the abuse of power by corporations is given by Professor Eugene Rostow, who is concerned that corporations in the name of social responsibility may use their great power to advance such dubious causes as "social credit and Buchmanism."[12] I do know what his contemporary examples might be, but limiting the responsibility of the corporation to its own economic well-being would be a way of keeping it out of such mischief! The extent to which one considers this a realistic danger is perhaps a function of one's political views: if right-wing groups in the churches were to use their clout in cooperation with right-wing elements in corporations, the issues that Professor Rostow raises would offer food for thought.

The Interfaith Center on Corporate Responsibility

In 1974, "The Interfaith Center on Corporate Responsibility" was established under the umbrella of the National Council of Churches with direct responsibility to a Board made up of representatives of a number of mainline Protestant agencies and to one Roman Catholic Order, the Atonement Friars. In an article explaining the work of this center, Timothy Smith, who is one of its executives, says that "the board decides policy and directs actions on such corporate responsibility issues as southern Africa, Latin America, the Philippines, equal-employment opportunity, strip mining, women, creative investment."[13] This is quite a large order. One of the chief functions of the Center is to be a source of information about the practices of corporations. It also helps to coordinate the efforts of many Protestant groups and agencies.

Both before and after this Center was established there has been a considerable record of action by units of the Church in relation to the behavior of corporations. Sometimes this action is taken officially by a denomination. Sometimes it is taken by a consortium of denominations. Sometimes it is taken by a board or agency within a denomination which has itself made corporate investments. Sometimes it is taken by an ecumenical body such as the World Council of Churches or the National Council of Churches. The action may be to sell stocks in protest against the policy of a corporation or a bank, but more often it is to mobilize support for a resolution to be presented at a stockholders' meeting. Quite as important, and perhaps more important in some cases, is consultation between representatives of churches and officers of corporations. This discussion helps to keep up persuasive pressure.

By mentioning some examples of what churches have done in this regard, I can suggest the wide range of activities in which they have engaged.

Examples of Church Power

One of the early examples of an effort by churches to change the policies of corporations was the pressures brought by several denominations upon Eastman-Kodak in 1967 in connection with the company's racial policies during a controversy in Rochester over an organization named "FIGHT" (the first letters referred to freedom and integration). Professor Powers says that these pressures from churches "seem to have made an important difference."[14] Much of the activity of churches involved not pressure on corporations but what has been called "creative investment"—the decision to invest funds with some degree of risk in projects controlled by minorities or designed for their benefit. During the Vietnam War there was much discussion of the involvement of churches in the war, even though they had opposed it, because of their investment in American companies which made weapons or other instruments of war, but I find little evidence that many actions were actually taken. The Church of the Brethren, which is governed by pacifist principles, did sell its stock in a number of corporations for this reason. There was also pressure on Honeywell because it manufactured napalm, but in general churches must have found that it was difficult to find corporations so pure that they had no part in the war.

A number of church boards and agencies in 1970 protested at stockholders' meetings against the operations of Gulf Oil Co. in Angola when it was still a colony of Portugal. There was an effort in 1971 on the part of agencies of six denominations, directed against American Metal Climax and the Kennecot Copper corporation, to protect the Puerto Rican environment.

Father Williams and Professor Houck, in their volume, *Full Value*, give an account of the action taken by the National Council of Churches together with two Catholic orders to get the Gulf and Western Industries to provide full disclosure of their activities as a major economic force in the Dominican Republic.[15] The company had been engaging in many educational and welfare activities which the critics regarded as a front for serious exploitation of the people. Twice the National Council and the Catholic orders pursued the matter through resolutions at stockholders' meetings. Eventually, the corporation bowed to pressure and provided the disclosure that had been requested.

In 1979 many church bodies in Britain supported a resolution at the annual meeting of the holding company of Royal Dutch Shell because that corporation had broken the oil sanctions against Rhodesia.

I am amazed by the massiveness of the attacks by American churches and churches in other countries on corporations doing business in South Africa. In his review of the activity of churches in this context Charles Powers traces the beginning of this pressure on corporations to demonstrations by students, especially those from Union Theological Seminary, in 1966 against the New York banks that loaned money to the South African government.[16] The United Methodist Board of Missions led the response to this by withdrawing $10,000,000 from the National City Bank. The Episcopal church in 1971, through its Presiding Bishop, John Hines, called on General Motors, in which it had stock, to cease its manufacturing operations in South Africa. In 1972, as an unusual result of consultations between an agency of a church and a corporation, Mobil Oil Corporation and the United Church of Christ Board of World Ministries jointly announced an agreement whereby the corporation would inform stockholders about the activities of its affiliates in the Republic of South Africa. In 1974, a coalition of ten American religious organizations which held stock valued at $700 million challenged twenty-two corporations doing business in South Africa to reveal the facts about their operations. In 1975, a large coalition of American religious groups took action in a stockholders' meeting to ask IBM to stop selling or leasing computers in South Africa. In 1978, the American Lutheran Church voted to require more aggressive monitoring of the employment policies of the seventeen corporations in South Africa in which it had investments.

The World Council of Churches in 1972 sold its stock holdings in firms directly involved in or trading with the white-dominated countries in southern Africa. The General Board of the National Council of Churches in the United States in 1977 withdrew all funds from banks that invest in or make loans to South Africa.

The General Assembly of the Church of Scotland in 1971 authorized its Church and Nation Committee to investigate its investments in South Africa and to look into the possibility of redeploying church investments to assist the economies of underdeveloped countries. The Council of Churches in The Netherlands in 1978 called for the total disinvestment by the churches of that country in South Africa. An ecumenical agency set up by several denominations in England in 1979 called upon the churches and missionary societies associated with it to withdraw funds from banks operating in South Africa. The Swedish Ecumenical Council called on Swedish companies operating in South Africa to reduce the disparity between the wages and salaries received by white and black people. The story goes on and on.[17]

There was no agreement about the desirability of disinvesting. Most often it was thought better policy to keep the stock and use the role of stockholder to bring pressure on the corporation to improve the position of the blacks from within the country. Charles Powers has a good discussion of the two different concerns that sometimes led to different policies—the concern to be pure and the concern to be effective.[18] Sometimes it could be argued that since to divest was the best way to call attention to an issue through publicity, there was no need to choose between those two goals.

There was an interesting response to all of this activity in 1978 by the South African Council of Churches (this does not include the Dutch Reformed Churches) which called upon foreign corporations to "revise radically" their investment policies in South Africa. The Council did not advocate the withdrawal of all foreign investments, but it did testify that foreign investments and loans had tended to bolster the apartheid system.

The Multinational Dilemma

Most of the corporations mentioned in the South African context are multinational or transnational corporations. I do not find that much is said in the name of churches about the multinational character of corporations. They are criticized for what they do in particular national situations. Yet there is a widespread concern that multinational corporations are at present accountable for their foreign operations to no one unless the host country has enough strength to discipline them. Even when they have partners within the country where their affiliates operate, they tend to exert influence in behalf of the corporation and against the interest of the majority in their own country. The country that is the home base for a multinational corporation has difficulty in exercising controls in the international public interest, but efforts seem to be being made in this connection. At present there is no international body to which such corporations are accountable.

In the first section of this chapter I referred to the strong statements made at the Nairobi Assembly of the World Council of Churches in criticism of the multinational corporations. Some of this criticism may seem demagogic, but multinationals in the Third World have become symbols of economic imperialism, even though in particular situations the contributions that they make in the transfer of capital and technology and skills to developing countries are accepted despite anxiety about the economic power that they represent.

In June 1977 a meeting on transnational corporations was held under the auspices of the World Council of Churches.[19] It was attended by corporate representatives, labor leaders, theologians, economists, and church administrators. It was the culmination of a series of ecumenical meetings on transnationals. And it was the beginning of a major new program of the World Council to study and evaluate transnationals and to find ways of counteracting what was perceived as the harm that they do to developing countries. Much was said at the consultation about the positive contributions of transnationals as "suppliers and transfer agents of employment, capital and skills," but the final report calls for a "critical stance against transnationals worldwide." The program was characterized, however, by an open attitude and a desire to study the actual effects of transnational corporations.

Despite such openness and the desire to avoid a propagandist spirit, there is no doubt that at present the dominant outlook is negative toward transnationals. One work-group report said to the consultation: "It is almost, if not entirely impossible for transnationals to conserve or promote social justice. The main pressures on transnationals are for survival and growth." The report speaks of the transnationals as "exploiting natural resources and cheap labour, amassing vast wealth and power without adequate control and responsibility, and applying capital intensive technology for large profits, against the best interests of the host country." Those who represent transnationals may regard that sentence as unfair diatribe, but it can be regarded as a sober checklist of problems with which those who control transnationals need to deal. They are the conditions that are bound to arise when the rich and the strong bring their power to bear on the poor and the weak. We can expect to hear much more from many Christian groups working under the auspices of the World Council of Churches on this subject. The concerns of the World Council are no different from those expressed in *Populorum Progressio* in which Pope Paul VI summarizes the effect of the relations between highly industrialized nations and less developed economies that have "only food, fibres, and other raw materials to sell" and then concludes the discussion with the words: "the poor nations remain ever poor while the rich ones become still richer."[20] Counteracting this tendency should be high on the agenda of all the churches. It should be high on the agenda of humanity. Is there hope that it will become high on the agenda of most corporations?

NOTES

1. J. H. Oldham (ed.), *The Oxford Conference — Official Report* (New York: Willett and Clark, 1937), Section 3, pp. 86-92.

2. W. A. Visser 't Hooft (ed.), *The First Assembly of the World Council of Churches: The Official Report.* See the report of Section 3.

3. W. A. Visser 't Hooft (ed.), *The Evanston Report* (New York: Harper, 1954). See the report of Section 3.

4. David M. Paton (ed.), *Breaking Barriers — Nairobi 1975* (Grand Rapids, Mich.: Eerdmans, 1975). See report of Section 6, par. 42.

5. Walter Rauschenbusch, *Christianity and the Social Crisis* (New York: Macmillan, 1907), p. 46.

6. "Basic Christian Principles and Assumptions," adopted by the Executive Committee of the *Federal Council of Churches of Christ in America,* September 1948.

7. "Christian Principles and Assumptions for Economic Life," adopted by the General Board of the *National Council of the Churches of Christ in the U.S.A.,* September 15, 1954.

8. "Christian Concern and Responsibility for Economic Life in a Rapidly Changing Technological Society," adopted by the General Board of the *National Council of the Churches of Christ in the U.S.A.,* February 24, 1966.

It is important to realize that all three of these statements were first discussed for long periods and then adopted by the Council's Department on the Church and Economic Life, which included representatives from the main segments of the economy together with theologians and church leaders and economists and representatives of the public.

9. For a summary of the facts about the report on the steel strike and the responses to it, see Robert M. Miller, *American Protestantism and Social Issues 1919-1939* (Chapel Hill: University of North Carolina Press, 1958), pp. 210-16). Professor Miller says of the report on the steel strike: "It is impossible to overestimate the importance of this study."

10. Two important studies of Gastonia, N.C., where there was a bitter strike with widespread reverberations in 1929, written thirty-four years apart, describe a very revealing case of the rejection of labor unions by both the employers and most of the middle-class ministers. Between 1929 and 1976 there was some mellowing of relations and considerable improvement of race relations, but little change in the attitude toward unions. I refer to Liston Pope, *Millhands and Preachers* (New Haven, Conn.: Yale University Press, 1942), and John R. Earle, Dean D. Knudson, and Donald W. Shriver, Jr., *Spindles and Spires* (Atlanta, Ga., John Knox Press, 1976).

11. Quoted in Charles W. Powers, *People/Profits—The Ethics of Investment* (New York: The Council on Religion and International Affairs, 1972), pp. 4-5.

12. Edward S. Mason, (ed.), *The Corporation in Modern Society* (Cambridge, Mass.: Harvard University Press, 1959). See the chapter by Eugene V. Rostow on "To Whom and for What Ends Are Corporation Managements Responsible."

13. Timothy Smith, "Church Agencies Step up Campaign for Corporate Responsibility," *The Christian Century* 91 (April 3, 1974): 369-71.

14. Charles W. Powers, *Social Responsibility and Investments* (Nashville, Tenn.: Abingdon Press, 1971), p. 100.

15. Oliver F. Williams and John W. Houck, *Full Value—Cases in Christian Business Ethics* (San Francisco, Calif.: Harper and Row, 1978), chap. 11.

16. Powers, *Social Responsibility and Investments*, p. 15.

17. For the facts about the involvement of churches I have depended on the files of *The Christian Century*, under "Church investments." Supporting the boycott of the Nestle Co. for its overseas promotion of its infant formula, an issue that has figured prominently in the news, may be the most recent activity of many agencies of the Church.

18. Powers, *Social Responsibility and Investments*, pp. 76-80. This is similar to Max Weber's famous contrast between the "ethics of ultimate ends" and the "ethics of responsibility."

19. This account of the consultation is based on a report in the *Ecumenical Press Service,* June 30, 1977.

I want to refer also to an article by J. Irwin Miller in *Worldview,* November 1976, entitled "The Future of the Multinationals." Miller, a widely known head of a multinational corporation, shows great sensitivity toward the feelings and interests of host countries. He has been an influential lay leader of both the World Council of Churches and the National Council of Churches.

20. *Populorum Progressio,* par. 57.

BIBLIOGRAPHY

Barnet, Richard J., and Ronald E. Mueller. *Global Reach—The Power of the Multinational Corporation.* New York: Simon and Schuster, 1974.

Bennett, John C., *The Radical Imperative.* Philadelphia: Westminster Press, 1975.

Bock, Paul. *In Search of a Responsible Society—The Social Teachings of the World Council of Churches.* Philadelphia: Westminster Press, 1974.

Bonino, Jose Miguez, *Doing Theology in a Revolutionary Situation.* Philadelphia: Fortress Press, 1975.

Earle, John R., Dean L. Knudson, and Donald W. Shriver, Jr. *Spindle and Spires.* Atlanta, Ga.: John Knox Press, 1976.

Handy, Robert J., *The Social Gospel in America 1870-1920.* New York: Oxford University Press, 1966.

Interchurch World Movement of North America. *Public Opinion and the Steel Strike.* New York: Da Capo Press, 1970 [1921].

Mason, Edward S., (ed.). *The Corporation and Modern Society.* Cambridge, Mass.: Harvard University Press, 1959.

Miller, Robert M., *American Protestantism and Social Issues 1919-1934.* Chapel Hill, N.C.: University of North Carolina Press, 1958.

Niebuhr, Reinhold. *Moral Man and Immoral Society.* New York: Scribner's, 1944.

———. *The Children of Light and the Children of Darkness.* New York: Scribner's, 1944.

———. *Man's Nature and His Communities.* New York: Scribner's, 1965.

———. *Faith and Politics.* New York: George Braziller, 1968. These volumes represent the thoughts of the most influential American Protestant thinker on social ethics since the Social Gospel. The first book is dated in many ways but is nonetheless an essential introduction to the author's Christian realism.

Obenhaus, Victor. *Ethics for an Industrial Society.* New York: Harper and Row, 1965. This is a summary of a study of economic ethics under auspices of the National Council of Churches. Another volume in the study is Bowen, Howard R. *Social Responsibility of the Business Man.* New York: Harper and Row, 1953.

Olds, Marshall. *Analysis of the Interchurch World Movement's Report on the Steel Strike.* New York: Putnam's, 1923.

Pope, Liston. *Millhands and Preachers.* New Haven, Conn.: Yale University Press, 1942.

Powers, Charles W. *People/Profits, The Ethics of Investment.* New York: Council on Religion and International Affairs, 1972.

———. *Social Responsibility and Investments.* Nashville, Tenn.: Abingdon Press, 1971.

Preston, Ronald H. *Religion and the Persistence of Capitalism.* London: SCM Press, 1979.

Rauschenbusch, Walter. *Christianity and the Social Crisis.* New York: Macmillan, 1907.

Temple, William. *Christianity and Social Order.* New York: Seabury Press, 1976.

Vernon, Raymond. *Sovereignty at Bay: The Multinational Spread of U.S. Enterprises.* New York: Basic Books, 1971.

Williams, Oliver F., and John W. Houck. *Full Value: Cases in Business Ethics.* New York: Harper and Row, 1978.

Wogaman, J. Philip. *The Great Economic Debates: An Ethical Analysis.* Philadelphia: Westminster Press, 1977.

4. Catholicism, Business, and Human Priorities

James V. Schall, S.J.

Still even from the relatively best organization of economic life, no paradise can be expected. Considering the weaknesses and the inadequacy of all models, flaws will always arise. The ideal of theory is hardly completely realized, and even the programs of practical economic policy are no magic formulae, even if they move along the proper path.

Heinrich Pesch, S.J.
Lehrbuch der Nationalökonomie

That the Gospels contain little if any formal economic theory is readily recognized, even though we are freely to give a cup of water to the thirsty, while our few talents, be they ten, five, or even one, are to be used for productive purposes, even for interest, if nothing else, and not buried in the ground for safekeeping. (Matt. 25:35–46; Luke 19:12–27). "I submit that orthodox Christianity is fairly non-specific and quite skeptical about *all* economic systems," economist David McCord Wright wrote in his essay, "Toward a Christian Approach in Judging Economic Systems." The New Testament, indeed, suggests that we can be drawn away from God as much by temptations to power as by temptations to money (1 Tim. 6:9); even "doing good" has the danger of letting the right hand know what the left hand is doing (Matt. 6:3–4; Gaylin, 1978). Professor Wright continued: "In these [economic and political] matters, individual Christians will always vary as to how many of the world's evils are removable. Men differ in optimism and there is always room for judgment. On the other hand, the one thing upon which all orthodox Christians should agree is that no system in the finite world is going to be perfectly 'just' or perfectly free from evil" (Wright, 1957, p. 123).

Such reflections foreshadow the major themes and lines that have been followed by Christians in confronting the world of economy, business, and politics. The life of truck, barter, and trade is itself good and normal, nothing is going to be perfect, the best does not always happen, but there are, nevertheless, certain practices and systems that are wrong, contrary to Christianity and the human good. And men can learn what these are.

John Paul II, speaking to the International Theological Commission, stated principles which also, in their own way, apply to the manner in which Christians view the ethical issues that arise in the world of business and economic systems. "It is already well-known," the Holy Father observed, "that in ancient times several schools of theology existed and even in this age diverse schools of thought and opinions are recognized as legitimate so that one can speak of a healthy pluralism. Nevertheless, care must be always taken to preserve intact 'the deposit of faith' and theologians must reject those philosophical tenets which are incompatible with the faith" (John Paul II, October 26, 1979). We find here, consequently, a "liberation" tempered by norms and values that prevent just anything from being true or wise.

In this context it is also well to recall John XXIII's famous passage about the difference between ideologies as such and the historically conditioned movements said to embody them. This passage, from *Pacem in Terris* (#159), is often used to establish some justification for socialism.

> It must be borne in mind, furthermore, that neither can false philosophical teachings regarding the nature, origin and destiny of the universe and of man be identified with historical movements that have economic, social, cultural or political ends, not even when these movements have originated from those teachings and have drawn and still draw inspiration therefrom.
>
> This is so because the teachings, once they are drawn up and defined, remain always the same, while the movements, working in constantly evolving historical situations cannot but be influenced by these latter and cannot avoid, therefore, being subject to changes, even of a profound nature. Besides, who can deny that those movements, insofar as they conform to the dictates of right reason and are the interpreters of the lawful aspirations of the human person, contain elements that are positive and deserving of approval?

However, the same passage can be seen in quite another manner. It was intended to establish the fact that ideas and systems deserve their own criticism on the basis of their own internal validity, while these same ideas, whether true or false, when put into practice, may be modified to reduce or eliminate their objectionable parts or even corrupt the good aspects. Yet, whether a happy or dehumanizing result takes place must be based on fact, as John XXIII intimated. This means that a dangerous theory might not be so bad in practice, but then again it might. It might change. Then again, it might not. Critical realism about real results and tendencies remains at the heart of any Christian intelligence about the actions and institutions of men.

A Catholic Social Doctrine?

While there may be no specifically Christian economics, there are still economic actions and principles that have been judged compatible or incompatible with Christianity, presumably because they are in conformity with or in violation of economic laws as these relate to an identifiable human dignity. The history of Christian thought about business and economic practices, even for the Church Fathers, was not so much an independent doctrine, derived a priori from faith or reason, as a series of historical and ecclesiastical judgments and decisions about specific crises or aberrations that were considered contrary to the Christian ethic on some specific point (Giordani, 1944, chaps. 10-13). On the basis of such experience, no doubt, there is ground for the development of a unique theory, or perhaps several divergent theories. But the essence of this experience is that, in the end, "not all things are permitted," that there are degrees of goodness and badness in our affairs that are not simply reduced to subjective opinion. The "human" and the "inhuman" are, then, definitely contradictory terms and can be known as such. The central line of Christian thought has held that intelligence is valid and, indeed, more itself because of faith.

However much contemporary Christians might presume to speak of moral and religious imperatives in economic or business affairs, therefore, they should not forget that Christianity long antedated modern political and business institutions, as well as the very science of economics itself. To be sure, economics owes a deep debt to the First Book of Aristotle's *Politics,* while ethical business practices recall Cicero's stern *Treatise on Duties,* both of which, of course, appeared before Christianity, as did the commandment "Thou Shalt Not Steal." This means at least that the memory of older virtues and vices ought to be retained in all of our practical analyses. In the course of this history, moreover, Christians have been accused of being at once too worldly and too other-worldly, accusations still often heard today. Both of these rather opposite positions arose, ironically, from certain economic theories. Cathedrals were monuments to ostentation and waste, not to Aristotle's magnificence or Pericles' civic beauty, while heaven, in the meantime, was said to distract men from their main task, that of feeding the poor and tending the Earth for as long as possible, under the Stars.

The intellectual import of this same contrast can, perhaps, be seen by following the contrasting views about Christian thought of Professor Frank Knight and Professor Joseph Schumpeter. For Knight, in a famous article in *Economica* in 1939,

> Our thesis is twofold. First, we point out the teachings of Christianity give little or no direct guidance for the change and improvement of social organization, and in fact, give clear *prima facie* evidence of not having been formulated to that end. . . . [Secondly], there is also little to be found in Christianity in the way of moral principle or ideals which can serve for the ethical guidance of deliberate political action. . . . Indeed, evil rather than good seems likely to result from any appeal to Christian religious or moral teaching in connection with the problems of social action. Stated in positive form, our contention is that social problems require intellectual analysis in impersonal terms, but that Christianity is exclusively an emotional and personal morality. (p. 339)

Christianity is, in this view, at least irrelevant and probably inimical to any properly just economic enterprise or system.

Professor Schumpeter, on the other hand, after his great study of economic doctrine and shortly before he died, remarked, in an Address to the American Economics Association: "A reorganization of society on the lines of the Encyclical *Quadragesimo Anno,* though presumably possible only in Catholic countries or in societies in which the Catholic Church is sufficiently strong, no doubt provides an alternative to socialism that would avoid the omnipotent state" (Schumpeter, 1950, p. 416; see also Solterer, 1951, pp. 12-23; Waters, 1961, pp. 133-41). The logic of the omnipotent state within economic theory led Schumpeter to a tradition that acknowledged the validity of economics without ignoring the perhaps more serious dangers of statism.

From such contrasting views it seems evident that here exists an issue of considerable consequence. For in either case, the assessment of Christianity and its impact on economic life will be crucial to any analysis of what kind of society we want, of what kind is possible, within a correct understanding of human nature and religious destiny. Thus, if we are hesitant to speak of a Christian economics or a Catholic business, we cannot forget that over the centuries, Christians have lived in and commented on the whole variety of economic and political organizations, from the absolutely totalitarian to the wide-open laissez-faire ones, with almost everything in between. This means, then, that there is a Christian reflection, indeed, a "Catholic Social Doctrine," as John Paul II was concerned to emphasize at Puebla in Mexico, against the widespread view that there is not (John Paul II, January 28, 1979, III.7). This Catholic Social Doctrine addressed itself to both religious and philosophical principles as well as to specific problems and questions that arose historically out of the economic activities of nations and men (Messner, 1949). And so for Christianity, as Chesterton suggested, while the environment of wealth was morally the worst in which to live, such that we were probably better off poor, we are still fond of Aquinas's dictum from Aristotle, that ordinary men and women need a certain sufficiency of worldly goods before they can comfortably practice the virtue expected of them.

Again, on hearing such evident contrasts, the critics of Christianity suspect that orthodoxy means that anything can be eventually true, while the orthodox have always insisted that certain things, perhaps not so many, yet definitely some, are clearly true while others are quite false, quite wrong. And yet, both Aquinas and Chesterton were probably right. The Christian spirit enjoins both a concern for the poor to have at least something, preferably as a result of their own exertions, together with a praise of poverty and a warning about riches. At the same time, however, it did not disdain beautiful and noble things, the lack of which in a culture or human life was seen as a loss and a lessening of the vision of mankind.

On this point, some remarks of Samuel Johnson, in Boswell's words, "On the subject of wealth, the proper use of it, and the effects of that art on what is called oeconomy," are well worth Christian reflection:

"It is wonderful to think how men of very large estates not only spend their yearly incomes, but are often actually in want of money. It is clear they have not value for what they spend. . . . A great portion of [their estates] must go to waste; and, indeed, this is the case with most people, whatever their fortune is."

Boswell. "I have no doubt, Sir, of this. But how is it? What is waste?"

Johnson. "Why, Sir, breaking bottles, and a thousand other things. Waste cannot be accurately told, though we are sensible how destructive it is. Oeconomy, on the other hand, by which a certain income is made to maintain a man genteely, and waste on the other, by which on the same income, another man lives shabbily, cannot be defined. It is a very nice thing: As one man wears his coat out much sooner than another, we cannot tell how." (Boswell, 1799, ii, pp. 200-201)

As there probably have not been three more Christian men than Aquinas, Johnson, and Chesterton, we must expect that there will be things in economics that "cannot be accurately told," as Johnson put it, while what is waste and what income will vary, "we cannot tell how," like the durability of our coats and the prudence of our use of what we inherit and produce.

Aristotle had already said, in fact, that in such matters, we should not expect more certainty than the subject matter allows. Those with very large estates—be they individuals, corporations, or states—are often in want of cash, while the poor, who are always with us, may very well be living quite comfortably, quite genteelly, thanks to their own virtues and, perhaps, to the nature of that most curious revolution, which we call the Industrial Revolution, the one that still, perhaps more than any other, influences our thinking about the levels of wealth and poverty, about the production and distribution of "goods," as they are paradoxically called.

The preliminary conclusion that might be drawn from these remarks on the relation of Christianity to the order of economics and business is that the world is so made that a mutual openness exists between the things of God and the things of this world. These are not the same, to be sure, but neither are they so exclusive that their inner-relatedness is not itself a cause of our understanding of one and the other. Josef Pieper, in commenting on Aquinas in his essay, "The Christian West," stated what Christianity presupposed:

> Worldliness always has the inner tendency to release itself from the constraints of theology and religion. Religion is steadily tempted to be exclusively "other-worldly." . . . Worldliness was a real danger, as St. Thomas clearly saw. But he also saw that [the] Aristotelian affirmation of the visible world was not something foreign or pagan; he recognized it as originally Christian. He claims it as Christian property on the strength of two theological arguments. . . .
>
> The first argument can be put in a single sentence: all things—the visible world, the body, the natural reason of man—

are good because God created them. The second argument occurs in an area which is in a more intensive sense theological, in the theology of the sacraments. If visible things become instruments and vehicles of salvation in the sacramental process — not only water, bread and wine but, once again and above all, the human body—how should these things not be good and therefore worthy of affirmation? . . . This theologically grounded affirmation of natural reality means that *eros,* the technological fields, political power, science, the whole realm of the worldly, together with their rights and claims, are declared to belong to the wide expanse of Christian experience. The argument does not, of course, forget the correlated challenge to these worldly elements to submit to a transformation and reshaping according to ultimate theological norms (Pieper, 1957, p. 608)

The idea that there is indeed some graced presence in the world challenging it to its *own* proper ends, as well as to ends beyond itself, yet not at the cost of neglecting its own proper being, is what motivates any authentically Christian approach to economic or political realities.

The Formation of Catholic Social Doctrine

Anderson's Law is said to go something like this: "I have yet to see any problem, however complicated, which, when you look at it the right way, did not become more complicated." Though it is not normally the purpose of academic exercise unduly to complicate things, nevertheless, a healthy respect for this particular subject matter of the Church's various judgments on the economic order, its reactions to business and industry, requires some attention to medieval and early modern issues relating to the development of commerce and business. Modern Catholic social thought formally consists of three elements: (1) official papal, conciliar, and at least some episcopal documents beginning with the last quarter of the nineteenth century, (2) scholarly philosophic and scientific reflection on these documents and the history and traditions behind them, and (3) the experience of Catholic citizens in various eras and countries who have sought in numerous ways to apply this doctrine so that it is not merely an abstract ideal, so that, in Pieper's terms, it becomes in fact "worldly" (Calvez, 1959; Mueller, 1963; Moody, 1963).

To understand the significance of all of this, however, it is clear that we cannot just begin with Leo XIII's famous social Encyclical of 1891, *Rerum Novarum,* though it is rightly considered to be, along with

Leo's earlier writings on the state in the 1880s, the first major papal statement in this area. Indeed, as Leo XIII himself remarked at the beginning of the same Encyclical, the condition of the working classes had something to do with the fact that "the ancient working men's guilds were abolished in the last century and no other organization took their place" (#2). This and similar lines in other social documents from the Church led many to suspect that the Catholic Church really "hankered" for the Middle Ages. Ths was, for many, reconfirmed by a streak of nineteenth-century romanticism in Chateaubriand or Coleridge and of twentieth-century Guild Socialism and Distributism, all of which were seen to embody this, presumably, outmoded heritage. This atmosphere lingered, in spite of efforts of historians such as Christopher Dawson to give a more balanced and sympathetic view of medieval organizations (Dawson, 1958).

Catholicism, in any case, was often seen as something which stood against "modernity," which, for the culture of the era brought up on progress and evolution, was the worst of backwardness. This kind of appreciation for the past was, indeed, generally frowned upon for a hundred years until someone like E. F. Schumacher, in his now famous book, *Small Is Beautiful,* a book grounded mostly in Catholic rather than Buddhist economics, made so many medieval ideas—fair price, smallness, craft, quality, fair wage—seem to be at the heart of the modernizing process of the Third World, a process that came, after John XXIII, to be the major focus of Catholic social thought.

Catholic Social Teaching: A Response to the Times

If we assume, then, that the reign of Leo XIII (1878-1903) was the beginning of a series of major documents and addresses by Leo himself and by subsequent pontiffs until John Paul II, upon which an authentic Catholic doctrine was built, we recognize that these pronouncements were made possible and indeed necessary because of the way the modern world developed. There are still some few who continue to presume that Catholicism, should it be true as it claims, should have anticipated science, capitalism, or the conditions of poverty. But if we follow the suggestion of Josef Pieper, we will admit that crises and problems and real issues must first arise in the world before religion can itself be expected to reflect on them. Christianity has been a faith that, in denying determinism, has accepted the consequences that there are some free things that follow, which we can only know when they happen. Professor Heinrich Rommen, in his great work on *The State in Catholic Thought,* made a similar point:

Catholic political philosophy remains a philosophy of man, not simply a philosophy for the believer. The state belongs to a human culture and to the secular order. Its root is the social nature of man. Its nearest end is the order of secular felicity or happiness, the *ordo rerum humanarum*. Therefore, the great doctors maintained at all times that the essential duties and rights of the citizens and of those in authority are independent of the state of grace. (Rommen, 1945, p. 12)

This would mean, a priori, that economic laws and institutions likewise have a certain autonomy, that men must learn by experience and judgment what they can do and how to do it, which institutions work and which do not.

In retrospect, the sequence of events that contextualizes the way Catholicism has understood the economic order proceeds from the Fall of the Roman Empire, to the conversion of the so-called barbarians, to feudalism, to the Crusades, with the reopening of Mediterranean trade and the growth of Hanseatic commerce from Venice to Bruges, with the French fairs in between. From these origins arose the new economic world made famous by the analyses of Henri Pirenne concerning the commercial nature of the medieval and early modern towns, in which guilds and limited markets replaced the manor and the fairs, in which Europe's center of gravity began to move North, began to accumulate capital and develop ideas and institutions to handle and understand and employ it (Pirenne, 1933).

Out of this background, the modern state appeared, with its theoretical origins in Machiavelli and Hobbes and its historical origins in the absolute monarchies of France, England, and Spain. This, together with the Reformation, meant the effective reduction of the two international institutions that made medieval society unified, in spite of its simultaneous internal factionalism. These institutions were, of course, the jurisdictional Church and the Holy Roman Empire. Thus, when Columbus discovered America and Henry the Navigator's followers sailed their way to the Orient about the Cape of Good Hope, the European territorial nation states, during the next few centuries, became, as they thought, the fashioners and civilizers of the whole world, a world which in so many ways still bears their scars and crowns.

The new states—which ironically were to become the models for all the new states founded or refounded in the nineteenth and twentieth centuries—denied any higher authority other than their own majesty, especially that of the papacy, and they gradually subdued within themselves all the varied entities—guilds, towns, and principalities—which the medieval world had produced in such abundance. It is not without irony, then, as Leo XIII hinted, that it was the French with their still enigmatic Revolution, who destroyed these institutions of buffer and spontaneity, and this according to a rational plan. On this point, it is essential to keep in mind that, partly because of this French experience, partly because of philosophical ideas, all subsequent Catholic social thought will include both a spirited defense and rationale for economic and political institutions lesser than the state, institutions both public and private and religious, along with a recognition of institutions beyond the state, institutions of legal, international, and ecclesiastical origins.

Furthermore, internally with the English Glorious Revolution of 1688 and the French Revolution of 1789, externally with the American Revolution and Declaration of 1776, the question of the proper political and economic structures of this independent nation-state and its capacity to gain and control areas beyond its frontiers arose in an ever more acute form. The issue was posed not only with regard to the proper constitutional forms of this state, but with regard to its limits, with the idea of human, civil, and eventually economic rights, for which and to which this state was responsible. Contemporary philosophic theory about this state has now begun, with Professor Leo Strauss and others, to wonder about and question whether human values are compatible with its evolution and the premises on which it was based (Strauss, 1953; Voegelin, 1952; Hallowell, 1950). Christian theory has long wondered about this same problem (McCoy, 1963).

During all this period, it is well to recall, the pope was at once a spiritual and a temporal ruler. As a temporal power, the papacy was strategically placed in central Italy (Hales, 1960; Hughes, 1961). In form, the papacy was an absolute monarchy, perhaps even the model of that ill-fated institution. This meant that it was caught up in the turmoil of the European factions while trying to exercise a spiritual power conditioned by this temporal burden in a world of growing dogmatic nationalism. The very task of keeping the papacy independent, which was defensible on historical grounds, came to mean a dependence not on the papacy's own small army but on the balance of power between Austria, Germany, France, Spain, England, Naples, and the Turks. Most of all, the papacy came to be seen as the major obstacle to the formation of an Italian state, itself conceived as a product of the modern idea that all men must live in a sovereign nation-state.

It is not pertinent here to recount the ups and downs of these Papal States from Napoleon's conquest of them, his imprisonment of Pius VI and Pius VII, to their restoration by Cardinal Consalvi's diplomacy at the Congress of Vienna, to their final suppression by the Italians in 1870, and on to the establishment of Vatican City by the Treaty of 1929 with Mussolini's state. But this history does serve to explain the nineteenth-century papacy's opposition to "democracy," especially to that absolutist kind of Rousseauean democratic institution that resulted, especially in Southern Europe, from the French Revolutionary tradition. This tradition did not base itself on or limit itself only to politics as that idea had been understood in the classical Western tradition (Rommen, 1954). We cannot read Leo XIII's encyclicals on the modern state without realizing that the kind of existing state he had most in mind was at the same time "democratic" and skeptical, anti-clerical and often quite anti-religious in the name of an absolute humanism. On the other side, however, we owe to Leo XIII's experience with the *Kulturkampf* in Germany and the anti-clerical legislation in France and Italy, along with Pius XI's later anti-totalitarian encyclicals in the 1930s, that hardheaded theme of Catholic social thought which, though in general able to justify the state, was simultaneously concerned to limit and restrict its legitimate exercise, to deny the state the right to politicize all aspects of life.

Religion: An Enemy of Progress?

In any case, just as the American and French revolutions had in very different ways raised the question of the relation of the form of the state to the rights of the people, so the commercial and industrial revolutions, both of which were conceived in some sense in opposition to the feudal and religious outlook of medieval Catholicism, finally challenged the Church to take a hard look at the kind of life that was resulting in European society some one hundred years after Adam Smith's *Wealth of Nations* and Watts's steam engine. Today, with our almost reactionary ecological notions and our dubious disaffection with science, it is difficult to recall that for most of the early modern world, particularly Catholic themes and outlooks—guilds, doctrines against usury, fair price, restricted hours, holy days—were considered to be enemies of *progress,* that great doctrine, as Bury and Becker were to declare and record, that became the secular salvation history of the modern world (Bury, 1932; Becker, 1932).

This is, of course, the shadow of the Weber-Tawney thesis about religion and capitalism, an argument by no means settled even today (Weber, 1920; Tawney, 1922). Thus, the Catholic position developed against a background of the relative lateness of the Industrial Revolution in predominantly Catholic countries, against the political reality of the Papal States, which were themselves considered to be notoriously retarded, and against the extreme ideologies of the French Revolution, which often had Catholicism as a major target. The first adequate Catholic responses came from Catholics of Northern Europe, with Bishop von Ketteler in Mainz, with social and intellectual circles in France, Austria, Switzerland, and Northern Italy, whose history Father Georges Jarlot, S.J., has so well recorded (Jarlot, 1973). The content of Catholic thought about proper institutions and values in the modern industrial world was greatly conditioned by a sense of inferiority, as it were, a suspicion that somehow Catholicism and industrialism were at odds, that the only way to develop was to reject its major religious premises, At the same time, this seemed also to prove that Catholicism was outmoded because who, after all, could doubt the worthiness of progress?

The basic argument was that Catholic countries were backward because of the nature of that very religion. The countries of Southern Europe in particular and their overseas colonies were thought to be incapable of appreciating the requirements of the Protestant Ethic, as it came to be called, because of their religious outlooks on life and work. In retrospect, this was the forerunner of an argument still raging on a scale broader than Europe, about how much does religion foster or hinder the evolution of sound business and commercial policies, over how much these latter, even at their best, contribute to the amelioration of all classes.

The idea that the Catholic countries were backward was eventually disputed by their own relative development in relation to other more backward societies. On a more intellectual and historical level, George O'Brien and Amintore Fanfani pointed out that most of the modern business methods were already in place in Genoa, Florence, and Venice, in the Catholic Rhineland and Belgium (O'Brien, 1944; Fanfani, 1935). Moreover, various economic historians suggested that the Spanish Jesuits pioneered a way to modify the medieval prohibition on usury, which had somehow become the symbol of the Catholic failures to grasp the nature of the modern commercial world (Dempsey, 1948; Schumpeter, 1954, pp. 73-123). Thus, Calvin alone was not responsible for this religious accommodation. Nevertheless, the Catholic church in the nineteenth century never shook the accusation of being backward and largely hostile to capitalism and development. Pius IX was thus condemned for a century for daring to say in his Syllabus that modern civilization and Catholicism were incompatible. Today, in not only the most radical circles, that very modern civilization is regularly seen as incompatible with human value. Pius IX, I am sure, would have enjoyed the irony.

The Reconstruction of the Social Order

By the time of Leo XIII, however, this heritage of disaffection with the results of modern industrial development did not look nearly so bad because, by the end of the nineteenth century, the issue was not so much over the Industrial Revolution itself, over its superiority to mercantilism and feudalism, but over its initial consequences. The Manifesto of 1848, along with the rise of socialism as an explanation of all of human life, placed the Church in the position of fighting on two fronts. Thus, something did seem wrong with the Industrial Revolution, but something even more dubious seemed to be attached to the socialist analysis and practice. The key country was undoubtedly Germany, as the second major power in Europe to reach the fullness of industrial development, largely with the aid of the national policy of the state. Politically, Bismarck's anti-Catholic *Kulturkampf* taught the Church, in a most graphic way, the value of political parties in a more democratic system. Socially, however, Bismarck himself realized that the Church was rather an ally against the socialists. Both were learning that concrete policies of the state could blunt the bad effects of the Industrial Revolution and undermine socialist claims. Bismarck's welfare and insurance policies created a lasting impression. And even the socialists under Bernstein were beginning to wonder why the workers were getting richer rather than poorer.

Anyone who reads Catholic social documents from Leo XIII to John XXIII will, in this context, be struck by the degree to which they are concerned with the internal structures and the economic processes in the industrialized countries. Thus, the main questions were those of property, fair and family wages, the right to organize, the authority of the state itself in the economy—in general, with what *Quadragesimo Anno* in 1931 began to call "the reconstruction of the social order." There seemed almost an unquestioned assumption—and Catholic thought was not unique in this—that the real issues of mankind were to be found within the structures of the European states, over the relation of capital and labor, over the attempts to prevent the excesses of liberalism and socialism, both of which were seen to contain some truth against a background of a more complete philosophy, but also errors on certain basic points. Indeed, socialism and liberalism were seen to be quite related: the former led almost necessarily out of the misunderstandings of the latter. This meant that the question of private property, its naturalism and its limits in relation to the industrial order, came to be seen as the theoretical grounds upon which an independent yet perennial Christian position was to be built, one that reached back to Aquinas and Aristotle and the whole idea of natural law.

Catholic Social Thought as a "Middle Way"

Catholic social thought, as a result, came to look upon itself as a "middle way" between laissez-faire and socialist positions. Practically every encyclical from Leo XIII to Paul VI is structured to some degree in this way. This led to an era of *Catholic social thought,* in which all seminaries and universities had courses based upon this assumption of a unique Catholic position. After the rise of a more ideological and pro-Marxist influence among Catholics after John XXIII, but having roots in French and Latin Catholicism earlier, this centrist tendency came to be looked upon as a defect, even though the function of John XXIII's two great encyclicals was to acknowledge the validity of much of the legislation and programs that had been evolved to soften Marxism and guide liberalism. Catholic social thought, it was then fashionable to argue, had no authentic position of its own; it was only a kind of critique of all secular social systems, which latter contained the "scientific" element of any genuine analysis, especially if they were in the socialist tradition (Schall, 1976, pp. 284-300). Generally, the idea of a legitimate *pluralism,* which itself had a long and valid argumentation behind it, was used to establish, first, that there was no *one* Catholic position, then, by a kind of perverse dialectic, that among the various plural options, there was only one "scientifically" legitimate. However, up until the middle 1960s, Catholic writers generally assumed that Catholic theory itself was a viable option, one which ought to be put into effect if social disintegration was not to be continued.

The general form this latter position took concerned the notion of a "vocational order" or the "industry-council plan," as it was generally called in the United States (von Nell-Breuning, 1936; Bruehl, 1939; McGowan, 1933; Masse, 1966). The Catholic position was itself argued within the older tradition that the Church was indifferent to a nation's precise political form, provided it was not simply corrupt. That is, the Church's official position was that a people was free on religious grounds to choose from a number of legitimate political forms, a choice which necessarily contained a great deal of historical contingency. This was not only the earlier medieval heritage, but also the prudential result of the Church's nineteenth-century confrontation with democratic ideas. This did not, evidently, mean, as Pius XII later argued in his famous 1944 Christmas Address and John XXIII stated in *Pacem in Terris,* that Christian social thought could not argue for the best system or form of rule, but it did mean a liberal interpretation of the many ways people could in practice organize themselves. Yet, almost at the very time this political attitude was being gradually embraced, the major problems that arose were those of the Depression of 1929 and the rise of the totalitarian states.

As the Church had not forgotten the French Revolution, Bismarck, and the various minor despotisms, it was not as unprepared as, say, Marxism to analyze the causes of fascism or nazism. Catholic social thought had behind it the largely German experience from Bishop von Ketteler to the great German Jesuit economist Heinrich Pesch, with his famous theory of solidarism (Mulcahy, 1952; Mueller, 1941; Alexander, 1953, pp. 407-17). Here was a genuine economic theory that accounted for the values of freedom, personality, initiative, and the need of public order.

Subsidiarity as a Key Concept

Yet, the Catholic response in the 1930s probably caused more confusion about the import of Catholic teaching than almost any other thing in its whole history, with the possible exception of usury. For almost at the very time the vocational groups theory was propounded as a response to monopoly capitalism, which was seen as the cause of the Depression, Mussolini proposed his apparently similar theory of the Corporate State. Indeed, the very proposal of Pius XI was often called "corporatism," so that with the Concordat and Lateran Treaties of 1929 and the subsequent economic theories, especially of Mr. Salazar in Portugal, Catholic thought was suspected of being statist, if not downright fascist.

The Catholic literature of the period is, naturally, rather appalled at this turn of events. Again and again, it was pointed out that it was not, like fascism or even like Franklin Roosevelt's NRA, a top-down organization, but rather that the principle of subsidiarity was the key concept of the whole Catholic approach. This principle insisted upon the naturalness and freedom of groups less than the state (von Nell-Bruening, 1951, pp. 89-110; Cronin, 1947, pp. 1-18; Alter, 1952, pp. 97-106). This was based both on the tradition of private property and on a denial of class conflict as an intrinsic philosophical necessity for social order. Capital and labor were not hostile but all fit together under a common principle of solidarity, under the philosophical idea of the common good. This denied the socialist/fascist position that the state ought to control all the economy. Rather, it followed the idea that the economy ought to arise out of the free initiative and interchanges of its members, that its component parts have a common interest, and that there should be corrective laws and rules of the state and the society to correct abuses of monopolies, labor, and the government itself.

Pius XII, in particular after World War II, devoted a good deal of attention to the kind of society that ought to result from what he considered the tragic results of earlier economic theories. He was primarily concerned with the question of the meaning of property and its relation to social policy as the key tool of analysis. Catholic thought had stressed property from Aquinas both as an expression of the worthiness of work and the normal way goods return to their ultimate social purpose. By Pius XII's time, this question appeared in the form of how modern business and industry are to be controlled. Did the labor contract, in particular, which itself was seen as just if it recognized the human dimension of the worker, if it did not consider the worker a mere "commodity," require "co-ownership" or even "co-management?"

Were these latter proposals even to be permitted, then, as they were being at the time proposed in Germany and Switzerland? Pius XII had constantly argued in favor of small- and medium-sized industry, for just wages so that property could be purchased by the worker. But he refused consistently to derive a "right" of co-ownership or co-management solely on the basis of the wage contract or of the right to unionize. He argued this mainly because economic responsibility must be able to be legally located, however much ownership and control were separated (Pius XII, June 3, 1950; January 31, 1952; July 7, 1952; September 14, 1952). In his later years, Pius XII was concerned with the problem of the "masses" as that idea was philosophically argued in critiques of totalitarianism, especially in the context of a presumed "de-personalization" that came from automation and technology (Pius XII, December 24, 1955; December 22, 1957). During this period also, there was much speculation about the nature of "work" as a personal human enterprise.

The International Perspective: Poverty in the Third World

In 1957, the Swiss economist Wilhelm Röpke wrote an essay on

"Liberalism and Christianity," in which he generally praised *Quad-ragesimo Anno* and its innovations, but voiced this hesitation:

> The Encyclical's point of view on monopolies which it imag-ines to be the creations of free competition [seems incomplete]; in my opinion, they are rather the result of insufficiencies in the legal framework and of a certain brand of state intervention. But I can only acquiesce with joy when the Encyclical goes to war against monopoly and its disastrous economic and political con-sequences. (Röpke, 1957, p. 131)

Röpke went on to make what, in retrospect, seems like a prophetic statement about the next turn in Catholic social orientation:

> Only now and then does the Encyclical mention the problems of the international economy. Considering the importance of this domain, this omission is regrettable. If I am not mistaken, the position of Catholic social philosophy is least definite with respect to these problems. (pp. 133-34)

In the context of Pius XII's discussions of coexistence, of the sub-sequent documents of John XXIII, *Mater et Magistra* and *Pacem in Terris,* Vatican II, and Paul VI's *Populorum Progressio,* the almost complete conversion of Catholic social thought to this "international" perspective, away from the internal needs of the industrial order in developed countries, is worthy of much reflection.

The discovery of the Third World, a discovery so unlike that original discovery by Christopher Columbus, was, in a way, to Catholic social thought what Lenin's *Imperialism* was to *Das Kapital.* By the time of Paul VI's *Octagesima Adveniens* (1971), there was even some hint that labor unions, which had been the test of social awareness in Catholic social thought in the post-World War I era, were themselves possibly at times obstacles to the well-being of society (#14). As yet, there is little analysis of the relation of the rights and costs of labor in the developed world, the legal ways they are protected, to the ability of the Third World people to develop themselves (Krauss, 1980).

In the period from John XXIII to John Paul II, the focus of attention has thus shifted from the internal social order of a prosper-ous developed country to the question of the poverty of the Third World. At first sight, this emphasis on poverty as a justifying criterion for social analysis might seem merely a reflection of certain Gospel priorities. However, anyone familiar with how the idea of poverty has served as the ideological basis for modern totalitarian thinking from Babeuf to Saint-Simon and on through modern revolutionary movements must be quite critically clear what is being argued in the name of poverty (Talmon, 1960; Arendt, 1963).

Moreover, practically the whole content of Christian analysis of business and the economy has been conditioned by this new orientation. There is little doubt that papal documents have reflected this shift, though there is a considerable controversy about whether this shift means a rejection of their former anti-socialist stance, particularly in the light of the rather poor performance of the various socialisms on this very point. It may also mean a reformulation of the earlier tradition of the limited state, freedom of the economic order, the value of initiative and lesser organizations, a theme that was pioneered in a way by the publication of Jacques Maritain's *Reflections on America,* a book more than any other which has divided Catholic thinking on what is to be done about poverty and how to eliminate it in freedom (Maritain, 1958). The situation is made doubly fascinating with a pope from a Marxist-controlled country and several segments of the Christian churches arguing, under the general rubric of liberation theology, that the "socialist" alternative is the only "moral" one, however little they have proved, as Solzhenitsyn has remarked, that it really removes poverty (Gutierrez, 1973; Solzhenitsyn, June 30, 1975; July 9, 1975).

The Socialist Alternative

J. L. Talmon, in *The Origins of Totalitarian Democracy,* situated the Enlightenment background of such alternatives as they most often appear in the contemporary argument. In the modern era, the dividing line has been this:

> Should the economic sphere be considered an open field for the interplay of free human initiatives, skills, resources, and needs, with the state intervening only occasionally to fix the most general and liberal rules of the game, to help those who have fallen by the wayside, to punish those guilty of foul play and to succor the victims thereof, or should the totality of resources and human skill be *ab initio* treated as something that should be deliberately shaped and directed, in accordance with a definite principle, this principle being—in the widest sense—the satisfaction of human needs? (Talmon, 1960, p. 149)

If the option be for the latter, injury to the weak, cupidity of the successful, all-round general confusion are stressed. But this in turn is, from the former point of view, criticized as a position that would stifle initiative, weaken the productive capacity which is needed by all, and result in a centralized system to control all human actions. "At bottom," Talmon concluded,

> the whole debate centers around the question of human nature: could man be so re-educated in a socially integrated system as to begin to act on motives different from those prevailing in the competitive system? Is the urging for free economic initiative nothing else than rationalized greed or anxiety, bound to die out in an order guaranteeing economic well-being as the collectivist ideology teaches? (p. 149).

Most of the lines of argument within subsequent Christianity are already here, though what seems missing is any adequate appreciation of the case for the alleviation of world poverty made within the kind of free economic system that is best argued in the context of a hard analysis of the performance of advanced socialism; rather than on the basis of high-sounding theory alone.

A Christian Realism

Roger Heckel's perceptive essay on *Self-Reliance* for the Pontifical Justice and Peace Commission bodes well here (Heckel, 1976). And Paul VI held in *Octagesima Adveniens* (1971):

> Too often Christians attracted by socialism tend to idealize it in terms which, apart from anything else, are very general; a will for justice, solidarity and equality. They refuse to recognize the limitations of the historical movements, which remain conditioned by the ideologies from which they originated. (#31; see also Kirkpatrick, 1979)

It is well to acknowledge the noble aspirations of any movement or religion, of course, but aspirations and historical practice are not "completely separate and independent." Their connection must be seen as part of the issue, so that any analysis of such movements should also keep intact the independent sources of Christianity's own approaches. These safeguard "the values, especially those of liberty, responsibility and openness to the spiritual which guarantee the integral value of man" (Paul VI, 1971, #31).

The Christian realism of this latter approach should not be underestimated. Professor Herbert Butterfield's statement is a pertinent one in this connection: "My whiggism is different from the liberalism on the Continent or in the American sense in that it is not utopian.

Apart from hoping that human beings will be virtuous, it does not operate by assuming that they are" (Butterfield, 1979, p. xxxi). Butterfield goes on to cite the metaphysical reason for this position from a passage in Lord Acton who said, "It is not organized society but the human being that has the eternal soul" (p. 241). Such priority of the soul or the person over the relational category of society is the beginning of all Christian reflection (Bochenski, 1972, pp. 83-101). Butterfield continues in this context: "It has always been fundamental to the Christian religion that no man can begin to approach this problem of human nature unless he has first of all tackled it inside himself, recognizing that he himself is part of the problem—he has his share of man's universal sin" (p. 263).

In confrontation with contemporary orientation toward the Third World, Catholic social thought has sought not to forget such admonitions about what is in man, yet also to endeavor to keep central the basic transcendent religious message: the primacy of the human person, his individual destiny as more than that of political society, his relation to God and neighbor, his realization of the many things that are not Caesar's. On a social level, two interests follow from this. The first arises from the value of human life itself. It was precisely here, as Hannah Arendt pointed out, that Christianity most emphatically overturned the classical ideas of the primacy of forms and abstractions over real people (Arendt, 1959). This has meant opposition to those theories, stemming largely from the developed world, that see the causes of poverty as people themselves. The second arises from the notion that the sole cause of poverty is the economic structure of the world that "exploits" the poor.

The Christian sense of the value and dignity of the person as central to all moral thinking about society has made the social thought of the Church highly critical of theories that reduce problems of war or poverty or disorder to people and their very existence. On the other hand, there has likewise been a rejection of the Marxist-oriented analyses which would presume that all problems are structural.

The Christian view has held, rather, that there is another "force" or orientation in the world that can fashion natural institutions and resources, as well as, and more importantly, human wills and intelligences (which are the principle resources and causes of action in the world), so that men can meet any problems or destinies that might arise. Christopher Dawson, perhaps more than any other writer, has sought to identify this difference. European experience cannot be seen only in terms of "imperialistic aggression" or "economic exploitation," he wrote in *Religion and the Rise of Western Culture.* Other cultures have exploited and expanded, but there is a difference here.

> The peculiar achievement of Western culture in modern times is due to a new element which was not present in the older type of imperialism.
>
> For, side by side with the natural aggressiveness and lust for power and wealth which are so evident in European history, there were also new spiritual forces driving man towards a new destiny. The activity of the Western mind, which manifested itself alike in scientific and technical invention as well as geographical discovery, was not the natural inheritance of a particular biological type; it was the result of a long process of education which gradually changed the orientation of human thought and enlarged the possibilities of social action. (Dawson, 1950, p. 17)

From this latter change derive ideas such as the following: that the common good includes man's spiritual reality, that men are not necessarily at war with one another, that justice is not sufficient, that there is a moral responsibility of the rich to the poor, and of the poor to all others, that political rule is above all a service, that law is a matter of conscience, that will lies at the heart of all change for good or for evil. This would recognize, then, that we do need political and economic structures. And if in asking what these are, we turn carefully to John XXIII or Vatican II, we find an analysis and summary of the rightness of the basic institutions and reforms that have been effected in the modern era in response to the social, political, and economic problems that originated in the Industrial Revolution and with the modern state. *Pacem in Terris* (1963) remains, in this regard, one of the best statements about the nature of rule coming from any source public or private in our era (Reed, 1965).

The Catholic Social Approach to the Poor

Generally, John Paul II has taken the view that there are certain deficiencies in the present international order. He has, however, insisted on a specifically Catholic social approach that is neither Marxist nor liberal in emphasis or origins. Following Catholic tradition, John Paul II has argued that the spiritual principle that is "new" in the world should and can lead to a better order, one authentically human, even though it need not do so. Here we are at the crux of the criticism that is made against Catholic thought by such scholars as Leo Strauss and Harry Jaffa, one to which Maritain, too, often addressed himself: that grace must lead to structures or values intrinsically unacceptable to the non-Christian (Strauss, 1953; Jaffa, 1952; Maritain, 1955). The Catholic and papal answer is important here, and this issue should be recognized as the primary philosophical problem that religion, particularly Christianity, addresses to the social sciences, namely, their practical adequacy in their own order to be themselves. This is the modern context of Aquinas's question in his Treatise on Law on the "necessity" of revelation (I-II. 91. 4).

The doctrinal point at issue, itself neither dogmatically optimistic nor pessimistic, was well stated by Professor John Finnis of Oxford, who, along with Professor Midgley at Aberdeen, is one of the most perceptive of English thinkers in this whole area. Professor Finnis wrote:

> The field of Catholic social teaching offers many examples which are "not expressly affirmed in revelation" but which "have their roots" in a revelation understood more profoundly through centuries of such personal experience and ecclesial life. . . . In the Catholic faith, eternity is not merely something whose "shadow" can be discerned here. . . . Rather, eternal life somehow begins here. And good works do not merely manifest the operation of faith; they themselves operate, not only to build up the world (in ways we understand and work for) but also (in ways now mysterious to us) to build the new heaven and new earth and new human family that are to come. (Finnis, 1979, pp. 317-18; see also Midgley, 1979; Schall, 1979).

This means that a standard of judgment upon the performance of the world order is claimed, one that guides and perfects the nature of science and the public order. What is at issue here, I think, is the social-science version of the conclusion that Stanislaus Jaki gave to his recent study on faith and the natural sciences. "It is our chief cultural task," Father Jaki wrote, "to transmit to the upcoming generation, that inspiration which will be theirs in the measure in which they, inspired we hope by our example, will keep in mind about scientific history a fundamental facet: the tie binding the road of science to the ways of God" (Jaki, 1978, p. 331).

John Paul II, then, in his *Redemptor Hominis* (#16) can call for "daring creative resolves in keeping with man's authentic dignity." This effort is not, therefore, to be viewed as an "impossible one." There are available "appropriate institutions and mechanisms to meet the serious needs of the poor." At the level of trade, "the laws of healthy competition must be allowed to lead the way." The effort to achieve a wider distribution must be approached gradually and efficiently to meet the real needs. Here, the Holy Father emphasized again the importance of each individual in each social order. Collectivities are not "saved," nor do they justify the sacrifice of individual persons to some future world order. This suggests that "the structure of economic life is one in which it will not be easy to go forward without the intervention of a true conversion of mind, will, and heart." The Christian sees change, however, not as a narrow self-interest, but as a "self-reliance," as Roger Heckel called it, which understands the source of human action and responsibility. This means a solidarity with others in union with those natural forms of community such as family, voluntary groups, the state, and the international order implied in the fullness of human social life.

The Threat of Totalitarian Theories

The contemporary priorities on a world scale are no doubt those having to do with minimal personal and political freedom and poverty. Poverty and the method of its alleviation — abundance is not incompatible with slavery — can very easily be the pretext for establishing and controlling a totalitarian state. This is why empirical evidence of an ideology's actual performance is a vital part of Catholic social philosophy. Many today have come to look on Christianity, potentially at least, as an apt instrument for achieving this latter goal of supporting an absolutist ideology (Norman, 1979; Lefever, 1979). The great threat that hangs over the Christian churches today is whether they will voluntarily become the major avenue by which totalitarian economic theories are imposed on the rest of mankind. Classical liberalism, itself not so immune from this same threat, has always found a sort of naïveté among Christians in this area. And there is very little in contemporary records to suggest that there is not a legitimate worry here. Intellectually, all one needs to do is grant that the "poor," however defined, cannot be "free" *until* certain structures are embraced, that freedom can only come *after* poverty is eliminated. With such views, the road to absolutism is all but paved.

Catholic social thought has had to speak to a world not only full of social and economic problems, but also full of ideologies designed to explain them (Heckel, 1976). I would hold that the major reason why poverty continues in the world today is the deliberate choice by developing countries of the wrong analysis of what is wrong with their situation. P. T. Bauer has stated the problem bluntly:

> While large-scale transfers can despoil donors, they cannot ensure any substantial specific level of income, rate of growth, or reduction of international income differences, since these depend largely on domestic factors. If these are unpropitious, no amount of external donation can secure any specified level of income. . . .
>
> Governmental policies are of course not the only determinants of income levels, differences, and changes. Economic attainment depends greatly on aptitude, motivation, mores, political arrangements, and objectives. Natural resources, climate, and accessibility to different societies also play a part, although their utilization depends on the personal, social, and political factors just noted. . . .
>
> The world is not divided into two distinct collectivities, separated by a wide gap reflecting external exploitation. The world comprises a very large number of societies that have emerged in varying degrees from a basis of material poverty. The earlier emergence or greater progress of some groups does not retard but facilitates the progress of others, who can take advantage of skills, knowledge, and markets of the more developed groups. (Bauer, 1979, pp. 462, 464; see also Beckermann, 1974; Macrae, 1975; Kristol, 1978)

Such approaches to nonclass warfare, sharing, common good, and innovation are the best context in which to think of poverty. They lie also at the heart of the Christian orientation, a fact too often unappreciated by Christians themselves.

Often we hear people—including popes—argue that if only we would spend on the poor the money we put into armaments, then we would quickly eliminate the problem. Aside from the fact that energies which support armament may not be easily transferable to other kinds of questions, this proposition itself remains true only if we would also choose the right way to spend the surplus that presumably might result. As Professor Bauer suggested, it may not be true that lack of external aid or markets is the explanation of why the poor are poor, as the "no more armaments" argument suggests. Furthermore, one can only talk realistically of getting rid of armaments if there is also a method of avoiding the evils armaments themselves were designed to meet. It is not at all clear that lack of social concern for the poor rather than ideological power ambition is the real motive in today's armaments races. Nor is it all that clear that wars are caused by poverty. If Solzhenitsyn has meant anything, it is that being well-fed is not the first or last human issue. Too many Christians and other religious people seem to talk today as if they do not understand these truths. This is why the popes have admonished us also to look at the record, not merely at the printed ideals.

Economic Growth and the Cause
of Human and Social Progress

The case for the elimination of poverty on a world scale by a sophisticated and responsible "business" philosophy within a limited modern state has never been adequately made in Christian circles (Novak, 1978; Sorge, 1973; Maritain, 1958). This is unfortunate, even though Christianity and the poor would both have had much to gain by it. Most of the critical tools for evaluating various business abuses in the Catholic literature have been taken from *Rerum Novarum*, if not from St. Thomas (Masse, 1944; Camp, 1971; von Nell-Breuning, 1962; Synod, Justice, 1971; Bishops Program, 1919). And there have been many practical statements that recognize the positive side of business achievement. Bernard Dempsey had this positive side in mind when he wrote an essay on Catholic thought entitled, "But Don't Call It Capitalism!" He wanted to prevent the modified, progressive experience of modern business and society from being identified with laissez-faire capitalism. Even as late as Paul VI's *Populorum Progressio* (1963), there is a Catholic aversion to the very word capitalism. Christopher Manion was probably correct in his suggestion that Paul VI did not misunderstand capitalism. But when capitalism means, as it so often does in Europe or Latin America, at least in the literature, an exaltation of "individual freedom by withdrawing it from every limitation," any pope will think that such capitalism "is merely the economic dimension of the Reformation heresy of individualism" (Manion, 1980).

What needs to be understood is rather how the self-reliant, nonabsolutist, empirical experience of modern institutions does not flow from this individualistic premise. Furthermore, almost invariably, the countries that have in fact developed since World War II are the ones that accept the ideas of personal responsibility and reward, sacrifice, innovation, social order, and usually very hard work (Macrae, 1978;

Schall, 1978). In saying this, then, I wish to reject the thesis that essentially the poor are poor because the rich are rich, and thus the only way to aid the poor is to take from the rich (Kahn, 1976; Macrae, 1975). This is a very attractive thesis in many quarters, but essentially a formula for disaster. It is unfortunately one that is widely promulgated in religious quarters.

Without denying the evil in the human heart and the fact of injustices, then, it remains true that our main problems still lie in production and in priorities arising freely from the populace in the form of adequate demand, intelligent demand. Nor is the variant that all we have to do is to "consume" less any less a danger to the specific problems at hand. A massive effort to consume less or invent less would be the single most certain way to guarantee that the poor will remain poor, poor and subject to ideology. The currently popular argument that a simple life—no consumption, no extravagance—would be the best policy, a kind of universal secular monasticism, which has great attraction to platonic and religious minds, is a formula for stagnation, when not placed within an environment of innovation, savings, growth, and personal achievement. This approach also largely ignores the higher forms of development, of beauty, liberality, and splendor, which are part of the human endeavor and potential. An equality of proportionate or enforced misery, an ideal put forth by certain ecological or revolutionary schools, is not an ideal demanded by the faith, or by our times.

The right approach, then, is rather that suggested by Roger Heckel:

> The atmosphere of crisis, which has been a constant characteristic of the last few years, has made the urgency for economic growth the major issue of our present day and age. The full legitimacy of this top priority concern is quite evident. . . . Care must be taken, however, to avoid confining our thinking to an overly exclusive economic logic. While economic growth does condition human and social progress, it does not automatically assure that progress. . . .
>
> Without prejudice to the specific nature of the objectives, its own means, and the various types of active participation which it requires of all economic growth must also enter the dynamic hope of the integral development of men and jointly responsible peoples. It must be receptive to the impulse and decisive discipline which flow from this higher logic. (Heckel, 1979)

Conclusion

Such an approach, in conclusion, allows us to admit that the present order is not adequate. Yet, it also allows us to recognize that many things are on the right path, that there are principles that are open to the kind of value and society that our philosophical and religious traditions lead us to think are objectively better, but which do not represent the full Kingdom of God, or even all we ought to do. There are, in the end, no magic formulas, nor does the Gospel put any brakes on authentic dynamism. The relation of Catholicism and modern business is, then, at a critical stage, both for religion and for business, because there really is a way to achieve the concrete ethical goals which Catholic thought and business practice have suggested to be open to man. The drama of history lies, as Professor Butterfield remarked, following Augustine, in our personal choices about these goals for which we think we act. Catholicism holds that the human person transcends in its essence all social orders, that it can survive in any order if need be. But it also argues that some environments are better than others. The business community has a great stake in convincing us that, for the achievement of the pressing ethical and moral goals of our era, its ways are the empirically best. What the Catholic and Christian tradition needs to show is precisely how its resources of grace and faith can guide and transform such institutions toward the very goal that most people consider the imperative of our century.

BIBLIOGRAPHY

Papal Documents

Leo XIII:
Diuturnum (On Civil Government), 1881.
Immortale Dei (The Christian Constitution of States), 1885.
Libertas Humana (Human Liberty), 1888.
Sapientiae Christianae (The Chief Duties of Christians as Citizens), 1890.
Rerum Novarum (On the Condition of the Working Classes), 1891.
Graves de Communi (Christian Democracy), 1901.

Pius XI:
Casti Conubii (The Christian Family), 1930.
Non Abbiamo Bisogno (Italian Fascism), 1931.

Quadragesimo Anno (The Reconstruction of the Social Order), 1931.
Mit Brenneder Sorge (On Nazism), 1937.
Divini Redemptoris (On Atheistic Communism), 1937.

Pius XII:
Summi Pontificatus (On the Unity of Human Society), 1939.
Christian Democracy, Christmas, 1942 and Christmas, 1944.
On Property, Co-Ownership and Co-Management:
    To Union of Catholic Employers, August 7, 1949.
    To International Congress of Social Studies, June 3, 1950.
    To Italian Catholic Owner-Managers, January 31, 1952.
    To French Social Week, July 7, 1952.
    To Austrian Katholikentag, September 1952.
    (Letter of Cardinal Montini, Papal Undersecretary of State to Italian Cath-
        olic Social Week, September 22, 1952)
Aid to Poor, Christmas, 1952.

(N.B. The previous addresses are found in English in the *Catholic Mind*, the
following are in *The Pope Speaks*.)

Population in True Perspective, September 9, 1954, Summer 1954, p. 265.
Coexistence, December 24, 1954, First Quarter 1955, pp. 3-16.
The Christian Way of Life among Workingmen, May 1, 1955, pp. 147-53.
The Savings Bank, May 16, 1955, Summer 1955, pp. 143-45.
The Spiritual and Temporal Welfare of the Workingman, June 26, 1955,
    Summer 1955, pp. 163-67.
Ideals for the Businessman, February 4, 1956, Spring 1956, pp. 45-49.
The Small Business Manager, February 25, 1956, Spring 1956, pp. 49-53.
The Catholic Employer, June 7, 1955, Summer 1955, pp. 154-58.
International Reconciliation, October 14, 1955, Winter 1955-56, pp. 315-26.
Food, Agriculture, and Human Solidarity, November 20, 1955, Winter 1955-
    56, pp. 327-31.
The True Basis for Men and Society, December 24, 1955, Winter 1955-56, pp.
    301-14.
Small Business in Today's Economy, October 8, 1956, Spring 1957, pp. 405-9.
Christ's Kingdom and the World of Labor, October 28, 1956, Spring 1957, pp.
    411-16.
The Contradictions of Our Age, December 23, 1956, Spring 1957, pp. 331-46.
Economics, the State, and the Personal Worth of Man, March 7, 1957, Summer
    1957, pp. 85-89.
The State and the Rights of Man, March 28, 1957, Summer 1957, pp. 20-25.
Poverty, the State, and Private Investment, May 3, 1957, Winter 1957, pp.
    205-9.
Automation: Its Problems and Prospects, June 7, 1957, Autumn 1957, pp.
    147-56.
The Divine Law of Harmony, December 22, 1957, Winter 1957-58, pp. 239-57.

John XXIII:
Mater et Magistra (Economics and Society), 1961.
Pacem in Terris (Political Order), 1963.

Paul VI:
Populorum Progressio (On the Development of Peoples), 1963.
Octagesima Adveniens (Social Problems), 1971.

Vatican II:
Gaudium et Spes (Christian Social Prospectus), 1965.
Dignitas Humana (Religious Liberty), 1965.

John Paul II:
Redemptor Hominis (The Redeemer of Man), 1979.
John Paul II's Addresses on his Mexican, Polish, Irish, and United States visits
    are published by the Daughters of St. Paul in individual volumes. These
    are also in *The Pope Speaks* and the English Edition of *Osservatore Romano*.

Other pertinent documents: The two justice documents of the Synods of Rome
    in 1971 and 1974; Cardinal Maurice Roy's Reflections on the 10th
    Anniversary of *Pacem in Terris*, 1973; and the Irish Bishops, *The Work of
    Justice*, Dublin, 1977.

Bishops Program of Social Reconstruction, 1919, with an Introduction by Cardinal
    Mooney in 1939, Washington, National Catholic Welfare Conference,
    1939.

Collections:
The Social Teachings of the Church, ed. A. Fremantle. New York, Mentor, 1963.
The Church Speaks to the Modern World: The Social Teachings of Leo XIII, ed. E.
    Gilson. Garden City, N.Y.: Image, 1954.
*The Church and the Reconstruction of the Modern World: The Social Encyclicals of Pius
    XI*, ed. T. McLaughlin, Garden City, N.Y.: Image, 1957.
The Papal Encyclicals in their Historical Context, ed. A. Fremantle, New York:
    Omega, 1956.
The Seven Great Encyclicals. New York: Paulist, 1963.
The Gospel of Justice and Peace: Catholic Social Teaching (Documents) since Pope John,
    ed. J. Gremillion, Maryknoll, N.Y.: Orbis, 1976.
Forell, George W., *Christian Social Teachings*. Garden City, N.Y.: Doubleday
    Anchor, 1966.

Books and Articles

Alexander, Edgar. "Church and Society in Germany." In Moody, *Church and
    Society*. New York: Arts, 1953, pp. 325–583.
Alter, Karl J. "The Industry Council System and the Church's Program of
    Social Order," *The Review of Social Economy*, September 1952, pp. 97–106.

Arendt, Hannah. *The Human Condition*. Garden City, N.Y.: Doubleday Anchor, 1959.

——. *On Revolution*. New York: Viking, 1963.

Bauer, P. T. "Commentary," in *Challenge to a Liberal International Economic World Order*, ed. R. Amacher. Washington: American Enterprise Institute, 1979, pp. 462–64.

Becker, Carl. *The Heavenly City of the Eighteenth Century Philosophers*. New Haven, Conn.: Yale University Press, 1932.

Beckermann, Wilfred. *Two Cheers for the Affluent Society*. New York: St. Martin's, 1974.

Bennett, John C. "Capitalism and Ethics," *The Catholic Mind*, May 1967, pp. 42–51.

Bochenski, J. M. *Philosophy, An Introduction*. New York: Harper Torchbooks, 1972.

Boswell's Life of Johnson. London, Charles Dilley, 1799.

Briefs, Goetz. "The Agony of the Mass Age," *The Social Justice Review*, September 1949, pp. 147–50.

Brophy, Liam. "Catholic Action and Political Action," *The Social Justice Review*, December 1948, pp. 359–62.

Bruehl, Charles P. *The Pope's Plan for Social Reconstruction*. New York: Devin-Adair, 1939.

——. "The State and the People," *The Social Justice Review*, July-August 1948, pp. 111–14.

Bury, J. B. *The Idea of Progress*. New York: Dover, 1932.

Butterfield, Herbert. *Writings on Christianity and History*. New York, Oxford University Press, 1979.

Calvez, Jean-Yves. *Eglise et Société Economique*. Paris: Aubier, 1959.

Camp, Richard L. "Corporate Reorganization or Comanagement? The Reform Program of Pius XII in the Hands of the Commentators." *The American Ecclesiastical Review*, May 1971, pp. 319–32.

Cronin, John F. "Economic Research and the Social Encyclicals," *The Review of Social Economy*, March 1952, pp. 16–31.

——. "Forty Years Later, Reflections and Reminiscences," *The American Ecclesiastical Review*, May 1971, pp. 310–18.

——. "Implementing the Social Encyclicals in America," *The Review of Social Economy*, June 1947, pp. 1–18.

Dawson, Christopher. *Religion and the Rise of Western Culture*. Garden City, N.Y.: Image, 1950 [1958].

Dempsey, Bernard. *Interest and Usury*. London: Dobson, 1948.

——. "But Don't Call It Capitalism!" *Social Order*, May 1954, pp. 199–208.

——. "The Economics Implicit in the Social Encyclicals," *The Review of Social Economy*, December 1942, pp. 12–18.

Drummond, William. *Social Justice*. Milwaukee: Bruce, 1955.

Ederer, Rupert. "The Industry Council in America," *The Review of Social Economy*, September 1961, pp. 155–65.

Fanfani, Amintore. *Catholicism, Protestantism, and Capitalism.* London: Sheed, 1935.

Fedotov, G. P. "The Church and Social Justice," *Cross Currents,* Fall 1964, pp. 417–32.

Fiero, Alfredo. *The Militant Gospel.* Maryknoll, N.Y.: Orbis Books, 1975.

Finnis, John. "Catholic Faith and the World Order," *The Clergy Review,* September 1979, pp. 309–18.

———. "Catholic Social Teaching Since *Populorum Progressio,*" *Social Survey,* August 1978, pp. 213–20.

Gaylin, Willard. *"Doing Good": The Limits of Benevolence.* New York: Seabury, 1978.

Gibellini, R. (ed.). *The Frontiers of Latin American Theology.* Maryknoll, N.Y.: Orbis Books, 1975.

Giordani, Inigo. *The Social Message of the Early Church Fathers.* Paterson, N.J.; St. Anthony Guild Press, 1944.

Goulet, Denis. "The World of Underdevelopment," *The Christian Century,* August 24, 1974, pp. 452–55.

Gutierrez, Gustavo. *Theology of Liberation.* Maryknoll, N.Y.: Orbis Books, 1973.

Hales, E.E.Y. *The Catholic Church in the Modern World.* Garden City, N.Y.: Image, 1960.

———. *Pope John and His Revolution.* Garden City, N.Y.: Image, 1966.

———. *Revolution and Papacy.* Notre Dame, Ind.: University of Notre Dame Press, 1966.

Hallowell, John. *Main Currents in Modern Political Thought.* New York: Holt, 1950.

Heckel, Roger. "Declaration of the Holy See," *Church Alert,* July-September 1979, pp. 1–3.

———. "Foi et Justice," *Fides et Justitia.* Rome: Pomel, 1976, pp. 42–60.

———. *Self-Reliance.* Vatican City: Justice and Peace Commission, 1976.

———. *The Universal Purpose of Created Things.* Vatican City: Justice and Peace Commission, 1977.

Hughes, Emmet John. *The Church and the Liberal Society.* Notre Dame, Ind.: University of Notre Dame Press, 1944 [1961].

Jaffa, Harry. *Thomism and Aristotelianism.* Westport: Greenwood, 1952 [1979].

Jaki, Stanislaus. *The Road of Science and the Ways of God.* Chicago: University of Chicago Press, 1978.

Jarlot, Georges. *Doctrine Pontifical et Histoire.* Rome: Gregorian, vol. I (1878–1922), 1964; vol. II (1922–39), 1973.

Kahn, Herman. *The Next 200 Years.* New York: Morrow, 1976.

Kenkel, F. P. "Towards the Vocational Order," *The Social Justice Review,* May 1948.

Kilroy, Patrick. "The Businessmen as Christian," *The Furrow,* May 1978, pp. 263–73.

Kirkpatrick, Jeanne. "Dictatorships and Democracy," *Commentary,* November 1979, pp. 34–45.

Knight, Frank. "Ethics and Economic Reform: Christianity," *Economica,* November 1939, pp. 398–422.

Krauss, M.P. "Social Democracy," *The Wall Street Journal,* February 1, 1980.

Kristol, Irving. *Two Cheers for Capitalism.* New York: Basic Books, 1978.

Lefever, Ernest. *Amsterdam to Nairobi: The World Council and the Third World.* Washington: Ethics and Public Policy Center, 1979.

Macrae, Norman. "America's Third Century," *The Economist,* London, October 25, 1975, Survey.

———. "The Brusque Recessional," *The Economist,* December 23, 1978, Survey.

Manion, Christopher. "Timelessness and the Itch of Modernism," *Chronicles of Culture,* January-February, 1980, pp. 20–24.

Maritain, Jacques. *Man and the State.* Chicago: University of Chicago Press, 1952.

———. *Reflections on America.* New York: Scribner's, 1958.

———. *Scholasticism and Politics.* Garden City, N.Y.: Image, 1960.

———. *Social and Political Philosophy of Jacques Maritain,* ed. J. W. Evans and Leo Ward. Notre Dame, Ind.: University of Notre Dame Press, 1955.

Masse, Benjamin. *The Church and Social Progress.* Milwaukee: Bruce, 1966.

———. *Economic Liberalism and Free Enterprise.* New York: America, 1944.

McCoy, Charles N. R. *The Structure of Political Thought.* New York: McGraw-Hill, 1963.

McGowan, Raymond. *Towards Social Justice.* New York: Paulist, 1933.

Messner, Johannes. *Social Ethics.* St. Louis: B. Herder, 1949 [1965].

Michel, Virgil. *Christian Social Reconstruction.* Milwaukee: Bruce, 1937.

Midgley, E. B. F. "Concerning the Modernist Subversion of Political Theory," *The Modern Schoolman,* Spring 1979.

Miller, Raymond. "Papal Pronouncements on the Entrepreneur," *The Review of Social Economy,* March 1950, pp. 35–43.

Moody, Joseph N. *The Challenge of Mater et Magistra.* New York: Herder and Herder, 1963.

———. *Church and Society, 1789–1950.* New York: Arts, 1953.

Mort, Ernest. "Christian Corporatism," *The Modern Age,* Summer 1959, pp. 245–49.

Mueller, Franz. "The Church and the Social Question." In Moody, *The Challenge of Mater et Magistra,* pp. 13–154.

———. *Heinrich Pesch and His Theory of Solidarism.* St. Paul, Minn.: College of St. Thomas, 1941.

Mulcahy, Richard. *The Economics of Heinrich Pesch.* New York: Holt, 1952.

———. "Equality Issues in the Economics of Individualism," *The Review of Social Economy,* 1962, pp. 45–68.

———. "Solidarism," *The New Catholic Encyclopedia,* vol. 13, pp. 419–20.

Newman, Jeremiah. *Co-Responsibility in Industry.* Dublin: Gill, 1955.

Norman, E. R. *Christianity and the World Order.* New York: Oxford University Press, 1979.

Novak, Michael. *The American Vision.* Washington: American Enterprise Institute, 1978.

O'Brien, George. *An Essay on the Economic Effects of the Reformation.*
Westminster: Newman, 1944.

———. "Capitalism in Transition," *Studies,* March 1944, pp. 33–47.

Pieper, Josef. "The Christian West," *The Commonweal,* March 15, 1957, pp.
607–9.

Pirenne, Henri. *Economic and Social History of Medieval Europe.* New York:
Harvest, 1933.

Reed, Edward (ed.). *Pacem in Terris: An International Convocation on the
Requirements of Peace.* New York: Pocket Books, 1965.

Röpke, Wilhelm. "Liberalism and Christianity," *The Modern Age,* Fall 1957, pp.
128–34.

Rommen, Heinrich. *The State in Catholic Thought.* St. Louis: B. Herder, 1945.

———. "Genealogy of Natural Rights," *Thought,* Autumn 1954, pp. 403–425.

Ryan, John A. "The Democratic Transformation of Industry," *Studies,*
September 1920, pp. 383–96.

———. and Joseph Husslein. *The Church and Labor,* New York: Macmillan,
1920.

Schall, James V. *Human Dignity and Human Numbers.* Staten Island: Alba House,
1971.

———. *Redeeming the Time.* New York: Sheed, 1968.

———. *The Sixth Paul.* Canfield, Ohio: Alba Books, 1977.

———. *Welcome Number 4,000,000,000.* Canfield, Ohio: Alba Books, 1977.

———. "The Death of Christ and Political Theory," *Worldview.* March 1972,
pp. 18–22.

———. "From Catholic Social Doctrine to the 'Kingdom of God on Earth,"
Communio, Winter 1976, pp. 274–300.

———. "Political Theory and Political Theology," *Laval Théologique et
Philosophique,* February 1975, pp. 161–74.

———. "The Non-Existence of Christian Political Philosophy," *Worldview,*
April 1976, pp. 26–30.

———. "The Re-Discovery of Charity," *Spiritual Life.* Winter 1979, pp. 195–
203.

———. "Rethinking the Nature of Government, *The Modern Age,* Spring 1979,
pp. 158–67.

Schnepp, Gerald. "An Estimate of *Quadragesimo Anno,*" *The Catholic Mind,*
November 1946, pp, 661–70.

Schumacher, E. F. *Small Is Beautiful.* New York: Perennial, 1973.

Schumpeter, Joseph. *A History of Economic Analysis.* New York: Oxford, 1954.

———. "The March to Socialism," *The American Economic Review,* May 1950;
also in the Third Edition, *Capitalism, Socialism, and Democracy,* 1950.

Shea, John. "Discussion of Dempsey," *The Review of Social Economy,* December
1942, pp. 19–21.

Solterer, Josef. "*Quadragesimo Anno:* Alternative to the Omnipotent State," *The
Review of Social Economy,* March 1951, pp. 12–27.

Solzhenitsyn, Alexander. Addresses of June 30, 1975 and July 9, 1975.
Washington: AFL-CIO, 1975.

Sorge, Bartolomeo. *Capitalismo, Scelta di Classe, Socialismo*. Rome: Coines, 1973.

Strauss, Leo. *Natural Rights and History*. Chicago: University of Chicago Press, 1953.

Talmon, J. L. *The Origins of Totalitarian Democracy*. Chicago: Praeger, 1960.

Tawney, R. H. *Religion and the Rise of Capitalism*. New York: Mentor, 1922 [1954].

Villey, Daniel. "Catholics and the Market Economy," *The Modern Age*, Summer 1959; pp. 256–61; Part II, Fall 1957, pp. 395–401.

Voegelin, Eric. *The New Science of Politics*. Chicago: University of Chicago Press, 1952.

von Nell-Breuning, Oswald. *Reorganizing the Social Economy*. Milwaukee: Bruce, 1936.

———. *"Octagesima Adveniens,"* *Stimmen der Zeit*, May 1971, pp. 289–96.

———. "Some Reflexions on *Mater et Magistra,"* *The Review of Social Economy*, Fall 1962, pp. 97–108.

———. "Vocational Groups and Monopoly," *The Review of Social Economy*, September 1951, pp. 89–120.

Vree, Dale. *On Synthesizing Marxism and Christianity*. New York: Wiley, 1976.

Waters, W. R. "Schumpeter's Contributions and Catholic Social Thought," *The Review of Social Economy*, September 1961, pp. 33–46.

Weber, Max. *The Protestant Ethic and the Spirit of Capitalism*. New York: Scribner's, 1920 [1958].

Wilhelmsen, Frederick D. *Christianity and Political Philosophy*. Athens: University of Georgia Press, 1978.

———. "Faith and Reason," *The Modern Age*, Winter 1979, pp. 25–32.

Wright, David McCord. "Toward a Christian Approach in Judging Economic Systems," *The Modern Age*, Fall 1957, pp. 121–27.

The following three Symposia are worth noting:
"On Reconstructing the Social Order," *Social Order*, January 1956.
"*Mater et Magistra:* A Symposium," *The Review of Social Economy*, Fall 1962.
"Eighty Years After," *The American Ecclesiastical Review*, May 1971.

5. The Rabbinic Tradition and Corporate Morality

Burton M. Leiser

The Pharisees have had a bad press. They have been called hypocrites, hair-splitting legalists, and worse. They have been accused of a lack of compassion for their fellow human beings, and of adherence to rigid legalisms at the expense of mercy and love of their neighbors. Their very name has become a common noun or an adjective denoting hypocrisy and sanctimoniousness, a stern and censorious attitude toward the manners and morals of others, and a conviction of one's own moral superiority. No doubt some Pharisees (like the members of other groups) had had such attitudes and deserved the reprobation their critics heaped upon them. But it is time for the truth to be faced: that the principal doctrines of Judaism, which is what Pharisaism is called nowadays, are founded upon reasonable and humane principles which are a sound guide for civilized behavior, not only between individuals and other individuals, but also between corporations and their customers, their suppliers, and the general public.

Uses of the Law

The Pharisees did emphasize the deep study of the law and its application to human affairs. They realized, as Hobbes did many centuries later, that without the restraints of law, the lives of men are likely to be poor, nasty, brutish, and short. The law, as they saw it, was given to man by God to help restrain man's baser impulses, to provide guidance in the ways of life, to give concrete expression to the ideals of the people, and to enhance the worth of human life. Far from being rigid and unbending in their application of the law to particular situations, they often found ways to bend it, interpreting it and reinterpreting it, much as our courts do today, to fit novel situations or to see that justice was done and that needless suffering was not inflicted upon innocent persons. But they were also prepared, where necessary, to apply the law rigorously, for law without realistic sanctions that are in fact applied in daily life is no law at all.

The Pharisees believed, rightly, that mere generalities, however beautifully phrased and however inspiring they might sound, are not sufficient guarantees for human safety, for the security of property, or for the respect due to one man from another; they were convinced that clear and specific norms were essential, and that nothing was more important than the education of their people in the meaning of those commands and in the importance of abiding by them. This is not to say that they believed that there was no room for moral virtue, as opposed to rote obedience to the law. Of course there was—and they had special words of praise for those who went *lifnim mishurat hadin*—beyond the limits of the law—in their daily conduct. Such persons were called *tzadikkim* or *hasidim*—righteous or compassionate persons. But not everyone has the makings of a saint. The law is made for the normal person in everyday situations, not for the extraordinary person in unusual situations. For that very reason, it is essential, for most of the time we all behave in rather predictable ways.

According to the Talmud, the first question a man is asked when he enters the next world is, "Have you been honorable in the conduct of your business?" Only afterward is he asked about his study of Torah and his attention to the other divine commandments.[1] Elsewhere, the rabbis of the Talmud said, "He who deceives or lies to a man is considered as one who attempts to deceive or lies to God."[2] In the Book of Exodus we read that God has promised to bless the people if they would "listen to the voice of the Lord [their] God, do that which is right in his eyes, listen to his commands, and keep all his statutes" (Exod. 15:26). On this, the rabbis commented, "This refers to doing what is right in business, or in buying and selling. And hence you may learn that he who conducts business, and buys and sells in truth and fidelity, and in whom the mind of man finds pleasure, is regarded as if he had fulfilled the whole Torah."[3]

Applications of Talmudic and Biblical Principles

These general sentiments found concrete expression in numerous laws, which were based upon biblical texts but were expanded and elaborated in the Talmud and in the legal and moral literature that followed. I shall concentrate here upon several broad areas of talmudic law that are directly connected with business ethics, and add a few remarks on specific cases, recent or current, to which talmudic and biblical principles might appropriately be applied.

Genevat Da'at—*Deceptive Advertising*

In talmudic times, the Hebrew language acquired a special term for deception, revealing as well as anything can the attitude of the rabbis toward it. It was called *"genevat da'at,"* theft of the mind, a notion that is derived directly from several biblical passages.[4] "There are seven kinds of thieves," they said, "but worst of all is one who deceives his fellowmen."[5] Fraud was in their opinion a greater crime than the defilement of the sanctuary of the Temple in Jerusalem.[6] Even one word of *genevat da'at* was forbidden. One ought to have a truthful tongue, an upright spirit, and a pure heart, they said. The sin of *genevat da'at* was worse than robbery in their eyes, for as they put it, truth is the foundation of the soul, while the lying tongue creates irredeemable guilt.[7]

"It is forbidden," the rabbis wrote, "to deceive your fellowmen in your business dealings."[8] It is perfectly permissible for a merchant to advertise his wares, of course. But in connection with advertising, Rabbi Alexander, some 1800 years ago, cited Psalm 34:13-14, "Who is the man that desires life? . . . Keep your tongue from evil and your lips from speaking guile."[9] A man may praise his wares and use reasonable means to persuade others to purchase them—but not at the expense of deceit or fraud. "You shall not wrong one another," said the Torah (Lev. 25:17), and Zephaniah had warned the people of Israel not to "do iniquity, nor speak lies; neither shall a deceitful tongue be found in their mouth" (Zeph. 3:13). The rabbis interpreted these passages as references to false advertising.[10]

One must not package his merchandise in such a way as to make it appear to be what it is not, though one may make it beautiful and attractive, they said—so long as its true nature is not hidden from the prospective purchaser.[11] For example, it is forbidden to paint old goods to make them appear new, but one may make new goods attractive by painting them with beautiful colors.[12]

A few examples of recent cases in which major corporations have been involved in deceptive advertising should give one a sense of the dimensions of the problem.

• The Block Drug Company recently consented to an FTC order to stop making false and misleading advertising claims for its Poli-Grip and Super Poli-Grip denture adhesives. The FTC found that the company had no scientific evidence to substantiate its claims that Extra

Effervescent Polident denture cleanser could clean better than Extra Strength Efferdent, a competitive product produced by another pharmaceutical manufacturer, and that it had falsely advertised that persons using its denture adhesives could eat foods such as apples or corn on the cob without difficulty.[13]

• The Warner Lambert Pharmaceutical Corporation has advertised Listerine for years, making numerous claims for it which were not true. Prior to 1922, the company advertised it as a suitable treatment for gonorrhea and for "filling the cavity, during ovariotomy," and later touted it as a safe antiseptic that would ward off cold germs and sore throat and guard its users against pneumonia. Still later, the company discovered halitosis. After literally decades of litigation, the company finally consented to an FTC order forbidding such fraudulent claims.

• General Foods Corporation falsely advertised that two Toast'ems Pop-Ups provide 100 percent of a child's minimum daily requirements of vitamins and iron.

• Warner-Chilcott Laboratories falsely advertised Peritrate SA as an effective remedy for the massive chest pain of angina pectoris. The FDA seized the drug. It has also seized Serax, a tranquilizer marketed by Wyeth Labs.; Lincocin, an antibiotic marketed by Upjohn; and Lasix, a diuretic marketed by Hoechst Pharmaceuticals—all for false and deceptive promotion directed to the medical profession. Searle, Mead-Johnson, and Syntex were all cited for having misled physicians as to the hazards of their birth-control pills. And the FDA demanded that Ayerst Laboratories send a "corrective letter" to some 280,000 doctors, retracting a claim that Atromid-S had a "beneficial effect" on heart disease.

The most insidious deception of all is committed upon children, who are, as the Talmud would have put it, the victims most likely to have no intellectual defense against campaigns devised by clever advertising agencies with the specific purpose of taking advantage of their vulnerability. The Hudson Pharmaceutical Corporation's advertising campaign for Spiderman Vitamins is perhaps the best example of this. The ads, associated with a superhuman cartoon hero on television, led children to believe that the product "has qualities and characteristics it does not have" and tended to "induce children to take excessive amounts of vitamin supplements which cause injury to their health." The FTC found that Spiderman Vitamins with iron were a deadly poison when ingested in large amounts by children. In one recent year alone, vitamins and mineral supplements accounted for more than 5,000 cases of poisoning among children under five years of age.

Advertisers often make contradictory claims for competing products which they must know cannot possibly be reconciled with one another. Sterling Drug's Bayer aspirin is advertised as "the strongest pain reliever you can buy," and as a drug which cannot be improved because it's 100 percent aspirin. But the same company advertises Vanquish as a product that has a "unique way" of relieving headache "with extra strength and gentle buffers. . . . It's the only leading pain reliever you can buy that does." Thus, Sterling Drug is both unable and able to produce a pain reliever that is more effective than Bayer aspirin.[14]

• Richardson-Merrell Pharmaceutical Corporation developed and marketed MER/29 (triparanol), an anticholesterol drug, with a vigorous promotional effort, claiming that it was "virtually nontoxic and remarkably free from side effects even on prolonged clinical use." The company was aware of side effects, but concealed them from the FDA. In response to FDA inquiries, the company's representatives said that there had been no blood changes in its tests of the drug on rats or monkeys when, in fact, most of the animals had developed cataracts and severe hair loss. Only after the FDA raided the company's premises and seized its records did the company withdraw the drug from the market. In the meantime, there had been numerous reports of cataracts developing in persons treated with MER/29—490 during the first year—as Richardson-Merrell realized $7 million in profits from the drug's sales.[15]

No one knows how much harm has been done to innocent persons by the false and misleading advertisements which are employed by major corporations of all kinds, both in this country and abroad. I do not wish to condemn the entire advertising industry. I have argued elsewhere that advertising is and rightly ought to be an important factor in our economy, and that it makes significant contributions to our well-being. But too many segments of the advertising industry and the marketing departments of the corporations which use advertising agencies or develop their own advertising strategies base their operations on *genevat da'at*—the stealing of people's minds—the deception which the rabbis of the Talmud found so abhorrent and so inconsistent with biblical ethics.

Middot—*Weights and Measures*

The prohibition against using false weights and measures (Deut. 25:13-16) followed immediately by the mention of Amalek, whose troops picked off the weak and feeble at the rear of the procession of

Israelites as they made their way through the desert, served as a warning, the rabbis said, figuratively to blot out the remembrance of Amalek—to bring an end to the abuse of the weak and the ignorant by fraudulent weights and measures, which they are unable to check by themselves. In the Midrash to Ruth,[16] they said that whoever measures or weighs goods is likened to a judge. His decision has to do with principles of right and wrong, justice and injustice. Hence, they concluded, one who abuses the trust reposed in him by employing false weights and measures or by engaging in any other deceptive practice in commerce perverts justice and is unrighteous and abominable. "He pollutes the land and profanes the name of God. But a judge who renders just judgment [and equally a merchant who gives honest measure] is a partner in His work of Creation."

"The penalty for one who violates the laws of just weights and measures is very severe," according to the Code of Jewish Law, "for it is impossible for one who has employed false weights and measures to do proper repentance," since he cannot restore to his customers what they have lost. "Such a person is like one who denies the exodus from Egypt."[17] According to one of the commentators on that passage, the reason for this is that anyone who engages in such deception hides what he does from his fellow men, and is not afraid of God, "for he thinks that God's providence does not extend to men's actions. Whoever denies divine providence denies the exodus from Egypt, for there was the great revelation of God's providence in all the signs and wonders he performed."[18] And still another commentator explained that such violations are even worse than those involving unchastity and idolatry, for the latter, being principally between man and God, can be atoned for.[19] But it is impossible for the commercial cheat to atone for his crimes, since he cannot locate all of his victims, and is thus unable to compensate them for all of their losses. Prayer, charity, and other forms of atonement are impotent when a particular human being has been injured. Genuine atonement can be achieved only when each individual who has been harmed has been compensated for his injuries and has forgiven the one who harmed him.

In the Talmud, grain merchants were enjoined to clean their vessels frequently in order to be sure they sold exact measures, and not less.[20]

Compare such attitudes and ordinances with the well-known practices of major grain merchants in the United States today. We are of course familiar with the great grain scandal a few years ago, in which major corporations involved in shipping, storing, and selling grain were found to have engaged in massive, systematic programs designed to cheat both their suppliers and their customers. Through elaborate devices rigged up in grain elevators, they paid for less than they actually purchased from the farmers and charged for more than they delivered to their customers. Moreover, they deliberately mixed a great variety of impurities into their grain, including sand and grain of lesser quality. Such adulterated grain, some of it unfit for human consumption, and in some cases unfit even for animal feed, was shipped to Third World nations that were desperately in need of food to feed their people. The governments of those nations paid for high-grade grain and received adulterated grain; and they paid for quantities far in excess of those they actually received.

One might have thought that the exposure of these fraudulent practices would have brought them to an end. But the companies that operate the elevators seem always ready to employ new devices to cheat those with whom they deal. An old saw in the trade, it is said, is "Buy on a Steinlite and sell on a Motomco."[21]

Steinlite and Motomco are the names of two devices, manufactured by different companies, which are used by the operators of grain elevators to determine the moisture content of grain. Corn with lower moisture content is purchased at a higher price than corn whose moisture content is higher, since there are certain costs involved in drying it to keep it from spoiling. The Steinlite moisture meter gives readings at least a percentage point higher than the federally approved test method, and the Motomco meter reads somewhat lower. By using the Steinlite meter when buying the corn, the elevator operator can cheat the farmer out of as much as a nickel per bushel; and by using the Motomco meter when selling it to his own customer, he is able to pocket a substantial differential. It is estimated that Iowa farmers alone have been bilked out of millions of dollars each year by elevator operators who employ this scheme.

In the long run, we are all victims of these sharp practices. But we need not go so close to the sources of our food. We may turn to the supermarket itself, where, not so many years ago, it was almost impossible to find the net weight on a package so that it might be compared to another. I remember well the days when General Foods, General Mills, and Kellogg complied with the rule that net weight be displayed on their packages by placing it in tiny, almost microscopic print in an obscure part of the label, against a background of color almost identical with the color in which the weight was printed. Even if the net weight is accurately printed on the package, it is *genevat da'at* if the consumer can't find it, or can't make sense out of it once he does find it. The practice of packaging products in odd and fractional ounces is undoubtedly being perpetuated in order to contribute to the consumer's confusion. From ancient times, Jewish law required the use of easily calculable measures, with all fractions divisible by 2 (e.g., 1/4, 1/8, etc.). If support of the metric system were forthcoming from American corporations, and if they would package their wares in weights and volumes that resulted in no remainder when divided by 10, there would be far less confusion and much more meaningful comparisons could be made by the consumer. The rabbis of the Talmud would have had no hesitation about enacting such requirements into law.

Major corporations rightly complain about excessive government regulation. Regulatory agencies wield their power with excessive zeal, and sometimes with insufficient appreciation of an industry's problems. But it may be fair to say that American corporations, because of their frequent insensitivity to ordinary norms of morals and simple justice, such as these ancient biblical rules, have brought their problems upon themselves.

Hassagat Gevul—*Unfair Competition*

Rabbi Yehudah issued a legal opinion, back in Talmudic days, according to which merchants would not have been permitted to distribute nuts and sweets to children to induce them to shop in their stores when sent by their parents on shopping errands. He felt that such practices violated the biblical injunctions against *hassagat gevul*—moving a neighbor's boundary marker in order to encroach upon his land.[22] His colleagues, however, permitted the merchants to engage in such practices, because they concluded that the same tactics were open to all, and therefore none would gain an unfair competitive advantage. But it is clear that if one merchant had an unfair advantage over another, the rabbis would have disapproved. This same doctrine was employed to create a copyright in one's intellectual creations, long before common-law copyright came into existence.[23] During the Middle Ages the doctrine of *hassagat gevul* was extended to include a prohibition against offering a landlord a higher rent than the current tenant could afford in order to have the tenant evicted and to take his place, when housing or places for commercial establishments were in short supply. The rabbis imposed a ban on such practices, and forbade the rental of the building for a year after it was vacated if the landlord acceded to such a deal.[24]

The rabbis of the Talmud decreed that (the same principle applied to business enterprises) a tradesman could not set up an enterprise in close proximity to that of a competitor if that would have the effect of driving him out of business, and a teacher was not permitted to entice another man's students into his own school.

The rabbis of ancient times and of the Middle Ages did not have to contend with the problems presented by gigantic corporations. But the principle upon which they operated is surely applicable to the modern scene.

Whenever Continental Baking, now a subsidiary of ITT, decided to move into a new territory, they would inform a small baker that they were interested in buying him out, but would offer him a price far below what his business was worth. If he refused to sell, they would sell bread at five cents a loaf, and wait until he had run out of money and the will—or financial ability—to fight. In some instances, Continental worked in tandem with union officials who harassed the small baker, or they bought off his employees, who would purchase their routes from their employer, the independent baker, on the pretext that they wanted to become independent businessmen themselves. They would then sell their routes to Continental. In addition, Continental would displace the small baker's products from store shelves by foisting huge quantities of its products on grocers and supermarkets with the promise that any leftovers would be replaced at no cost—a practice which the small baker could not afford to duplicate. Once the competition disappeared, Continental raised its prices and cancelled its special deals. Continental Baking has been assessed millions of dollars in penalties through the years, and has been convicted of violating federal statutes time after time. But such lawsuits and penalties seem to be nothing more than a petty annoyance to this giant corporation.[25]

In addition to such tactics, competitors have misrepresented the competition's goods or prices, defamed their characters, harassed salesmen or other employees, intimidated customers, organized boycotts, stolen trade secrets, and engaged in even more imaginative and unscrupulous tactics. Consider the following cases, which cover a rather diverse set of sins:

• *Orgel* v. *Clark Boardman Co.*, 301 F.2d 119 (2d Cir. 1962): Clark Boardman published a text on the law of eminent domain, 35 percent of which was plagiarized from a text written by the plaintiff.

• *University Computing Co.* v. *Lykes-Youngstown Corp.*, 504 F.2d 518 (5th Cir. 1974): The defendants paid an employee of Leonard's Department Store in Fort Worth, Texas, $2,500 to induce him to steal the store's copy of a computer software system for inventory management. Although, on trial, they conceded that their behavior was not "lawful or even defensible," they argued that the system was not unique and attempted to deprecate its value, and also denied that it was a trade secret within the meaning of the law.

• *Julius Hyman & Co.,* v. *Velsicol Corp.,* 563, 233 P.2d 977 (1951). Some of Velsicol's employees were induced to leave and join the Julius Hyman Company. The employees knew the formulas and procedures for manufacturing chlordane, an extremely effective insecticide. They turned their knowledge over to their new employer, who proceeded to manufacture the product and to sell it at a reduced price, forcing Velsicol either to meet the lowered price or go out of business. The court found that Hyman Company had gained $1,563,499.40 as a result of its theft of Velsicol's trade secrets and infringement of its patents.

• *Matarese* v. *Moore-McCormack Lines,* 158 F2d 631 (2d Cir. 1946): Matarese was an uneducated Italian immigrant who worked as a part-time stevedore at Moore-McCormack's pier. He invented some devices which were designed to load and unload cargo from ships more efficiently and more safely than the procedures then in use on the docks. One of the shipping concern's agents visited Matarese's home in Brooklyn and was shown working models of Matarese's invention. He was so impressed by them that he promised Matarese one-third of the savings Moore-McCormack would realize from its employment of his invention. He also offered Matarese the job of supervising construction of the devices. The devices were so successful that Moore-McCormack put a large number of them into use — but when Matarese began to press for his share of the company's savings, he was fired. The court found that the company saved about $140,000 per pier per year over the seven years from their initial installation, and that the company was operating ten piers.

• *Truck Equipment Service Co.* v. *Fruehauf Corp.,* 536 F.2d 1210 (8th Cir. 1976): Fruehauf appropriated the design of a TESCO twin-hopper-bottomed grain or bulk-commodity semitrailer, and manufactured one exactly like it, even to the nonfunctional aspects of the design. Fruehauf also used photographs of the TESCO trailer in its sales literature to promote its own product. In its defense, Fruehauf pointed to the fact that Sears, Roebuck & Company had marketed a lamp whose design was appropriated from a lamp manufactured by the Stiffel Company.

• In 1976, Microdot, Inc., was the target of a hostile tender offer by General Cable Corporation. Irving Trust Company, one of Microdot's banks, financed General Cable's offer. At a seminar on tender offers sponsored by Irving Trust, an Irving vice president said, "I can assure you that a responsible bank will remain loyal to its present customer and certainly wishes to avoid choosing sides." A former vice president of Microdot, who had attended that seminar, said later that when he learned of Irving's role in the takeover attempt, he was flabbergasted. "We couldn't believe that a bank with Irving's reputation—a bank that said it would never do that kind of thing— turned right around and did it to us. It's unethical, immoral and barbaric. If it isn't illegal, it should be."[26] A vice president of another firm said, "You assume that your banks are treating your information with total confidentiality, but you can never be sure. You can ask for assurances, but if one of those banks thought it was going to lose a billion-dollar customer that wanted to buy us out, you have to wonder how strong those assurances are unless you've got them in writing from the chairman of the bank."[27]

Some of these cases involve not merely *hassagat gevul,* intrusion into another's territory, but outright theft. The religious authorities of Judaism would have made short shrift of them. They were contrary to divine law, they would have treated them as involving violations of major principles of Judaism and universal moral law, and they would have been condemned. Those who participated in such practices would undoubtedly have been required to make restitution to the injured parties if they had been brought before a rabbinical court, and possibly also would have been assessed punitive damages for having violated such important legal and moral principles, in order to deter others who might consider following their example.

Labor Relations

The Talmud was concerned with both the laborer and his employer. Both had rights, and each had duties to the other. For example, the Code of Jewish Law specifies that if a person has been hired for a particular job and finishes it in half the time contracted for, he may be asked to do similar work, or easier work, to fill up the time for which he had been hired. But if the employer has no additional work to give him, he must pay the full day's wages. On the other hand, if the worker knew in advance that he could finish the job in less time than that which was agreed to, and did not so inform the employer, then the employer may ask him to complete the time with harder work or withhold payment for the excess.[28]

An employee is entitled to certain fringe benefits—such as lunch if he works in a food-service establishment. But he has no right to insist that his wife and children be given a free lunch, even if he chooses not to eat what he is entitled to.[29] And if he dines at any time other than lunchtime, or takes home the food he was supposed to eat on the premises or gives it to another, he is guilty of theft. The food was given to him for the employer's convenience, not for his own, and he is obliged to use it in accordance with the conditions laid down by the employer.

Moreover, an employee is not permitted to moonlight if doing so will so weaken him that he is unable to perform his regular job at maximum efficiency. He owes his employer, not only his time, but his best efforts while on the job; and these may not be compromised by holding some other position when he is off duty.

"The worker must not take off a little time here and a little there. He must be very strict with himself, . . . working with all his strength. As the righteous patriarch Jacob said, 'I have worked with all my strength for your father,' and for that reason he reaped his reward in this world, for it is written, 'And the man prospered very much.' "

"It is a divine command to pay a man's wages on time—and if the employer withholds them, it is equivalent to endangering his very life, and is a violation of six divine laws."[30]

Ha'anakah is a legal principle derived from the command in Deut. 15:13-14, which enjoins the slaveowner to see that his slave does not leave his premises empty-handed when he is freed at the beginning of the sabbatical year. The principle was extended to include hired laborers, who were to be given severance pay when they were released from service. As early as the thirteenth century, severance pay was recognized as a moral obligation. More recently, experts in Jewish law have argued that it is a legal right enforceable by the courts, and not merely a moral duty. Rabbinical courts in Israel have ruled that severance pay is to be set by the courts wherever there is no customary rate, and that an employee who has worked for two years or more is entitled to it. An employer must give his employee a month's notice prior to dismissal or a month's remuneration in lieu thereof. This position has been accepted by the Supreme Court of Israel, and has been enacted into statutory law by the Knesset. The law provides that an employee is entitled to a month's severance pay for every year of full-time employment, if he is laid off or if he resigns due to significant deterioration in conditions of his employment, health problems, or a change of residence. If he dies, his survivors are entitled to his severance pay. And severance pay, like wages, takes precedence over all other debts of the employer.

Under these principles, featherbedding, so beloved by American unions and the cause of such serious economic losses to so many industries—particularly the railroads—would not be permissible. But at the same time, certain standards of conduct would automatically be imposed upon employers — standards designed to protect the welfare of their employees. Economic hardship would not be a sufficient excuse for placing employees into situations where their lives or health were endangered without offering them the maximum possible protection. Although some of the standards imposed by the Occupational Safety and Health Administration [OSHA] may be onerous, the principal reason for the agency's establishment in the first place was the failure of employers, or their absolute rejection of any efforts, to improve the working conditions of their employees so as to minimize risks to their health and safety. Such attitudes are unconscionable. Under Jewish law, they would not be tolerated.

Our unemployment benefits are similar to the benefits of *ha'anakah,* or severance pay, that were granted to Hebrew slaves 2,000 years ago and to employees of Jewish employers who followed Jewish law from the Middle Ages onward.

But we still have a long way to go before all of our workers in all of our industries — particularly restaurants and agricultural labor — are given the benefit of all the protections to which every worker is entitled under ancient principles of decency and humane treatment.

Excess Profits

According to the Talmud, any profit greater than 1/6 of the cost of an item (including overhead) is excessive — and on demand, the seller must return the excess to the purchaser.[31] The exaction of such excess profits is called oppression, and profiteers (those who cornered the market in any essential commodity and raised the price beyond this standard) were said to violate the injunction against endangering the lives of one's fellow men.[32] During talmudic times, some rabbis issued special edicts designed to drive the prices of such profiteers down and to deprive them of their ill-gotten gains. In the seventeenth century, R. Menachem Mendel Krochmal of Moravia, incensed by a conspiracy of fish merchants to jack up the price of fish just before Passover, when it was customary to serve fish, issued an emergency ban on the consumption of fish for a period of two months, including the holiday of Passover, thus breaking the monopoly.

The assumption prevailing in American board rooms today seems to be that corporations have the right to as much profit as they can extract from the public, regardless of the personal hardships and social consequences of their greed. The regulation of utilities was brought about at least partly for this reason. The most notable examples of such attitudes at the present time are, of course, the great energy corporations, which have diverted enormous sums of money, derived from their excess profits, into advertising campaigns designed to persuade the public that there is no such thing as an excess profit.

Bal Tashhit—*Preservation of the Environment*

The Talmud and later Jewish law contain many provisions designed to protect the environment. Indeed, one might argue that the Bible itself contains such legislation. The first instance of ecological concern might be the story of Noah—but on the legislative side, we might turn to Deut. 23:13-15.[33]

The rabbis recognized a law which they called *Bal Tashhit,* after an expression that is found in the Bible. It means literally, "Lest you destroy," and first appears in the injunction against destroying fruit trees during a military siege. The Mishnah enjoined against burning certain kinds of wood because such burning was considered to be a threat to the natural environment. Others argued that the prohibition was designed to protect people against the emission of excessive smoke. In the Talmud, the rabbis discuss legislation requiring the establishment of tanneries at a distance from inhabited areas, in order to avoid emission of noxious odors near residences.[34] Moreover, when they were established, they were to be placed in locations where the prevailing winds would blow their fumes away from the cities. The Mishnah bans sheep and goats in cultivated areas of Israel to avoid waste to the land.[35] And other passages in the Talmud forbid the waste of animals,[36] oil,[37] and all human artifacts that might be useful. "Not only trees, but all things come under the ban against wanton destruction. Thus, anyone who needlessly breaks any human artifacts, or tears clothing, or destroys a building, or plugs up a source of water, or causes food to be spoiled, violates the injunction against wanton destruction."[38]

The rabbis went so far as to say that even when one destroys something which may be lawfully destroyed, because it is needed for some worthy purpose, he should be careful, since grave danger may follow. For this reason, they said, God commanded Moses to construct the tabernacle of acacia wood—to teach men that when they build their own houses, they should not use the wood of fruit trees. When a fruit tree is cut down, they said, its voice rings out from one end of the world to the other.[39] "If you are engaged in a long siege of a city, attempting to overthrow it by warfare, you may not destroy the trees that surround it by setting your axes against them. For you may depend upon them.

You must not cut them down. For man depends upon the trees of the field" (Deut. 29:19).

Even in time of war, men do not have the right to destroy the countryside. The Torah declares that man is so totally dependent upon his natural environment that he must respect it, and not devastate it, for there is no guarantee that it will be restored in time for those who depend upon it to survive or to benefit from the restoration. If men are forbidden to destroy even the forests of their enemies in wartime, how much more obvious must it be that we have no right to destroy our natural birthright for a temporary economic advantage. "Man *is* the tree of the field." Without the trees of the field, without the wilderness, the lakes, the streams, and the wildlife that all depend upon the tree for their existence, man ceases to be man. Therefore, the Torah warns us that we must guard our natural environment as we would our own lives. For in fact, our very lives and the lives of our children depend upon the preservation of nature in the pristine and virgin state in which it was bequeathed to us. "If man damages the field or the vineyard of his neighbor by sending some destructive element there, he must pay with the best of his field and the best of his own vineyard. If fire spreads, and, finding some flammable substance, consumes the crops of another, he who is responsible for the destruction shall surely provide compensation for the loss" (Exod. 22:4-5).

The Torah speaks in general terms, but the lesson is obvious. If any man causes the destruction of another's property by permitting fire or any other destructive agent to escape from his property into the other's, then he is responsible for the damage, and must compensate his neighbor. It matters not whether the destructive substance is fire, or mercury, or carbon monoxide, or sulfur dioxide, or any other poisonous gas or fluid that deprives others of their right to sustain themselves by fishing or even to enjoy the pleasures of fishing in unpolluted waters; to bathe and swim in clear lakes and on clean beaches; to preserve marble monuments without the corrosive effects of acids that are deposited upon them from the atmosphere; to breathe clean air without the fear of slow asphyxiation or deadly asbestos fibers, to walk through the streets of one's own city, or to enjoy the privacy of one's own home, without the intrusions of poisonous gases and disturbing noises. He must compensate the victims of his irresponsible conduct. This is a *standard*, and not a matter of individual opinion.

The responsibility of the Hooker Chemical Corporation for the harm done to residents of the Love Canal area in Niagara Falls, and of the Allied Chemical Corporation for the great kepone disaster should not be blinked away or permitted to be submerged by years of protracted litigation. Under the principles of talmudic law, these companies would have been required to compensate their victims long ago.

Conclusion

R. Israel Meir Hakohen, also known as the Hafetz Hayim, after the title of his first book, kept a general store. He refused to handle any merchandise except that which was fresh and perfect.

He always added a little over the amount ordered and paid for by his customers to be sure that he had not failed to give them full measure.

In order to avoid committing *hassagat gevul*—the sin of competing against his neighbors unfairly and depriving them of income that they needed and were entitled to—he closed his store early every day, so that some of the people who might have patronized his establishment would go to those of his competitors.

When one customer left behind an item which he had purchased and the Hafetz Hayim couldn't identify him, he gave all his customers an identical item free on the following market day, to be sure that he had not profited unfairly from another's loss.

And when his books were published, he personally checked the conditions of employment at the printing plant to be sure that the employees of the printer were treated justly and fairly—that they received proper wages, that the conditions of their employment were safe and healthful, and that they enjoyed all the fringe benefits to which they were entitled by the laws of the Torah. He refused to patronize any establishment that did not meet his exacting standards.

It would be unreasonable to expect every businessman to adopt all of the Hafetz Hayim's practices. But it is not unreasonable to expect them to adopt all of his standards, and to try, as best they can, to live up to them. Not everyone is a saint. But we can learn from such saintly men that it is possible to live well, to live happily, and at the same time to live decently and honorably, without harming one's fellow men, with genuine concern for their well-being, and with constant attention to principles other than those of profit alone, while conducting a profitable and successful business.

NOTES

1. *Shabbat* 31a
2. *Sifre Num.,* Naso, Sec. 2.
3. *Mekilta* 2, *Vayassa', Beshallah,* Sec. 1.
4. E.g., Abimelech's complaint against Abraham for having deceived him about Sarah, in which he charges the Patriarch with having "stolen my heart," deceived him. Gen. 31:26, and similarly, it is said that Absalom "stole the hearts of the people of Israel" 2 Sam. 15:6. The most important of these was the command, "You shall not steal," in Lev. 19:12, which the rabbis interpreted as referring to deceptive business practices.
5. *Mekilta Mishpatim,* chap. 13.
6. *Baba Batra* 88b.
7. *Shaare Teshuva* of R. Yonah, 184.
8. Quoted by Maimonides in *Yad* (his Code of Jewish Law), *H. Mechirah,* 80.18.
9. *Avoda' Zara* 19b.
10. M. H. Luzzatto, *Mesillat Yesharim,* chap. 11.
11. *Yad, H. Mechirah,* 80, 18.
12. *Baba Metzia* 60a–b.
13. *Wall Street Journal,* October 28, 1977, p. 5.
14. For references to cases and sources, see Burton M. Leiser, *Liberty, Justice and Morals,* 2d ed. (New York: Macmillan, 1979), chap. 9.
15. *Toole* v.*Richardson-Merrell, Inc.,* 251 Cal. App. 2d 689, 60 Cal. Rptr. 398 (Ct of Appeals, First Dist., 1967) is one of many cases that resulted from the marketing of this drug.
16. 1:2
17. *Shulhan Arukh, Hoshen Mishpat* 231:19.
18. *Beer Hetev* ad loc.
19. *M'irot 'enayim* ad loc.
20. *Baba Batra* 88b.
21. *Des Moines Sunday Register,* April 13, 1980, p. 1, col. 1.
22. Deut. 19:14. *Baba Metzia* 60.
23. *Sifre Deut.* 188.
24. Cf. M. Elan, *Hassagat Gevul, Encyc. Judaica,* 7, 1462.
25. Cf. for example *Utah Pie Co.* v. *Continental Baking Co.,* 396 F.2d 161 (10th Cir. 1968); *Continental Baking Co.* v. *Old Homestead Bread Co.,* 476 F.2d 97 (10th Cir. 1973).
26. *Wall Street Journal,* March 16, 1979, p. 19, col. 1.
27. *Ibid.*
28. *Shulhan Arukh, Hoshen Mishpat* 335.
29. *Ibid.* 337.
30. *Ibid.* 339.
31. Derived from Lev. 25:14.
32. *Hoshen Mishpat* 231.

33. Cf. *Maimonides H. Kings* 6:14–15, *Baba Kamma* 82b, *Baba Batra* 2:8–9, prohibiting dunghills within the city limits of Jerusalem, and prohibiting the establishment of a threshing floor within 50 cubits of the city limits of any town because the chaff would jeopardize the health of nearby residents. Also *Baba Kamma* 82b, outlawing the use of open furnaces within the city because of the fumes and smoke.

34. *Baba Batra* 30a.
35. *Baba Kamma* 7.7
36. *Hullin* 7b.
37. *Shabbat* 67b.
38. *M'lachim* 86, 5.
39. *Pirke d'R Eliezer*, 33.

BIBLIOGRAPHY

Elon, Menachem. *"Mishpat Ivri"* and articles cited there on such topics as *Ha'anakah, Hassagat Gevul,* Contract, Labor Law, *Ona'ah,* Partnership, etc. Jerusalem: *Encyclopedia Judaica,* 1971, 12:109-151.

Jacobs, Louis. *What Does Judaism Say About . . . ?* New York: Quadrangle Press, 1973.

Kellner, Menachem M. *Contemporary Jewish Ethics.* New York: Sanhedrin Press, 1978.

Luzzatto, Moses Hayyim. *Mesillat Yesharim: The Path of the Upright,* trans. Mordecai Kaplan. Philadelphia: Jewish Publication Society, 1936.

Vorspan, Albert, and Eugene J. Lipman. *Justice and Judaism.* New York: Union of American Hebrew Congregations, 1956.

PART THREE

The Interface Between Corporate and Religious Values

The three essays in this section are all by authors who are well-versed in religious social thought, and yet they each take a decidedly different standpoint in assessing the crucial issue for the relationship between corporate and religious values. For theologian Michael Novak, moral and religious convictions have a role to play in informing corporate practice, although his overriding concern is that theologians and religious leaders may have incorrectly identified the moral threat of our era. In his judgment, it is not the power of the corporation, but rather "the growing power and irresponsibility of the state" that must be addressed. Chapter 7 follows with an essay co-authored by economists Charles Wilber and Kenneth Jameson. From their perspective the significant problem today is that the economic system in the United States has little chance to be successful in meeting future public expectations both at home and abroad. In marked contrast to Novak's analysis, Wilber-Jameson argue that "business-as-usual will become impossible," and they offer some guidelines from the Judeo-Christian tradition to reform the system. In Chapter 8 Denis Goulet, economist and specialist in transnational corporations, accepts transnational corporations (TNC's) as a fact of life and asks whether they might play an increasingly positive role in the formation of a more just world order. If there are men and women of character shaping the corporate world, Goulet is hopeful that TNC's will play a significant part in the quest for world justice. However, some important changes in the theory and practice of TNC's may be required.

Three Perspectives: Capitalist,
Socialist, and the "Middle Way"

Whether it is because of the magnitude and complexity of the world-poverty problem today, or simply because we are finally within reach of solving it, it is clear that there is increasing discontent among intellectuals and religious persons with "big business" and its part in the poorer or less developed countries (LDC's). Noted Christian scholars Yves Simon and Jacques Maritain, writing almost fifty years ago, argued that the best hope of realizing the vision of a just and humane world, inspired by religious social thought, was in a liberal democracy. Maritain was particularly hopeful about the total organizing system of the United States: ". . . if a new Christian civilization . . . is ever to come about in human history, it is on American soil that it will find its starting point."[1] Certainly that sort of optimism is not prevalent among religious social thinkers today.

Traditionally, within the United States there have been strong disagreements about the precise roles for the state and for business. Often this conflict is posed in terms of choosing between the tyranny of the giant corporations or the tyranny of the state. As Father Schall notes in Chapter 4, Catholic social theory offers a "middle way" between these stark alternatives, and it does this with a threefold focus: the dignity of the person, the principle of subsidiarity, and a respect for pluralism in social groupings. Protestant and Jewish writings present a similar theme.

The ever-recurring theme of Church social encyclicals and the writings of theologians in social theory is the dignity and the social and relational character of the person. In order to thrive and to develop as persons, people need others, and they naturally come together in various groupings—families, church groups, neighborhood associations, professional associations, social clubs, unions, corporations, and so on. These groups or "mediating structures" together comprise what we know as "society." The state exists to be *in service of* society, that is, its role is to initiate and facilitate cooperation, to promote and protect the common good.[2] This position on the role of the state is distinct from both the laissez-faire capitalist and the socialist view.

Capitalist theory takes the state to be a necessary evil, an entity charged to police the marketplace to insure that economic competition proceeds according to the rules.[3] The goal is to provide an environment where fair economic competition can be sustained. Sometimes this may require intervention in order to keep key competitors in the running (the Chrysler loan guarantees by the U.S. government are an example), but the state is fundamentally a police officer charged to check the worst of human selfishness and is *distinct from* society.

While socialism emphasizes the cooperative dimensions of human nature, it oftentimes, in both theory and in practice, *identifies* the state and society. The state organizes and controls almost all aspects of life—the arts and sciences, morals, politics, economics, and so on. Though some socialists look forward to the time when social structures will so modify human nature that people will be almost selfless, thereby lessening the role of the state,[4] religious social theory continues to insist that human nature was, is, and always will be flawed. There are good and evil in every person, and one of the roles of the state is to facilitate the growth of the good character traits (compassion, generosity, cooperativeness, and so on) and mute those that are less noble.

Again from the perspective of religious social thought, competition, an avowed virtue of capitalism, is always set in a wider context of cooperation because people are rooted in families, neighborhoods, and other groupings which provide a humane meaning and value for their lives. Edward Trubac, in Chapter 1, makes the point that large-scale organizations cannot exist without eliciting the cooperative dimension of the individual, and William Sexton, in Chapter 2, portrays the corporation as potentially a humane environment fostering cooperation par excellence. In the final analysis, even the most diverse groups have a mutuality of interests which would engender cooperation. The best image for the state in this vision is not that of the police officer, as in capitalism, or of the all-pervasive mother, as in socialism, but rather that of the facilitator. The notion that the U.S. government ought to facilitate collective bargaining between labor and management is the sort of idea that follows from this view. This is the kind of activity that should be intensified, for example, in stimulating the private sector to find jobs for the hard-core unemployed.

Religious social theorists have a fundamentally different understanding of human nature than either doctrinaire capitalists or socialists. For the "middle way," the state, as the *agent* of society, must both enhance human freedom and curtail human selfishness for the common good of society. However, there is a confidence that the goodness, the cooperative dimension of the person, can be evoked with the appropriate environment, the contours of which are delimited by legislation. Social constraints by the state are viewed as engendering cooperative tendencies rather than restraining "capitalist" selfishness. On the other hand, a religious view, following upon the insights of the ancient doctrine of original sin, could never envision the flawless individual posited by some socialist theory.[5]

The Need for an Explicit Theory

Seldom is our practice in complete accord with our theory, and it is to the business of theory that our first author, Michael Novak, turns. Novak is convinced that Jacques Maritain was correct in his judgment that democratic capitalism in the United States might very well be the closest any system has come to the teachings of the Gospels. The problem is that although the system works well—"in its attainment of political liberties, broad distribution of benefits, and productive achievements"—there is no full-blown theory to describe its workings. Only when politicians, religious leaders, and business executives consciously reflect on how the total system actually works, should we expect helpful direction to make it better.[6]

Novak uses the term "democratic capitalism" to refer to the way of life in the United States, a way which is understood to be comprised of three sources of meaning: political, moral-cultural, and economic. Thus, for example, a U.S. corporation is sustained in meaning and value not simply by some theory of free enterprise, but rather by a theory of democratic capitalism, and this theory is actually three systems in one—a political system, a moral-cultural system, and an economic system. "Business enterprises are, as it were, plants that cannot flourish independently of the trebly differentiated roots from which they have sprung."

In Novak's view, there is a role for religious leaders and theologians (members of the moral-cultural system) to criticize, protest, and persuade the corporate leaders (members of the economic system), for the "three interdependent but autonomous systems of democratic capitalism are accountable to each other." Yet he is not impressed with statements by church leaders and theologians on economic matters because, in his judgment, these statements demonstrate little understanding of the economic system. Novak lists six specific "sorts of ideology" he finds present in these statements; many readers will find this section provocative. The position of his essay is that church documents and theological writings have not seriously grappled with economic principles and realities, and that, until this task is accomplished, corporate executives can expect little in the way of helpful advice from the churches. Novak goes on to sketch his answer to the problem with his "theology of economics" and "theology of democratic capitalism."

There is a tension in Novak's essay that continues to spark discussion.[7] His definition of democratic capitalism with its threefold source of meaning seems, for many, to capture a reality present in the United

States. When it comes to delineating exactly how the three systems interact with each other, however, there is less agreement. Novak insists that the economic system is "accountable" to religious values, but that it cannot be "subordinate" to them. He also acknowledges the need "for leaders in the moral system or in the political system to place constraints upon the economic system." Yet he goes on to caution "lest one of the systems becomes excessively subordinated to another."

To a large extent, the conflict over the interface between corporate and religious values stems from differing positions on just when one crosses the line from "accountable to" to "subordinated to." For example, is a capitalism that is not "subordinated to" a moral-cultural system, a laissez-faire capitalism, and is this desirable for the common good of society? Since each person, whether he or she be a politician, a corporate executive, or a theologian, embodies meaning from all three systems, it seems that there would be a hierarchy of values, both for individuals and for the organizational cultures that they form. Would not this, in the practical order, imply a subordination of key values from one or both systems to that of the third?

Perhaps the most interesting question here is just what is Michael Novak's understanding of the role of the state in religious social thought. Many commentators on his paper noted that he seems to suggest that the state ought to have little, if any, role in facilitating cooperative behavior in the society. Passages such as the following are cited: "But an economic order in a pluralistic society cannot be based upon principles and ideals of any single church. It must be based upon assumptions which permit all who participate to define their own values." If *all can define their own values,* does not this preclude the state from legislating against certain practices of a laissez-faire capitalism, and thus deny any significant role to the "political system" in constraining behavior of the "economic system" taken to be unjust by the "moral-cultural system." It is difficult to see how the economic system can be *accountable* to the political and moral-cultural systems without in some instances being *subordinated* to these systems. Without denying that "big government" has failed to deliver on all the promises of its social programs in the last two decades, many who are advocates of religious and humane values in public and private policy continue to see a large role for the state, either as "policeman" or "facilitator," in extending the common good in economic matters.

To be sure, it would be unfair to Novak to portray his intentions as anything other than to enhance the common good. For example, Novak is concerned that business corporations help in solving the world poverty problem. Yet he insists that the problem has been cast incorrectly. Before talking about distributive justice, one ought to talk about growth and productivity, for "what is not produced cannot be distributed, and choices about production condition choices about distribution." A pivotal concept in Novak's thinking here is Bernard Lonergen's notion of emergent probability;[8] this is a way of saying that human ingenuity has a hand in shaping (not always controlling) history, that practical intelligence can unlock the secrets of creation implanted by the creator. For example, in his oral presentation, Novak reminded his audience that 100 years ago most of the things we call resources today, were not known to be resources. The first oil well was drilled in 1859, and prior to that time having oil on your property was thought to be a nuisance rather than a resource. Given the will to do it, Novak is confident that the corporations of democratic capitalism can meet the challenge of fostering the growth of a more just world.

"Business-as-Usual Will Become Impossible"

Chapter 7 is an essay by economists Charles Wilber and Kenneth Jameson. The authors first delineate what they take to be reasonable goals of an economic system: "Overcoming scarcity, generating and extending freedom of choice, and fostering the conditions for right relations among people—fellowship." In the authors' judgment, while the economic system in the United States has been successful in overcoming scarcity, it has not made satisfactory headway on the other two goals. In fact, the essay argues that it is highly unlikely that the U.S. economic system can continue to overcome scarcity without some important reforms.

Wilber and Jameson argue that capitalism today is dominated by mega-institutions, and that this largeness and the high concentration of firms in each industry call for some fresh thinking. The traditional theoretical model of capitalism, based as it is on Adam Smith's insights from a much smaller market system, is outmoded, and today there is, in fact, a new model better termed "corporate capitalism." The root of the growing malaise in the U.S. economy is that its operating premise, continuing economic growth, assumes a ready supply of cheap natural resources, and the salutary workings of self-interest as the motive power for this growth. In "corporate capitalism," both of these assumptions are false, according to the analysis, and thus the times are faced with physical and social limits to growth.

Under physical limits to growth, the authors consider issues such as the higher costs of energy supplies and natural resources, the style of competition based on programmed obsolescence, individualist-oriented consumer growth, and the additional expense involved with firms internalizing pollution costs. In the authors' judgment, these new factors make it highly unlikely that the economic system in the United States can continue as we know it. Under the social limits to growth, the authors argue that an economy which relies on "positional" goods, goods which display status and "set the owner apart from the crowd," breeds conflict and frustration in society, and hence undermines fellowship and distorts free choice. They go on to offer a radical critique of Adam Smith's key insight that individuals acting out of their self-interest will enhance the common good. This Smithian point assumed that individuals would be basically moral and consider it wrong to lie, cheat, steal, and so on. The religious base kept the whole process on course, in Smith's view, and insured an efficient and productive economy. One cannot assume a common acceptance of fundamental religious and moral convictions today because there has been an erosion of the traditional religious ethic. Where religion is present, it often is a privatized religion with little or no social dimension.

In the light of their analysis of the physical and social limits to growth, the authors predict the continuing deterioration of economic performance, and suggest three themes from the Judeo-Christian heritage to guide reform: stewardship, jubilee, and smallness. Stewardship is an ancient biblical theme. The Book of Genesis (Gen. 1:26-31) has God telling humankind that they are stewards (not owners) of *his* world, and are charged to be resourceful in their caretaker role. The authors focus on ownership of corporations and suggest that more public control would insure that people, not profits, are the dominant concern. In traditional religious social theory, the right of private property, while not an absolute right, is taken to be an effective way to insure the dignity of the person and a just society.[9] Wilber and Jameson argue that with the advent of "corporate capitalism" a fresh perspective is demanded, and increasing public-control measures are more likely to enable the stewardship task.

The Jubilee Year is described in the Book of Leviticus (Lev. 25:23-55). Held once every fifty years, it was understood to be an occasion to remind the Jewish people that ultimately all wealth and power are the Lord's and that persons vested with these goods are only his agents. Leviticus describes the jubilee year as a time when debts are forgiven, slaves are freed, and all land is returned to the community. While many scholars doubt if the events proscribed for the jubilee year ever actually took place, there is a consensus that the point of the work is to remind persons of their accountability to each other and to their God. Wilber and Jameson suggest that the import of this biblical theme is a mandate to address income inequalities by lowering salaries of senior executives and providing minimum income and jobs for all who want to work.

A final consideration is termed "smallness." While Michael Novak sees big government as the threat of our age, Wilber and Jameson argue that all mega-institutions—business, unions, government— make life less humane than it might be. While they do not call for the dismantling of mega-corporations, they do outline the way in which the social fabric is destroyed without smaller institutions, and make a strong plea for the revitalization or creation of smaller "mediating structures" which would be more responsive to individual needs. This theme has been traditionally addressed under the rubric of "subsidiarity."[10] The wisdom of the heritage was that institutions ought to be no larger than *necessary*. Just how large is necessary, for example, to produce airplanes, is open for discussion. In any event, the authors note that satisfactory solutions to major societal problems will often not be found in either big government or big corporations. "Smallness" meets the needs of meaning and intimacy; vital mediating institutions between persons and large institutions are essential.

In the terms of Novak's essay, the Wilber-Jameson study is an analysis of the economic system combined with a critique from the moral-cultural system. What Wilber-Jameson define as the "economic system" with its three goals is more akin to Novak's "democratic capitalism." Novak uses the term "economic system" to refer to one of three systems of democratic capitalism, the system concerned with the wealth-producing capacity of a society. A crucial question for many is just how much one can alter the economic system without impairing its ability to provide goods and services efficiently. In Novak's terms, the economic system must be "accountable" to the Judeo-Christian heritage, but *not* "subordinate" to it. Do the Wilber-Jameson suggestions (more public-control measures, lowering senior executives' salaries, less reliance on the corporate sector for solutions, and so on) render the economic system subordinate to the moral-cultural system? And, more importantly, is this a good posture for assessing the suggestions for reform?

New Social Roles for Transnational Corporations

In the final essay of this third part of the volume, Denis Goulet presents his perspective on the interface between corporate and religious values. He first provides a list of ten assumptions about how a person within transnationals, coming from the Judeo-Christian tradition, ought to approach economic development and global justice. He takes a definitive moral stance when he, first, sets out the goal "neither to maximize economic growth nor to aggregate wealth, but to improve the living conditions of all people. . ." Next he pinpoints the basic needs of the globe's poorest population as the first priority target, which should be the concern of governmental, business, and religious persons. This moral horizon inspires all of Goulet's ideas; he will compromise over method or means, but never over goals or ends.

Goulet recognizes the dilemmas confronting businessmen and women who are trying to implement this moral perspective. He observes that business confers "rewards of success" on individuals whose moral traits contrast sharply, often with religious moral values. Still he holds out that, to use his term, the moral schizophrenia can be overcome. He goes on to describe the sometimes heroic task of witnessing to religious values in business. Without rejecting the magnitude of the dilemmas described by Goulet, it is appropriate to point to the pivotal role of *trust* for religious persons who affirm in all aspects of their lives, including business, "the ultimate power by which our lives are ruled is the personal reality of God, whose loving mercies surround and sustain us."[11]

Next, the essay provides a helpful survey of the literature on transnational corporations including critics, advocates, and visionaries. In the final section Goulet explicitly discusses ways in which religious values might interface with corporate values. He provides some examples of firms exploring new social roles for transnational corporations, such innovative ideas as joint long-term planning that would bring together corporate executives, government officials, and local community representatives to discuss the various aspects of corporate strategy in Third World countries.

The "contract of solidarity," a scheme to develop sovereign states and other institutions by forming exchanges between strong and weak partners, is also presented. Here the stronger partner forms a special relationship with the weaker one in order to strengthen it. Many will find Goulet's discussion of new social roles of transnational corporations a creative instance of the "middle way" in which government serves as a facilitator to enhance the common good. This kind of innovative thinking is only in its infant stage, and it is too early to make any final judgments. Some would oppose these measures since they substitute a planner sovereignty for the consumer sovereignty of traditional economic theory; ultimately, the critical question is: who will make the final decisions for the plan? In Novak's terms, do the new social roles for transnational corporations suggested by Goulet "subordinate" the "economic system" to the "moral-cultural system," or are these measures simply concrete ways by which the former system is accountable to the latter? These questions, and the moral vision implied by them, will continue to challenge men and women of competence and goodwill for a long time.

NOTES

1. Jacques Maritain, *Reflections on America* (New York: Charles Scribner's, 1958), p. 188.
2. The 1931 encyclical *Quadregesimo anno* uses the verbs direct, watch, urge, and restrain "as occasion requires and necessity demands," when speaking of the role of the state (#80). *Mater et Magistra,* the social encyclical of Pope John XXIII, identifies the role of the state as to "encourage, stimulate, regulate, supplement and complement" (#53). The function of the state is always seen as promoting the common good. See Thomas Aquinas's treatise *On Kingship.*
3. The term "capitalism" is used here to refer to the economic theories of such contemporary thinkers as Milton Friedman. For example, see his *Capitalism and Freedom* (Chicago: University of Chicago Press, 1962).
4. For a detailing of socialist thinking that recognizes the dangers of totalitarian socialist states, such as the Soviet Union, and plots a more hopeful course, see Erich Fromm (ed.), *Socialist Humanism: An International Symposium* (New York: Doubleday, 1965).
5. For an elaboration of this religious view of the person, see Oliver F. Williams, C.S.C., and John W. Houck, *Full Value* (San Francisco: Harper & Row, 1978), esp. chap. 3.
6. Novak's concern for a theory of democratic capitalism parallels Maritain's concern. See Jacques Maritain, "Too Much Modesty—The Need for an Explicit Philosophy," *Reflections on America* (New York: Scribner's, 1958), pp. 101-20.
7. For example, a *New York Times* religion editor reporting on Michael Novak's presentation at the University of Notre Dame wrote: "Mr. Novak seemed to find a new absolute in something called 'democratic capitalism' . . . ." Cf. Robert Blair Kaiser, "Morality of Working in Modern Business is Argued," *New York Times,* April 20, 1980, at A 26.
8. Bernard J. Lonergan, *Insight: A Study of Human Understanding,* rev. ed. (New York: Philosophical Library, 1965).
9. Thomas Aquinas advocates a system of private property, and his discussion forms the basis for much of the subsequent discussion in the churches. Cf. *Summa Theologica,* II-II, 66, 2. For a good summary of the tradition, see E. Duff, "Private Property," *New Catholic Encyclopedia,* 2:849-55.

10. Subsidiarity is discussed in a number of encyclicals and theological writings. See *The Gospel of Peace and Justice: Catholic Social Teaching Since Pope John*, ed. Joseph Gremillion (Maryknoll, N.Y.: Orbis Books, 1976), pp. 154, 168, 231, and 322.

11. Avery Dulles, S.J., "The Meaning of Faith Considered in Relationship to Justice," *The Faith That Does Justice* ed. John C. Haughey (New York: Paulist Press, 1977), p. 13.

6. Can a Christian Work for a Corporation? The Theology of the Corporation

Michael Novak*

Few theologians have yet attempted to reflect systematically upon economic activities and economic systems. While there do exist mature "theologians of history" and fledgling "political theologies," there is as yet no theology of economics. In particular, within the theology of economics, there exists no theological description and critical evaluation of democratic capitalism. Most theologians of the last 200 years have approached democratic capitalism in a premodern, precapitalist, predemocratic way, or else they have been socialists (usually of a romantic and utopian, rather than an empirical, type). Lacking both a theology of economics and a theology of democratic capitalism, it is difficult, indeed, to launch a third-order inquiry into the theology of the corporation.

The corporation is an invention of democratic capitalism or, to put it another way, the corporation represents an invention of law which made democratic capitalism possible. Neither participatory democracy nor capitalism could exist without the corporation. The existence and practice of the corporation, on the other hand, give the lie to all theories of democracy and capitalism which focus exclusively on the individual to the neglect of human sociality. The corporation is an expression of the social nature of humans. Moreover, it offers a metaphor for the ecclesial community which is in some ways more illuminating than metaphors based on the human body ("the mystical body") or metaphors based on the family, the clan, the tribe, or the chosen people.

Paul Johnson has pointed out that the origins of the corporation lie in the twofold need of religious communities, whose purpose

*Special thanks are due to John W. Cooper for his research assistance.

transcends the life of the individual, for independence and self-subsistence.[1] Their motive was "profit," in the sense that they needed to be sufficiently productive to have time for other things (prayer, honoring the dead) than mere subsistence. They also needed independence and continuity over time. Pre-Christian religious communities in New Kingdom Egypt (ca. 1300 B.C.) owned property corporately, as did perpetual mortuary foundations in later Egyptian history. From Egypt, these corporations influenced the incorporation of the late-Roman Christian monastic communities, which benefited by the land deeds pioneered by late Roman Law. The Benedictine monasteries, in turn, provided economic models for the lay guilds of the fourteenth and fifteenth centuries, whose legal structure was imitated by the merchant adventurers of the sixteenth century. These merchants, to raise capital and to share risks, then developed the joint stock company. Thence came the modern corporation—a communal institution whose purposes and continuity must in the nature of the case transcend the limits of individual life. The lineage of the modern multinational corporation may likewise be traced in legal and economic history to the internationalism of the Benedictines and other general congregations of religious men and women whose activities were multinational. As leisure is the basis of culture, so "profits" exceeding the needs of subsistence underlay the economics of the independent, multinational religious orders. Often, to be sure, these self-sufficient congregations took their "profits" as time for prayer and study, subsidized by their own excess productivity.

In a word, the modern economic corporation is a fruitful *locus* for theological inquiry, even though a full exploration of the theology of the corporation would depend upon a prior theology of democratic capitalism, which in turn depends upon a prior theology of economics.

Unfortunately, the necessary preliminary investigations cannot be set forth here; I hope to have an inquiry into such matters ready for publication in a year or two. The question addressed to me today is quite specific. It is also laden with denigrating bias.

Introduction

I have been asked: *Can a Christian work for a corporation?* Under the logical paradigm for this question other vocations fall as well. *Can a Christian work for the state? Can a Christian work in a university? Can a Christian be a bishop?* Being a Christian is a high vocation—a vocation to grow in the holiness of Jesus Christ. Living before the age of democratic capitalism, which for convenience may be thought to have been fully distinguished from mercantilism with the publication of Adam Smith's *The Wealth of Nations* in 1776, Jesus did not work for a corporation. He did, apparently, work for a small business as a carpenter. His disciples appear to have been mostly independent small businessmen, as well, working as fishermen, some of whom presumably hired others to help them.[2] To be an economic animal is as much a part of human nature as to be a political animal or a religious animal. Human life is inconceivable, indeed, apart from the economic activities necessary to create housing, gather food, build roads, and establish markets.

A majority of lay Christians in approximately 30 of the world's 156 nations, including the United States, Japan, Hong Kong, Sri Lanka, most nations of Western Europe and others, now live out their lives under systems reasonably designated as analogues, at least, of democratic capitalism.[3] By *democratic capitalism*, one means a society no longer structured like a traditional society, in Max Weber's sense,[4] but rather a society differentiated into three social systems: a political system, an economic system, and a moral-cultural system. As the church is separated from the state, so also the economic system has a certain independence from the political system and the reverse. If we are ever to have a credible theology of work, theology of the laity, and theology of the world, we will have to construct a sound fundamental theology of economics and a critical theology of democratic capitalism. For our present purposes, however, we will be obliged to focus attention upon the actual *praxis* of economic corporations, within which sizable numbers of Christians now perform their daily work and earn their daily bread.

The preliminary answer to the question, *Can Christians work for a corporation?*, must therefore be answered: In fact, many of them do. By *corporation* in this context is meant a legal body chartered and empowered by law to perform specifically designated functions under the restraint of law.[5] The existence of corporations depends upon the evolution of a body of law, upon such differentiation of society as permits corporations a certain independence from the state, and upon that free entering into social contracts which constitute the corporation as a legal person and active agent in history.[6] In a more fundamental sense, the coming into existence of corporations depends upon at least an implicit metaphysics of "emergent probability," as Bernard Lonergan has defined it;[7] upon the cultural evolution of notions of individual liberty, voluntary association, and formally free labor; and upon the invention of systems of accounting, including double-entry bookkeeping.[8] Max Weber's reflections upon these last points in *The Protestant Ethic and the Spirit of Capitalism* (1904) suffice for preliminary survey of the social preconditions for the emergence of economic corporations in history.

Not all corporations are economic, of course. Political parties are incorporated. So are labor unions, universities, foundations, charitable organizations of many sorts, and many institutions of research, invention, science, and the arts. The development of corporate law opened human history to the action of social institutions freely entered into. These "mediating structures," larger than the individual but smaller than the state, make possible where they appear the flowering of human initiative, cooperation, and accountability.[9] They are of considerable historical significance. The traditions on which corporate law is based are not universal. Not all Christians live under such traditions today. Is it good for Christianity that such corporations exist?

Six Sources of Distortion

Some theologians today write as if corporations were evil forces and, indeed, as if democratic capitalism as a whole were incompatible with Christianity. In 1864, Pius IX enshrined an analogous view in his "Syllabus of Errors," declaring that same modern civilization to be incompatible with Catholicism. Declarations by church leaders and theologians on secular matters are always worth attending to, but those who issue them are not always as knowing or wise as they imagine. Insight into the organization of the secular world is not their strength. Regarding the understanding of economic matters produced by Christian leaders in the World Council of Churches, the National Council of Churches, and the Catholic Church's Peace and Justice Commission, even the most stalwart partisans can scarcely deny a great gap between the views of centralized leadership and those of rank-and-file Christians.[10] One explanation for this gap may be that the rank and file are less educated, less informed, or less knowledgeable about economics and Christianity than the writers of ecclesiastical statements. Yet given the rather broad distribution of education and experience among local clergy and laity today, such an explanation hardly seems convincing. An alternative explanation may be that church commissions are managed by a special social class of Christians with its own understandable bias.[11] What cannot be assumed in advance is that the writers of ecclesiastical documents have superior knowledge of economics and Christianity and their proper relation. Their views, too, must face the relentless drive to raise questions.

A theology of economics which wishes to be critical must, then, establish a point of view from which to submit to criticism all propositions, whatever their origin, about the relation of the Christian people to economics. Church leaders are more likely to err in this territory than in most others.[12] The gospel itself provides little guidance. Neither do theological traditions formed by traditional social orders. So church authorities have only a very weak authority, indeed, for their pronouncements in this area. Moreover, church leaders and theologians may be among the least well prepared of all Christians in training and experience to speak about economic matters in modern societies.[13]

A student of statements by church leaders and theologians on economic matters is likely to notice the unusual shape of such literature. Six specific sorts of ideology are frequently imported into it without argument or justification.

The Ideological Use of "Poverty"

Poverty is highly praised in the Bible, so there is reason for church leaders to focus on it. But how? What is the meaning of poverty? What is its religious meaning? What is its economic meaning? After the Protestant Reformers slammed the monastery doors behind them, as Max Weber describes,[14] are we to understand that ascetic poverty ought now in the name of Christianity to be imposed upon the peoples of the world? Modern churchmen and theologians, oddly, seem to regard poverty not as a state to be praised but as a state to be eliminated. They often suggest that poverty is a scandal, that it is due chiefly to hardheartedness or to exploitation by the rich. They seldom distinguish among theories of poverty.[15] They seldom recount its historical dimensions, its universal persistence, or the methods by which at some times and in some places it has been alleviated. They use the concept ideologically, not empirically. They seldom seem to recognize, as J. L. Talmon does, how the ideological use of "poverty" lies at the origins of "democratic totalitarianism."[16]

Is poverty more widespread today than in the time of Jesus? Is famine as common?[17] Are rates of infant mortality higher? Is life expectancy greater? Are there wider disparities between rich and poor than in the time of the Pharoahs and the Caesars? The sources of poverty may lie as much in nature and in culture as in economic structures. If "the Kingdom of God" in this world demands the elimination of poverty, it may also impose correlative demands upon the production of wealth. Indeed, empirical and critical inquiry may suggest that the relevant intellectual problem is not poverty, which is widespread and immemorial, but how to produce wealth. If theologians are serious about poverty, they must develop an empirically founded theory about it.

The World View of Traditional Societies

Church leaders are tempted to think in terms appropriate to a traditional society rather than to a modern, differentiated, pluralist society.[18] Thus, they are more likely to imagine that the economic order should be suffused with charity and justice from above or from some central focus.[19] They often imagine themselves to be prophets, utopians, visionaries, "improving" society by their lights. Yet a modern social order must be pluralistic, permitting many different Christian, Jewish, Muslim, atheist, and other sorts of visions about its character. A modern social order necessarily regards church leaders as equal, but not privileged, participants in the common dialogue. Their visions of how justice and charity ought to be observed in the economic order do not, cannot, and should not determine the rules of the economic order, for others who hold other visions must also be free to work for their visions. The problem of order in a differentiated society has not been adequately addressed.

Naiveté About Transfer Payments

Led by the models of the Christian past which stressed paternalism and charitable giving, religious leaders are inclined to think that income gaps between humans are (a) unjust, and (b) best eliminated by "transfer payments."[20] In other words, those who have will better help the poor if they give of their abundance to them. This approach is doubtful.[21] Supposing that gaps between poor and rich are immoral, it does not follow that, in the empirical world of actual practice, the most useful method of equalizing incomes is by transfer payments. The effectiveness of such a remedy must be demonstrated, not asserted.

The Anti-Capitalist Bias of the Intellectuals[22]

Given the anti-capitalist bias of the Roman Catholic church, of major American and European Protestant theologians in this century, and of the pronouncements of the Protestant churches, church leaders are vulnerable to systematic misperceptions about the nature of democratic capitalism. Few if any theologians or church leaders have set forth a theoretical understanding of democratic capitalism which is intended to be descriptively true. Commonly, they accept what Max Weber called "kindergarten" notions about the system.[23] Before describing it accurately, they are already in an adversary position. Many speak of "individualism," "acquisitiveness," "greed," "self-interest," "money," "success," "competitiveness," as though these underlie the actual practice of democratic capitalism. For example, the Oxford Conference of 1937 described the system as follows:

> When the necessary work of society is so organized as to make the acquisition of wealth the chief criterion of success, it encourages a feverish scramble for money, and a false respect for the victors in the struggle, which is as fatal in its moral consequences as any other form of idolatry.[24]

Do people in practice live this way? How many? A great many people clearly do not. Perhaps theologians merely borrow from economists' descriptions of *economic* behavior. But economists note explicitly that they are speaking abstractly about "economic behavior" and "economic man," not about real persons enmeshed in the real social order. Theologians commonly criticize economists for excessive abstraction. Theologians themselves are bound, then, to describe the real world of ordinary experience. For example, the basic institution of capitalism is the corporation—a social organism. Indeed, entire schools of criticism fault corporate life for an excess of social pressures toward conformism rather than for an excess of individualism.[25] Church leaders are prone to rely on ideology rather than on accurate phenomenological descriptions of the forms of fraternity, sympathy, fellowship, and cooperation practiced in democratic capitalist societies, and also in corporations.[26]

Guilt-Mongering

The profession of church leaders and theologians requires them to criticize leaders of other institutions for falling short of religious ideals. But an economic order in a pluralist society cannot be based upon the principles and ideals of any single church. It must be based upon assumptions which permit all who participate to define their own values. Moreover, a just economic order in a pluralist society cannot be based solely on the concepts of virtue, innocence, and motivation taught by church leaders. The fact that democratic capitalism is based upon *rational* self-interest[27] does permit Christians and Jews, rationally choosing their own vision of virtue and justice, to take part in it. But it does not permit such believers to impose their own view of what is "rational" upon nonbelievers. A democratic capitalist economic order does *not* assume that human beings are depraved, so as to be motivated by self-interest, acquisitiveness, and greed. Its basic concept is *rational* self-interest, defined as each participant chooses to define it.[28] Thus, many participants seek through their work satisfactions that are far from monetary, selfish, or materialistic. The social order is much enhanced by such choices. Philanthropy, the arts, universities, research centers, and many other altruistic activities are expected to flower and do in fact flower under democratic capitalism.

The Constantinian Temptation

In traditional societies, church leaders (whether in Rome or in Geneva) were able to impose their own values upon the entire civil society. It is difficult for church leaders to play such a role within a differentiated society. Thus there is often a secret hankering, a lingering nostalgia, for a planned society which would once again permit church leaders to be in alliance with civil leaders in suffusing an entire society with their values.[29] Today the new Constantinianism appears as socialism in totalitarian states and as statism in mixed economies. Democratic capitalism functions as three systems in one, and it is altogether proper for leaders in the moral system or in the political system to place constraints upon the economic system. But those constraints must be as jealously watched as those flowing in other directions, lest one of the three systems becomes excessively subordinated to another. Leaders in each system tend to manifest typical bias. Theologians and church leaders must learn to detect their own characteristic bias. If "evangelical" leaders tend to be biased toward economic leaders, "liberal" churchmen tend to be biased toward the state. Each such bias may be dangerous to the common health.

In the spirit of these warnings, let us turn now to some matters of fact about corporations in the United States.

Some Observations on Matters of Fact

How many corporations are there in the United States? Some 2 million economic corporations now report to the Internal Revenue Service.[30] According to the Small Business Administration, there are an additional 13 million unincorporated small businesses.[31] (Since the active labor force in the United States numbers nearly 100 million persons, this means that there is, on average, one business corporation for every six or seven workers.) Defined in terms of the number of laborers employed by each enterprise, by the total assets of the enterprise, and by the annual sales volume of the enterprise, there are approximately 15 million "small businesses" in the U.S. and about 700,000 "large businesses."[32]

In recent years, the level of employment in industrial corporations has been relatively static, or even declining, while the number of jobs in the service sector and in government employment has been growing rapidly. During the period from 1969-76, for example, nearly all the 9 million new jobs added to the economy were added in government employment (3 million) and in small businesses, mostly in the service sector (6 million).[33] Employment in large businesses has been static; the Small Business Administration claims that 87 percent of all new jobs in the private sector are created by small businesses.[34] One sees many of these small businesses, from rock groups to boutiques, spring up among college-age students.

Where Americans Work

Of the 100 million Americans who work, some 16 million work for government (federal, state, and local). Another 10 million work on contract to the government. Some 41 million of the workers in the private sector work for taxi fleets, local dairies and bakeries, retail stores, auto dealers, restaurants, and other small businesses.[35] About 33 million work for "large" corporations. Since there are about 700,000 large corporations, on average "large" corporations employ about 47 persons each.[36] The New York Stock Exchange, the American Stock Exchange, and the Over-the-Counter Market together list some 5,250 corporations, whose shares are owned by the public and publicly traded. All of these corporations rank as "large businesses," but many of them number only a few hundred workers.

Each year, *Fortune* magazine lists the 500 largest corporations in America. Over the years, some of these corporations disappear and rankings change, as new technologies spawn new giants and old technologies and methods of operation result in the obsolescence, decline or bankruptcy of others. The tenth-largest corporation, the Chrysler Corporation, for example, appears to some to be in its death throes. Of "the *Fortune* 500," the top 100 are truly giants; the bottom 100 rank dramatically lower in net worth, annual gross sales, and numbers of employees. Altogether, the top 500 corporations employ about 14 million Americans, 2 million fewer than those employed by the state, 2 million more than those who attend American colleges and universities as graduate students and undergraduates.[37] The average work force of the top 500 corporations is 28,000, approximately the number of students enrolled on the campuses of some major universities.

Some Characteristics of the Top-500 Corporations

If we limit our discussion for a moment to the top-500 industrial corporations, several of their characteristics may be worth pointing out. These corporations are spread out over some 25 industries, from aerospace to food processing to publishing.[38] Although from industry to industry and from year to year, there is some variation, the annual return upon investment of such companies in 1978 was 14.3 percent.[39] As frequently happens, the television industry led all others that year with an annual return on investment of about 22 percent. Since it has been possible in recent years to get a return on investment of about 10 percent—lately, in an all-time peak, 15 percent—simply by putting one's money in the higher-ranked bank instruments, with virtually no risk, the incentive for investing capital in American industry is not at present very high. Technological innovation is falling off; productivity is falling off dramatically. It requires about $30,000 of capital investment to create each new job. The drop in capital investment has limited job creation for several years now.

Corporations are normally started by a few persons pooling their capital—often only a very little in the beginning, as when Hewlett and Packard began making electronic instruments in a small garage in Palo Alto just after World War II—in order to bring *some new idea* "to market." Practical insight is the first and indispensable constituent in the formation of a corporation. There has to be a practical idea. Everything else depends upon that. That idea cannot be realized in goods and services, of course, until someone puts up the money (capital in the secondary sense) to provide the instruments of manufacture and delivery. But money alone can be as easily lost as increased, as easily squandered as invested productively. In addition to the money, and prior to it, is the *idea,* the organizing original *insight.* In their book, *The Responsible Society,*[40] Eugen Loebl and Stephen B. Roman have perspicaciously underlined the primacy of intelligence to the workings of democratic capitalism.

While large corporations have been important since the founding of America—from the British companies that founded early colonies to the hunting and transportation firms, canal builders, and railroads—large corporations did not become a conspicuous part of the American landscape until after the Civil War and, especially, after the creation of a national, transcontinental society in the twentieth century.[41] From the Revolutionary War, at least, Americans properly feared the large, all-encompassing state. For the last century, this fear of bigness has been redirected at the growing number of large corporations. The giant among corporations, General Motors, with nearly 800,000 employees, is much smaller than the federal government. Still, a single corporation employing more persons than are to be found in several of our sovereign states is a formidable economic force. Most large corporations are far smaller than General Motors. Of "the *Fortune* 500," 429 have under 50,000 employees; 300 have under 23,000 employees; the fifth 100 each have under 8,200 employees. Yet even the smallest of the 500 (529 employees) faces enormous problems of innovation, continued vitality, and organization in order to function at all. We academics are somewhat more familiar with the problems of morale, financing, quality, and management in the running of a large university. As citizens, we have some understanding of the problems of managing the truly gigantic work forces of the government. Still, we tend to react to corporations as to foreign bodies largely outside our lived worlds.

The Need for Creative Practical Intelligence

It is a common mistake of academics to believe that anyone can manage a large corporation. Academics value a type of intelligence, important for its own sake but not necessarily adequate to the demands of the economic order.[42] Indeed, experience teaches academics that the sort of work and ideas they value most highly are less likely to be successful in "the market" than lesser work. The ideals of scholarship have more of an affinity with aristocratic than with commercial thinking. The market is disdained in preference to judgments made in the light of long-held, traditional values.[43] Yet creative practical intelligence must also go against the market; it aims to *change* the market. An economic system like ours rewards such dissent, anticipation, and innovation. It also penalizes mistaken strategic decisions, which can bankrupt even the tenth-largest company, Chrysler. At the time when corporate decisions must be made, it is not at all certain which of many competing decisions will be the "correct" one. Practical intelligence of a high order is often obliged to fight its way through legions of doubters who "know" from the conventional wisdom that novel proposals "can't work."

Lenin once expressed the view that any citizen could manage the government, just as any one of them could in a short time be trained to work as a postal clerk. There is a systematic bias on the part of intellectuals that denigrates the order of intelligence required for the successful management of a business enterprise. Corporate executives normally do not own the corporations they manage.[44] They are professionals of an uncommon talent. The average length of service of a chief executive officer is about that of a professional football player: six years. The pay—for the *Fortune* 500 it averages $400,000 per year—is about commensurate with that of top professionals in sports, entertainment, television journalism, or writers of best sellers. It is rarely as dramatic as that of some television and movie producers, inventors, and others. About 3 percent of the 77 million American households receives a one-year income in excess of $50,000. Only 275,000 persons, on average 5,500 in each of the fifty states, receive a one-year income in excess of $100,000.[45] (Certain academic authors of certain widely used textbooks are to be found in this number.)

The imagery surrounding corporate leaders is mainly negative; it seems to be ideologically (and even ethnically) inspired. Few write about "fat-cat" professors or journalists. Successful movie actors are seldom subjected, as are businessmen, to ridicule by cartoonists. In *The View from Sunset Boulevard*,[46] Ben Stein has reproduced interviews which dramatize quite starkly the anti-business attitudes of the makers of television and the ideological distortions of their perceptions. In the American past, there were reasons for "the huddled masses" to regard the "robber barons" as their class, ethnic, and even religious enemies. Such passions have continued in more moderate form into the present. Religio-ethnic resistance to Catholics and Jews in major corporations seems to have persisted until after World War II, but it largely collapsed under the onslaught of talented professional managers like Thomas A. Murphy of General Motors, Lee Iaccocca of Chrysler, Irving Shapiro of DuPont, and many others.

Rather distinct from the class of professional managers is the smaller class of corporate executives around whose inventions or insights the corporation they founded was built. Such persons commonly benefit not only by the salaries paid them but by a substantial interest in the company they own. Indeed, building a company, even a small company like an auto dealership or a small chain of retail stores, is a far surer path to wealth than working as a professional manager.[47]

Ownership in the firm enables the owner to accumulate wealth as capital; it is not paid him in salary. The limousine service from New Haven to LaGuardia and Kennedy airports was sold recently by its founder, for example, for a reported $13 million.

The largest industries are in almost all cases the most heavily unionized. Their businesses usually pay the best pension benefits, medical benefits, vacation benefits, and the rest. Smaller businesses rarely have the cash flow, security, or permanence to do nearly as well.

Some Observations on Multinational Corporations

In an interdependent world, economic enterprises—like churches, scientific associations, and other institutions—have become multinational. Within the United States, many multinational corporations founded and based in other lands compete with American firms: British Petroleum, Volvo, Sony, Olivetti, Volkswagen, and many others. In 1970, the Department of Commerce surveyed 298 U.S. firms with operations overseas.[48] Sperry Lea and Simon Webley note that, under a stricter definition of the term, there are only about 200 multinational corporations based in the U.S., out of 300 worldwide.[49] These U.S. firms make roughly two-thirds of their sales in the developed countries and one-third in developing countries.

Multinational corporations encounter many moral dilemmas in doing business overseas. In most traditional societies, bookkeeping is not public, nor bound solely by law. Custom and tradition have a familial base.[50] Ruling families consider it a right, perhaps a duty, to take a percentage of all commercial transactions, much as the governments of developed states levy taxes. In developed societies, such extralegal but traditional payoffs are considered bribes, and are both illegal and immoral. In traditional societies, neither custom nor tradition so regard such activities. The effort by Americans to impose American standards of commercial behavior on foreign authorities is not in all nations regarded as wise. Moral conflicts are inevitable in an interdependent world, whose systems of law and morality are not as interdependent as are economic activities.

Favored by nature, the United States is itself actually dependent on foreign trade for relatively few commodities. It depends heavily on oil, although some argue that the U.S. should long ago have cut its dependence on foreign oil to a small fraction of its present proportion. The U.S. is even more dependent on certain specialty metals indispensable to advances in high technology, like chromium, titanium, and a score of others.[51] In addition, some U.S. industries, especially high-technology industries like aerospace, but also agriculture, depend heavily on exports. In both imports and exports, then, the U.S. economy is interdependent with the world economy. Would those who oppose multinationals simply ban them? This can and has been done. No multinational corporation is as strong as a foreign state. Only a state has armies. Even small states have confiscated the properties of major corporations and banned such corporations from their territory. They restrict and tax such corporations as they will. Thus many corporations refuse to do business overseas, except under unusually stable conditions.

Meanwhile, the litany of accusations against the activities of U.S. corporations abroad demands case-by-case intelligent judgment.[52] No doubt corporations are often wrong. No doubt they have been unprepared for the complexities of their interaction with host cultures. The clash between modern and traditional societies would be ridden with moral conflict under the most favorable conditions. Methods and attitudes suited to the United States often have unfortunate effects abroad.

An interdependent world creates many moral dilemmas for corporations, and moral costs accrue whichever course they take. The absence of investment from abroad may be more morally damaging to traditional societies than is the activity of multinational corporations. One thing is certain: democratic capitalism needs to attend as much to cultural systems as to economic and political systems. On these matters, theologians may have something to contribute; but it would be arrogant to think that we can—Solomon-like—resolve all perplexities. Should corporation X invest in a new plant in underdeveloped nation Y? Does it have the human resources to do so with cultural wisdom? What ought a Christian corporate executive to consider in making such a decision? We do not at present, I fear, offer much light.

Why not?

Elements of a Theology of Economics

One of the reasons why theologians have little say about the practical dilemmas of corporate executives is that the theology of economics is at present the least sophisticated branch of theological inquiry. Few theologians who address the social order (for example, Jurgen Moltmann today or Paul Tillich a generation ago) have paid extensive attention to economic matters. The official documents of the popes and of Protestant ecumenical bodies (the World Council and the National Council) are notably strong in moral vision, much less so in their description of economic principles and realities. The coming generation will inherit as a task the need to create and to set forth in a systematic way a theology of economics. This theology will have to deal critically with several key concepts. Among them will be the following:

(1) *Order.* There is a difference between the way a *traditional society* orders the cosmos of human meaning (political, economic, moral) and the way a modern *democratic, pluralistic, capitalist society* orders meaning.[53] To judge modern democratic, pluralistic, capitalist societies by the norms of traditional societies is to make a categorical mistake. Those who do so often falsely describe the risk, danger, and terror inherent in personal liberty ("the experience of nothingness")[54] under pejorative notions like alienation, anomie, and privatization. "Order" in a nontraditional society necessarily seems like disorder to those whose ideal is the order of a traditional society. The resentment against modernity among traditionalists in Iran illustrates the point. Socialist societies like Cuba, the U.S.S.R., and China offer a single system of meaning ("justice") far closer to traditional societies than to a fully differentiated modern society.

(2) *Emergent probability.* Many theologians are fascinated by the future, by utopian thinking, by prophecy, and by the myth of the avant-garde. Moreover, the phrase "the economy of salvation" suggests to some that history moves forward by a kind of moral imperative (and inexorable necessity) toward self-improvement. By contrast, a theology of economics requires a critical philosophy of history. A promising candidate appears to be the theory of "emergent probability"[55] sketched by Bernard Lonergan: a world order moved neither by necessity alone nor by human will alone, neither wholly open to intellectual insight nor wholly closed to it, neither guaranteeing that the future will be better than the present nor ruling out all hope of some improvement. A theology of emergent probability is to be contrasted with Moltmann's theology of hope.[56]

(3) *Sin.* Any social order which intends to endure must be based on a certain realism about human beings and, therefore, on a theory of sin and a *praxis* for dealing with it. However sin is defined, its energies must be given shape, since sinful energies overlooked in theory are certain to find outlets in practice. Thus some hypothesize that democratic capitalism is based on self-interest, greed, acquisitiveness, egotism.[57] Others hypothesize that socialism—particularly in its egalitarianism—is based upon envy and resentment.[58] Since no realis-

tic social order can be based on expectations of heroic or even consistently virtuous behavior, it seems that a realistic social order must be designed around ideals rather lower than Christian ideals. In a pluralist social system, in particular, the rules should not be so defined that every participant must, in effect, be a practicing Christian. (It is possible but not likely that Christian rules might be arrived at consensually.)

(4) *Practical wisdom.* The practical world depends as much on insight and intelligence as does the intellectual world. Certainly the economic system does. The role and conditions of insight in particular societies need close and concrete study.

(5) *The Individual.* The most distinctive contribution of Judaism and Christianity to social theory is the identification of the individual conscience as a major source of social energy. Not all energy comes from authority, as the ancients held; nor from social structures, as the Marxists hold; nor from historical necessity; nor from "class struggle," etc. The individual is an originating source of insight, decision, and action.

(6) *Community.* Human experience is by destiny familial. Primordially, it has been centered in family, clan, tribe, people. As the institutions of social organization become differentiated, human sociality has also moved outward into the institutions of the state, the society, the economy, the universities, the churches, etc. In the economic sphere today, forms of sociality seem far more prevalent than individualism. In democratic capitalist nations a variety of social organisms (including the business enterprise and the corporation) have replaced or have been added to loyalties of family and clan. For some persons today, colleagues in the workplace are closer to them than family. The business corporation, in particular, is a relatively new organism in social history. It is, perhaps, the single best secular analogue to the church. It is a legal person, a unitary being, constituted by voluntary contract, animated by social purposes, and subject to pervasive disciplines. Churches themselves are often incorporated. The kinds of community and sociality which corporations make possible within corporations and in the social field around them deserve concrete description.

(7) *Distribution.* The classic moralist's principle for the economic order is distributive justice. This principle was a first principle in traditional societies which had no moral decision to make about growth. Traditional societies were, on the whole, static. When the sum of worldly goods is finite, limited, and already known, traditional

ethicists properly concentrate attention upon how the known store of goods ought to be distributed. Until the rise of democratic capitalism, a permanent condition of poverty was taken as a given. Indeed, in the France of the 1780s four-fifths of all French families spent 90 percent of their incomes simply on buying bread—only bread—to stay alive. In 1800, fewer than 1,000 people in the whole of Germany had incomes as high as $1,000. In Great Britain from 1800 until 1850, after the sudden capitalist "takeoff" which began in 1780, real wages quadrupled, then quadrupled again between 1850 and 1900.[59] The world had never seen anything like it. After World War II, the internationalization of such methods enabled dozens of other nations—but not all nations—to experience even more rapid growth. The fact that economic growth has suddenly become a matter of human freedom has introduced an ethical principle prior to distributive justice. Moral decisions about growth and productivity are prior, both in logic and in the real world, to questions of distribution. What is not produced cannot be distributed, and choices about production condition choices about distribution.

(8) *Scarcity.* In the current lively debate about "the limits of growth"—recently summarized brilliantly by Seymour Martin Lipset[60] —three separate issues are involved. One is a question of fact and empirical probability. Here the critics of "the Club of Rome" seem to be gaining the upper hand. The second concerns the role of technology and science. It seems odd that so soon after the disastrous struggles between religion and science in preceding generations so many theologians, like Jurgen Moltmann,[61] should be trying to enlist the Christian church in opposition to growth. This is doubly odd since there are many new directions in which technology and science can yet turn, depending largely on the wisdom, needs, and investments of individuals and societies. Slowdowns in some directions do not entail slowdowns in others. Thirdly, some hold that democratic capitalism is based on an assumption of plenty. Nothing could be further from the truth. As Peter Clecak shows,[62] the distributive ethics of socialism do depend upon economic abundance and become irrelevant under conditions of scarcity. A market system, by contrast, is designed to deal efficiently either with scarcity or with abundance. A "no-growth," "limited," "economy of scarcity" is not at all incompatible with a market system; scarce items have long been allocated by markets. Scarcity can offer cruel dilemmas. It does not make democratic capitalism impossible; indeed, democratic capitalism—and modern economics—were invented as methods for escaping the Malthusian trap of scarcity.

Democratic Capitalism and the Corporation

For reasons of space, I am not able to include here a section on the theology of democratic capitalism. From very general considerations about the theology of economics, we must move in an abbreviated fashion to the question at hand. Yet a few words of elucidation are necessary. For, to encourage young people, precisely as Christians and Jews, to turn their idealism and longing for service to the corporate world, without at the same time offering them a reason why democratic capitalism is, from a theological point of view, an acceptable or even a good system, would be to plunge them into bad faith. Put with exquisite succinctness, that reason is the connection, in practice and in theory, between political liberty (human rights) and democratic capitalism.

A Justification Based on Freedom

Even those monks of old who washed dishes, did the laundry, swept the floors, pruned the living vines in the vineyards, milked the cows, or copied manuscripts in tedious labor knew that they served the Kingdom of God and the liberation of humankind. So it is also with the contemporary laborer, however humble, in the contemporary corporation, however modest or even frivolous its product. To serve human needs, desires, and rational interests is also, in its fashion, to serve human liberty, conscience, and God. Only if we can make an affirmative theological judgment about democratic capitalism can we develop a plausible theology of the lay world and a theology of work. Otherwise, no one is in good faith except those determined to destroy an evil system.

In this respect, the Freedom House charts of the 156 nations of the world dramatize graphically a fact that is slowly becoming well known: There are no instances of socialist states which are also democratic.[63] De facto, there appears to be a clear relationship between political liberty and economic liberty. Human rights seem clearly to depend on a differentiated system in which the economic system is relatively free, the political system relatively free, and the moral-cultural system relatively free. But this relationship appears to be a relationship of theory as well as of fact. It is difficult to see, even in theory, how a political system can be free if individuals are not free to make their own economic decisions. If printing presses are not free of government economic controls, for example, it is not likely that ideas can circulate freely. Indeed, the Polish government maintains totalitarian control less by the use of police and armies (although these there are in abundance) than by total legal control over wages, prices, interest, contracts, and every other aspect of economic behavior.[64] Economic totalitarianism is constituted by total public control and total public "accountability."

Accountability vs. Subordination

Under democratic capitalism, "accountability" must be clearly distinguished from "subordination." The churches must not, through institutional controls, be made subordinate to the state in their decisions of conscience. The political system must not be subordinated to economic institutions. The economic system must not become subordinate to the political or religious system. To return to state or church control over economic behavior would be to return to mercantilism or, as Weber called it, *patrinomial capitalism:* a collapsing of the tripartite differentiation of the economic, the political, and the moral-cultural systems. The three interdependent but autonomous systems of democratic capitalism are accountable to each other, and to the citizens through whom they each have their historical existence. But no one of them can be permitted to become subordinated to the other two.

Each of the three systems may properly, and often must, criticize the other two, inject new ideas into them, and impose many legitimate sanctions upon them short of subordinating the other two to itself. For each of the three systems, "laissez-faire" is impermissible. Those of us who believe in a strong state, active even in the economic sphere, must be especially alert to the dangers of confusing "accountability" with "subordination." A great deal can be accomplished through persuasion, public criticism, and public protest. Each of the three systems is vulnerable to public opinion, for each depends for its daily functioning on a good reputation and a favorable climate of ideas. Each must appeal to voluntary support from citizens free to choose against them. Each must be accountable to its own internal system and, on the basis of autonomy and equality, to the other two systems from which it has been differentiated—but not by any means been given carte blanche.

An Empirical Perspective

In the real world, utopian theories of liberty are out of place. No perfectly free, just, or rational society has existed or ever will exist. This fact and this expectation are wholly consistent both with Christian conceptions of original sin and with the nonutopian liberal political philosophies of the West. Democratic capitalism is not without sin. Yet no one can plausibly claim that the tripartite system of democratic capitalism is inferior in its political liberties, broad distribution of benefits, and productive achievements to any historical alternative yet experienced by the human race. It need not fear empirical comparisons with traditional and socialist societies.

In the U.S., the largest proportion of workers in America, among them many Christians and Jews, work for small corporations. In so doing, they build the material economic base on which a society of liberty depends for its political and cultural liberties. Another large proportion of Christians and Jews work for "large" corporations, but most of these are rather modest in size. They, too, serve liberty as well as their own rational self-interest. About 14 million work for the top-500 corporations, and of these some 8.5 million work for the 100 largest corporations. While these giants carry with them the dangers of great size, they are absolutely essential to the tasks set before them. The airliners that carried most of us to this meeting could not be built by small corporations. Nor would such corporations be less dangerous if they were owned and operated by the state. Indeed, it is almost certain that such corporations, if owned by the state, would run at deficits and perform far less humanely and far less efficiently than at present. Those who have had experience with government-owned and government-controlled enterprises have had reason to observe the difference in morale and performance prevalent in such industries.

The Moral Threat: Corporate Power or State Power?

What Christians and Jews who labor for large corporations most lack is an intellectual and moral theory which would (1) express the high spiritual vocation their work serves; (2) articulate the ideals of democratic capitalism which would enable them to judge and to improve upon their present practice; and (3) provide concrete guidance in the many decisions they must reach every day. Executives have considerable discretion over such decisions. With a set of principles and case studies, they could no doubt tilt many of their decisions so as to align them better with the ideals put forward by the moral-cultural system which plays so important a role in the tripartite system by which we live. Such executives are played false by moral-cultural leaders who misunderstand the ideals of democratic capitalism, and who manifest so many forms of naïveté and utopianism about government officials.

While moral-cultural leaders speak earnestly about the need for "accountability" in the economic system, they have not yet shown evidence of thinking clearly about the consequences of vesting such systems of accountability in the state. There is a serious imbalance in the analysis put forward by ethicisits about the moral dangers of selfishness, immorality, and corruption in the economic system. No parallel analysis has yet been put forward about the moral dangers of selfishness, immorality, and corruption in the political system.[65] From one point of view, the public interest is best served by an economic system powerful enough to resist and to restrain the political system. For the classic danger to liberal ideals comes far more from the tyranny of the public sector than from the sins of the private sector. Scholars determined to be as neutral as possible between the claims of large corporations and the state must, in fairness, begin to analyze the specific lack of accountability, the specific corruptions, and the specific evils endemic to the public sector, as they already do those of the private sector.

I would advise intelligent, ambitious, and morally serious young Christians and Jews to awaken to the growing dangers of statism. They will better save their souls and serve the cause of the Kingdom of God all around the world by restoring the liberty and power of the private sector than by working for the state. I would propose for the consideration of theologians the notion that the prevailing moral threat in our era may not be the power of the corporations; but that it may well be the growing power and irresponsibility of the state.

The health of the Christian church and the Jewish people in the next century will depend to an extraordinary degree on the perspicacity of the present generation in discerning where the greater danger lies, and in throwing its weight with the weaker party. Merely to follow the conventional wisdom on these matters would be to betray the unrestricted drive to understand.

The Praxis *of Democratic Capitalism*

Even though space is limited, it would be intellectually unsatisfying to leave this subject without making some comments on the moral practice that flows from the theology of the corporation outlined so briefly above. Since democratic capitalism is a tripartite system, it is wrong to think of it as merely a free-enterprise system. The economic system is only one of three systems, each of which has claims upon our loyalty, each of which is indispensable for the functionings of the other. Although there is much to be gained when the leaders of each system respect the relative autonomy of the other two, and when each system fulfills its own specific responsibilities first, no one of these three systems stands alone. As a human being, each of us is at once a citizen of a democracy, an economic worker, and a moral agent within a culture. Not only is it possible for an economic system to be suffused with moral purpose and religious belief; Max Weber argued that democratic capitalism is distinctive among other commercial systems in the world *because of* the religious and moral value it attaches to commerce. It is one thing to tolerate commerce and to regard it as a vulgar necessity. It is another to regard it as the fulfillment of a vocation from God and a way of cooperating in the completion of Creation as God intended it.

To be sure, a fully differentiated type of democratic capitalism cannot impose a religious vocation and a religious self-understanding upon all who partake in it. Pluralism requires openness to other motivations and understandings. There are in all cultures and at all times persons who believe that "in the real world," power and wealth are actual subjects of realistic strivings, despite the efforts of moralists to insist upon the importance of virtue and high-mindedness. Otherwise, the dialogues of Socrates and Thrasymachus and the dialectical arguments of Aristotle about the nature of "true" happiness would have no relevance for the ages.

The Moral-Cultural System Supplies a "Way of Life"

In their useful case book, *Full Value,* Oliver F. Williams, C.S.C., and John W. Houck mention two categories of moral flaws often cited by a public "losing confidence" in the moral integrity of business:
1. Numerous violations of legal codes that have come to the attention of the public, such as price fixing, tax law violations, and bribery.
2. Breaches of the professional code of ethics by business persons, such as deceptive advertising, selling company secrets, and dishonesty in expense accounts.[66]

These problems are immemorial. No system will ever eliminate them. They are encountered analogously, in the professions of politics, government service, the academy, and others. Yet every immorality must be struggled against. Father Williams and Professor Houck quite successfully juxtapose the power of "the Christian story," in its biblical immediacy, to concrete problems Christians in the world of business are likely to meet. This is an excellent example of the way the moral-cultural system shapes the attitudes and behavior of those within an economic system. It vivifies, directs, and restrains the latter not by subordinating it institutionally but by supplying it with a "way of life" that gives it spirit.

There is another category of moral problems which the cases they present open up, however: the problem of a democratic capitalist system in interaction with an entire world of other cultures and other economic and political systems. They mention, for example, the problems of Gulf and Western in the Dominican Republic, an American hotel chain in Jamaica, a resolution of the U.S. Senate on world hunger, and a corporation with branches in South Africa. In these cases, Williams and Houck raise important points.

Conclusion

From the theology of economics sketched above and even more from the notes offered toward a theology of democratic capitalism, it follows that U.S. business enterprises abroad represent not simply an economic system alone but also a political and a moral-cultural system. They are, willy-nilly, agents of democratic capitalism, not only of free enterprise. Moreover, unless they succeed in establishing on foreign soil at least some of the political culture and some of the moral culture in which democratic capitalism can be incarnated, they are doomed to lose spiritual legitimacy. Without the latter, freely bestowed, they are bound to be regarded as illegitimate enterprises. In the long run—and, often enough, even in the short run of five or ten years—such moral status is bound to have damaging consequences, first to the business enterprises themselves, but also to the political system and the moral-cultural system which they represent.

On the one hand, impossible political and cultural burdens cannot be imposed on business enterprises. They have not been constituted as primary agents of the political system or of the moral-cultural system. To ask them to do well with what they are not set up to do is to ask too much. On the other hand, they cannot escape the burden of carrying with them the presuppositions of their own native political system and moral-cultural system. To these, too, they must do at least rough justice.

Direct political interference on the part of American enterprises abroad would be fiercely, and properly, resisted. So would a sort of tacit moral-cultural imperialism. Yet the international "war of ideas" cannot be evaded. In cultures which are not democratic capitalist, the differentiation between an economic system, political system, and moral system is not observed. Regimes of both the traditional authoritarian type and the socialist type have unitary theories and practices of control. The differentiation required by democratic capitalism is currently attacked from the side of traditional authoritarianism and from the side of socialist authoritarianism. Corporations must become far more intellectually aware of the maelstrom of ideas, beliefs, and practices into which they are entering.

In this respect, the debate about the "social responsibility" of business has been badly drawn. Business enterprises are not designed to be either political institutions or moral-cultural institutions, But they are, as it were, plants that cannot flourish independently of the trebly differentiated roots from which they have sprung. Their responsibility *to themselves* entails sophisticated attention to the political and moral-cultural requirements of their own existence. Such are the facts of life of democratic capitalism.

World Poverty and Hunger

The most urgent question posed by Father Williams and Professor Houck concerns world poverty and hunger. They borrow from Father Hesburgh's *The Humane Imperative*[67] the image of five spacemen in a space ship, one of whom (representing the populations of the democratic capitalist lands) produces and uses nearly 80 percent of the world's goods. Two centuries ago, the United States and Western Europe were not democratic-capitalist lands, nor had they escaped from poverty. They were state-controlled mercantilist societies. Poverty within them was widespread. Famines had not been eliminated. Transport, living conditions, and diet were "underdeveloped." These nations, like others, were threatened with "the Malthusian trap." How did they escape the poverty, disease, ignorance, and material precariousness they then shared with most of the rest of the world.

They did it by following an *idea.* Many scoffed at the idea. Many rejected it. It is not an idea complete once and for all time. It is a dynamic idea. It is experimental in temper. It is rooted in the differentiation of the economic, the political, and the moral-cultural systems. It interprets human society as composed by the Creator so as to have its greatest source of social dynamism in the imagination, initiative, and liberty of the human individual. It is an idea intended for all nations. It is an idea whose express purpose is to increase the material wealth of nations, and at the very least to eliminate famine and poverty.

There are today no examples of democratic capitalist nations which cannot feed themselves. Major socialist nations, which used to be

net exporters of food, are no longer able to feed themsevles.[68] Many
traditional societies, down through history subject to recurrent famine,
still endure famine. None of this hunger is necessary. It is not due to
ignorance about agriculture. Its sources are pre-eminently to be found
in economic and political institutions which needlessly stifle elementary economic growth.

Facing hunger and poverty, no person of conscience can remain
indifferent. The great intellectual and moral argument of our time is
not whether we should do all we can to raise the material wealth of all
nations. The great questions are *what* we ought to do and *how*. The
greatest irresponsibility of all would be to pretend that we know
nothing about the secrets of how to produce wealth, or that such secrets
were not implanted on this earth by the Maker of all things, so that his
creatures, by trial and error, would in due course discover them.

It is the ethical responsibility of Christians who enter the business
corporation to recognize that their way of life has a twofold importance
for the entire world: the spiritual importance of a set of ideas and the
material importance of showing all nations a way out of famine and
misery. Now that the secrets of how to produce wealth are known,
famine and misery spring not from the will of God but from the will of
man.

NOTES

1. Consultation at the American Enterprise Institute, April 2, 1980. See
also Weber: "The modern rational organization of the capitalistic enterprise
would not have been possible without . . . the separation of business from the
household . . . The indispensable requisites for this independence . . .
[include] our legal separation of corporate from personal property." Max
Weber, *The Protestant Ethic and the Spirit of Capitalism,* trans. Talcott Parsons
(New York: Charles Scribner's Sons, 1958), pp. 21–22.

2. "We shall view the [early] Christian movement . . . not as a proletarian
mass movement but as a relatively small cluster of more or less intense groups,
largely middle class in origin." Robert M. Grant, *Early Christianity and Society*
(New York: Harper & Row, 1977), p. 11.

3. For a convenient analytic breakdown of the social systems of the world's
156 nations consult: Raymond D. Gastil (ed.), *Freedom in the World 1979* (New
York: Freedom House, 1979), pp. 40–41.

4. "A system of imperative coordination [authority] will be called 'traditional' if legitimacy is claimed for it and believed in on the basis that the sanctity
of the order and the attendant powers of control as they have been handed

down from the past 'have always existed.' " *The Theory of Social and Economic Organization*, trans. A. M. Henderson and Talcott Parsons (New York: Free Press, 1947), p. 341.

Weber contrasted "traditional" society with two other types, *charismatic* and *legal-rational:* "In traditionally stereotyped periods, charisma is the greatest revolutionary force. . . . It may . . . result in a radical alteration of the central system of attitudes and directions of action with a completely new orientation of all attitudes toward the different problems and structures of the 'world.' " *Ibid.*, p. 363. "In legal [rational] authority, submission does not rest upon the belief and devotion to charismatically gifted persons, like prophets and heroes, or upon sacred tradition . . . [It] is based upon an impersonal bond to the generally defined and functional 'duty of office.' The official duty . . . is fixed by rationally established norms, by enactments, decrees, and regulations . . ." Max Weber, "Social Psychology of the World's Religions," in H. H. Gerth and C. Wright Mills (eds.), *From Max Weber* (New York: Oxford University Press, 1958), p. 299. See also Little, n. 18 below.

5. "The law is prone to emphasize that the corporation is a body chartered or recognized by the state; that it is a formal agreement, in the nature of a contract, among people joined in a common purpose; that it can hold property, contract, and sue and be sued in a common name; and that it has a length of life not subject to the lives of its members." Edward S. Mason, "Corporation," *International Encyclopedia of the Social Sciences*, 3:396. Cf. also: John P. Davis, *Corporations* (New York: Putnam, 1961), reprint of 1905 edition; A. Berle and Gardiner C. Means, *The Modern Corporation and Private Property*, rev. ed. (New York: Harcourt Brace Jovanovich, 1968); Peter F. Drucker, *Concept of the Corporation* (New York: Day, 1946); Richard J. Barber, *The American Corporation* (New York: Dutton, 1970). This last makes severe criticisms of the corporation. By contrast, Robert Hessen argues that the state does not create corporations, but only registers their "birth certificates." See *In Defense of the Corporation* (Stanford, Calif.: Hoover Institution Press, 1979).

6. "Modern rational capitalism has need . . . of a calculable legal system and of administration in terms of formal rules . . . Such a legal system and such administration have been available for economic activity in a comparative state of legal and formalistic perfection only in the Occident." Weber, *The Protestant Ethic*, p. 25.

7. Bernard J. Lonergan, *Insight: A Study of Human Understanding*, rev. students' ed. (New York: Philosophical Library, 1965), pp. 121–28.

8. Weber, *The Protestant Ethic*, pp. 21–22.

9. Peter L. Berger and Richard John Neuhaus, *To Empower People* (Washington: American Enterprise Institute, 1977). Berger and Neuhaus specifically exclude the large corporations from their list of "mediating structures." Yet most of the 700,000 "large corporations" outside the top 500 are no larger than individual universities. Thus, most "large" corporations and all "small businesses" presumably do qualify as mediating structures. In my view, even the largest corporations are significant defenses against the power of the state. In an extended but real sense, General Motors is a "mediating structure" (it is

smaller than the Lutheran church), and its individual units are as much "mediating structures" as parishes are.

10. Among representative documents one might consult, for Protestantism: J. H. Oldham (ed.), *The Churches Survey Their Task* (London: Allen & Unwin, 1937); see chap. 3, the Oxford Conference (forerunner of the World Council of Churches) "Report on Church, Community, and State in Relation to the Economic Order"; and from the General Board of the National Council of the Churches of Christ in the U.S.A., "Christian Concern and Responsibility for Economic Life," February 24, 1966. For Catholicism: Joseph Gremillion (ed.), *The Gospel of Peace and Justice* (Maryknoll, N.Y.: Orbis Books, 1976). Questions are raised about this theology by, among others: Ernest W. Lefever, *Amsterdam to Nairobi* (Washington: Ethics and Public Policy Center, 1979); Edward Norman, *Christianity and the World Order* (New York: Oxford University Press, 1979); Michael Novak, "Liberation Theology and the Pope," *Commentary* 67 (June 1979): 60–64, and "The Politics of John Paul II," *Commentary* 68 (December 1979): 56–61.

11. For a survey see B. Bruce-Briggs (ed.), *The New Class?* (New Brunswick, N.J.: Transaction Books, 1979). The notion of the new class was first employed by writers on the left: David T. Bazelon, *Power in America* (New York: New American Library, 1967); John Kenneth Galbraith, *The Affluent Society*, 3d rev. ed. (Boston: Houghton Mifflin, 1976), chap. 14; Michael Harrington, *Toward a Democratic Left* (New York: Macmillan Co., 1968), chap. 10. See also my "Needing Niebuhr Again," *Commentary* 54 (September 1972): 52–60.

12. See Garry Wills, *Politics and Catholic Freedom* (1964, out of print).

13. This point was made to me recently by the provost of a major university, who cited in evidence the transcripts of students and faculty of the divinity school on campus. Few, he asserted, had rigorous intellectual training in economics or public policy.

14. ". . . Asceticism, the more strongly it gripped an individual, simply served to drive him farther away from everyday life, because the holiest task was definitely to surpass all worldly morality. Luther . . . had repudiated that tendency, and Calvinism simply took this over from him. . . . Now every Christian had to be a monk all his life. . . . Those passionately spiritual natures which had formally supplied the highest type of monk were now forced to pursue their ascetic ideals within mundane occupations." Weber, *The Protestant Ethic*, p. 121.

15. See, e.g., P. T. Bauer, "Western Guilt and Third World Poverty," *Commentary* 61 (January 1976): 31–38.

16. J. L. Talmon, *The Origins of Totalitarian Democracy* (Chicago: Praeger, 1960).

17. There have been "over 750 famines spanning nearly six millenniums . . . Mediterranean Europe was the region of highest famine occurrence in the 501 B.C.–A.D. 500 time period. Famines were recorded prior to 450 B.C., some lasting twenty years, but the first century A.D. was noted for disastrous famines. Thousands perished in the famine of A.D. 6 . . . Eastern Europe was the region

of highest famine occurrence in the A.D. 1501–1700 time period. . . . More than 150 famines were recorded here in a 200-year period. . . . Asia was the region of highest famine occurrence from 1701–1974. . . . The twentieth century has been the era of the great Russian/USSR famines." *Food and Social Policy I*, ed. Gary H. Koerselman and Kay E. Dull (Ames: Iowa State University Press, 1978), pp. 14–16. ". . . the super-death-rate from acute famine and epidemics virtually disappeared during the 18th century in Western Europe because of agricultural advances, international trade that improved the availability of all resources, and better hygienic defenses (the famine of 1847 in Ireland was atypical)." *Encyclopaedia Britannica*, 15th ed., s.v. "Population."

Citing E. Parmalee Prentice, *Hunger and History* (New York: Harper & Bros., 1939), Henry Hazlitt writes:

> The dwellings of medieval laborers were hovels—the walls made of a few boards cemented with mud and leaves. Rushes and reeds or heather made the thatch for the roof. Inside the houses there was a single room, or in some cases two rooms, not plastered and without floor, ceiling, chimney, fireplace or bed, and here the owner, his family and his animals lived and died. There was no sewage for the houses, no drainage, except surface drainage for the streets, no water supply beyond that provided by the town pump, and no knowledge of the simplest forms of sanitation. 'Rye and oats furnished the bread and drink of the great body of the people of Europe . . . Precariousness of livelihood, alternations between feasting and starvation, droughts, scarcities, famines, crime, violence, murrains, scurvy, leprosy, typhoid diseases, wars, pestilences and plagues'—made part of medieval life to a degree with which we are wholly unacquainted in the Western world of the present day.

Citing William Farr, "The Influence of Scarcities and of the High Prices of Wheat on the Morality of the People of England," *Journal of the Royal Statistical Society* 9 (February 16, 1846), Hazlitt continues:

> And, ever-recurring, there was famine: 'In the eleventh and twelfth centuries famine (in England) is recorded every fourteen years, on an average, and the people suffered twenty years of famine in two hundred years. In the thirteenth century the list exhibits the same proportion of famine' . . . One writer has compiled a detailed summary of twenty-two famines in the thirteenth century in the British Isles, with such typical entries as: '1235: Famine and plague in England; 20,000 persons die in London; people eat horse-flesh, bark of trees, grass, etc.' 1005: famine in England. 1016: famine throughout Europe. 1064–72: seven years' famine in Egypt. 1148–59: eleven years' famine in India. 1344–45: great famine in India. 1396–1407: the Durga Devi famine in India, lasting twelve years. 1586: famine in England giving rise to the Poor Law system. 1661: famine in India; no rain fell for two years. 1769–70: great famine in Bengal; a third of the population—10 million persons—perished. 1783: the Chalisa famine in India. 1790–92: the Deju Bara, or skull famine, in India, so called because the dead were too numerous to be

buried. This list is incomplete—as probably any list would be. In the winter of 1709, for example, in France, more than a million persons, according to the figures of the time, died out of a population of 20 millions.

Henry Hazlitt, *The Conquest of Poverty* (New Rochelle, N.Y.: Arlington House, 1973), pp. 14–15.

18. On conceptual differences in kinds of "order," see David Little, *Religion, Order, and the Law* (New York: Oxford University Press, 1970), chap. 1.

19. ". . . Free competition, however, though justified and quite useful within certain limits, cannot be an adequate controlling principle in economic affairs. . . . All the institutions of public and social life must be imbued with the spirit of justice, and this justice must above all be truly operative. It must build up a juridical and social order able to pervade all economic activity. Social charity should be, as it were, the soul of this order." Pope Pius XI, *Quadragesimo Anno*, par. 88.

20. "Disturbing factors are frequently present in the form of the frightful disparities between excessively rich individuals and groups on the one hand and, on the other hand, the majority made up of the poor or, indeed, of the destitute . . . Everything will depend on whether these differences and contrasts in the sphere of the possession of goods will be systematically reduced through truly effective means. . ." Pope John Paul II, Address to the United Nations General Assembly, October 2, 1979. The pope insisted in another talk in America that the wealthier nations should "give of their substance, not only of their plenty."

21. "Foreign aid . . . to underdeveloped countries . . . has had far-reaching and sometimes brutal consequences, enormous costs, little success, and virtually no adverse criticism . . . Economic achievement depends primarily on people's aptitudes and attitudes (e.g., interest in material success) and their social institutions and political arrangements . . . not on handouts." P. T. Bauer, "Foreign Aid, Forever?" *Encounter* 42 (March 1974): 15, 17–18.

22. There is already a small body of literature unmasking this ideology. Yet much remains to be done. See Ludwig von Mises, *The Anti-Capitalistic Mentality* (South Holland, Ill.: Libertarian Press, 1972); F. A. Hayek (ed.), *Capitalism and the Historians* (Chicago: University of Chicago Press, 1954); Ernest van den Haag, *Capitalism: Sources of Hostility* (New Rochelle, N.Y.: Epoch Books, 1979); Michael Novak (ed.), *The Denigration of Capitalism* (Washington: American Enterprise Institute, 1979).

23. "The impulse to acquisition, pursuit of gain, of money, of the greatest possible amount of money, has in itself nothing to do with capitalism. . . . It should be taught in the kindergarten of cultural history that this naive idea of capitalism must be given up once and for all." Weber, *The Protestant Ethic*, p. 17.

24. J. H. Oldham (ed.), *The Churches Survey Their Task* (London: Allen & Unwin, 1937), pp. 104–5.

25. See Sloan Wilson, *The Man in the Gray Flannel Suit* (Cambridge, Mass.: Robert Bentley, 1979); see also the concept of the "other-directed" personality

in David Riesman et al., *The Lonely Crowd* (New Haven, Conn.: Yale University Press, 1950).

26. A few leads for further exploration are suggested in my own *The American Vision: An Essay on the Future of Democratic Capitalism* (Washington: American Enterprise Institute, 1978).

27. "The impulse to acquisition . . . has in itself nothing to do with capitalism. . . . Capitalism *may* even be identical with the restraint, or at least a rational tempering, of this irrational impulse." Weber, *The Protestant Ethic*, p. 17.

28. ". . . [Unlike Smith] the Sentimental School assumed and asserted that there were natural and self-correcting limits to the pursuit of self-interest." Irving Kristol, "Adam Smith and the Spirit of Capitalism," in *The Great Ideas Today 1976* (Chicago: Encyclopaedia Britannica, 1976), p. 289. In *The Theory of Moral Sentiments* (Part III, chap. 1), Adam Smith described the perfection of human nature as something far beyond self-interest, unless the latter is seen to include sympathy, benevolence, and altruism: "We endeavor to examine our own conduct as we imagine any other fair and impartial spectator would view it. . . . [It follows that] to feel much for others, and little for ourselves, that to restrain our selfish, and to indulge our benevolent, affections, constitutes the perfection of human nature." Cf. Garry Wills, "Benevolent Adam Smith," *New York Review of Books*, February 9, 1978.

29. The hidden premise in many discussions of the free market and of "private selfishness" is that public officials are less selfish, more public-spirited, *by definition.* Little in the history of state tyranny and state bureaucracy supports this premise. One must distinguish, further, two quite different types of rationality. One is the rationality which emerges as the calculus of individual choices in the market. The other is the rationality imposed by planners. Evidence suggests that, while neither form of rationality is complete, the former is more worthy of rational trust. Those who criticize the rationality of the market are usually utopian with respect to the rationality of planners. This is the new Constantinianism. A traditional Catholic culture like that of Latin America is especially prone to it. An alliance between commissars and clerics under "Christian Marxism" is a modern version of a traditional society imposing a unitary moral vision on the political system and the economic system.

30. U.S. Bureau of the Census, *Statistical Abstract of the United States, 1979* (Washington: U.S. Dept. of Commerce, 1979), p. 272.

31. U.S. Small Business Administration, *Facts About Small Business and the U.S. Small Business Administration* (Washington: U.S. Small Business Administration, n.d.), p. 1.

32. According to the chief economist of the National Small Business Association (telephone inquiry).

33. SBA, *Facts*, p. 4.

34. According to an economist at the U.S. Small Business Administration (telephone inquiry).

35. SBA, *Facts*, p. 3. and Bureau of the Census, *Statistical Abstract, 1979*, p. 392.

36. Extrapolation from quoted data, *ibid.*

37. The top-100 firms hold 65 percent of the assets of "the *Fortune* 500," make 65 percent of the annual gross sales, and employ 58 percent of the workforce. The fifth 100 hold 4 percent of the assets, make 4 percent of the sales, and employ 5 percent of the workers. *The Fortune Directory* (New York: Time, Inc., 1976). See also, Bureau of the Census, *Statistical Abstract*, 1979, pp. 160, 313.

38. *The Fortune Directory*, 1976.

39. Bureau of the Census, *Statistical Abstract*, 1979, p. 572.

40. Stephen Roman and Eugen Loebl, *The Responsible Society* (New York: Regina Ryan Books/Two Continents, 1977).

41. "The forces that made this industrial growth possible were released by the Civil War, but they were bound in any event to have made their influence felt." Foster Rhea Dulles, *The United States Since 1865* (Ann Arbor: University of Michigan Press, 1959), p. 52. Most historians write rather negatively of business and the corporations in the U.S. Scholars should perhaps reconsider the evidence in the light of the prevalence of anti-capitalist bias, so that the evidence may speak for itself.

42. See Lonergan's discussion of insight in various forms of common sense and its systematic biases. *Insight*, chaps. 6 and 7.

43. "The intellectual's hostility to the businessman presents no mystery, as the two have, by function, wholly different standards, so that the businessman's normal conduct appears blameworthy if judged by the criteria valid for the intellectual's conduct. . . . The businessman offers to the public 'goods' defined as anything the public will buy; the intellectual seeks to teach what is 'good,' and to him some of the goods offered are things of no value which the public should be discouraged from wanting." Bertrand de Jouvenal, "The Treatment of Capitalism by Continental Intellectuals," in Hayek (ed.), *Capitalism and the Historians*, pp. 116–18.

44. Berle and Means, *The Modern Corporation and Private Property*. Cf. Crawford H. Greenewalt, *The Uncommon Man: The Individual in the Organization* (New York: McGraw-Hill, 1959).

45. U.S. Bureau of the Census, *Household Income in 1977* (Washington: U.S. Dept. of Commerce, 1977) p. 1. Bureau of the Census, *Statistical Abstract*, p. 266.

46. Ben Stein, *The View From Sunset Boulevard* (New York: Basic Books, 1979).

47. In describing corporate wealth, socialists commonly fail to distinguish newcomers to wealth from older families of wealth. In each generation, new fortunes are being made (McDonald's, Xerox, Polaroid, Texas Instruments) as new technologies are invented and new services organized, while fortunes based on obsolete technologies are often dissipated. Downward mobility is an important feature of the system, and may have only a slightly smaller frequency than upward mobility. There is also a fascinating "circulation of elites" in all three systems (economic, political, moral-cultural). Each generation of successful people, moreover, has great difficulty in passing on its

talents, skills, drive, motivation and success to the next generation. It is easier to give children "every advantage money can buy" than to pass on qualities of intelligence and character.

48. U.S. Bureau of Economic Analysis, *Special Survey of U.S. Multinational Companies, 1970* (Washington: U.S. Bureau of Economic Analysis, 1970).

49. Sperry Lea and Simon Webley, *Multinational Corporations in Developed Countries* (Washington: British-North American Comm., 1973), p. 1.

50. See Jeanne Kirkpatrick, "Dictatorships and Double Standards," *Commentary* 68 (November 1979): 44.

51. James F. McDivitt and Gerald Manners, *Minerals and Men,* rev. ed. (Baltimore: Johns Hopkins University Press, 1974), pp. 59–62.

52. See, e.g., Richard J. Barnet and Ronald E. Miller, *Global Reach: The Power of the Multinational Corporations* (New York: Simon & Schuster, 1974). Also see: Ralph K. Winter, *Government and the Corporation* (Washington: American Enterprise Institute, 1978), chap. 3; Barber, *The American Corporation.*

53. See Little, *Religion, Order, and the Law,* chap. 1.

54. Michael Novak, *The Experience of Nothingness* (New York: Harper & Row, 1970).

55. Lonergan, *Insight.*

56. See Jürgen Moltmann, *Theology of Hope* (New York; Harper & Row, 1967).

57. R. H. Tawney is typical in this regard. " . . . The quality in modern societies which is most sharply opposed to the teaching ascribed to the Founder of the Christian Faith . . . consists in the assumption . . . that the attainment of riches is the supreme object of human endeavor and the final criterion of human success. . . . Compromise is as impossible between the Church of Christ and the idolatry of wealth, which is the practical religion of capitalist societies, as it was between the Church and the State idolatry of the Roman Empire." R. H. Tawney, *Religion and the Rise of Capitalism* (New York: New American Library, 1926), pp. 234–35. In contrast to Tawney, Milton and Rose Friedman write: "Narrow preoccupation with the economic market has led to a narrow interpretation of self-interest as myopic selfishness, as exclusive concern with immediate material rewards. Economics has been berated for allegedly drawing far-reaching conclusions from a wholly unrealistic 'economic man' who is little more than a calculating machine, responding only to monetary stimuli. That is a great mistake. Self-interest is not myopic selfishness. It is whatever it is that interests the participants, whatever they value, whatever goals they pursue." Milton and Rose Friedman, *Free to Choose* (New York: Harcourt, Brace, Jovanovich, 1980), p. 27.

58. See: Helmut Schoeck, *Envy,* trans. Michael Glenny and Betty Ross (New York: Harcourt, Brace & World, 1969); Leszek Kolakowski, *Main Currents in Marxism,* 3 vols. (New York: Oxford University Press, 1978), esp. the epilogue.

59. Paul Johnson cites these numbers in *Will Capitalism Survive?,* ed. Ernest W. Lefever (Washington: Ethics and Public Policy Center, 1979), pp. 4–5. See also his *Enemies of Society* (New York: Atheneum, 1977).

60. Seymour Martin Lipset, "Predicting the Future of Post-Industrial Society," in *The Third Century*, ed. Seymour Martin Lipset (Stanford, Calif.: Hoover Institution Press, 1979), pp. 1–35.

61. See his comments on economic growth in Jurgen Moltmann, *The Church in the Power of the Spirit* (London: SCM Press, 1977).

62. Peter Clecak, *Crooked Paths* (New York: Harper & Row, 1977), pp. 153–55.

63. ". . . Freedom is directly related to the existence of multiparty systems: the further a country is from such systems, the less freedom it is likely to have." Gastil (ed.), *Freedom in the World 1979*, pp. 39–42.

64. I visited Poland for the first time November 17–December 5, 1979, and described this point in "A Lesson in Polish Economics," *Washington Star*, December 15, 1979.

65. See Charles Wolf, Jr., "A Theory of Non-market Failures," *The Public Interest* 55 (Spring 1979): 114–33.

66. Oliver F. Williams and John W. Houck, *Full Value: Cases in Christian Business Ethics* (New York: Harper & Row, 1978), p. xv.

67. Theodore M. Hesburgh, *The Humane Imperative* (New Haven, Conn.: Yale University Press, 1974), p. 101; quoted in Williams and Houck, *Full Value*, p. 135.

68. Ideological blinders cause much needless suffering. Soviet planners know what works but cannot admit it. "By law, no Soviet citizen can farm a private plot larger than 1 acre. Nevertheless, private farmers working 1.4% of the country's arable land produce 61% of its potatoes, 34% of the eggs and 29% of the meat, milk and vegetable output." *Newsweek*, April 7, 1980, p. 21.

7. Goals of a Christian Economy and the Future of the Corporation

Charles K. Wilber and Kenneth P. Jameson

The starting point for any consideration of the role of the corporation in our economic system must be an examination of the purpose of an economic system. At a general level an economic system is a collection of social institutions and behavioral patterns that enable many people to work together to achieve goals, only some of which are material, which could not be attained as well by acting individually.[1]

There are many ways to classify goals, but the following should enjoy widespread support among Christians and others who are concerned with the conditions of humankind in the modern world:

1. Overcoming scarcity (providing for basic human needs) both collectively and individually;
2. Generating and extending freedom of choice;
3. Fostering the conditions for right relations among people — fellowship.

Every society — past, present, and future — has the task of organizing a system for producing and distributing the goods and services it needs for its own perpetuation. It must overcome scarcity by devising social institutions which will mobilize human energy for productive purposes. This productive effort must be able to provide the quantity of goods and services needed and must be allocated so that the desired kinds of goods and services are produced. To maintain its ability to produce what it needs, the economic system must distribute the production among its members in such a manner that they will have both the capacity (health and skills) and willingness (incentive) to continue working.

It is common to categorize "economic systems" with terms such as slavery, feudalism, capitalism, or socialism. All of them have had to devise social institutions to carry out these tasks. A key social institution under capitalism is private property (embodied, most importantly, in corporations) coupled with free exchange in markets. In theory it can be relied upon to overcome scarcity. Under socialism a system of public property coupled with central planning is understood as playing the same role. Both systems have had substantial success in dealing with scarcity, especially in the postwar period.

The second goal—freedom of choice—has not been achieved by most societies in history. Freedom of choice means freedom to choose which consumer goods to buy, which occupation to pursue, which leader to help select, and so on. In traditional and feudal societies freedom of choice was a moot point. Tradition determined occupation, self-sufficiency and poverty meant that few consumer goods were purchased, and rulers were selected by tradition or force. Proponents of capitalism argue that its chief virtue is that it is not only productive but it maximizes freedom of choice. Proponents of socialism argue that meaningful freedom of choice requires worker control of production, minimum income levels for all, and a political mechanism to give us the kinds of communities and environments we want and need to survive.

The third goal has never been achieved and may never be fully achieved in the future; but it remains a goal to be sought. The social institutions devised to ensure adequate production and to enable freedom of choice should also foster fellowship among the people of that society which will allow each to develop his/her potential. Fellowship thrives where people are led to cooperate in social endeavors and where there is time and opportunity to relate with each other as loving, sharing human beings. Fellowship is encouraged where social forces that erect barriers among people are minimized. For example, extreme inequality, be it in income, position, or power, makes fellowship next to impossible. Emphasis on individual self-advancement makes fellowship and solidarity difficult to maintain. Race, class, and sex discrimination generate hostility, which destroys the possibility of satisfying relationships among people.

It should be noted at the outset that it may be difficult to reconcile the conflicting demands of these three goals, and any set of social institutions will embody them in an imperfect way. Like freedom and order or justice and peace, they coexist with a degree of tension even though it is a creative tension. Different peoples at different times will assign greater value to one of the goals over another. For example, proponents of capitalism place great value on overcoming scarcity and freedom of choice; in fact, they argue that the latter makes the former possible. Fellowship is seen either as a by-product of freedom of choice or, when pursued directly, in conflict with the first two goals. Many socialists, on the other hand, argue that fellowship fosters productivity, and for them the key element in freedom of choice is its implementation in the workplace, with other aspects following from that.

Our claim is that neither of the systems is highly successful in balancing these goals, and that their success is likely to diminish as they move into the future. We suggest that a search for new and more successful paths can be enhanced by drawing upon elements of the Judeo-Christian heritage. Since we are interested in the U.S. primarily, we will start with a description of that economic system.

Adam Smith and Corporate Capitalism

The roots of capitalist economic systems can be traced to the breakup of the traditions and legal restrictions of feudalism at the end of the Middle Ages. They were replaced by an expanding system of private property in which those who did not own productive property sold their labor to those who did. Pursuit of self-interest was the motivating force of this new system. Since a person could be depended upon to act rationally to maximize his/her individual self-interest, it was thought possible to set up an automatic, self-regulating mechanism to manage economic affairs. Thus one of the goals, freedom of choice, could become a means to achieve the goal of overcoming scarcity.

From Adam Smith to today, mainstream economists have argued that the best way to overcome scarcity and to maximize personal freedom is to rely on the individual's pursuit of self-interest in a private property system regulated by the force of market competition, in which the government acts as the neutral umpire of the rules of the economic game. In order to maximize his/her income each person would have to produce something (product, service, or labor) which others wanted and were willing to pay for, and this in turn would maximize over-all production.

What prevents a system of private property based on self-interest from degenerating into a jungle where the powerful oppress the weak? According to most mainstream economists competition is the great regulator of economic life. The forces of competition insure that the economy produces those goods which people desire in the quantities that are desired. Although economists are not blind to the faults and machinations of business people, they argue that little harm can be done in a society dominated by freely competitive enterprise. If producers tried to sell products at a higher price than the market price, customers would buy from others. No one would buy at a price above the market price. On the other hand, if one attempted to pay workers less than the going wage, they would leave to take higher-wage employment. Therefore, the force of competition insures that workers are paid the going wage and consumers get their products at the lowest possible price.

As each individual attempts to maximize income and become wealthy, society, made up of the individuals living in it, benefits. Thus, private profit and public welfare become reconciled through the impersonal forces of competition.

However, this private property system as it actually developed turned out to have an Achilles' heel: competition tended to destroy itself. Competition turned out to be a foot race with the winner getting larger and larger and the losers dropping out. As a result the U.S. economy today is characterized both by largeness and by high concentration of the firms in each industry. As a result, price competition has been replaced by competition in advertising and product differentiation. In addition, of course, government has taken on a role far greater than that of an umpire.

As a result, the U.S. economy deviates substantially from the theoretical model of capitalism and has assumed a new form, called by some "monopoly capitalism" or "corporate capitalism." It is less successful in meeting the three goals we have outlined. The inequalities in income, power, and wealth make claims to fellowship highly dubious. While there is ostensibly a high degree of freedom of choice, this is true only for those in the upper levels of society. Someone without skills or a stable job has few decent choices: to eat a little more or buy a few more clothes, to continue in a dead-end job or try to get some type of dole, to vote for someone who is bound to neglect your interests or to abstain.

Thus without overlooking the accomplishments of our economy, it is apparent the three main goals are not likely to be met through business as usual.

The case can be stated even more strongly. The major accomplishments of the economic system have been in overcoming scarcity, but a look to the future suggests that even in that area performance is likely to deteriorate.

Physical and Social Limits to Growth

The American economy, particularly the corporate sector, operates on the premise of continuous economic growth. That premise is based on the assumption of continued cheap natural resources. In addition, it has been assumed that self-interest would power this economic growth without undesirable side effects. Since both assumptions are false, the American economy faces both "physical and social limits" to continued growth. Since the corporation by its very definition is dependent on growth, its future is clouded by the existence of these limits.

Physical Limits to Growth

The first limit which must be faced is based on the availability of natural resources. Note in what we say below that we are not adopting the Club of Rome stance in which the whole world system collapses at a certain point. We are saying that growth will become increasingly harder to achieve, and the U.S. will be less successful in its efforts. There are four reasons why growth based on a profligate use of natural resources is no longer a valid expectation.

First, exhaustible energy and natural-resource prices have not reflected their true scarcity because the market system has not costed them out properly. The market price reflects today's cost of obtaining the resources and ignores the fact they may be exhausted tomorrow. The implicit assumption always has been that technology will provide a substitute—so don't worry. The result is an economy based on cheap energy and natural resources. As the demand increases around the world, the resultant scarcity will limit a continuation of this resource-using style of growth.

Second, corporate capitalism has compounded the problem by competing through product innovation and differentiation and thus encouraging stylistic and physical obsolescence. When goods are designed to be "thrown away" after use, or to be used less than their physical capacity warrants because of style changes, or constructed to fall apart sooner than necessary, the result is increased wastage of energy and natural resources. Physical limits to the maintenance of this style of competition pose serious challenges to the viability of corporate capitalism.

Third, economic growth has been based on the ideology of individual consumption. The awesome power of modern advertising has spread the capitalist gospel—the good life comes from increases in consumption of individually marketable goods and services. People are urged to believe they *must* have individual washers and dryers instead of laundromats, and private automobiles instead of public transportation. Individually owned consumer durables that sit idle most of the time use up resources that would not have been necessary if they had been provided on a collective basis, i.e., laundromats, community recreational centers. This phenomenon is particularly important when viewed in a worldwide context. The earth's resources simply cannot sustain the corporate style of individualist-oriented consumption.

Fourth, pollution abatement poses physical limits to continued reliance on traditional economic growth. Corporations attempt to minimize private costs of production. Since the cost of polluted air and water have been borne by the public, production processes have tended to ignore social costs—i.e., pollution. As public awareness forces firms to internalize these costs, further limits will be imposed on continued growth.

These physical limits to growth pose difficulties and challenges to corporate capitalism. "Business-as-usual" will become impossible. Increasing scarcity of energy and natural resources will result in ever higher prices that will undermine the corporate emphasis upon product competition and individual consumption and will call for new insights and new approaches.

Social Limits to Growth

The second set of limits to growth—social limits—pose even greater challenges. The current style of corporate growth not only exacerbates physical limits but also engenders social limits that further undermine the viability of accepted patterns. These social limits are of two types. First, growth has been based on the production of "positional goods," which is self-defeating. Second, growth has relied on self-interest as its motivating force. This in turn has undermined the general "moral base" necessary for the economic system to remain viable. Let us take up each of these in turn.

First, as economic growth continues "positional" goods become an ever larger portion of total production. These are goods whose consumption is available only to those who have reached a certain economic position. But the pursuit of positional goods is self-defeating because by definition they can be enjoyed only if you have them and others don't. Growth allows others to obtain them, undermining your satisfaction while adding little to theirs since the goods have become less positional. There are two types of positional goods. One kind— large diamonds, a one-of-a-kind designer dress, etc.—are those enjoyed solely for snob appeal. They set their owner apart from the crowd. But if everyone has access to them they lose their ability to reflect supposed status. A second kind are those goods—quiet beaches, uncongested roads, servants—which are unavailable if many have access to them. If we all can afford to take a vacation, the beaches will no longer be quiet. If we all can afford cars, the roads become congested. And as we all gain more income from growth, no one has to be a servant.

The result is that peoples' expectations are constantly disappointed. This drives them to seek new goods to capture "positional" advantages. Thus the majority are constantly left frustrated and the resource-using nature of the economy is reinforced. Furthermore, this constant frustration of peoples' dreams increases disharmony and conflict among social groups. An ever more fierce struggle among social classes and occupational groups for larger shares of per capita GNP is the result. This struggle may be a key factor in the present inflationary situation and may require controls that undermine the social system. But in terms of the goals of an economic system, this struggle obviously undermines fellowship and certainly forces a reconsideration of the meaning of free choice in consumption.

The second social limit reminds us that traditional economics has forgotten one of Adam Smith's key insights. It is true he claimed that self-interest will lead to the common good if there is sufficient competition; but also, and more importantly, he claimed that this would be true *only* if most people in society accepted a general moral law as the guide for their behavior, i.e., if there were a moral base for the society.[2]

The assumption that self-interest in a competitive environment is sufficient to yield the common good is an illusion. An economy, capitalist or socialist, in which everyone—buyers, sellers, workers, managers, consumers, firms—constantly lied, stole, committed fraud and violence, etc., would neither yield the common good nor would it be stable. Yet pushed to its logical extreme, individual self-interest would suggest that it would usually be in the interest of an individual to evade the rules by which other players are guided. Similarly, the "free-rider" concept suggests that it is in an individual's interest not to cooperate in a situation of social interdependence if others do cooperate, for he/she will obtain the same benefits without any sacrifice. Therefore, why don't individuals in societies always operate in this fashion? The answer is not because of fear of the police power of the state but rather because our selfishness or tendency to maximize our material welfare at the expense of others is inhibited by a deeply ingrained moral sense, one often based on religious convictions.

Peter Berger reminds us that "No society, modern or otherwise, can survive without what Durkheim called a 'collective conscience,' that is without moral values that have general authority."[3] Hirsch reintroduces the idea of moral law into economic analysis: "truth, trust, acceptance, restraint, obligation—these are among the social virtues grounded in religious belief which . . . play a central role in the functioning of an individualistic, contractual economy . . . The point is that conventional, mutual standards of honesty and trust are public goods that are necessary inputs for much of economic output."[4]

The major source of this social morality has been the religious heritage of the precapitalist and preindustrial past. However, this legacy of religious values has diminished over time because of a twofold change: (1) the repudiation of the social character and responsibility of religion has meant its banishment to a purely private matter;[5] and (2) the elevation of self-interest as a praiseworthy virtue in turn has undermined that privatized religious ethic.

In our present-day capitalist countries, the erosion of this preindustrial, precapitalist moral legacy has proceeded slowly for two reasons: (1) economic growth has spread over a very long time period, and (2) that growth has for the most part relied on decentralized decision-making. This slow and seemingly natural process has facilitated popular acceptance and has also permitted adjustment in the moral base of the society. However, the limits to this process are now being reached in the United States, and conflict will be an inevitable result.

Capitalist development was far from conflict-free in the past. But one of its advantages was the absence of an identifiable villain behind the disruptions that occurred. Such changes resulted from the independent decisions of thousands of persons acting rationally. None could rig the rules to his or her benefit, so inequalities appeared legitimate and the undermining of religious values had no identifiable cause. The centrality of government in most developed countries today, however, provides a target for dissatisfaction. In such circumstances the legitimacy of inequalities and changes in values are open to question and to challenge. The gradual disappearance of the moral base of society forces government to attempt to act as a substitute and to provide a context that will encourage principled action among the elite while at the same time ensuring acceptance of the outcome by the majority. Thus, government must create or in some sense embody a "civil religion." But as Bellah points out, "No one has changed a great nation without appealing to its soul, without stimulating a national idealism, as even those who call themselves materialists have discovered, culture is the key to revolution, religion is the key to culture."[6]

Let us summarize the argument thus far. The erosion of the inherited moral base under the onslaught of continuous growth and spread of individualism creates the following situation: the economic actors, especially the entrepreneurial elite, have been freed of the old religious and moral values; but the individualistic growth process does not provide any ready social morality that will substitute. Thus the previously effective inhibitions on lying, cheating, and stealing have lost their effectiveness, and the functioning of the private sector is likely to be much less effective and acceptable than in the past.

The central role played by the state in managing the economy is a second factor which generates social limits to growth. There is a central flaw in the current approach of planned capitalist growth which calls for the pursuit of self-interest by individuals in the private sector but forbids it in the public sector. The expectation that public servants will not promote their private interests at the expense of the public interest reinforces the argument that the economy rests as importantly on moral behavior as on self-interested behavior. "The more a market economy is subjected to state intervention and correction, the more dependent its functioning becomes on restriction of the individualistic calculus in certain spheres, as well as on certain elemental moral standards among both the controllers and the controlled. The most important of these are standards of truth, honesty, physical restraint, and respect for law."[7] But the more self-interest progresses and the more the original moral base of the society is undercut, the less likely these conditions are to be met.

Attempts to rely solely on material incentives in the private sector and more particularly in the public sector suffer from two defects: in the first place, stationing a policeman on every corner to prevent cheating simply doesn't work. Regulators have less relevant information than those whose behavior they are trying to regulate. In addition, who regulates the regulators? Thus, there is no substitute for an internalized moral law that directs persons to seek their self-interest only in "fair" ways.[8] Secondly, reliance on external sanctions further undermines the remaining aspects of an internalized moral law.

In summary, the erosion of society's moral base under the onslaught of self-interest has important practical results. As Hirsch says:

> Religious obligation performed a secular function that, with the development of modern society, became more rather than less important. It helped to reconcile the conflict between private and social needs at the individual level and did it by internalizing norms of behavior. It thereby provided the necessary social binding for an individualistic, nonaltruistic market economy. This was the non-Marxist social function of religion. Without it, the

claims on altruistic feelings, or on explicit social cooperation, would greatly increase, as was foreseen, and to some extent welcomed, by a long line of humanists and secular moralists. Less love of God necessitates more love of Man.[9]

Guides for Coherent Policy

To sum up our position so far: corporate capitalism in the U.S. faces physical and social limits to continued economic growth which imply a deterioration in performance even in the goals which have been met with some success previously. So what is to be done?

The starting point is to consider again the purposes of an economic system:

1. Providing for basic human needs (overcoming scarcity);
2. Generating and extending freedom of choice;
3. Fostering the conditions for good human relations—fellowship.

In the face of deteriorating performance, how can these goals be reached in the changed climate of the 1980s? We do not want to suggest a whole new economic system. It is all too easy to talk in terms of "end states" which are perfect systems in theory. We want to be more realistic and to take from our Judeo-Christian heritage three moral canons which should provide a coherent direction for a public and private policy aimed at moving toward greater success in attaining economic goals.

The three areas of thought, reflection, and action, are the following:

Stewardship

Private ownership is still important for the 12 million small businesses in the United States; but in the largest corporations, ownership and incentive are weakly related because executives now operate corporations with minimal interference from owners. Ownership of these corporations should be vested in the hands of townships, states, workers, and similar collective bodies, for they will be sensitive to needs which are beyond the maximizing individual or the "satisficing" executive.

The guiding criterion should be stewardship, not ownership.[10] Corporations may hold property and use it as they see fit—as long as the public interest is served. In this way the acquisitive motive is not eliminated, but is muted and more carefully channeled for the public welfare. Competition should be supplemented with public control measures designed to allow fellowship to develop—through worker self-management, for example.

Jubilee

We do not need extreme income inequalities in the U.S. to mobilize human energy. Would corporate chief executives quit if their incomes were lower than the 1977 median of $471,000? Hardly. They would still be rewarded well in monetary terms and in psychic income: pride, challenge, power, status. A major redistribution of income from the top levels is desirable, plus a minimum income guarantee and jobs for all who want to work. While this redistribution would improve the situation of the bottom 20 percent of income earners, its greater importance would lie in counteracting the social limits to growth that are engendered by inequality.

Smallness

Only about half of the eligible electorate bothered to vote in the last U.S. elections. Yet, there has been an incredible proliferation of neighborhood groups. National institutions have become too large, too uncontrollable, too unresponsive. We must develop smaller institutions more responsible to individual needs if we are to broaden areas of free choice and nurture fellowship.

U.S. society today is characterized by largeness of firms, unions, and government institutions. Exxon, GM, the Teamsters, UAW, and the Carpenters Union are all mega-institutions. Government agencies such as HEW are even larger. Socialist economies share this characteristic. Their economic institutions are even larger and more bureaucratized than ours.

The development of the U.S. economy (and most other industrialized economies) has created a fundamental dichotomization of social, political, and economic life.[11] Put most simply, the dichotomy is between the mega-institutions and the private life of the individual. These two divisions of our society are experienced and apprehended by the individual in quite different ways. The GMs, DODs, UAWs, HEWs, UCLAs, AMAs are "remote, often hard to understand or downright unreal, impersonal, and ipso facto unsatisfactory as sources for individual meaning and identity. . . . By contrast, private life is experienced as the single most important area for the discovery and actualization of meaning and identity."[12]

People could cope with these mega-institutions if the dichotomization process had not so deinstitutionalized the private life of individuals. People have always found their identity through and, in turn, impressed their values on, the mega-institutions, through what Berger calls "mediating structures." However this interlocking network of mediating institutions—family, church, voluntary association, neighborhood, and subculture—has been severely weakened by the rampant growth of the mega-institutions that have taken over many of their traditional functions.

The Crucial Role of Mediating Institutions

In the face of this dichotomization of modern life the Christian concepts of stewardship and fellowship fall on infertile soil. There are a number of reasons why this is true.

People feel helpless in the face of the mega-institutions. Their sheer size is so alienating that the individual retreats to private life believing that nothing can be done about THEM out there. However, private life is becoming less of a refuge as mediating institutions continue to decay in the face of the expansion of the mega-institutions. As Berger says, "The situation becomes intolerable . . . when, say, my wife leaves me, my children take on life styles that are strange and unacceptable to me, my church becomes incomprehensible, my neighborhood becomes a place of danger, and so on."[13] The result is a turn to hedonism and me-firstism at the worst, and quietism at the best. And, of course, this further weakens the mediating institutions of private life.

Not only do people feel helpless, but in fact, as individuals, they are unable to make any difference. With the mega-institutions "taking care" of the hungry, the thirsty, the stranger, the naked, the ill, and the prisoner, and with the family, church, voluntary association, neighborhood, and subculture weakened and defensive, the individual finds it difficult if not impossible to be a steward and find fellowship.

There is also a direct relation between the problems of fellowship and stewardship and the social limits to growth which are causing difficulties in overcoming scarcity. As noted above, the moral base of the society has progressively been undermined.[14] The religious source of this collective conscience or moral law has generally operated through the mediating institutions of private life. Because of their remoteness and sheer size, the mega-institutions are "consumers" not "producers" of this type of morality. A general moral code cannot rest on the activities of individuals either. The experiments with "life styles" of "consenting adults" is too unstable and unreliable a basis for the generation and maintenance of a collective conscience. However, without it, the ethic of stewardship and the possibility of fellowship must languish even as success in overcoming scarcity wanes.

Our modern political philosophies—liberalism, conservatism, socialism—have failed precisely because they have not understood the importance of mediating institutions. Liberalism has constantly turned to the state for solutions to social problems, while conservatism has sought the same in the corporate sector. Neither has recognized the destructiveness to the social fabric caused by relying on mega-institutions. Socialism suffers from this same myopia. Even though it places its faith in renewed community, it fails to see that socialist mega-institutions are just as destructive as capitalist ones.

Mediating institutions which may aid in attaining our three goals should be fostered in two ways. The first is through public policy. Berger suggests two basic propositions: "One: *Public policy should protect and foster mediating structures. Two: Wherever possible, public policy should utilize the mediating structures as its agents.*"[15]

More importantly, ways must be found to revitalize mediating institutions from the bottom up. The old Catholic concept of subsidiarity and the Latin American "basic communities" provide some guidelines. The local level, not the national level, provides the best alternatives for sustenance and fellowship. A good example is the efforts of the Youngstown coalition to provide for the well being of the citizens of that area.

Conclusion

The road ahead is not easy and the precise directions of change are still unclear. One thing is certain: the national level will not be the most effective arena for achievement of the three goals of the U.S. system. At this point many of the programs which had favored these goals, such as full employment and a decent level of security, are about to be jettisoned in the name of controlling inflation. We are moving backward.

To be sure, the thrust we suggest will not be accepted immediately, and if it were, it would not result in a miraculous attainment of the goals of an economic society. But it is less improbable than the complete transformation of society envisioned by radicals, and it can lead to a more humane society than the existing one, which is so tenaciously defended by conservatives.

NOTES

1. It should be apparent that this view is fundamentally different from that of authors such as Michael Novak, who see a separation of economic, political, and moral spheres. We feel our view to be historically correct as well as a good description of present reality.

2. See Adam Smith, *Theory of Moral Sentiments* (London: Henry Bohn, 1861), and A. W. Coats (ed.), *The Classical Economists and Economic Policy* (London: Methuen, 1971). It is interesting that Milton Friedman, in his *Essays in Positive Economics* (Chicago: University of Chicago Press, 1966) has a similar starting point when he says "Differences about policy among disinterested citizens derive predominantly from different predictions about the economic consequences of taking action . . . rather than from fundamental differences in basic values" (p. 5).

3. Peter Berger, "In Praise of Particularity: The Concept of Mediating Structures," *Review of Politics* (July 1976), p. 134.

4. Fred Hirsch, *Social Limits to Growth* (Cambridge, Mass.: Harvard University Press, 1978), p. 141. We owe him the idea of social limits to growth. Roy Weintraub says the same thing in his book but doesn't seem to recognize its significance for applied economics. See Roy Weintraub, *Microfoundations: The Compatibility of Microeconomics and Macroeconomics* (New York: Cambridge University Press, 1979).

5. See R. H. Tawney, *Religion and The Rise of Capitalism* (New York: Harcourt, Brace & World, 1926), and Charles K. Wilber, "The New Economic History Re-examined: R. H. Tawney on the Origins of Capitalism," *The American Journal of Economics and Sociology*, 33 (July 1974): 249–58.

6. Robert Bellah, *The Broken Covenant: American Civil Religion in a Time of Trial* (New York: Seabury, 1975).

7. Hirsch, *Social Limits*, pp. 128–29.

8. This casts new light on the recent attempts to construct theories of justice that are acceptable to all. See John Rawls, *A Theory of Justice* (Cambridge, Mass.: Harvard University Press, 1971), and the literature spawned by that work. The whole endeavor can be seen as an attempt to create a substitute moral law based on rationality rather than religion.

9. Hirsch, *Social Limits*, pp. 141–42.

10. For a number of treatments of aspects of stewardship see M. E. Jegen and C. K. Wilber, *The Earth is the Lord's: Essays in Stewardship* (New York: Paulist Press, 1977).

11. We are indebted to the work of Peter Berger for the following material. See his "In Praise of Particularity."

12. *Ibid.*, p. 133.
13. *Ibid.*, p. 134.
14. The importance of such a moral base has been widely recognized. Gary Wills, "Benevolent Adam Smith," *New York Review of Books,* February 9, 1978, finds a moral system based on cooperation as central to Smith's views. Edward Banfield, *The Moral Basis of a Backward Society* (Glencoe, Ill.: Free Press, 1958) located the moral base in small groups, in this case the family. James C. Scott, *The Moral Economy of the Peasant: Rebellion and Subsistence in Southeast Asia* (New Haven, Conn.: Yale University Press, 1976), finds it in a subsistence insurance ethic and shows that its destruction is likely to lead to rebellion.
15. Berger, "In Praise of Particularity," p. 138.

8. Goals in Conflict: Corporate Success and Global Justice?

Denis Goulet

"Can transnational corporations contribute to a just World Order?" This is the central question posed by this essay.

No attempt will be made in these pages to defend a set of basic assumptions on development and global justice that have been formulated by the author in earlier writings. Ten of these assumptions, however, are briefly stated: they provide the context for examining ethical tensions between corporate efficiency and global justice.

Assumptions

1. The goal of sound development is neither to maximize economic growth nor to aggregate wealth, but to improve the living conditions of all people and to enhance possibilities of personal and community fulfillment at all levels — cultural, political, and spiritual, as well as material.[1]

2. Meeting the basic human needs of the poorest populations should be the first priority target of national development strategies and international resource transfers.[2]

3. For political leaders, keeping in close touch with the aspirations of the general populace and maintaining a commitment to endowing their societies with equitable incentive systems are essential ingredients to success.[3]

4. Development strategies ought to build from within the latent dynamisms found in traditional value systems throughout the world.[4]

5. Standard economic measures of development are poor indicators of qualitative social progress.[5]

6. Correlatively, all national societies are poorly developed in some essential respects.[6]

7. Change strategies must operate to solve problems within existing systems as well as to effect abrupt discontinuity with these systems when circumstances warrant rupture.[7]

8. Technology and other resources which circulate globally must be made available to needy groups on more favorable bargaining terms than those now prevailing.[8]

9. Notwithstanding dismal performance in recent decades and widespread disenchantment with most development models, considerable scope still exists for increasing welfare and justice in most societies.[9]

10. New international legal, political, and economic arrangements are indispensable features of sound development efforts.[10]

The present essay will not reopen debate on the merits of these premises. Its specific purpose is to inquire whether transnational corporations (TNC's) are to be judged as positive or negative forces in the quest for a more just international order. I shall conduct this inquiry by analyzing three related points:

(a) ethical dilemmas facing Christian corporate personnel in their efforts to be both successful and faithful to their religious ideals;

(b) conflicting judgments as to whether corporations are good or bad for the development of poor nations; and

(c) explorations into new social roles for corporations.

Ethical Dilemmas for Corporate Personnel

More than twenty-five years ago Adolf Berle wondered if the modern corporation could have a soul, or at least a conscience. He observed that:

Our grandfathers quarreled with corporations because, as the phrase went, they were "soulless." But out of the common denominator of the decision-making machinery, some sort of consensus of mind is emerging, by compulsion as it were, which for good or ill is acting surprisingly like a collective soul.[11]

Berle was quick to add:

The really great corporation managements have reached a position for the first time in their history in which they must consciously take account of philosophical considerations. They must consider the kind of a community in which they have faith, and which they will serve, . . . In a word, they must consider at least in its more elementary phases the ancient problem of the "good life," and how their operations in the community can be adapted to affording or fostering it.[12]

By the early 1970s business firms in the U.S. had begun issuing "social audits" to supplement their annual financial reports. The officers of Abt Associates, a Cambridge-based consultant firm which pioneered in the social audit, explain that:

> Until the 1970's, the social performance of organizations, including business organizations, was a widely discussed topic, dealt with primarily by qualitative arguments shrouded in ideological rhetoric. Concern for the social performance of business and other organizations is as old as the Medieval Church's regulations of usury, the English Common Law, the U.S. Constitution and the Sherman Anti-Trust Act of 1890. What is new about social audits is both a fresh approach and a specific method for measuring the social impacts of organizations in quantitative terms.[13]

Corporate reflection on the obligation to include social and political "externalities" in their decision-making has spread rapidly in the last decade. One major stimulus for self-examination and innovation has been provided by the United Nations study on the impact of transnational corporations on developing countries. For the U.N. the problem arises not simply because large multinational corporations command more resources or wield greater economic power than entire nations. It also resides in "their ability to shape demand patterns and values and to influence the lives of people and policies of governments, as well as their impact on the international division of labor."[14] Generally speaking, corporations have been placed on the defensive by an aroused international public opinion which demands answers to ethical and value questions surrounding corporate abilities.

Four Levels of Ethical Conflict

Discussions of ethical responsibility in corporate personnel can be conducted in four distinct normative arenas.

1. The first domain is that of personal and professional behavior within the context of presently accepted ethical ground rules and organizational values. Examples are such issues as truthfulness and honesty in handling expense accounts, the avoidance of illegal bribes or favors in order to win a contract, and the delivery of stipulated model and quality of goods purchased by a customer and not some slightly different (and cheaper) substitute.

2. A second realm bears on corporate policy decisions, usually pertaining to complex issues of societal justice. Examples include such questions as investment in South Africa (Does corporate investment help oppressed blacks or buttress the unjust *apartheid* system?). Another issue is whether corporations may responsibly "export pollution" to a Third World site, thereby creating environmental damage even though host-country laws may allow pollution. Still another instance is the choice of not making an otherwise desirable investment lest it wipe out local employment opportunities, etc.

3. The third arena of ethical conflict deals with the over-all systemic effects (good and bad) of corporate activity in the world. Here the moral issues are whether, on balance, corporate activities benefit poor countries or poor populations, or whether, as some argue, they make things worse by widening gaps between privileged and deprived groups, by reinforcing technical and economic dependency, and by destroying vulnerable cultural values.

4. A fourth and final level of ethical conflict focuses on competing images and standards of success operative in business circles, on the one hand, and in the Christian religion, on the other. Expressed in stark biblical terms, the question is whether one can be faithful to both God and Mammon.

Most writings on corporate ethics concentrate heavily on levels (1) and (2). The present paper, however, proposes to address itself more directly to arenas (3) and (4). In this author's view, the moral responsibilities of Christian corporate personnel are not adequately discharged unless they make sound value decisions in all four domains just listed.

The Christian in the Corporate World

The broadest ethical conflict of all turns on whether corporate goals can, ultimately, prove compatible with sound developmental objectives for society. More specifically, growing demands for equity and social justice in development cast doubts on the validity of arguments invoked by corporations to prove that organized profit-seeking truly contributes to development. My purpose here, however, is not to resurrect sterile polemics about corporations as "good guys" or "bad guys." The debate needs to be taken one step forward by focusing on ethical dilemmas faced by corporate personnel who also profess ethical allegiance to Christian values.

These dilemmas are traceable to the radical tension existing between the measures of success adopted by business, on the one hand, and by Christian religion, on the other. Competitive business confers the rewards of success on individuals displaying moral traits which are sharply opposed to those preached by the masters of Christian spiritual perfection. Success goes to aggressive sellers and organizers, to single-minded servants of the goals (and sensitivities) of managerial hierarchies, to sharp operators who pounce on fleeting opportunities to maximize their firm's competitive advantage. It also helps if a corporate person is convivial in a mode that will never offend others—thereby encouraging such habits as shallowness in discourse and linguistic sail-trimming. All in all, the personality profile of successful business people, as portrayed by both sociologists and novelists, and as experienced impressionistically by those within and those outside corporate bureaucracies, is not calculated to warm the hearts of moralists or teachers of spiritual perfection. Too great a premium seems to be placed by business on external characteristics, the perquisites of rank and office, the cultivated image of the supreme coper, with the attendant risk of superficiality or the atrophy of inner virtues.

Yet suffering, tragedy, and self-abnegation form an integral part of the Christian vision of success: one must die with Christ if one is to be fit to rise with Him. To Christians, what "the world" or even their own ego calls failure is often a providential aid to greater self-knowledge, to deeper humility, to greater reliance on God's grace, and to more prayerful daily living. The Christian profile of the virtuous man or woman has little in common with the dominant image of successful corporate executive as one who is "on top of things" and confidently issues orders which galvanize a worldwide array of actors into efficient action. Consequently, one needs to be skeptical of heady optimistic claims that career professionalism can be easily reconciled with the cultivation of genuine Christian values.

In recent years the Transcendental Meditation Movement has gained many adepts among business executives, military officers, and professional athletes. Perhaps the reason for this recruiting success is that the movement makes no profound moral demands on its devotees. Any serious religion or ethics, however, will socialize people into believing that material success and a good name among peers are relatively unimportant values, as compared with fidelity, truthfulness, and patience under trial. This is obviously not to argue that it is impossible for one to be a good manager or financier while also being a virtuous Christian, any more than it is to contend that Christianity rules out being a good bricklayer or electrician. It would clearly be foolish, wrong, and slanderous to claim that the exercise of these professions is intrinsically immoral. The point, however, is that being committed to monetary values in order to succeed in business places one in a psychological stance which pulls one sharply and powerfully away from the exigencies of Christianity. One simply cannot serve well two different masters: God and Mammon. The ability to obtain profit for one's employer, or to maneuver peers into granting consensus, or to convince customers of the "superiority" of one's product are all skills which rely heavily on promoting an image of oneself as assertive yet collaborative, afraid of risk, morally cautious. Over time these traits readily induce "compromising" habits in one's moral personality; and these habits are in little harmony with true Christian commitment.

Understandably, therefore, the tensions inherent in devoting one's major energies to pursuing profit in highly competitive arenas and being gauged "successful" according to business norms tend to place conscientious practitioners in a state bordering on ethical schizophrenia. It is evidently no easy thing for a corporate official to be compassionate and, as the Bible recommends, "no respecter of persons." One must refrain from being a "bleeding heart" when it comes to firing incompetent people, and one is encouraged to be a respecter of persons when "cultivating" a big client. The psychological and behavioral strains imposed on persons operating under such a double allegiance are enormous. And they are multiplied tenfold for those who pay serious moral attention to the systemic effects of corporate activity on societies at large, particularly on Less-Developed Countries (LDC's).

A Role for an "Ethics of Distress"

Large firms, especially transnational corporations (TNC's), strive unremittingly to convince the public that they contribute to social welfare in the very process of enriching themselves. The necessity of engaging in such special pleading leaves them vulnerable to self-deception, at the very least. The sociology of interests[15] works powerfully to create rationalization systems. Similar dangers doubtless face political rulers, military officers, and ministers of religion. But it must be recognized that the business world is structurally beholden to a conception of societal welfare (namely, that abundant buying and selling of material goods will generate a common good) which pulls in directions contrary to the image of welfare grounded on such values as Aristotle's political friendship, the ideal of distributive justice preached in papal encyclicals, or the Basic Human Needs model of development.

Perhaps one exaggerates very little in stating that corporate personnel are necessarily positioned in what the French theologian Regamey calls an "ethics of distress" situation.[16] This concept refers to a situation of moral choice in which it is impossible to avoid dehumanizing options without being morally heroic or sacrificial. Regamey developed the concept of the ethics of distress in the context of the morality of warfare, violence, and conscientious objection. What I am suggesting here is that, while observing differences in kind and degree applicable to business ethics, something analogous to an ethics of distress situation may habitually confront corporate personnel. Unless such persons are exceptionally lucid and ethically courageous, they will easily be led by the rationalization systems operative within business circles to reduce Christian virtue to a kind of ornamental patina aimed at winning for them the social respectability they need to succeed in business. In short, my argument states that the main ethical dilemma faced by corporate personnel is the antagonism between competing images and criteria of success as portrayed by business and by the Christian religion.

No facile resolution of this dilemma is possible: indeed the only acceptable resolution may be to accept life in a state of creative tension in the teeth of the dilemma. In order to do this, however, one must constantly acknowledge that the tension between the two value systems *perdures* and cannot be dissolved.

A serious problem exists because professional efficiency and competence, like excellence in any human endeavor, are genuine and positive values. Clearly, business persons, like any others, must not bury their talents in the ground: any work to be done by them ought to be done well. Nevertheless, there is no denying that the demands of professional efficiency in corporate profit-making often place individuals in contradiction to their vocation, as Christians, to bear witness to the value of each person—even unproductive ones. Moreover, excessive dedication to wealth-getting (even for stockholders) readily generates quasi-idolatrous corruptions.[17] Traditional invocations of the stewardship ethic simply skirt the issue: what is at issue is the loyalty system which binds the heart and soul of the steward. "Where your treasure is, there is your heart."

It must not be supposed, however, that ethical problems faced by corporations can be reduced to these subjective dilemmas of personal conscience, however acute and important they be. These personal difficulties are invoked here to show how easy it is to explain away the radical tension which both separates and links two competing value systems. A similar tension likewise can be found in the public arenas in which corporations must be judged: this is the tension between the institutional values of corporations and the values postulated by a just world order. The question, simply put, is: Can corporations truly help make societies more just and more humane? No one can even ask the question seriously without first acknowledging that the dominant values of just and humane societies and of successful corporations lie in sharp opposition one to another. In order to provide a preliminary sketch of this opposition, I shall now briefly examine a few competing views of corporations as good, or as bad, for the cause of development in the Third World. This, then, is the burden of the following pages.

TNC's: Good, Bad, or Indifferent?

Transnational corporations have not lacked for champions, even as attacks upon them have escalated in number and intensity. Recent defenses of TNC's all conclude that, on balance, large corporations contribute to genuine development and that, therefore, they are basically good. All witnesses for the defense urge critics, however, to recognize TNC's frankly for what they are: namely, efficient profit-making global institutions, not national governments seeking societal welfare, or philanthropic organizations dispensing charity.

Corporate Champions

Neil Jacoby's book, *Corporate Power and Social Responsibility,* reflects the late author's lifelong convictions.[18] An eaclier work of his, *U.S. Aid to Taiwan,* portrayed Taiwan as a paradigmatic developmental success story made possible, in large measure, by U.S. governmental aid.[19] Still earlier, Jacoby had served as an economic counselor to President Dwight Eisenhower. Jacoby's sturdy Republicanism translates into a no-less-sturdy, albeit an enlightened, defense of capitalism and of the corporate system. Most criticisms leveled at TNC's, Jacoby claims, are unfair: they are based on erroneous information, tendentious inter-pretations, and ideological myths. As a reformer who believes in the values of pluralist democracy, Jacoby pleads for new alliances of government and corporations in order to achieve a more just, efficient, creative, and democratic society. But as a corporate apologist, however, he optimistically assumes

> that the economies of the Western nations will continue to be based mainly on the institutions of private property, free enter-prise, open markets, and profit incentives. The manifold draw-backs of socialist economies are serious enough to allow us to

assume that people will not support the replacement of capitalism by socialism.[20]

And Jacoby's optimism leads him to predict that:

> [T]he continued growth of multinational enterprise will be a potent force for the development of supranational organizations and the harmonization of national policies and actions. Although some scholars have predicted a sharp clash between the multinational company and the nation-state, resulting in national restrictions on multinational business, a much different course of events is probable. *National governments will find that the most effective way to prevent multinational firms from benefitting from differences in national policies is to harmonize those policies. . . . We would suggest that multinational business is the most powerful institution in the forging of a world order.*[21]

On balance, Jacoby judges TNC's to be a beneficent and enduring social institution which plays a very positive role both for development and for the evolution of global governance institutions. While he grants that some criticisms directed at corporate institutions may be valid, he denies that they are generally applicable: documented abuses, in a word, are but exceptions to the rule. And the rule itself is beneficial for everyone concerned. In the face of criticisms, Jacoby retorts that "improvements in the American political system are even more urgently needed than reforms of the corporate system, if we are to attain the Good Society."[22]

Richard Farmer, professor of international business at Indiana University and formerly general manager of a construction-transportation company in Saudi Arabia, is the author of another iconoclastic book entitled *Benevolent Aggression.* His earthy style comes through immediately in the Preface, where we are told that:

> The stink of poverty is everywhere—no one can quite get away any more. I've seen it in the Middle East, in Mexico, in Japan, in Europe, in California, and about ten blocks from where I now live in the center of Mid-America. And it bothers me, as it bothers lots of people who keep running into it wherever they turn. The enjoyment of affluence is everywhere too. . . . Maybe we're all a bunch of uptight, neurotic organization men, but at least we don't have to worry about being poor. As someone said, "money may not be everything, but it sure as hell beats whatever comes in second."[23]

Farmer thinks that the entire world, especially its poor sections, would do well to learn their lessons from successful corporations. As he puts it:

> Visiting the headquarters of an American-based multinational corporation in a less-developed country is like moving into another world. One moment you're out on a hot street, swarming with flies, kids, beggars in rags, vendors, beat-up taxicabs, and dirt; the next you're in the quiet, clean, air-conditioned office building, with its calm atmosphere of workmanlike efficiency, attractive secretaries, and images of progress and wealth. It's almost impossible not to think about what's just outside the door. "If only the whole country ran like this," you ponder, "what a difference it could make!"[24]

After reciting a litany of standard complaints against multinational corporations, Farmer offers this rebuttal:

> It's a tough life being poor, and few of us will ever admit that it just might be our fault. Better to blame the devil foreigners, to demand more, to suggest darkly that some international cartel is screwing us all in ways we cannot quite understand. But the image of enormous competence lingers. The firms are good. No question about it. Now, why can't they get to work and fix up the world everywhere?[25]

He answers his own question by explaining that private firms are so efficient because they pursue simple, direct goals. In contrast, public institutions are inefficient because they pursue complex, overlapping, and often contradictory objectives. After their creation both types of organizations quickly acquire a vested interest in surviving. The key difference is that private enterprises cannot survive unless they make money, thereby proving their efficiency. But unfortunately, Farmer laments, public firms are not subjected to this reality test: they can be grossly inefficient and still survive.

Richard Farmer advises Third World governments to imitate the efficiency and focused goal-orientation of private firms, particularly small, flexible private firms. Entire countries need to learn, he argues, "the total marketing concept"[26] which is nothing other than comparative advantage. As an intelligent and practical man who recognizes the limited resources available in poor countries, Farmer wants more small-scale capitalism in the Third World nations. He tells their leaders: Don't be infatuated with large organizations, because it is too difficult to manage them well with a dearth of skilled people. His words are these:

Get your investments, your organizations, your technologies, and all the rest meshed in well with whatever the country has to offer *now*—not what it wished it had. If there are masses of illiterate peasants, then try to figure out things to do which illiterate peasants can really do and which will enable them to learn more while they are doing.[27]

We have here, admittedly, a maverick champion of corporations. In common with other defenders of corporate capitalism, he rejects all criticisms leveled at TNC's by exuberantly praising their efficiency, realism, and competitive success.

No business scholar has mounted a more sophisticated defense of multinational corporations, however, than Harvard's Raymond Vernon, author of *Sovereignty at Bay* and the more recent *Storm Over the Multinationals*.[28] In essence, Vernon's contention is that large corporations have brought major benefits to Third World countries which they could not have gotten otherwise. He admits their self-interested motives, but claims that sovereign countries, even poor and small ones, have the legal basis and the political power to negotiate more acceptable terms. Their only other option, is to do without corporations, thereby sacrificing the benefits these bring. That so few nations do in fact make this choice convinces Vernon that even hostile governments admit that TNC's bring to them needed investment capital, technology, managerial skills, jobs, and entries to profitable markets. These benefits, he asserts, would simply not be available if profit-seeking corporations were kept out. No less importantly, according to Vernon, the major evils associated with multinationals—"hegemony, corruption, inequity, pollution, and indifference to consumer interests were endemic in mankind's history long before the multinational enterprise existed. Moreover, nations that have placed severe limitations on the subsidiaries of multinational enterprises operating in their areas do not seem to have escaped these ills; at best, such countries have only altered the source and form of the problems."[29] Why, Vernon asks, do Third World nations blame TNC's for the general ills attributable to the industrialization process itself? The reasons, he replies, are that TNC's are highly visible, large in size, and plurinational in scope; therefore, "public opinion in many developing countries is bound to link the seamier side of the industrialization process with the operations of the multinational enterprises."[30] Nevertheless, corruption, pollution, and shoddy production "are much in evidence in all sorts of industrializing societies, both socialist and capitalist."[31] Vernon counters negative data or accusations leveled against TNC's by declaring the data to be unrepresentative or insufficiently researched. Alternatively, he traces proven abuses to unique or unusual conjunctures. This is how he explains away the huge transfer price increases detected in the Colombian pharmaceutical industries by Constantine Vaitsos. Because Vaitsos used exceptional figures, Vernon argues, he "produced various exotic estimates of the costs of overpricing to the Latin American economy."[32]

In short, Vernon asserts that TNC's are highly beneficial to LDC's, that available alternatives are unattractive, and that "[T]he inherent power of the state to control monopoly practices has always existed; the substantive question is whether the developing countries have the will and energy wisely to apply that power."[33] Although the most severe problem is the tension between aspirations to national autonomy and the internationalization of production, this tension, says Vernon, will probably decline as weak governments institute greater controls. Yet, he adds that:

> The real role of the multinational enterprise may not decline in some critical respects, such as control of the channels by which a developing country gains access to foreign markets. But the tone and form of participation on the part of developing countries could change sufficiently to take the sharp edges off the tension.[34]

John Kenneth Galbraith is another highly prestigious defender of the multinational company. In his 1978 *Harvard Business Review* article entitled "The Defense of the Multinational Company,"[35] Galbraith advises TNC's to acknowledge that they wield huge power, but to declare their public commitment to wielding it responsibly, and to go on doing their beneficent job of providing capital, skills, jobs, products, and market access to the world. This, he says, is the best way TNC's have of being socially useful.

Galbraith's article was later reprinted by the United States International Communications Agency and distributed all over the world. Paradoxically, Galbraith has been seen by many as a sharp critic of capitalist enterprises; he complains about their distorted priorities and insensitivity to social needs, about the alienating effects of affluence and credit-buying, and errant managerial practices. In the hour of truth, however, Galbraith comes out resolutely on the side of the corporate angels.

In an October 1979 interview appearing in the *New York Times*, Galbraith was asked if a repeat of the 1929 Great Depression was possible. He replied:

Basically I'm an optimist. The nice thing about capitalism is that it lends itself to an infinity of patching up. If it were subject to the rigors of principles assumed by either the Right or the Left, it would have ended long ago. So we may have more convulsions and more pragmatic patching up, and the patching up will enable it to survive. Now you have my final bit of wisdom, capitalism will survive."[36]

The last champion of multinational corporations receiving mention here is philosopher-theologian Michael Novak, presently a Resident Scholar at the American Enterprise Institute, a private research center. Novak is one of the thinkers so well profiled by Peter Steinfels in *The Neo-Conservatives*.[37] In an essay entitled "Irony, Tragedy, Courage," prepared for the *Smith-Kline Forum for a Healthier American Society*, Novak makes the case that capitalism is the best economic system among existing, or realistically conceivable, alternatives. "Irony dominates our era," Novak writes:

A socialist system which is a dismal economic and political failure stirs tremendous ideological fervor around the world, while democratic capitalism, based firmly on a record of unparalleled liberty, equality, and prosperity, is rejected as morally unworthy.[38]

Capitalism's greatest crime is the success it has earned from its high productivity: "our prosperity is used by our enemies and detractors as proof of our guilt." The real ethical challenge, for Novak, is not to reform capitalism but to find a more eloquent defense of the system.

If democratic capitalism does perish, it will not be because its economic system produced a lesser prosperity. It will not be because its political system permitted a lesser range of liberties and civilities. It will be because its cultural leaders never perceived, never expressed, and too poorly defended its moral ideals.[39]

So much, then, for the champions of market capitalism, the system upon which TNC's rest their claims to legitimacy. We can now turn our attention to representative critics of TNC's.

The Critics

A much briefer discussion of critics of TNC's will suffice for our purposes here, if only because both their arguments and their names are well-known. Richard Barnet and Ronald Müller, for example, argue that TNC's are intrinsically exploitative and expansionist.[40] Worse still, they are structurally incapable of avoiding a train of ills: economic inequity, destruction of local cultures, the perpetuation of humiliating dependency, and the curtailment of governmental autonomy in Third World countries. For all these reasons, TNC's constitute the main institutional vehicle of neocolonialism. The Barnet-Müller book *Global Reach* is a scathing indictment of corporate injustices and exploitative practices. It traces these evils to the systemic and inevitable workings of international business competition.

An earlier study by the Canadian economist Kari Levitt, entitled *The Silent Surrender,* blames U.S. corporations for taking over control of Canada's economy and diluting the sovereignty of that nation's government, threatening, in the process, to transform Canada itself into little more than a subsidiary of American corporate enterprise.[41] The dilution of national sovereignty in host countries and the control of their economy by foreign actors are recurring themes in Third World literature. By globalizing production and marketing, TNC's are charged with imprisoning nominally sovereign countries in bonds of chronic economic dependency. In this way, therefore, TNC operations are inherently exploitative. Latin American dependency literature, however, makes use of new imagery—the metropolis and the periphery—and new terms (for example, "dependent development").

In *The Uncertain Promise* I have traced what appears to be a *sequence of dependency* following certain patterns.[42] At first poor countries depend on outside sources for capital. Even after obtaining capital of their own, they remain dependent on foreign sources for technology. Even if they develop technological capabilities of their own, however, they continue to depend on imported managerial know-how, the ability to coordinate large productive enterprises. The fourth and final stage in the sequence of dependency is competitive access to markets. This sequential analysis of dependency owes much to the produce-cycle theory linked to the names of several Harvard scholars: Raymond Vernon, Robert Stobauch, and Frederick Knickerbocker. According to these theorists, products and the competitive edge that comes with them last only a certain period of time during which the first corporate actors in the field enjoy a period of quasi-monopolistic market advantage. This advantage, however, gets progressively diluted and finally disappears, after which the competitive edge shifts to some other product or technology. The point, of course, is that dependency takes many forms.

Classical Marxists view imperialism and exploitation as the unavoidable fruits of expansionist capitalism, which functions by appropriating to a ruling (and owning) class the surplus value created by wage slaves.[43] Marxist theorists declare that minor improvements or even major reforms imposed, let us say, by mandatory, ethical codes of conduct, change nothing. In their view, corporations are intrinsically evil instrumentalities of exploitative practices. Without doubt one finds in many Third World settings a strong residual condemnation or at least distrust of corporations traceable to Marxist class-conflict theory. Hence corporations are widely viewed as essentially privileged institutions perpetuating the privilege of exploiters. Some contemporary revisionist democratic Marxists, notably Michael Harrington (in *The Vast Majority*[44]) argue that U.S. imperialism is the product of a cruel innocence which produces undemocratic behavior abroad. Thus imperialism by the U.S. is "accidental," the result of erroneous policy and not the necessary expression of American capitalistic interests. Whatever be the nuances on even substantive differences among them, however, all critics of TNC's concur in judging that TNC's harm the cause of development, exploit people, and promote injustice, both within developing countries and in the global circulation systems that govern the flow of resources across national borders.

TNC's: An Opportunity

Numerous analysts, however, have grown impatient with polemical defenses or denunciations of TNC's. They prefer to portray the corporate institution as one which channels a mixture of good and bad effects.

The United Nations, for instance, in its publications by the Group of Eminent Persons and others accepts the fact that transnational corporations simultaneously bring both benefits and harm to LDC's.[45] Therefore, a wise policy course for poor nations consists in trying to minimize the harmful effects and maximize the good impacts as much as possible. This is also the approach adopted by World Bank economist Paul Streeten, a foremost advocate of Basic Human Needs (BHN) development strategies.[46] Streeten urges LDC's to engage in selective linkage and delinkage with the positive and negative impulses which flow from the center to the periphery, that is, from rich-world institutions to those of poor lands. The key, in short, is a new bargaining stance. Severyn Bruyn, an American sociologist and author of *Social Economy: People Transforming Modern Business,* advocates reform of TNC's on the grounds that they are firmly entrenched—and cannot be removed from the scene.[47] More importantly, he says, TNC's are potentially beneficial to all societies, poor and rich alike. Bruyn seeks to re-charter corporations in ways designed to assure their social responsibility. New charters would promote the decentralization of corporate activity and lead, by an evolutionary process, to the creation of what he calls "social federalism and an economic republic." He attaches great significance to worker management and public accountability.

This third group of analysts shares the conviction that, whether one defends or condemns TNC's, they cannot be wished, or decreed, out of existence. Therefore, they must be regulated, controlled, and reformed. Obviously, since TNC's wield great power, regulation, control, and reform are possible only if their agents exercise countervailing power. The chief sources of such countervailing power are: national governments, international public opinion, and critical pressure from a variety of organizations, ranging from churches to political parties to labor unions. These very pressures have begun generating new models, both theoretical and practical, of social roles for corporations. A brief examination of these new roles is now in order.

Exploring New Social Roles for TNC's

Corporations are fictitious legal persons authorized by government charters to engage in stipulated activities for profit. In earlier times the only requirement imposed on chartered entities was that they obey the general laws of society. Thus, in effect, a charter was a hunting license allowing firms to make money, provided they paid their taxes and conformed to the ground rules of societal governance. Nowadays, however, we are witnessing a vigorous process of debate, criticism, and regulation which, taken cumulatively, is undermining the legitimacy of the charter or license originally issued to corporations. At issue is nothing less than a new social compact binding governments to corporations and to a widening array of articulate public-interest groups. Many countries doubtless have weak national governments, and their public opinion on issues of social responsibility is poorly articulated. Moreover, given the dominant position of TNC's in the national economy of many LDC's, demands on them rarely control corporate activity in ways deemed more acceptable to the population at large, or at least to politically organized groups within that population. Nevertheless, by and large, the ground rules governing corporate profit-seeking are beginning to change. Frankly recognizing such changes, conservative economist Harry Wallich pleaded with businessmen several years ago to cast off their obsolete image of capitalism.[48] Wallich argued that the future of capitalism and the continued profitability of corporate enterprise are not linked to continued ownership of the means of production by private capital. He explained that the tide of nationalism in the Third World, and the requirements of greater social accountability in other nations, powerfully impel governments to nationalize key productive facilities. Accordingly, he advises business leaders to keep themselves competitive in market arenas: if they do so, he predicts, they will survive. It is access to markets within a competitive framework that is the key to capitalism, not the ownership or even the management of capital goods. That a conservative economist like Wallich should have to argue his case for the business community reveals how slow that community is to understand the great changes occurring in the sociopolitical climate within which capitalists must legitimize their operations. Wallich, in effect, is warning corporations that they must find new social roles for themselves if they are to survive; otherwise, they will be eliminated as intrinsically exploitative or parasitical organizations.

Joint Long-term Planning

One of the most tireless advocates of new social roles for TNC's is André van Dam, a Dutch economist employed by Corn Products International and director of that company's Latin American regional planning activities. For over a decade, in countless articles appearing in development journals, management newsletters, U.N. publications, and futurist magazines, van Dam has insisted on the urgent need to institute collaborative long-term planning among TNC's, LDC governments, and local communities affected by production decisions.[49] Such planning would engage all parties in debates on criteria for investment, norms for what is produced and for whom, methods for setting employment policy and salary scales, and upgrading personnel. Marketing strategy, managerial practices, considerations of social justice and ecological responsibility, and the manner in which control over technological creation is to be effectively transferred to nationals would also be part of the agenda. Van Dam deems joint planning essential if corporations are to survive, if their managerial and technical skills are to be harnessed to the cause of sound development, and if nonrenewable resources are not to be catastrophically depleted.

Van Dam advocates the creation of a "Multinational Corporation Development Institute" which would be a sociopolitical research enterprise sponsored and operated by a confederation of TNC's.[50] The Institute should be a Non-Governmental Organization (NGO) enjoying affiliate status with the U.N. family of organizations. Its mission would be to provide a factual, legal, and moral framework for reaching agreements among TNC's host governments and local populations. Van Dam wants the new institute to engage in projections for the future in order to expect the unexpected under alternative scenarios. Among specific tasks the Institute should undertake are the following:

(1) Conduct a feasibility study of the southward transfer of R & D facilities for labor-intensive and export-oriented manufacturing industry. TNC technology, originally developed for capital-rich and large-scale markets, needs to be adjusted to LDC conditions in which unemployment is massive, capital scarce, and internal markets small. At present barely 3-4 percent of industrial R & D is carried out by LDC's, although their population accounts for 77 percent of the world's total.

(2) Appraise the catalytic role of TNC's in the future fusion of petro-currencies, the huge labor reservoirs of LDC's, and urgent needs for increased food production in poor lands. Van Dam urges that the organizational and technical excellence of TNC's agribusiness be used to recycle petro-currencies through the World Bank or other multilateral financial agencies.

(3) Study the feasibility of establishing, jointly with UNITAR (United Nations Institute for Training and Research) and universities, numerous LDC management training centers in Asia, Latin America, and Africa. The objective is to reverse the brain-drain in LDC's and build up local talent by a pragmatic, case-study-oriented schooling facility geared to the locality.

Van Dam defends his vision, not as a piece of wild-eyed or bleeding-heart idealism, but as the most realistic and enlightened way to renegotiate the social mandate of TNC's, given the long-range aspirations to development found in the world at large.

The Practice of "Social Architecture"

A number of business scholars have likewise urged corporations to take steps far beyond merely humanizing the workplace: they aim at establishing a new basis for partnership with society at large. Among those exploring new social roles for corporations are Tagi Sagafi-nejad of the University of Washington, and Howard Perlmutter of Pennsylvania's Wharton School. Perlmutter, author of *Towards a Theory and Practice of Social Architecture,* calls for new multidisciplinary approaches to designing, and operating, institutions which assign primacy to human objectives and values in society.[51] It is not enough to succeed with limited objectives, such as realizing a profit or producing goods efficiently. Institutions must also contribute to a more viable system of human organization which promotes the achievement of diverse political and cultural goals. Perlmutter is presently studying models enabling TNC's to move "from paternalism to parity" in their dealings with other actors in social arenas. Large corporations, he argues, must not simply refrain from doing harm: they have a positive obligation to contribute to a humane industrial system. To do so, they must exhibit qualities which the new interdiscipline of "social architecture" can help outline. Perlmutter explores how health delivery systems and other concrete activities can meet these requirements. Sagafi-nejad, an early colleague of Perlmutter's, has worked more recently on control systems used by host governments to harness technology to their broader developmental purposes.[52] These purposes include the desire of LDC's to gain eventual control over their own technological destinies. Hence the importance they attach to guarantees that "transfers" will confer upon them effective control over R & D, and not simply over technological products and processes. Clearly, then, in realms of technology transfer, TNC's are being invited to play a pedagogical role in the technological initiation of their weaker partners.

The studies mentioned thus far are highly congenial to new models of cooperation advocated by development specialists. One thinks here of such proposals as the "planetary bargain,"[53] commitments to ally rich and poor nations in a partnership to abolish the worse aspects of absolute poverty by the year 2000,[54] and efforts to institute a future world order mutually beneficial to rich and poor alike.[55]

Contracts of Solidarity

I should now like to examine briefly one new concept, at once theoretical and practical, which is now beginning to circulate in arenas of development debate and which creates a backdrop for more specialized research into new roles for TNC's. This is the notion of "contracts of solidarity" devised by Albert Tévoédjrè, an African scholar presently employed by the International Labour Office. Tévoédjrè is a citizen of Benin and the author of a suggestive book entitled *Poverty, Wealth of Mankind*.[56] The book, whose title is clearly inspired by Adam Smith, advances the thesis that poor people, duly enlightened and organized in modes of solidarity, constitute the greatest wealth of poor nations. True wealth is neither finance capital, natural resources, nor technological expertise, but people. And in the final chapter of the work Tévoédjrè outlines his views on contracts of solidarity.

The basic idea of the contract is simple: it is to use all available channels of exchange among strong and weak partners as occasions for strengthening self-reliance in the weak in ways which satisfy some basic developmental need. Therefore, says Tévoédjrè, binding contracts ought to be instituted in multiple arenas—bilateral aid, technical exchange, investment, scholarship programs, etc.—with a view to establishing eventual parity among partners. The ILO (International Labour Office) is now conducting research on the concrete and specific terms of such contracts in several problem-solving domains. In January of 1976, at the International Institute for Labour Studies World Symposium on the Social Implications of a New International Economic Order,[57] Tévoédjrè introduced the "contract of solidarity" idea in its dual aspects, "combining standard-setting with operational activities, [which] constitutes both an indispensable ethical point of reference and an instrument for securing its acceptance."[58] He explains that:

The contract of solidarity is based firstly on a diagnosis of the present state of the world and secondly on a new view of the development of nations . . . the instrument capable of remedying the most serious ills of our time—famine, unemployment, endemic disease, destructive urbanisation, unequal terms of trade, marginalisation of certain populations, violence, drug addiction, etc. All these phenomena are basically attributable to the centralisation of power and the way in which it is shielded by the minorities which hold it.[59]

"Solidarity," we are told, "can become effective only if it *recognizes* that inequalities exist and if it leads to the *will* to eliminate them."[60] Consequently, the contract

can designate only those commitments in which material gain is neither the prime objective nor the determining factor. The contract of solidarity is motivated principally by the search for a higher interest common to the parties concerned. Consequently, it transcends current forms of solidarity—pertaining, for instance, to family, profession or class—to embrace an awareness of belonging to one world and the resulting sense of sharing a common destiny.[61]

Not only sovereign states, but other institutions as well should be parties to such contracts. Moreover, even when the state is a signatory, it must engage in prior consultation with its populace to assure that it truly serves the causes of solidarity and self-reliance it professes to champion. Tévoédjrè considers it obvious that a TNC must:

> fulfill certain requirements if it is to be allowed to take part in the implementation of a contract of solidarity. Although the big firms are beginning to accept the idea of a code of conduct with regard to the countries in which they operate, they wish to retain their initiative and negotiate the conditions for its exercise bilaterally on a case-by-case basis with each of the states directly concerned. However, there can be no contract of solidarity in this field without the promulgation of a strict code obeying new rules for the world economy and binding on all countries. It will be the responsibility of the latter to secure its observance by companies wishing to establish themselves on their territory. Provision should also be made for an arbitration body with powers to control the application of contracts of this kind and to issue legal rulings.[62]

The ideal model of partnership embraces "conflict plus cooperation," to borrow a phrase from the French economist François Perroux.

Limited contracts applicable to specific problem arenas will clearly not be accepted unless they rest on the pillar of principled agreement over a larger framework. For this reason Tévoédjrè recommends the drafting and acceptance of a "Charter of Cooperation" to provide such a framework. Considerations of mercantilism and the desire for hegemony must give way to the will to build solidarity among equals.[63] The main objective of a charter is to engage the energies of all major actors in the global system in creating

> a tool for supporting the efforts of nations to keep their needs to a minimum and to satisfy them within their own environment in the most direct manner possible . . . the international division of labour, which is at present the tangible evidence of unequal distribution of production capacity on a world-wide scale, would thereby be reduced and would take the form of a contractually planned complement to the creative self-reliance of nations.[64]

The French sociologist Alain Birou notes that contracts of solidarity

> serve as experimental outlines for a new law under which co-operation is directed toward the basic objective of securing for all individuals, social groups, nations or regions the possibility of controlling their environment.[65]

Contracts of solidarity are seen by their proponents as a choice instrument for the operational legitimization of that new "law of development" which is beginning to emerge in the international community. That emerging law is, in turn, itself seen as the vehicle for implementing the acknowledged "right to development" vested in all nations and peoples.[66]

Obviously, winning agreement on a general charter of cooperation is not enough: if contracts of solidarity are to be effectively institutionalized, further research on *model agreements* in crucial problem arenas is required. Among arenas deemed especially important by Tévoédjrè are: the mushroom growth of towns, the defense of regional particularities in the context of national planning, international cooperation in all domains of resource transfers, and the ocean-bed regime.[67] Model agreements have as their purpose to analyze the role and status of all parties affected, setting forth their respective commitments and fixing procedures to be adopted.

Let me now summarize the argument made thus far: it is evident that TNC's need to obtain a new moral legitimacy for pursuing profits. Whether TNC's obtain a revalidated mandate by moving from "paternalism to parity," by conducting long-term planning jointly with affected parties, or by binding themselves to "contracts of solidarity" which meet Basic Human Needs (BHN) in a mode of self-reliant development, one conclusion stands out sharply. It is that TNC's will be obliged to alter both their philosophy and institutional procedures in substantial ways simply in order to adapt to a world in evolution. TNC's will have to adopt, and bend themselves to, new incentive systems which combine new mixes of material and moral inducements to engage in responsible activity. Moreover, they will have no choice but to begin "internalizing new externalities"[68] in their efficiency calculus and in their cost-benefit equations. If TNC's fail to evolve in this direction, any overtures they make to public opinion and to an aroused body of international actors will be correctly perceived as mere palliatives not commensurate to the world's pressing problems.

An Example of the New Social Roles for TNC's

Sophisticated business officials pride themselves on being practical. And the more enlightened among them acknowledge that there can be no sound practice over the long term without good theory. Thus far in this section I have been describing theoretical models for new corporate behavior. I should now like to present one practical example, drawn from a recent decision-making dilemma in corporate circles, which illustrates the values and principles underlying this theoretical discussion. This example involves NABISCO, a prestigious international agribusiness firm.

In 1977 NABISCO faced a difficult choice.[69] The company had sought permission from the government of Mexico to build a fourth manufacturing plant in that country. A feasibility study had shown that the Mexican market was ready to absorb more Ritz crackers, Saltines, Oreo cookies, Fig Newtons, pet food, candy bars, and shredded wheat. But Mexico's government, newly alerted to recent discussions of BHN (Basic Human Needs) in development strategy, and eager to win greater autonomy in its R & D technology creation, offered NABISCO a counterproposal. Would the company agree to build a different kind of plant, at a different site, and to produce different goods? Specifically, could NABISCO harness its R & D capacity to develop a protein-enriched cracker, which it would then produce cheaply and sell at a very slight profit to impoverished local populations suffering from nutritional deficiencies? Would the company also agree to train Mexican researchers in this technology and transfer control over the R & D laboratory to Mexican owners in a stipulated number of years? In exchange for these new modes of cooperation, the Mexican government would authorize NABISCO to raise prices on its other products elsewhere in Mexico by 10 to 15 percent. This concession would be made in the knowledge that it is mainly middle- and upper-class customers who purchase traditional NABISCO products, but it would be poorer people with low buying power who would purchase the nutritional cracker.

Company officials were of divided mind over the response to give the Mexican government. Profits, after a few years, would equal those under the conventional mode of operations. The great advantage to accepting Mexico's plan was obvious: a public-relations windfall allowing the company to state truthfully that it had cooperated with a Third World nation to meet a vital Basic Human Need in development. Nevertheless, after several months, NABISCO rejected Mexico's proposal because it did not wish to set a precedent for transferring to outsiders an effective voice over what is produced, where, and for whom. Mexico, they granted, was a "reasonable, moderate country sympathetic to the U.S." But, if a precedent were set, what might happen if some other country, less reliable, moderate, or friendly than Mexico, were to insist on similar terms?

Nevertheless, NABISCO joined producers of 90 basic goods in Mexico committing themselves to a production program which would provide a set volume of relevant items at a special low price. Seventeen large retailing companies signed a related agreement.[70] Moreover,

Commerce Secretariat officials in Mexico have also negotiated with dozens of local and foreign-owned manufacturers. In return for voluntary pacts from companies, guaranteeing their collaboration on producing priorities and pricing policies, government authorities provide to corporations compensatory incentives, ranging from relaxation of price controls on products falling outside the alliance program, help in obtaining low-cost credit, and technical assistance from government agencies. What we have here, clearly, are experimental probes into new patterns of harnessing corporate abilities to social purposes, under the guidance of a government that is critically reexamining its own assumptions about development.

Conclusion

The general argument of this paper can be summarized in two propositions.

The first of these states that Christian corporate personnel should try to resolve their ethical dilemmas, at all four levels analyzed earlier, by making history while witnessing to transcendence.[71] They must plunge into history's tasks, including those of production and management, while bearing witness to higher values which often contradict prevailing norms of success invoked to judge accomplishment in those same tasks. The term witness, in Greek, is "martyr." Quite literally, Christians launched in any professional endeavor, must be prepared to lose their lives in order to find them. Speaking less dramatically, but perhaps more realistically they must be spiritually and psychologically indifferent to success if they are to achieve it truly. And at times not of their choosing, the higher destinies of Providence may even summon them to give up everything they treasure. Unless they prepare themselves by moral habits of daily virtue and detachment far beyond what society requires in exchange for conferring approval and good reputation on people, Christian business persons will fail these tests.

The second ethical proposition is that Christian corporate personnel have a duty to struggle endlessly to transform the very structures of corporate life within which they operate. As suggested earlier, profit-seeking and the very definition of corporate efficiency must be revolutionized in order to meet the true developmental needs of the world's poor majorities. Market competition, therefore, can no longer be accepted as the *organizing principle* of economic life. At best such competition may serve as a *regulatory mechanism* to counter tendencies toward duplication, waste, excessive centralization, and insensitivity to final demand. The vital distinction between organizing principle and regulatory mechanism is drawn from the work of Karl Mannheim, who almost thirty years ago wrote:

> Competition and co-operation may be viewed in two different ways: as simple social mechanisms or as organizing principles of a social structure.
>
> Competition or co-operation as mechanisms may exist and serve diverse ends in any society, preliterate, capitalist, and non-capitalist. But in speaking of the capitalist phase of rugged individualism and competition, we think of an all-pervasive structural principle of social organization.
>
> This distinction may help to clarify the question whether capitalist competition—allegedly basic to our social structure— need be maintained as a presumably indispensable motivating force. Now, one may well eliminate competition as the *organizing principle* of the social structure and replace it by planning without eliminating competition as a *social mechanism* to serve desirable ends. . . .
>
> Most arguments in favor of competition apply to competition among equals; it is fallacious to suggest that beneficial effects exist in present-day society governed by competition among unequals.[72]

Corporate personnel who take their Christianity seriously, and who take seriously their vocation to transform structures of privilege into structures of reciprocity will often be thorns in the side of their employers. They must reconcile themselves to promoting the long-term good of the corporation by, in fact and in the shorter term, undermining its present legitimacy structure and conventional wisdom. Christians will not be content with obsolete and trite pieties about the merit system, the rewards of productivity, and the necessity of efficiency at any cost. As Barbara Ward insists, equality of opportunity is not enough: we need institutions which guarantee some measure of equality of results. She writes:

> A market system, wholly uncorrected by institutions of justice, sharing, and solidarity, makes the strong stronger and the weak weaker. Markets as useful tools in a functioning social order have a positive and decentralizing role to play. Markets as masters of society enrich the rich and pauperize the poor.[73]

The ethical challenges outlined here may appear too demanding for most corporate personnel. They will appear too demanding, however, only if Christian corporate persons lose sight of the essentially spiritual nature of the struggle they must wage. Ultimately, it is in spiritual arenas that true success is always measured. This is true not only in terms of one's individual soul, but also in terms of building up history and making the earth a better place to live. The English historian Christopher Dawson does well to remind us that

> the true makers of history are not to be found on the surface of events among the successful politicians or the successful revolutionaries: these are the servants of events. Their masters are the spiritual men whom the world knows not, the unregarded agents of the creative action of the Spirit.[74]

NOTES

1. Denis Goulet, "The Challenge of Development Economics," *Communications and Development Review*, 2, no. 1 (Spring 1978): 18–23.

2. Mary Evelyn Jegen and Charles K. Wilber (eds.), *Growth With Equity: Strategies for Meeting Human Needs* (New York: Paulist Press, 1979), see Denis Goulet chapter on "Strategies for Meeting Basic Needs," pp. 47–68.

3. Denis Goulet, "Looking at Guinea-Bissau: A New Nation's Development Strategy," *Occasional Paper No. 9*, Washington, D.C.: Overseas Development Council, March 1978.

4. Cf. Denis Goulet, "Development as Liberation: Policy Lessons from Case Studies," *World Development*, 7, no. 6 (June 1979): 555–66; Denis Goulet, "Development Experts: The One-Eyed Giants," *World Development*, 8, no. 7 (July–Aug., 1980): 481–89; and Denis Goulet, "Drawing Strength from Traditional Values, Indigenous Practices and Community Institutions," introductory chapter of book to be published by the Overseas Development Council.

5. Morris David Morris, *Measuring the Condition of the World's Poor: The Physical Quality of Life Index* (New York: Pergamon Press, 1979).

6. Denis Goulet, *The Cruel Choice, A New Concept in the Theory of Development* (New York: Atheneum, 1971); Denis Goulet and Steven H. Arnold, "The 'Abundant Society': Dominant Life Styles in the U.S. and the Search for Alternatives," *Alternatives*, 5, no. 2 (1980).

7. Denis Goulet, "Is Gradualism Dead?" *Ethics in Foreign Policy* (New York: Council on Religion and International Affairs, 1970).

8. Denis Goulet, *The Uncertain Promise, Value Conflicts in Technology Transfer* (New York: IDOC/NORTH AMERICA, 1977); "Can Values Shape Third World Technology Policy?", *Journal of International Affairs*, 33, no. 1 (Spring/ Summer 1979): 89–109.

9. Denis Goulet, "Is Economic Justice Possible?" to be published by the

University of Notre Dame Press as a chapter in forthcoming book *Economic Justice*, ed. Stephen T. Worland and Roger B. Skurski.

10. Denis Goulet, "Development and the International Economic Order," *International Development Review*, 16, no. 2 (1974): 10–16; "An International Support System for Meeting Basic Needs," *Review of Politics*, 43, no. 1 (January 1981), 22–42.

11. Adolf A. Berle, Jr., *The 20th Century Capitalist Revolution* (New York: Harcourt, Brace and Co., 1954), p. 183.

12. *Ibid.*, p. 166.

13. *Abt Associates Inc. Annual Report and Social Audit 1973* (Cambridge: Mass., 1973), p. 23.

14. United Nations, Department of Economic and Social Affairs, *Multinational Corporations in World Development* (New York: UN, 1973), Doc. no. ST/ECA/190, p. 2.

15. On the sociology of interests see, e.g., Karl Mannheim, *Ideology and Utopia: An Introduction to the Sociology of Knowledge* (New York: Harcourt, Brace and World, 1936); see also Peter L. Berger and Thomas Luckman, *The Social Construction of Reality* (Garden City, N.Y.: Doubleday and Co., 1966).

16. P. R. Regamey, *La Conscience Chretienne et la guerre* (Cahiers Saint-Jacques, n.d.).

17. On the structural tensions between the pursuit of wealth and the demands of Christianity see Jacques Ellul, *L'Homme et l'argent* (Paris: Delachaux et Niestle, 1954).

18. Neil H. Jacoby, *Corporate Power and Social Responsibility* (New York: Macmillan, 1973).

19. Neil H. Jacoby, *U.S. Aid to Taiwan; A Study of Foreign Aid, Self-help and Development* (New York: Praeger, 1967).

20. Jacoby, *Corporate Power*, p. 251.

21. *Ibid.*, pp. 261–62.

22. *Ibid.*, p. xix.

23. Richard N. Farmer, *Benevolent Aggression: The Necessary Impact of the Advanced Nations on Indigenous Peoples* (New York: David McKay, 1972), p. vii.

24. *Ibid.*, p. 185.

25. *Ibid.*, p. 188.

26. *Ibid.*, p. 303.

27. *Ibid.*, p. 310.

28. Raymond Vernon, *Sovereignty at Bay: The Multinational Spread of US Enterprises* (New York: Basic Books, 1971); *Storm over the Multinationals: The Real Issues* (Cambridge, Mass.: Harvard University Press, 1977).

29. Raymond Vernon, *Storm over the Multinationals*, p. 145.

30. *Ibid.*, p. 14.

31. *Ibid.*

32. *Ibid.*, p. 155.

33. *Ibid.*, p. 167.

34. *Ibid.*, p. 204.

35. John Kenneth Galbraith, "The Defense of the Multinational Company," *Harvard Business Review*, March–April 1978, pp. 83–93.

36. John Kenneth Galbraith, interview with the *New York Times*, "The Crash: Congress Will Investigate," October 21, 1979.

37. Peter Steinfels, *The Neo-Conservatives* (New York: Simon and Schuster, 1979).

38. Michael Novak, "Irony, Tragedy, Courage," *The Smith-Kline Forum for a Healthier American Society*, 2, no. 1 (March 1980): 2.

39. *Ibid.*, p. 4.

40. Richard J. Barnet and Ronald E. Müller, *Global Reach: The Power of the Multinational Corporations* (New York: Simon and Schuster, 1974).

41. Kari Levitt, *The Silent Surrender: The Multinational Corporation in Canada* (New York: St. Martin's Press, 1970).

42. Goulet, *Uncertain Promise*, pp. 38–39, 66–67.

43. See, e.g., V. I. Lenin, *Imperialism: The Highest Stage of Capitalism* (New York: International Publishers, 1939).

44. Michael Harrington, *The Vast Majority* (New York: Simon and Schuster, 1977); *Toward a Democratic Left, A Radical Program for a New Majority* (Baltimore, Md.: Penguin Books, 1969), chap. 8, "The Almost-Imperialism," pp. 186–218.

45. United Nations, *Multinational Corporations in World Development*.

46. Paul Streeten, "Transnational Corporations and Basic Needs," in Mary Evelyn Jegen and Charles K. Wilber (eds.), *Growth with Equity* (New York: Paulist Press, 1979), pp. 163–74.

47. Severyn Bruyn, *The Social Economy: People Transforming Modern Business* (New York: John Wiley & Sons, 1977).

48. On this see Henry Wallich, "The Future of Capitalism," *Newsweek*, January 22, 1973, p. 62.

49. See, e.g., André van Dam, "The Management of Global Resources," *Industria*, April 1978, pp. 10–13; "The Third World: Poised to Become a Partner in World Commerce," *Industrial Development*, March/April, pp. 18–22; "Global Development: From Confrontation to Cooperation?", *Planning Review*, 2, no. 5 (August/September 1974): 1–3, 20–23; "The Multinational Corporation Vis-à-Vis Societies in Transformation: The Case for Intermediate Technology in the Developing Countries," *Technological Forecasting and Social Change*, 5 (1973): 281–93; and "Growth Without Pain," *Bulletin of the Atomic Scientists*, April 1978, pp. 28–30.

50. In André van Dam, "A Hearing Aid, or How to Amplify the Dialogue between Multinational Corporations and Developing Countries," paper submitted to a special colloquy at the World Conference of the Society for International Development, Abidjan, August 1974.

51. Howard Perlmutter, *Towards a Theory and Practice of Social Architecture* (London: Tavistock Publications, 1965); cf. Howard V. Perlmutter and Taghi Saghafi-nejad, "Process or Product? A Social Architectural Perspective of Codes of Conduct for Technology Transfer and Development," in Susan S.

Holland, (ed.), *Codes of Conduct for the Transfer of Technology: A Critique* (New York: Council of the Americas, 1976), pp. 95–129.

52. Two-volume report on "Technology Transfer Control Systems: Issues, Perspectives, Implications," Worldwide Institutions Group, The Wharton School, University of Pennsylvania, February 9–10, 1979, and The Graduate School of Business Administration, University of Washington, April 6–7, 1979.

53. Cf. John McHale and Magda Cordell McHale, *Human Requirements, Supply Levels and Outer Bounds: A Framework for Thinking about the Planetary Bargain* (Aspen, Colo.: Aspen Institute, 1975); John McHale and Magda Cordell McHale, *Basic Human Needs: A Framework for Action* (New Brunswick, N.J.: Transaction Books, 1977); and Harland Cleveland (ed.), *The Planetary Bargain, Proposals for a New International Economic Order to Meet Human Needs* (Aspen, Colo.: Aspen Institute, 1975).

54. Martin M. McLaughlin, (ed.), *The United States and World Development Agenda 1979* (New York, 1979); James P. Grant, *Disparity Reduction Rates in Social Indicators* (Washington, D.C.: Overseas Development Council, Monograph No. 11, September 1978).

55. Cf. Saul H. Mendlovitz (ed.), *On the Creation of a Just World Order: Preferred Worlds for the 1990's* (New York: Free Press, 1975); Richard A. Falk, *A Study of Future Worlds* (New York: Free Press, 1975).

56. Albert Tévoédjrè, *Poverty, Wealth of Mankind* (Oxford: Pergamon Press, 1978).

57. Held in Geneva, Switzerland, January 19–23, 1976.

58. Albert Tévoédjrè, "Introduction" to "Contracts of Solidarity," *Labour and Society*, 3, nos. 3/4 (July/October 1978): 267.

59. *Ibid.*, p. 268.

60. *Ibid.*, p. 270.

61. *Ibid.*, p. 271.

62. *Ibid.*, p. 274.

63. On the difference between true interdependence and its counterfeits, see Denis Goulet, *World Interdependence: Verbal Smokescreen or New Ethic?* (Washington, D.C.: Overseas Development Council, Development Paper No. 21, March 1976).

64. Tévoédjrè, "Introduction," p. 275.

65. Alain Birou, "Concluding Remarks," in "Contracts of Solidarity," p. 493.

66. The twin themes of "right to development" and "law of enforcement" were debated at The Hague Academy of International Law in a symposium on "The Right to Development at the International Level," held at The Hague October 16–18, 1979. This author attended the symposium.

67. Tévoédjrè, "Introduction," p. 275.

68. On this see Goulet, *The Uncertain Promise*, pp. 25–27.

69. Details of the case described in these lines are drawn from discussions by the author with corporate officials during a seminar in which he was a

participant on "Corporations and Developing Countries," held at corporate headquarters in East Hanover, N.J., on March 15, 1977. These exchanges are complemented by oral and documentary information obtained from Dean A. Peterson, an economist and corporate official at NABISCO headquarters.

70. On this see, "Mexican Price Curb Plan Based on Voluntary Pacts with Companies," *Business Latin American,* March 2, 1977, pp. 66–68.

71. On this see Denis Goulet, *A New Moral Order* (Maryknoll, N.Y.: Orbis Books, 1974), final chapter.

72. Karl Mannheim, *Freedom Power and Democratic Planning* (London: Routledge & Kegan Paul, 1951), pp. 191, 194.

73. Cf. Barbara Ward, Foreword to *The Poverty Curtain,* (New York: Columbia University Press, 1976), p. xii.

74. Christopher Dawson, *Dynamics of World History* (New York: Sheed & Ward, 1957), p. 364.

PART FOUR

The Corporation and Social Responsibility

Early in the twentieth century, Walter Rauschenbusch, a pioneer of the social-gospel movement, expressed a concern that continues to trouble many observers today.

> Organizations are rarely formed for avowedly evil ends. They drift into evil under sinister leadership, or under the pressure of need or temptation. For instance, . . . a trust, desiring to steady prices and to get away from antiquated competition, undersells the independents and evades or purchases legislation. This tendency to deterioration shows the soundness of the social instincts, but also the ease with which they go astray, and the need of righteous social institutions to prevent temptation.[1]

> A realization of the spiritual power and value of these composite personalities must get into theology, otherwise theology will not deal adequately with the problem of sin and of redemption, and will be unrelated to some of the most important work of salvation which the coming generations will have to do.[2]

While the pressing problems of Rauschenbusch's time differ, perhaps, from those of our own, organizations and those wielding power in organizations continue to be held accountable for the social effects of their decisions. Today Rauschenbusch's "most important work of salvation" for business organizations is often discussed under the rubric of "the social responsibility of business."[3] The assumption is that there is a common core of values that we as a people hold, and that these social values are shaped and affected by the decisions and activities of business corporations. In this final section of the volume, Part Four, various dimensions of this theme are explored.

Where the Law Ends

The first essay, Chapter 9, is by Christopher D. Stone, a professor of law. His opening question sets the agenda: "Exactly what are socially responsible corporations supposed to do and why?" The thrust of his essay is that "profit-maximizing decisions must yield to 'responsible' positions." He uses the term "profit-maximizing" to refer to that behavior of an organization which single-mindedly focuses on *its* goals to the exclusion of any consideration of morals or society's best interests.

The thorny questions come in deciding just what a "responsible" position is. Some argue that morality and society's interests are best served by allowing the free market to produce and allocate resources; should the market encourage behavior that is undesirable to society, then the law is the appropriate tool to correct the situation. For those who take this position, market and legal signals are sufficient, and no moral or social constraints are appropriate. This is not to say that there are no ethical concerns in the market model; in fact, in order for the market mechanism to work effectively and thereby provide ample goods and services at the best price, there must be "ethical" and "responsible" behavior. For example, the market mechanism assumes adequate information to consumers so that intelligent choices are possible. False advertising, price fixing, honesty in honoring contracts, integrity in providing financial information for shareholders and in developing capital markets — these are all essential ethical concerns of the market model.

The basic responsibility of corporate leaders operating with this market mind-set is expressed well by one of its leading spokespersons today, Milton Friedman: "to make as much money as possible while conforming to the basic rules of the society, both those embodied in law and those embodied in ethical custom."[4] For Friedman, "ethical custom" means the honesty, fidelity, and integrity required for the market mechanism to function. Ethical custom does not include bringing human and social values into economic decisions. But the integration of these concerns into the economic affairs of the corporation is precisely what is advocated by those concerned with the "social responsibility of business." Friedman argues that bringing human values into economic decisions will ultimately lead to a transfer of power from the market mechanism to the political mechanism, and that such excessive governmental power brings with it all the evils of socialism. He thus labels social responsibility a "fundamentally subversive doctrine."[5]

Stone gets right to the heart of the matter with his incisive criticism of this position. For Stone, there is a basic assumption in our society that people will act responsibly—that is, they will act self-consciously, for a reason and in light of some valued goal. To put Stone's argument in Friedman's terms, Stone is arguing that "ethical custom" includes more than the honesty and integrity required to maintain the market, that as "an autonomous, moral human being" one necessarily goes through a cognitive process when making a decision on a complex issue. Stone lists some characteristics of this cognitive process: reflecting before acting, assessing consequences of contemplated action, scanning one's environment for its morally significant features, and weighing alternatives in moral terms. He also notes that a responsible person possesses a moral inclination to do the right thing. Thus, for Stone, one cannot depend on a utilitarian convergence of business and social values à la Smith's "invisible hand." One must self-consciously reflect and act in the light of a valued objective; that is, one must be responsible.

Friedman argues that business corporations ought to do what they are qualified to do—make money—and that this is their responsibility. Other institutions of society can take on the social roles. Yet economic decisions of business corporations have social and political ramifications and, Stone argues, insofar as possible, these ought to be considered when making a decision. Stone's position is that it is not sufficient simply to follow legal and market signals, rather, one ought to consider the good of "society at large." Charles Powers makes a similar point: "To argue that a corporation should take no responsibility beyond profit-making is to fail to see that our social systems cannot be neat because human dignity is so complex and because the distinctions between the social roles of institutions are too blurred."[6]

Stone also discusses whether it makes sense to ascribe moral predicates to corporate entities. For example, does it make sense to say that "Ford was morally blameworthy to have designed the Pinto gas tank the way it did"? He argues that such questions are meaningful precisely because they are likely to draw attention to the corporate behavior that is called into question—"that is, [to bring] about desirable changes in the internal rules, policies, organizational attitudes, and so on, that appear to be connected to the undesired conduct." Because of poor communication and overlapping networks of responsibility, it is conceivable that immoral outcomes can come about even when it is hard to distinguish any particular agents whose conduct is clearly immoral. The structure of the organization, its attitudes, ethos, and so on, may be the problem. In Stone's view educating persons regarding society's values and goals and delineating what is to be taken as right and wrong behavior are important functions of moral discourse.

"Law as a Floor, but not a Ceiling"

There are some interesting parallels between Stone's position on the role of law and that of a tradition of religious thinkers. Stone argues that in some cases, for the good of society, the corporate leader is required to do more than meet the letter of the law. He must engage in reflection as an "autonomous moral human being" and attempt to discern the right thing to do — even when it goes beyond or supersedes the current law. In the general introduction and the introduction to Part Two of this volume, mention was made of the natural-law position of the medieval religious scholar, Thomas Aquinas (1225-1274). Aquinas understood law to be "an ordinance of reason for the common good made by the authority who has care of the community and promulgated."[7] Law is thought of as a tool in service of realizing the good; it is as an instrument to protect the quality of life of a society. Citizens who might not otherwise do good will at least abide by some minimum standards when the coercive force of law is present. The law, however, is a means to an end, the good of society.[8] According to Aquinas, persons ought to cultivate the skill of discerning the inner meaning of the law, and be creative in devising ways to realize its intention, even when the law itself fails to protect and adequately promote the common good. Aquinas calls this skill of discerning the spirit of the law *epikeia* (from the Greek word meaning equity).[9]

For Aquinas, the human law is an attempt to make the natural moral law concrete and particular in order to have a harmonious society. For example, he would hold that a tenet of natural law is that justice requires that all persons give others their due. This commonly held principle, arrived at by reason and experience, is taken by some religious thinkers to be God's intention for humankind implanted in creation to be discovered by inquiring minds. Yet what is this "due" that we owe each other? Societies attempt to detail the working out of the basic natural law for a specific time and circumstance. However, since human laws may be inadequate and incomplete, disciplined critical reflection rather than following the letter of the law in lockstep fashion is essential. From one point of view, Stone's work may be seen as a retrieval of these important insights on law for our time in a creative and original fashion.

A Case Study

Chapter 10 is authored by a distinguished corporate leader, Catherine B. Cleary; she is the former chief executive officer of a major bank, and is currently a member of the boards of directors of General Motors, AT&T, and several other large firms. Her essay is an excellent illustration of the two different senses of responsibility discussed in Christopher Stone's article. Stone distinguishes between two kinds of responsibility—R_1 and R_2. R_1 refers to the responsibility entailed in following prescribed canons of behavior that have been established and routinized in an organization. For example, we have come to expect certain conduct from a judge, a professor, or a priest, and each of these is "responsible" (R_1) when he or she meets expectations and fulfills the duties of the role. R_2 is the sort of responsibility already highlighted here; it involves conscious reflection by a moral human being who is following more "open-textured and general" rules.

Cleary achieved success in a man's world long before there were incentives structured into corporate practice to encourage justice to women. In the oral introduction to her paper, when it was initially presented, she told how, after graduating from law school some thirty years ago, she applied for jobs in law firms and was invariably asked if she could type! Her point was that most men in the legal profession at that time had had no experience with women colleagues, and had no role models for women lawyers; a woman might be a secretary, but a lawyer!

Although there were no legal sanctions encouraging firms to hire women when Cleary began her career, she was fortunate in that she finally encountered some executives who were operating according to Stone's R_2, men who were willing and able to depart from the standard operating procedures of the day, R_1, and bring along a talented woman. She notes that there are many moral reasons for continuing to reform corporate behavior toward women: justice, respect for human dignity, religious convictions on equality, and so on. These reasons are brought together with the term "stakeholder." For, as she says:

In my opinion most large publicly held corporations in this country today recognize that the corporation has an accountability beyond its accountability to stockholders for financial results.

The new word to describe these groups [owed accountability] is "stakeholders," a term which recognizes that they have some claim on the corporation.

Cleary notes the need for some structural changes in corporate life in order to insure that women employees have an equal opportunity at work, and that society continues to be enriched with the stable institutions of marriage and the family. Finally, she points out that, at root, the women's issue is a human issue, and that attending to it will be of benefit to all of society.

A Religious Dimension to Business Life

The third essay of Part Four, Chapter 11, is a unique exercise in collaboration between a premier theological ethicist, James M. Gustafson, and an experienced senior-level corporate lawyer, Elmer Johnson. Their dialogue provides some crucial insight into the ethical resources of religion for the corporate leader today. Johnson argues that "modern managerial capitalism" needs a new ethic of corporate leadership which relies less on self-interest incentives and more on moral incentives. For example, he cites the case of top executives who are so motivated by short-term financial-incentive plans that they often make decisions which are economically and socially costly in the long-run; perhaps they know that they will not be around when the day of reckoning finally comes! Johnson's point is that this sort of executive strives for the short-term financial gain at the expense of the common good, both of the corporation and of society.

The essay provides an idea of the sort of person who is needed in the executive ranks today, a person with professional competence, personality, respect for others, maturity of judgment, and productive capacity. Drawing on the best of religious social thought, Johnson notes that institutions must rely more on evoking the cooperative tendencies of human beings and less on coercion. This means that corporations may have to look seriously at structural reform, and that lawmakers may have to be more creative in legislating their concerns for the common good.

In offering his proposals and comments on the role of law in society, Gustafson draws on the rich resources of the Judeo-Christian tradition. While he is well-versed in the work of Thomas Aquinas and the Scholastic tradition, his own stance is a modified natural-law position stemming from the writings of John Calvin and others.[10] Here it is necessary to note an important distinction in Protestant thought between the position of Martin Luther and that of John Calvin on the role of law. For Luther, law has two primary functions. The first is the spiritual role of reminding one of personal inadequacy, and hence of the need for a radical trust in Christ if one is to achieve salvation. The Decalogue (Ten Commandments) and the injunctions of the Christian Scriptures fulfill this function; when our many failures in living up to these laws become apparent, we are driven to rely on Christ for salvation.[11] The second use of the law, according to Luther, is called the "civic use," the ordinances of society that protect common life from falling into chaos. Luther saw the civic use of the law as a "dike against sin," a way to maintain a semblance of order in a corrupt world.[12] Unlike Aquinas, he was not optimistic that law could promote and protect the common good, for that seemed beyond the possibilities for this corrupt and darkened world.

Calvin, while accepting Luther's two uses of the law, dwelled more on what he called the "third use," the function of law in exhorting and instructing. Calvin vividly describes his understanding of this role: "The law is to the flesh like a whip to an idle and balky ass, to arouse it to work."[13] His approach to law has much in common with Aquinas and the Catholic tradition. Calvin also believed that there was a natural moral law, the Decalogue, which revealed the divine intentions for humankind. Calvin's thinking appears to have influenced some of Gustafson's proposals. For example, Elmer Johnson suggests some "rules and procedures of action" to guide corporations in maintaining a superior ethical environment. Gustafson responds that these are to be taken not simply as a "dike against sin," but also as "a way of ordering institutions that is more in accord with the 'divine governance.' " He goes on to elaborate his view of law as a tool to enhance the common good, and notes that Johnson's proposals "align the institutions with those powers that are directed toward realizing a larger social and human good than narrow self-interest permits."

Gustafson's constructive work provides theological underpinings for Stone's conviction (Chapter 9) that it is through a cognitive process, examining the situation in all its dimensions, that a person discerns what it means to be responsible. In Gustafson's words, "it is in and through events that moral requirements are developed and that a moral consciousness is raised." In his other writings, Gustafson elaborates the theological warrant for such a position; he contends that the fundamental belief is "the presence of the ultimate and purposive power in events and in experience."[14] Thus by reflecting on experience, considering the accrued wisdom of the community, and, in this light, forming moral judgments, one actually perceives "some signals about what God is requiring humans to be and to do.[15] This is a natural-law position with some similarities to Aquinas. Aquinas understood the moral law in nature to be grounded in creation, a participation in the eternal law of God, and the human mind as capable of discerning this knowledge.[16] Gustafson shuns Aquinas's use of Aristotelian epistemology and metaphysics and speaks rather of the "signals" of God's will discerned through moral judgments.

To be in tune with God's intentions, however, requires a certain sort of person. Religion has always been a significant resource for shaping the character, and Gustafson argues that this moral nurturing task must be recovered by the churches. Specifically, he suggests that the corporate leader would be enobled by the community, the theology, and the personal faith that is shared in the churches. A person formed and sustained in this way would be alert to try to discover God's intentions for the society and the time. Finally, Gustafson closes the dialogue with some intimations that all has not been said, that further, more radical probings into the possibilities of a more just society might be a fruitful endeavor.[17]

The Ethical Resources Within the Corporation

Chapter 12 is written by Kirk Hanson, of the Graduate School of Business of Stanford University. Chapter 11 considered the resources of religion in forming the conscience of corporate men and women; Kirk Hanson, drawing from his experience as consultant to major corporations, examines in a very practical way the institutional structures and resources available within the corporation to enhance its ethical sensitivity. Like the other writers in Part Four, he rejects the argument that the problem of corporate ethics will be solved solely by hiring morally good people. Hanson sees that the modern corporation is far too complex internally for such a simplistic answer. He argues for a corporate culture augmented by policies and procedures which will insure an effective balance of social and ethical concerns with the traditional business mentality of productivity and profitability.

This balance will be difficult to obtain, and some argue further that it would distract corporations from the business dynamic growing out of such practical values as growth, productivity, market exploitation, and profitability (the virtues which Edward Trubac described in Chapter 1). Certainly this conservative point of view, "that business ought to stick to its knitting," has been strengthened by the inflationary decade of the seventies and the malaise of industrial societies like the United States and Great Britain.[18] In addition, the idealism of the sixties—with economic growth apparently guaranteed—has given way to a new realism of the eighties: How do we maintain our industrial base? How do we provide jobs and careers for the postwar baby-boom generation moving into adulthood? How do we finance huge social programs like social security and national defense? How do we maintain our fidelity to biblical and ethical values of compassion and social justice in difficult times?

Kirk Hanson believes that the best of American corporations can fulfill the tasks created by this New Realism without a return to a "business-as-usual" climate. He is optimistic that businessmen and -women are adaptable enough, as well as sufficiently competent, to handle this challenge. These people are experienced in making tough decisions about "trade-offs between impacts on various constituencies," which for Hanson is the essence of the discipline of ethics. He quotes one business executive who saw his role as fundamentally that of a "practicing ethicist." Hanson goes on to make the point that most unethical business practices of the recent past were not caused by malevolence, but by shoddy management, that is, "the executive didn't do his or her homework." Hanson's paper is actually a call for a greater sense of professional responsibility by management which can avoid a return to "business as usual" or a new wave of government regulation.

In his essay, Kirk Hanson asks this question: "How do you manage a company in a way that all your managers, every day, will make good, consistent, and ethical decisions?" In other words, how do you raise and maintain the corporate ethical consciousness? He details nine techniques that should be present if the company is serious about ethical issues. His techniques point to the need to institutionalize ethical concerns by making them an integral part of the workings of a corporation. Social and ethical issues must receive the same attention as the traditional means of communication and decision-making within the company: financial and operational reports, strategic planning, policy-making, goal setting, and performance evaluation. To do otherwise, would indicate that social and ethical concerns take a "back seat." Finally, he describes how Atlantic Richfield Company demonstrates its seriousness by inviting outsiders to examine the corporation's internal policies and procedures, and, uniquely, by allowing public disclosure. Thornton Bradshaw, the recent president of Atlantic

Richfield and the newly appointed chairman of RCA, has this explanation of the innovative social-responsibility audit:

> One company issues an annual social responsibility report
> which includes a balance sheet of the year's activities (both debits
> and credits) prepared by a business writer-social activist. The
> arrangement precludes editing by the corporation and guaran-
> tees publication. This may be a startling departure by some
> corporate standards, but it is really a small step and hardly
> scratches the surface of the problem.
>
> Some who have reflected on the problem lean toward yearly
> issuance of so-called social responsibility audits, but little has been
> done beyond a few brief descriptions in annual reports. However,
> a widening recognition that people will judge corporations by
> poor standards if better ones are not available may lead to the
> development of better reporting in the future.[19]

It is important to recognize that there are considerable differences
in ethical perception from the top, the executive suite, and the middle-
and lower-management levels. Oftentimes, top management cannot
understand why some unit or division committed actions that are later
judged either unethical or illegal: "We don't want that kind of conduct
here!" or, "These people had only to read our corporate code of
conduct to know that they were getting out of line." But consider these
examples from the *Wall Street Journal*:[20]

> In response to ambitious but unrealistic targets of output and
> profit for next year, middle management resorted to deceptive
> bookkeeping, which for a time allowed the division to reach its
> goals.
>
> In violation of a labor-management contract, a secret speedup of
> an assembly line was carried out by middle management to meet
> goals set by the home office. Later, when asked why, the mana-
> gers responded: "We tried to explain our problems to higher-ups
> in the company, but we were told, 'I don't care how you do it—just
> do it.' "
>
> In order to pass a government emission standards test, some
> engineers of one company performed unauthorized mainte-
> nance, which was later discovered. The explanation: "When
> senior management puts the squeeze on, it encourages
> shortcuts."

There can be an excitement in plotting new "highs" in performance for the next quarter or year that will make top management look good in the eyes of peers, stockholders, and the business press. But to management lower in the corporate hierarchy, these goals become heavy burdens, and the cause of many unethical business practices. Kirk Hanson calls for an environmental scanning to determine the impact of the corporation on its various constituencies: labor, stockholders, consumers, and community groups. What can be forgotten within the organization is the impact of growth and performance on the managerial ranks themselves. The recently retired chairman of General Motors, Thomas A. Murphy, while generally optimistic that business could live up to high ethical standards, did indicate a major concern about this kind of internal pressure:

> Every person in authority must know his people. He must be sensitive to the pressures they're working under. Not everyone will complain if they're assigned a seemingly impossible goal. Some will simply go ahead and cut corners, ignore their conscience, even commit illegal acts, in the mistaken belief that they are expected to do so by their superiors. I am not talking about the occasional crook or outright criminal now. I am talking about otherwise honest people who respond in an unfortunate way to pressure.
>
> A manager's responsibility in this matter cannot be ignored. The success of an undertaking demands that the people involved be put under pressure to excel, granted. But a good manager must be careful not to put more pressure on a person than he or she can handle. And the only way a manager can hope to do that is by knowing the person. It's not a question of what I could accomplish or how I would go about it in a given situation; it's a question of what this particular subordinate, this particular person, will probably do and probably accomplish. This is a management responsibility, and from an ethical standpoint, it's one of the most serious anyone in a position of authority must meet.[21]

The Manager as a Professional

In discussing the sort of person who is desirable to manage corporations today, Gustafson in Chapter 11 highlights the importance of professional training. The crucial need is for persons who have a professional or moral character, a person with developed habits of thought and patterns of conduct. This sort of person has a standpoint, a vision from which to be responsive, Gustafson argues. The many themes of this volume can be woven together under the rubric of "the manager as a professional." A professional is defined as a person displaying four essential attributes: (1) training in a systematic body of knowledge ("professed" special knowledge); (2) dedication to values that will enhance the common good; (3) voluntary adherence to norms of practice established and enforced by colleagues; and (4) participation in a system of rewards, monetary and honorary, which acknowledge excellence in performance.[22] In various ways, the twelve essays assembled here point to the need for all of these attributes in corporate leaders today.

With the image of "the manager as a professional" as a guide for life, a corporate leader comes to understand him- or herself as one who is ultimately accountable to the society and its view of the good life. This self-perception of the executive will preclude making decisions based solely on economic criteria. Peter Drucker suggests that managers today adopt the standard for young physicians set out by the Greeks some 2,500 years ago: *primum non nocere* — "Above all, not knowingly to do harm."[23] A professional must *try* to do good, but, more importantly, he or she must *promise* not consciously to do harm. This key insight from the Hippocratic oath is as relevant today as it was for the ancient Greeks.

Conclusion

The overarching theme of the twelve essays in this volume is perhaps best summed up by the call "to be responsible." And, in all of this there is much guidance and sustaining power in our religious traditions — virtues, habits, attitudes, a way of life, and so forth. Should we choose to face the future with the strength of the past, there is much hope. Should we not, the future is questionable. The Pulitzer Prize-winning historian, Oscar Handlin, writing with his wife Mary on the American experience, put the question well:

> The communities of farmers, merchants and artisans which two hundred years earlier brought the nation into being are gone beyond retrieval. The hustling men and women who built its industrial structure in the nineteenth century have moved off stage. The elaborate enterprise they left behind, infinitely intricate, composed of innumerable interdependent parts, spins on. But whether the pieces will long remain in place without guidance or purpose — that is the ultimate question.[24]

NOTES

1. Walter Rauschenbusch, *A Theology for the Social Gospel* (Nashville: Abingdon Press, 1945), p. 72.

2. *Ibid.*, p. 76.

3. For an account of the historical development of the concept of the social responsibility of business, see Howard R. Bowen, "Social Responsibilities of the Businessman—Twenty Years Later," *Rationality, Legitimacy, Responsibility: Search for New Directions in Business and Society,* ed. Edwin M. Epstein and Dow Votaw (Santa Monica, Calif.: Goodyear Publishing Company, 1978), pp. 116–30.

4. Milton Friedman, "The Social Responsibility of Business is to Increase its Profits," *New York Times Magazine,* September 13, 1970, p. 33. This article is reproduced in *Ethical Issues in Business: A Philosophical Approach,* ed. Thomas Donaldson and Patricia H. Werhane (Englewood Cliffs, N.J.: Prentice-Hall, 1979), pp. 191–97.

5. Milton Friedman, *Capitalism and Freedom* (Chicago: University of Chicago Press, 1962), p. 133.

6. Charles W. Powers, "Can the Market Sustain an Ethic?: An Assessment of the Questions We Ask of Economic Systems," in *Can the Market Sustain an Ethic?,* ed. Yale Brozen, Elmer W. Johnson, and Charles W. Powers (Chicago: University of Chicago Press, 1978), p. 74. Peter Drucker makes a similar point: "Yet the 'pure' position of Milton Friedman, the Chicago economist and Nobel Prize winner—to avoid all social responsibility—is not practical either. There are big, urgent, desperate problems . . . Business and the other institutions of our society of organizations cannot be pure, however desirable that may be. Their own self-interest alone forces them to be concerned with society and community and to be prepared to shoulder responsibility beyond their own main areas of task and responsibility." *Management* (London: Pan Books Ltd., 1979), p. 281.

7. Thomas Aquinas, *Summa Theologica,* I-II, 90, 4.

8. Aquinas understood law in terms of finality, that is, in terms of Aristotle's "final cause," the cause which has reference to the end or purpose of a thing. Thus, a law has meaning and validity if it does what it was designed to do, protect and promote the common good.

9. Thomas Aquinas, *Summa Theologica,* II-II, 120, 1-2. Karl Rahner, S.J., develops the theme that the justification of law is the common good. See "The Dignity and Freedom of Man," *Theological Investigations II* (Baltimore: Helicon Press, 1963), pp. 235–64. Also Timothy E. O'Connell, *Principles for a Catholic Morality* (New York: Seabury Press, 1976), esp. chap. 18, "The Theology of Human Law," pp. 184–95.

10. See James M. Gustafson, *Can Ethics be Christian?* (Chicago: University of Chicago Press, 1975), esp. chap. 6, "Religious Beliefs and the Determination of Conduct," pp. 145–68.

11. Luther, *The Bondage of the Will* (1526), ed. Philip Watson, in *Luther*

Works, vol. 33 (Philadelphia: Fortress Press, 1972), p. 121: "For human nature is so blind that it does not know its own powers, or rather diseases, and so proud as to imagine that it knows and can do everything; and for this pride and blindness God has no readier remedy than the propounding of his law. . . ."

12. Luther, *Temporal Authority: To What Extent It Should Be Obeyed,* ed. Walther I. Brandt, in *Luther Works,* vol. 45 (Philadelphia: Muhlenberg Press, 1962), p. 90: "To put it here as briefly as possible, Paul says that the law has been laid down for the sake of the lawless [1 Tim. 1:9], that is, so that those who are not Christians may through the law be restrained outwardly for evil deeds, as we shall hear later. Now since no one is by nature Christian or righteous, but altogether sinful and wicked, God through the law puts them all under restraint so they dare not wilfully implement their wickedness in actual deeds."

13. John Calvin, *Institutes of the Christian Religion,* bk. II, chap. vii, sec. 12; in Henry Beveridge, trans., *Institutes,* 2 vols. (London: James Clark, 1949), 1: 309. Cf. David Little, "Calvin and the Prospects for a Christian Theory of Natural Law," *Norm and Context in Christian Ethics,* ed. Gene H. Outka and Paul Ramsey (New York: Scribner's, 1968).

14. James M. Gustafson, *Can Ethics Be Christian?* (Chicago: University of Chicago Press, 1975), p. 158.

15. *Ibid.*

16. Cf. Thomas Aquinas, *Summa Theologica,* II–II, 90–108.

17. A retired senior executive who attended the conference where ten of the essays of this volume were originally presented commented on his impressions: "Recently I attended a conference on the subject of 'The Judeo-Christian Ethic and the Modern Business Corporation.' There were about twenty-five theologians of the major faiths present. In the papers and the discussions there was frequent reference to 'unfair' competition, but I do not recall a single question by a theologian about competition per se." Cf. Robert K. Greenleaf, *Servant: Retrospect and Prospect* (Peterborough, N.H.: Windy Row Press, 1980), p. 28.

18. For a fuller treatment of this argument, see Norman Macrae, "America's Third Century," *Economist* (London), October 25, 1975. In addition, see "The Reindustrialization of America," *Business Week,* June 30, 1980, pp. 55–142. This special report argues for "sweeping changes in basic institutions . . . and in the way the major actors on the economic scene—business, labor, government, and minorities—think about what they put into the economy and what they get out of it."

19. Thornton Bradshaw, *Corporations and Their Critics,* ed. Thornton Bradshaw and David Vogel (New York: McGraw-Hill Book Company, 1981), p. xxii.

20. George Getschow, "Some Middle Managers Cut Corners to Achieve High Corporate Goals," *Wall Street Journal,* May 12, 1980, p. 1.

21. Thomas A. Murphy, "Reflections of a Retired Businessman," *The Eugene B. Clark Executive Lecture Series* (Notre Dame, Ind.: College of Business Administration, 1981), p. 15.

22. These points follow from Bernard Barber, "Is American Business Becoming Professionalized? Analysis of a Social Ideology," in *Sociocultural Theory, Values and Sociocultural Change: Essays in Honor of Pitirim A. Sorokin,* ed. E. A. Tiryatian (New York: Free Press of Glencoe, 1963). See also A. M. Carr-Saunders and P. Wilson, "Professions," *Encyclopedia of the Social Sciences* (New York: Macmillan, 1933), and Emile Durkheim, *Professional Ethics and Civic Morals,* trans. Cornelia Brookfield, (London: Routledge and Kegan Paul, 1957).

23. Peter Drucker, *Management,* pp. 296–303.

24. Oscar and Mary F. Handlin, *The Wealth of the American People* (New York: McGraw-Hill, 1975), p. 250. See also Gerald F. Cavanagh, *American Business Values in Transition* (Englewood Cliffs, N.J.: Prentice-Hall, 1976), and Oliver F. Williams, C.S.C., "Christian Formation for Corporate Life," *Theology Today,* October 1979, pp. 347–52.

9. Corporate Accountability in Law and Morals

Christopher D. Stone

During the past decade, along with a perceived growth in corporate power and the increased publicity given to corporate misconduct, there has been renewed interest in corporate social responsibility as an antidote. Indeed, to say that corporations should be socially responsible sounds at once so laudable and so limp that the notion has won broad support from both leaders within the corporate community and critics hammering from without. Corporate social responsibility is something we need, something whose "time has come"—but no one is being especially clear as to what it *is*. Exactly what are socially responsible corporations supposed to do, and why?

Certainly, in the space of these remarks, a complete and satisfactory set of answers is not forthcoming. But I hope to provide a few basic observations that are precise enough to steer the debate in a more productive direction. Specifically, I set out with an attempt to define the grounds under dispute: where do the proponents and opponents of corporate social responsibility agree, and where are they at odds? (Part I). In Part II, I outline what I take to be the strength of the opponents' position, that is, the reasons why one might prefer that the managers orient themselves to market and legal signals to the exclusion of extraneous moral and social constraints. In Part III, I give what I consider to be the proponents' best response to these arguments, and in Part IV, I indicate more exactly the sort of corporate responsibility that I believe defensible, one that calls for "responsible" reflection in certain circumstances. In Part V, I support both the intelligiblity, and prudence, of my position that we should increasingly hold corporate bodies (rather than, or in addition to their agents), morally accountable by drawing on some parallels presented in law, where analogous questions arise as to holding corporate bodies accountable legally.

I. The Profits Position vs. Voluntarism

Some of the confusion in the corporate-social-responsibility literature begins with its choice of the term itself. To say that one is advocating "corporate social responsibility" is highly misleading, if it suggests that those who disagree favor corporations being irresponsible, in the sense of indifferent to the satisfaction of human wants. In truth, there probably exists, between the two camps—those who favor and those who oppose the talk about corporate social responsibility— some differences as to what each would regard as the ideal society. But I suspect that the differences between them are less significant than the common bonds. Both groups want to see a productive and sober use of society's resources. Neither wants to see people going around unfed, much less poisoned by toxic wastes. Hence, the basic dividing line is not over ends, but means. Those who demur to "corporate social responsibility" believe by and large, that corporations are most likely to satisfy human wants when they are seeking profits within the bounds of collectively agreed-upon constraints in the form of legal rules. By contrast, the "responsibility" advocates believe that the social welfare requires corporate managers to give some consideration to social-moral concerns that are not adequately captured in the profits-law signals.

In order not to "load" the issue in favor of the proponents, I will temporarily[1] drop the term "responsibility," and divide the contending camps into advocates of the *profits position,* and advocates of *voluntarism.* The issue can be put as follows: Is society generally better off if corporate managers decide among alternative courses of action on the basis of which choice promises to be most profitable? or should they, in certain defined circumstances, select a course that voluntarily subordinates profit maximization to the realization of some other value that is not the organization's? It is the first of these positions that I term the profits position; the second is what I shall call voluntarism.

As with any other introductory, fundamental dichotomy, this one blurs some distinctions that others might wish to account for. For example, the notion of profit maximization is itself indefinite. The choices that maximize short-term profits are not the same as those that will maximize profits in the long run. The set of strategies that are ideal for some investors—the bondholders, say—is not the same as that which will be most "profitable" for the common shareholders. Moreover, some will point out that most major American corporations are not pure profit maximizers in any of the above senses, anyhow.

Over some range of output, they probably aim to maximize some other goal the corporation seeks—such as expanding into new fields, or increasing market position—even if doing so entails some foregone profit at the margin, i.e., even if it is not profit maximizing.

I am thus aware that, by taking several distinguishable strategies, and lumping them all into "profits maximization," I risk overburdening a single notion. I do so, first, because I suspect that, by and large, the distinctions one can make in theory fail to translate into large differences in practice. In most companies, in the face of almost all decisions, the significance of one theoretically available definition of "profit" over another, or of one institutional, probably short-term goal (profits), over another (sales volume), is likely to be too sophisticated and refined to be accounted for by the rough decisional data. Even more important, the distinction that lies at the heart of the debate is not so much one between seeking profits, on the one hand, and sacrificing profits, on the other—although that is a handy way to put it, which I will generally adopt. At the heart of the controversy, there is no less critical an issue of "corporate social responsibility" whenever the corporation finds conflict between its own, self-defined goals (profits and/or expansion), on the one hand, and exogenously (socially) defined criteria of welfare, on the other. Indeed, recognizing the conflict in these broad terms allows us to generalize from "corporate responsibility" in the for-profit sector to the ordinarily neglected issues of corporate responsibility among not-for-profit corporations. Consider, for example, the case of a charitable corporation whose self-defined organizational goal is to distribute food to starving people in Southeast Asia; suppose further that the charity cannot get the food through (realize its primary goal) unless it bribes local officials. How different is the issue faced by the managers of the charitable corporation from those faced by the officers of the business corporation, operating in the same region? I cannot, in the space of this paper, analyze all the similarities and contrasts. But we do well to keep the broader range of "corporate" problems in mind as we press ahead.

Hence, little is lost, and there is perhaps something to be gained, if we extend the notion of profits maximization slightly, using it as a sort of shorthand to include all those things the company wants to do to advance its own welfare (however *it* would define its welfare autonomously, without independent consideration of morals or society's best interests).[2]

One reason why the distinction between the profits position and voluntarism is not more clearly drawn in the literature is that it is so often unclearly drawn in practice. In many situations in which the corporate managers, scanning the unknowable future, decide a concrete case, several alternatives will hold equal promise of yielding the most profit (or providing the corporation whatever else it may be seeking to maximize). Of course, it would be easy to argue that at least in these cases, in which the managers face an array of alternatives equally promising from the perspective of profits, they ought to select from the group that choice which ranks best from some moral perspective. However, I do not want to be diverted by this set of cases (although it may possibly turn out to be a large and significant group), because to get at the fundamental issue, we have to postulate situations in which the conflict between the profits position and voluntarism appears clear-cut.

Making the conflict clear-cut is not easy, however, even in an illustration. Part of the problem stems from the fact that what is "morally" the right thing to do—considering the things the voluntarist wants the manager to account for—often comes out the same as "good business" considered simply from the vantage of profits. Consider, for example, a company that is considering "pulling up stakes" from the community that has been dependent upon it for many years, without giving warning, in order to head off community countermeasures. Obviously, the decision can be seen to raise considerations not only of ethics, but of profits, inasmuch as the proposed action has an adverse effect on profits—through loss of goodwill, jeopardization of government contracts, increase in wage costs necessary to retain employees in a firm with a "bad name," and so on. However, there is a firm conceptual distinction that we have to keep in mind. If the company looks to the unfavorable public reaction *as evidence of strongly held moral values,* and decides against the action *on those grounds,* we would be justified in labeling its decision voluntarist. If, on the other hand, it considers the unfavorable publicity only through the lens of, and to the extent of, *the impact on corporate profits,* to be weighed in the balance with the moving vans and all the other costs of the move out of town, then the company's decision would be animated not by voluntarism, but by the profits position, as we are employing the term.

Let us proceed to examine the theoretical foundation for each view: first, for the profits position, then—by way of rejoinder—for the voluntarist.

II. The Case for the Profits Position

Voluntarism has broad appeal. For no one—perhaps the new

breed of business executives coming out of the management schools, in particular—likes to believe that there is nothing to their job beyond making money. In fact, however, the case for the managers to set their sights on profits, and therefore benefit the entire society, has considerably broader appeal than most of the corporate responsibility advocates—both in and out of business—generally acknowledge. In fact, the case for the profits position has in its favor three arguments, all with—and this has to be emphasized—strong moral appeal. Each of these arguments would seem to place the burden of rebuttal on the voluntarists.

(1) *The Market Argument.* First, the voluntarists have to account for the presumptive capacity of the market both to produce and to allocate resources in a way that is morally superior to alternative social arrangements. In general, businesses make profits, or fail, in proportion to how adequately the goods and services they provide benefit society. This is not a presumption that is rebutted by showing—what I assume to be obvious to everyone—that the pursuit of profits leads to "excesses" that most of us oppose. For the issue that divides the advocates of the profits position from the voluntarists is one of selecting alternative *systems*. The profits defender may respond that, whatever the failings of profits-oriented managerialism, voluntarism, established as a general principle of managerial orientation, would engender more "evil"—less social product, and less equitable distributions of what is produced. The managers, the way this point is ordinarily put, are trained to manage businesses. They are neither social accountants, nor politically accountable.

(2) *The Law "Corrections."* But the profits position need not stand or fall upon the much-vaunted, and often exaggerated virtues of "the market system" per se. Even the most diehard "market" advocate recognizes the need for occasional political action to keep certain abuses in check. If, under prevailing market conditions, a certain course of corporate conduct that society collectively disapproves of turns out to be profitable, society can "correct" the market signals through law. Consider, for example, a firm that finds it profitable— under pure market conditions—to dump its toxic wastes into the handiest marsh. If this state of affairs is widely disapproved of, society can make the firm civilly liable for all the damages its wastes cause. The conduct having been made that much less profitable by the prospects of damage suits, the company is induced to respond by installing pollution-abatement devices, or by redesigning its production processes so that the wastes are recycled. If, even in the face of this level of "correction," the pollution continues in an amount society deems "still

too much," a second and even third level of "corrections"—in the form of punitive damages and criminal fines—can be superimposed on the civil damages.[3]

The point is that there is a politically legitimate response to undesired corporate conduct which does not involve uprooting the managers from their orientation to profits. If the course of conduct that the market makes profitable is the "wrong" one, the law is available to make the course of conduct less profitable, in proportion to society's aversion to it. In this manner, the corporate managers do not have to weigh independently the costs and values of different courses of conduct. ("Is *this* much pollution, at *these* costs, more valuable than *this* level of pharmaceutical production, at *these* costs?") That weighing process is left to society, through the agreed-upon, democratic decision procedures.[4]

(3) *The Promissory-Agency Argument.* Third, the voluntarists have to account for the managers' obligation to their shareholders as an independent basis for the profits position. Here, the argument is not that social welfare, as such, obligates the managers to pursue profits, but that their principal obligations are to the shareholders, who are presumed to prefer profits. This argument is ordinarily garbed in the language of "agency,"[5] which is something of a misstatement, since in some technical legal sense, the directors are not the pure "agents" of the shareholders.[6] And certainly there is no express promise to maximize profits running from the managers to the shareholders. Indeed, shareholders do not typically buy their shares directly from the corporation, through the managers, at all; most shareholders have purchased their shares from prior stockholders through impersonal market transactions in which nothing is said but "buy" and "sell."

Nonetheless, a colorable, if not quite so rigorous, argument can be made to the same effect, based on an implied promise in the circumstances, fortified by rightful expectancies and reliance. The "top" managers of the corporation, the directors, are elected by the shareholders. The shareholders have come, through tradition, to expect the managers to resolve ambiguities on their behalf. These expectancies have even found sanction in the rules of fiduciary duties, which recognize the priority of the investors' claims. And, in purchasing their shares, the investors have, in anticipation of the superiority of their claims, paid more for their shares than they would have otherwise. Thus, while a strong, literal agency-promise basis of obligation is missing, a case remains that the shareholders have a moral right to expect the managers to give their interests preference.

In summary of the profits position, the voluntarist has a hard row to hoe. He must be prepared to identify circumstances in which the corporation ought to subordinate profit maximization to the advancement of some exogenous value in the face of (1) the presumptive capacity of market signals to express collective desires, (2) the presumptive capacity of society to "correct" for any defects in these market signals by providing appropriate liability rules, and (3) the not unreasonable preference that the managers, at the least, resolve any lingering ambiguities in favor of the investors.

III. The Counterarguments of the Voluntarists

In my view, none of the arguments is adequate to displace the need for the corporation to take into account values exogenous to the corporation's "self-interest." Let me take up the third argument—the promissory/agency argument—first.

Even if we were prepared to infer from the circumstances that the managers made a constructive "promise" to the shareholders to give priority to their claims, the inference would hardly settle the issue. As a moral matter (which is what we are discussing here), the practice of making promises provides for the justifiable breaking of them in certain circumstances. It is sometimes morally justifiable to break promises in the furtherance of higher social and moral interests. Hence, promises—or the assumption of an agency role—can advance moral arguments, by way of creating prima facie cases in favor of conduct, but few of us believe that a promise or agency, per se, can put an end to moral discussion. Moreover, promises always have to be interpreted; we have to decide what a promise *means*, before we even reach the question of whether to *follow it*. Thus, even if managers were to make—as I observed they do not—an express promise to their shareholders to "maximize your profits," I am not persuaded that the ordinary investor would interpret it to mean "maximize *in every way you can possibly get away with*, even if that means polluting the environment, breaking the law if you will not get caught," etc. Nor if there *were* a promise that could be interpreted as such a commitment, would I lightly suppose there to be a moral argument that it must be kept.[7]

In the last analysis, the strength of the profits position turns not on the promissory-agency claims, but on a combination of the first two arguments. Indeed, the issue over which the profits supporter and the voluntarist divide is one of the most fundamental in any society: the *ability* and *desirability* of law as a means of organizing human conduct. The profits position comes down to a strong—but I think overly strong—preference for law as the way to "correct," i.e., restrict the incidence of, profitable, but undesired behavior. The voluntarist wants to allow for, even to foster, alternative self-imposed constraints. It is largely because I, although a lawyer, harbor misgivings about our society's increasing reliance on law, that my own sympathies are divided.

Why might one harbor misgivings about law as a control device? First, as to the *abilities* of the law to transmit the desired signals to corporate managers, there are several serious drawbacks. There are, to begin with, the problems of what I call information gap and time lag.[8] To illustrate, the first clues as to the existence of some corporate-connected hazards will often reach corporate managers before they reach, and can be acted upon by, the authoritative lawmaking bodies. For example, scientists in a company's laboratory are likely to suspect, and be able to evaluate, the dangers that some new product poses, long before governmental agencies get wind of them. In these circumstances, there would seem to be a strong case for the managers, at the least, to notify the appropriate agencies so as to set the lawmaking machinery in motion.[9] Observe that such a moral obligation seems defensible whether or not the disclosure is the most profitable course for the managers to pursue, and even if the supplying of the data is not required by law. One can also imagine extending the argument to maintain not only that the managers should notify lawmakers, but that they should hold some particularly hazardous courses of action in abeyance until the legislative process has had a reasonable time to react. In other words, one might well take the basic presumption of the profits position—that anything profitable goes until the law says clearly "no"—and reverse it in some circumstances: one does not hazard some things (destruction of the ozone layer) unless and until the law clearly says "yes."

Moreover, it seems weak to argue that the corporation's obligations do not extend beyond *obeying* the law, when corporations are exerting so much influence on the laws that they are subject to. The voluntarist may be concerned to affect corporate behavior in the lawmaking process. The profits advocate is tempted to respond that the lawmaking context need present no exception to his general formula. After all, the participation of corporations in lawmaking can be made subject to its own laws—of lobbying, political contributions, and so on: let corporations maximize profits within *those laws*.

But this response has several defects. To begin with, it is somewhat circular, inasmuch as the political participation laws about corporate lobbying, and so on, are themselves subject to corporate influence. Moreover, even if the legislature were willing to enact tough restrictions on corporate political speech, it is not free to do so. Any legal constraints that touch on participation in the lawmaking process are themselves subject to superior constitutional restrictions, i.e., the First Amendment's guarantees of free speech, and the right to petition the government. As a consequence, even if we assume, for purposes of argument, that the law can provide a relatively acceptable response to abuses of commercial advertising for which First Amendment restrictions are less stringently applicable,[10] the law cannot—and ought not—be as restrictive when the corporation is engaged in political participation. When the corporation is acting as citizen, and not touting its products, we are committed to deal with it less through law, and more through trust. In this context, the case can be made that the managers are committed, reciprocally, to react in kind: to exercise self-restraint that is in some measure *voluntary;* to bring into the legislative and administrative process their own grievances about "overregulation," and their own expertise—surely; but in doing so, to temper pure profit seeking with some measure of civic responsibility.

A further inadequacy of law (hence, a further toehold for voluntarism) is apparent when we shift from a consideration of features of lawmaking (above), to features of corporations as targets of the law. There are special reasons to doubt the adequacy of law when corporations are its target. Most obviously, some of the sanctions that society deems appropriate penalties for truly heinous wrongdoing, such as imprisonment and the death penalty, are simply unavailable when the corporation is the law's quarry. Other skepticism stems from the fact that the incentives of "the corporation"—which the law typically threatens—are distinct both from those of the managers, on the one hand, and the shareholders, on the other. The salaries of the managers are likely to be relatively unscathed by fines and damage awards that fall on the corporation.

The defect in law reliance vis-à-vis the shareholders is a consequence of limited liability. Suppose, for example, a company engaged in making toxic substances. The law's sanctions—the civil- and criminal-liability rules aimed at the corporation—may pose a threat to the corporate coffers of, say, $100 million, if the company recklessly skimps on safety measures with the result that communities are endangered. But if the catastrophe happens, and the penalties are invoked, the losses will be so severe that the company will fail. In this event, the shareholders—those who stand behind the firm—are, by virtue of limited liability, immune from personal judgment. Hence, in many of the most threatening situations, the law's threats are hollow: no one will have to pick up the tab.

Thus there is considerable reason to doubt that the law can provide a complete and reliable set of rules for constraining corporate misconduct. Something more is needed.

Not only is the profit position insensitive to the limits of the law as an *effective* constraint on corporate misconduct, it makes questionable assumptions about the *desirability* of law as a control device. That is, even if (contrary to the assumptions above) the legislators were adequately informed and competent, the legislative process was unaffected by corporate influence, the rules of limited liability were not in question, and so on, there would be lingering reasons to search for some other control techniques.

It must be kept in mind that there are a number of techniques by which social behavior is constrained; the law is only one of them, sometimes reinforcing, sometimes supplementing, other, less authoritative social constraints. If we turn to ordinary human conduct, for example, we find it continuously being given direction and hedged by customs, manners, mores, and so on.[11] All these "looser" controls derive their source of authority not from the threat of the state's force, but through the internalized dynamics associated with feelings of shame, guilt, anxiety about the censure of others. Indeed, when it comes to ordinary mortals, these dynamics shoulder the largest brunt of social control: we rely on people acting *responsibly.* We would certainly think it odd for anyone to suggest that people ought to do whatever their id impulses tell them to do, within the bounds of what the law specifically condemns. The burden would seem to be on the profits advocate to tell us why it should be otherwise with corporations.

This, I think, is the central burden that the profits advocates have failed even to acknowledge. And it is not an easy burden to meet.

Consider, for a moment, why it is that we relegate so much "control" over ordinary human conduct to good manners and mores, and not simply to law. Of course, there is no single explanation, but there are several contributing reasons. One—theoretically complex, but highly significant—stems from analyses of social-choice theory by Kenneth Arrow and others. Arrow has shown the impossibility of devising any collective-choice mechanism (for example, democracy's rule of one-person, one vote) that is capable, *even in theory,* of combining individual preferences (what each person wants) into collective preferences (what the combination of citizens wants) in a manner that does not violate at least one of several basic requirements thought ideally desirable.[12] Others have demonstrated the inability of various collective-choice mechanisms, including democracy, to account for varying intensities of preference—for example, A and B, although only slightly favoring rule x to rule y, can outvote C, whose preference for y to x is essential to his whole way of life.[13] For these and various related reasons, it appears that the shortcomings of a law-oriented society are not mere infirmities of our existing institutional arrangements which we might hope to repair by appropriate amendments. Reliance on law cannot be perfectly satisfactory, because no collective-choice mechanism we can design is capable of meeting ideal criteria.[14]

There are, moreover, costs of various sorts associated with relying on law as a means of organizing social relations. Some of these are the costs of making laws (expenses of legislative staffs, of hearings) and enforcing them (expenses of police, administrative agencies, and courts). Then there are the costs imposed on those made targets of the law—the costs not of legislation and administration, but of compliance. True, where we are concerned with highly immoral conduct, such as murder, we are relatively indifferent to how much compliance "costs" the complier. But most conduct—pollution, for example—is not so unambiguously blameworthy, nor can it be so readily severed from beneficial activity, that we can afford the luxury of indifference to economic efficiency. The more rigid we make the rules, and the more forbidding the penalties, the more we risk "overdeterring"—that is, imposing on the actor (and, through the actor, on all of us) more costs than benefits.[15]

It often appears, too, that the further the law goes in laying down precise "bright-line" standards of permissible and impermissible conduct, the more it may tempt people to press their behavior to the very bounds of what is allowed. Clear legal rules may induce more unwanted activity than no rules at all.[16] Indeed, we might say that the most serious "costs" of a law-ridden society involve the toll such reliance exacts from its citizens, measured in moral timbre. One thinks of the Confucians' objection to the codification of laws: "A litigious spirit awakes, invoking the letter of the law, and trusting that evil actions will not fall under its provisions."[17]

I cannot trace out how each of these infirmities may serve to shift some of our reliance on law to a reliance on morals and manners. But let me give an illustration to suggest some of the connections. Let us suppose that a majority of voters today would prefer that people do not smoke in public places. Yet, in recent referendums, the voters have consistently refused to ban smoking in public places by law. In my view, it would be a mistake to interpret these refusals to ban smoking as a vote in favor of letting anyone who wants to smoke do so whenever and wherever they want to. On the contrary, I suspect that what is being expressed is a preference *against law,* a decision to relegate the matter of smoking control to a complex social code of morals and manners. The minority who want to smoke are allowed to smoke so far as the law is concerned. But underneath, control is being relegated to a network of conventions. These include "mandates" that, before lighting up, the smoker look around to see if others are smoking; he is not to smoke if no one else is doing so; he is to make an inquiry of his neighbors to measure the intensity of feelings in the circumstances ("do you mind if I smoke?"); he is to adjust, flexibly, by finding a table as far away from nonsmokers as possible, or ideally situated, considering air circulation. Thus certain adjudicatory responsibilities fall, not on the judge, but on the maître d'.

In this context, more people may smoke, and more may be offended by smoke than otherwise. But notice the savings in enforcement costs and the quality of personal conduct and human interchange that are fostered. And might there not be some value in the fact that nonsmokers can feel that those who are resisting their impulses to smoke are doing so because they *care,* not because the law compels them?

In all events, if we look closely at the smoking example, and the pattern of control based on morals and manners, I think we will find that something is going on that is more complicated than what the term voluntarism suggests, i.e., something more than simply asking the smoker voluntarily to forgo his desire to smoke.

IV. Responsible Reflection

I want now to argue that the flavor of this something extra *is* best captured by the term responsibility, which, while dropped earlier to avoid "loading" the issue, is therefore appropriate to reintroduce at this point. For when we begin to analyze what is going on, one can identify two separate, although related sets of techniques, both of which involve "responsibility" in different senses.

The first sense of responsibility—which I will call R_1—emphasizes following prescribed rules of conduct. It is in this sense that we judge someone "responsible" who follows the law, who abides by the rules—legal and moral—of his social office (as judge, prosecutor, or citizen). The second sense of responsibility—R_2—emphasizes cognitive process, reflection, how one goes about deciding, particularly when no special, clear-cut prescriptions of the R_1 sort are available. That the two senses of responsibility are separable is easy to demonstrate, inasmuch as the same act can, depending upon which sense one employs, be either "responsible" or "irresponsible." For example, a judge in Nazi Germany who carried out the orders of his superiors might be seen as "responsible" in sense R_1—in that he carried out the orders of his superiors, according to rules and the dictates of his office; and yet, we might say of him also that he was "irresponsible" in the sense—R_2—that he inadequately reflected as an autonomous, moral human being.

Despite the fact that these two senses of responsibility can be conceived as diametrically opposed in some circumstances, the fact that the same term is applied suggests that in most cases no such conflict actually exists. In fact, we can argue that, despite appearances, the two senses of responsibility are not so disparate at all. At bottom, R_2 involves following rules no less than R_1, but the rules that structure R_2 are simply more generalized and open-textured.[18] That is to say, there is a perspective from which they differ only in degree of specificity and autonomy. At one extreme of R_1, there are "mere conventions," highly specific and relatively free of any moral content: men are—or were—to light a lady's cigarette: A step beyond mere conventions there are "good" manners," equally specific and of clear moral derivation: "Don't blow smoke in someone's face." At the far end there is a set of R_2 rules, vague in the direction they entail, but highly freighted with moral content. These rules, of which the Golden Rule is the paragon, have been variously stated by Kant, Sidgewick, Hare, and Rawls. But all are invitations to engage in a form of thinking which in one way or another involves requiring the responsible person to place himself in the position of others, to see whether he can generalize his contemplated action into a general rule of conduct. Of course, unlike the rules ("don't blow smoke in someone's face"), the general principles of ethics do not determine any particular outcome. They operate, instead, by generating what might be called an intellectual style and analytical procedure. The characteristics of this approach include:

1. Reflection before action; the responsible person does not immediately implement his initial, hedonistic impulse: to vent rage, or, in our smoking example, to "light up." Responsible behavior, viewed through its cognitive emphasis, involves holding these impulses in check while reflecting.

2. The reflection that responsible behavior requires entails assessing the consequences of the contemplated action (smoke will spread across the room). One takes the full measure of one's own *accountability* for those consequences (there may already be some smoke from other people's cigarettes, but depending upon the exercise of my will, smoke will or will not be added).

3. Responsible behavior involves a willingness to scan one's environment for its morally significant features: other persons, and other creatures—their needs, their feelings, their interests; in our example, one must recognize that the health of others will be jeopardized, their comfort diminished, and their feelings invaded.

4. Being responsible involves the weighing of alternatives, and weighing those alternatives in moral terms: is it "just," or "unjust," for me to light a cigarette in these circumstances, considering the strength of my desires and the number of people affected? Am I under an "obligation" to recognize their "rights" by asking them whether they mind? Do I have a "moral duty" not to smoke, or to defer smoking until after the meal is finished, etc.? If *I*, with my feelings, and needs, were in their place, could I justify performing an act of comparable character?

5. And, of course, one must have, in addition to the moral vocabulary, a moral inclination—a desire, as much internalized as conscious, to "do the right thing," not to impose upon others unduly.

It is true that this sort of responsible reflection over a moral problem, unlike reflection over a mathematical problem, is not destined, when "finally understood," to yield a unique solution—that is, the "one right answer."

The advocates of the profits position may argue that the sorts of rules that make up R_1 responsibility—the counterparts to "don't smoke a cigar during meals"—are not easily transferred to the typical corporate setting.[19] There is certainly a good case to be made that if hard-and-fast rules of conduct can be agreed upon, they ought to be legislated; and therefore that the commercial counterparts of rules of proscribed etiquette and good manners, e.g., professional and trade-association canons of ethics and codes of conduct, probably have limited utility.

As regards R_2 responsibility, the same people may argue that here, too, even after all the moral analysis is said and done, in many circumstances there will be so many competing, equally defensible outcomes, that the presumption in favor of profits will persist. Here, too, they have an argument; but I do not believe that as regards R_2, the comeback is quite as satisfactory.

Let us take, as an example that illustrates the misgivings of the profits supporters, a product safety case. Suppose that the managers of an automobile company are considering a design that will entail 3.4 fatalities from impact on crash per 100 million vehicle miles traveled (the current industry average). If they alter the designs slightly, incorporating a stronger, heavier frame at a cost of $500 per car, the projected fatalities would be reduced by approximately 10 percent, to 3 per 100 million vehicle miles. What guidance can responsible reflection, as I have described it, provide in these circumstances?

To begin with, a moral rule that required the managers, in essence, to put themselves in the place of the consumers would hardly be calculated to yield an unambiguous decision. If, as we are assuming, the decision to add the extra safety costs will reduce profits, there is already some rather good evidence that if the managers were in the consumers' place they would reject the marginal increases in safety at the marginal costs of providing it. True, this probability of what the consumers want does not settle the matter. Thinking about one's responsibilities sometimes produces paternalistic action — that is, sometimes we feel that we are morally obligated to do something in the interest of someone else in disregard of their own preferences, such as a parent or the state sometimes exercises on the behalf of a child. The argument might take the form that if the consumers *really knew*, as vividly and in the detail that our test data indicates — .e.g, how much more solidly the proposed design resists impact — they would decide in its favor.

But this is hardly a strong reed to lean on, particularly since we recognize that, in a decision liks this, the consumers are not the only other group whose place the managers ought responsibly "to stand in." There are many people other than the consumers who are variously and often conflictingly affected by the decision to strengthen or not to strengthen the car. For example, the increased weight of the car will reduce fuel efficiency. This will translate into an adverse impact not only on consumers; if the managers are to put themselves "in the place of" the society at large, they will have to think about the implications for increased dependency on oil, and for inflation. The new design would also contribute to inflation through increased demand for steel and labor, and consequent higher auto prices. Moreover, the additional coal and steel required to strengthen the cars will exact its toll in injuries among coal workers and steelworkers: how are the managers to feel if they put themselves in the places of these workers, balancing off the effect of increased wages, increased inflation, and increased injuries?

I think that this exercise is significant in reminding us that in many cases a "responsible" corporate decision, even one undertaken in the best of faith, is going to be indecisive, and the presumption for profits, when all is said and done, quite rightly remains. But the example is also, in its way, misleading. Much of what corporate responsibility advocates, such as myself, are seeking is not reducible to a binary decision such as whether to trade off $500 per car for 0.4 lives per 100 million miles traveled. What the responsibility advocates should be concentrating on is a *concern for safety,* and the willingness to design *an ongoing, internal corporate system* that advances safety concerns.

A corporation that consistently and fairly considers safety factors will undoubtedly come up with many possibilities of trade-offs that are, like the example employed above, in a range too ambiguous to overcome the profits presumption. But over time a company that sets up such a system may also discover the possibility of trade-offs that resist casuistry. For example, a company may come up with a lighter, safer, material that can save thousands of lives with virtually no increase in costs. To this, the profits defenders will respond that profit considerations alone will be enough to provide the incentives; "responsibility" is not required to institute such research since "safety sells." But such a response misses an important legal rub. Under present law, the very fact that a company undertakes to give thorough consideration to safety risks may operate to intensify corporate liability, should there be accidents, and encourage law suits seeking to exact criminal and punitive damages.[20] Hence, it may not be *profitable* for a company to give full and responsible consideration to safety; but I would be prepared to argue that—profitable or no—a company should be obligated to press ahead in its safety research beyond the dictates of law-corrected market signals. This is particularly so when we consider that the company is the most efficient investigator of safety problems; it presumably can learn more about the problem and its solution, at less cost, than the rest of us.

Moreover, the auto-safety case we have just examined is not the only paradigm with which the responsibility advocate may be concerned. Many other cases seem to lie beyond the capacity of all but the most diehard profits defenders to complexify. In these situations, it is possible that "responsible" reflection will unearth several defensible decisions. But it is wrong to suppose that, once a multiplicity of defensible outcomes has been identified, we have no choice but to throw up our hands and revert to profits. Any one of the "responsible" outcomes may be clearly preferable to the outcome dictated by profits.

Consider, for example, a company that operates a cotton mill in the South. It is informed by a privately hired epidemiologist that its operations pose severe risks of cotton-dust disease (byssinosis) to their workers. The workers, who have not seen the report, suspect that there is some risk, but are unaware of the degree of damage indicated: that they will suffer, over the years, damages equivalent to $10 million in present value.[21] If the workers were informed of the probable risks, some would quit, and others demand higher wages. (There would be some shift to machines.) Because the workers are risk-averse, the $10 million in damages they are actually expected to suffer, taking into account the net present value of their additional wage demands over the years, would come to $15 million in damages.

If the company takes no action on the report, conceals its findings, and continues with "business as usual," then, presumably, over the years, a number of workers will die, and others will become disabled. Of course, the legal system provides some avenue for relief in civil-action and wrongful-death suits. But many deaths and disabilities may occur before the connection between the work and the disease is appreciated. Even when people think to bring suits, plaintiffs will often lose. They will bear the burden of proof, and will have to negate defenses of joint causality (smoking, for example, can contribute to lung damage), and so on. Recall, too, that the plaintiffs will have to expend large sums to come up with a report equal to that already produced—and in management's hands. For all such reasons, if suits are brought, the net present value of the distant, contingent recoveries is even less than the $10 million that the employees will actually suffer—perhaps $9 million. We can well imagine that the company could, through a change in the physical conditions of production in the plant—say, the installation of a better air circulation and filtration system—cut the damages in half at a cost of only $5 million.

Now, observe that in this situation, the dictate of the profits position is to say nothing and suffer legal losses probably amounting to $9 million. This is considerably less than the wage costs the workers would impose if they knew the facts ($15 million) and less than the actual damages that the workers will suffer ($10 million). Under these circumstances, to pay the $5 million to halve the damages is not dictated by the profits position, inasmuch as, to the company, halving the damages is "worth" only $4.5 million. But in such a situation, is it really so "ambiguous" whether the company ought to follow the prof-its-maximizing decision: to say nothing and go ahead with business as usual for as long as it can get away with it? Several alternative "responsible" positions are indicated, any and all of which would seem clearly preferable:

(1) to turn over the data that the company has privately received to the workers' representatives, i.e., to make full disclosures of the report;

(2) to change the air-circulation and filtration system at a cost of $5 million;

(3) to institute a screening system so that workers who show signs

of the disease at early stages can be specially assigned (or, yes, perhaps bring law suits);

(4) to undertake and sponsor investigations of new methods that would improve the state of the art in dealing with the disease; and/or

(5) to disclose to the legislature the information on hand in order to assure safer treatment of all workers in all the mills, not just their own (this approach minimizes the competitive disadvantage that the company would suffer if it alone exposed itself to the additional costs of safety).

V. The Accountability of the Corporation

There are, of course, several conceptual difficulties in carrying forward the analytical framework we have outlined. Not the least of these is that it seeks to impute concepts like "accountability" and "responsibility" to the corporation itself, rather than (or in addition) to individual persons, as in more customary usage. I should like to conclude by suggesting some insights into this problem that may be gleaned from a close look at the relationships—the contrasts and similarities—between accountability in morals and accountability in law, where the notion of a corporation's (legal) accountability has accumulated something of a history.

When I speak of corporate accountability in morals, I refer to moral rules that govern the ascription to corporations of moral terms, such as "X Corp. was 'blameworthy,' " "Y Corp. acted 'wrongly' [in the moral sense]." Legal accountability involves the rules that govern the ascription of legal terms, e.g., "X Auto Corporation was guilty of manslaughter," the "Y Oil Company bribed Z."

The two systems of accountability can be detached (and often ought to be detached to achieve a clear understanding of the different conventions that may govern the application of the identical term, such as "person" in ordinary moral discourse, and "person" in legal discourse). But there are informative similarities between the two systems as well.

To begin with, when we undertake to examine accountability in either the moral or the legal realm, two common questions emerge. First, there is the threshold question of *intelligibility:* does the ascription of moral or legal predicates to a corporate body (as opposed to a corporate agent, a person) even make sense? Second, there is the question of *prudence:* even if we can "make sense" of the ascription intelligibly, does it "make sense" pragmatically? That is, is it a way of speaking that we ought to adopt in furtherance of social aims?

These common questions are not peculiar to the ascription of moral and legal terms to corporate bodies; they are raised, with equal significance, when we are concerned with the rights and claims of noncorporate entities, e.g., infants, persons of limited mental capacity, or, for that matter, nonhuman entities, such as animals, lakes, and mountains. For example, one can ask whether it is morally and/or legally intelligible to say of a person who is insane that "he acted 'immorally' — or 'committed murder' — in killing X"; and if the locution can be defended as intelligible, we can go on to ask whether the implications of the ascription (to extend blaming and legal responsibility to the insane, to minors, and so on) can be fitted into a defensible view of society.[22]

Accountability in Moral Discourse

Let us first examine corporate accountability in the moral realm. Is it intelligible to say that "Ford was morally blameworthy to have designed the Pinto gas tank the way it did," or, for that matter, that "Russia was morally 'wrong' to have invaded Afghanistan"?

There is in the philosophical literature a growing body of articles that examine the intelligibility of such ascriptions, most of which focus on the reductionist alternative: can't we say exactly what one might be trying to say by simply analyzing the action of "the corporation" into the actions of its various tangible agents, reserving the moral ascriptions for them?[23]

The questions raised are complex. In the space of this paper, I can do little more than state my own view that a complete reduction is not possible — that is, that there exists corporate conduct of a sort that can intelligibly be labeled "immoral" even in circumstances where we would be hard-pressed to locate any agent or agents whose personal conduct we could justifiably call immoral. This outcome flows from certain characteristics of corporate decision-making. For one thing, certain acts, such as the declaration of a dividend, a merger, the corporation's repurchase of its shares, are in some senses inherently *corporate;* that is, the acts cannot be performed by individual human beings, but only by corporate bodies pursuant to corporate rules. More important than the implications of formal organizational characteristics and rules, we do well to consider the informal authority relationships and attitudes. These constitute significant determinants of the organization's behavior, yet cannot be traced to particular markings on the organizational chart, much less to any particular actor or actors. Consider Corporation A which distributes to its company an internal memo insisting upon strict compliance with antibribery laws. Corporation B distributes the exact same memo. Is it not quite possible that the same words, originating from the same place in the hierarchy (the president's office), passing through the "same" channels, will be "interpreted" quite differently?—that in one company we will have compliance, and in the other not? And trying to explain this outcome, can one with confidence limit one's analysis to the individual employees— or is there some "corporate" residue: different *corporate* policies, different *corporate* character, different *corporate* ethos?[24]

Let us assume, for example, that it is immoral (as well, incidentally, as unlawful) for the corporation to declare a dividend if, after the dividend has been paid, the corporation will be so drained of cash that it cannot satisfy its obligations as they come due. Suppose that Corporation Z is under an obligation to produce and deliver uranium to one of its customers. The company's chief mining engineer knows that the ore in its own mines that it has been relying upon for delivery is "thinning out"; the Vice-President for Personnel knows that the miners are threatening a work stoppage; the foreman in its principal mine #7 knows that there may have to be a shutdown for safety repairs; the Vice-President for International Operations knows that world uranium prices are rising, with the implication that to purchase other uranium to "make up" their own contract obligation is becoming increasingly unfeasible; the Vice-President, Marketing, knows that the company they have promised to deliver to will be insistent on timely deliveries; the corporation's computer—alone, perhaps—has a firm grasp on the delivery schedule.

In these circumstances, in the face of the likelihood that the corporation will be seriously in debt, the declaration of a dividend would be immoral. Conceivably, though, at the time the directors of the corporation meet to declare the financially jeopardous dividend, no one of them—indeed, no single person in the corporation—knows enough of the relevant facts to warrant the judgment that he is morally "to blame." We could *say* that we blame them; the term is probably elastic enough that it would be intelligible to do so. But would such a stretching of the term not wear it thin, rob it of some of its force in cases where people are *really* to blame? Consider, however, the alternative of deeming Z, in these circumstances, an immoral corporation, *itself* blameworthy? To adopt the locution of "the blameworthy corporation" would not be unintelligible. We could well intend to fault, in a quite meaningful way, failures of *the organization* to gather, assess, and advance to the board room the various independent disparate items of information that, together, would have painted the appropriate picture. What was wrong, for example, might have been the corporation's formal and informal authority structure, its audit policies, its information network, and so on.

One may wish to respond that *some individual* was theoretically responsible for shaping the organization appropriately; but that response supposes the supremacy of an individual's will over the organization's inertia, which is certainly, in any case, quite open to question. Surely the corporate organization, like a nation state, has a culture, structure, and history that persist, through time, in the face of the various individuals who come and go. Why should it not be these peculiarly organizational characteristics that we wish to call attention to in moral discourse, that is, *to blame?*

What the illustration points up is the ultimate, underlying interdependence of the intelligibility questions and the prudence questions. In the last analysis, my argument that it is *intelligible* to blame the corporation draws on considerations that it is *useful* to speak in that manner. The validity of this claim, in turn, depends on what one supposes to be the function of moral discourse. If one agrees that it is the function of moral discourse to educate about what society considers right and wrong conduct (as opposed, for example, to reporting natural moral qualities, as G. E. Moore claimed), then it makes perfectly good sense to speak of the company—the corporate entity—as blameworthy, if doing so can be grounded in the advancement of societal goals. In other words, one wants to know what effect holding the corporation "to blame" will have—on those in the "outside" world, on the one hand (the ascribers), and on the agents "inside" the corporation—in terms of both altering conduct and affecting self-perception. Will entering into a moral discourse with "the corporation" be an effective way to alter those features of the organization that seem objectionable—that is, of bringing about desirable changes in the internal rules, policies, organizational attitudes, and so on, that appear to be connected to the undesired conduct? Or will ascribing blame to the corporation simply deaden the employees' own senses of responsibility? There are certainly no satisfactory answers to questions such as these in the social -science literature. And, frankly, I doubt that people are inclined to rely on empirical data in these areas, anyway.

Accountability in Law

As I have already indicated, the law has already acquired considerable "practice" and skill in the ascription of accountability to corporate bodies. Indeed, there has been a rich and complicated history from which those engaged in philosophy could well benefit.

In its earliest stages, the law took a fairly consistent position that the corporation itself could not be legally accountable for misconduct, particularly for intentional wrongdoing that required some specified mental state as a predicate. Sometimes the objection was that the corporation had no mind, and therefore (as opposed to its agents) could not be guilty of any offense that required intention, most importantly, of crimes that required, as an element, what lawyers call *mens rea*, or deliberate criminal intent. At other times, the objection seems to have been based on the unauthorized character of the act. Inasmuch as the corporation, qua corporation—a creature of the state—could do only those things that the state authorized it to do, and since the state would never authorize the corporation to violate its own laws, it was assumed that any wrongdoing was "ultra vires," i.e., beyond the powers authorized to the corporation. It was said to follow, therefore, that the corporation could not be liable.

Whatever the fascination that these and similar doctrinal qualms still hold for legal historians, it is safe to say that in most jurisdictions today there are very few delicts for which a corporation cannot be held legally answerable.[25] In other words, the intelligibility of ascribing wrongdoing to the corporate body, once so lively an issue in the law, is today mainly of historical and perhaps some lingering theoretical interest.

By contrast, if we turn to the questions of prudence, we find that, on the legal side, they are as alive—perhaps more alive—than ever. That is to say, assuming, as the law now does, that it is intelligible to hold corporations accountable as "persons" within the legal system, there is still a question whether, and in what circumstances, we ought to indict the corporation for some misconduct, when we should try to locate some responsible agent, the "culprit," and when we ought to coindict, i.e., pursue both the entity and one or more agents.

Note how closely these questions track the questions raised a moment ago regarding ascriptions in the moral realm: when should we blame the corporate entity, and when the agent? Here, the pragmatic side of the issue involves the likely effect of holding the corporate body legally accountable. One wants to know how making the corporation the law's quarry will affect those both "outside" the corporation and those who labor "within," in terms of their perceptions (most importantly, their self-perceptions) and behavior. Will our holding the corporate body answerable for the wrongdoing (diffusing the fine among investors) simply reinforce the agents' already-deadened sense of responsibility for the injuries that "the corporation" is—somehow, so impersonally—doing to others?

I cannot, in this space, do justice to all the subtleties that are involved.[26] But it is worthwhile to observe, as a first approximation, that whether we wish to hold the corporate body accountable in law, or whether we should insist upon pursuing certain individuals, cannot be determined without observing some fundamental differences among categories of misconduct. Specifically, some human conduct is regarded as so unambiguously immoral that we should always prefer to locate the individual agents and hold them accountable, even at higher costs of investigation and conviction. Indeed, for the most reprehensible offenses, the remedies are often fit only for individuals, and would not be applicable to organizations, e.g., imprisonment, or even the death penalty.

On the other hand, a considerable amount—indeed, an ever-increasing portion—of corporate-related misconduct that society wishes to deter is not immoral in traditional terms (independent of its unlawfulness, which always carries a presumption of immorality). Nor is the intent of the actors calculated to harm anyone. More often, any injuries that result from the violation of society's rules will be unforeseeable. Hence, the more the society determines to hold individuals accountable, by creating strict liability offenses, for example, the more it risks being itself "immoral," undermining the ethical bases of the criminal law.

In these circumstances, holding the enterprise accountable may give the society the opportunity to make its "statement"—that conduct of such-and-such a character is distasteful and unacceptable to the collective majority—while avoiding the imposition of penalties on agents whose conduct, individually, is not morally blameworthy. Indeed, making such a "statement" to the corporation may have a particular virtue of bringing about a revision in corporate, i.e., organizational, procedures and policies, in circumstances where those are to blame, and where the misconduct might thereby continue even where constituent individuals were replaced, one by one, and marched off to jail.

In other words, as we move into the area of enforcing rules that are increasingly "technical" (abstracted from any clear moral basis), society finds itself tugged in different directions by somewhat opposed moral and practical vectors. It is quite conceivable that in many circumstances, the best accommodation can be realized by pursuing the corporate body in law, and trusting to influence the individual agents only indirectly, through the corporation's "own" reaction to "its" sanctions.

Indeed, it is worth recalling in this regard a number of cases in which corporate misconduct has led to a joint prosecution of the corporate entity and its most responsible agents, and which have resulted in the jury convicting the corporation but excusing the agents.[27] Some commentators in the legal literature regard such outcomes as senseless—how could the corporation be liable if no agent was? But I believe, to the contrary, the jurors were trying to make a moral statement. In the context of a giant bureaucracy, none of the agents possessed the awareness requisite to a criminal conviction. Nonetheless, the result—an admixture of human action and organizational form—was socially unacceptable. The conviction of the corporation, even while extenuating the individuals, transmits its own signals that may be quite appropriate and significant: something has to be changed. Let the corporate managers, in their superior expertise, figure out exactly how this is best done.

But all this raises, as I say, a whole host of questions that need further exploration. And when we have a better handle on them—on the comparative virtues of corporate and individual accountability—we will still have to return to the larger issue raised at the outset: In light of the capacities and limitations of the social signals transmitted by the two legal techniques, viewed as overlays on the more pervasive market signals, what is the appropriate space for corporate social responsibility, i.e., for the managers to disregard the generally reliable, law-qualified profit messages, and steer the organization under their control in the direction of various social benefits not captured in the profit signals?

It is an area that demands, and deserves, much more clear thought than it has received. I am confident, however, that discussions of this very sort, bringing together an exchange of views among philosophers, theologians, businessmen, lawyers, and management experts, is a long step along the road of understanding, and dealing with, these many problems.

NOTES

1. Later in the text I will restore the term "responsibility" to the debate, but only after I have demonstrated the important senses that responsibility captures, while terms like "voluntarism" and "altruism" do not.

2. Perhaps because the social-responsibility issue has attracted the attention of economists, and economists tend to identify moral issues with welfare maximization, the literature generally assumes that, if there were moral choices for the managers, they would be resolved by a utilitarian calculus. I want to leave open the question, only touched on in the text below, whether there might not be moral decisions appropriate for managers to make, but on nonutilitarian, deontological grounds.

3. I assume that most opponents of corporate social responsibility would agree that, once some form of conduct has been criminalized by the legislature, the managers ought not to engage in it, even if, though criminal, it remains profitable—either because conviction is unlikely, or because the profits to be made for lawbreaking exceed the penalties. David Engel has argued, however, that the presence of the criminal-liabilty rule ought not, in and of itself, preclude the corporation from performing the forbidden act, if doing so is profitable. He argues that there are only a few crimes so heinous as to be unacceptable under any circumstances; many fines are like business expenses. Where some form of criminal conduct is not absolutely clearly condemned by strong consensus in all cases, the managers would wrongly arrogate legislative power if they desist from a profitable course of lawbreaking. Suppose for example, a company that from some course of conduct will earn $12,000 and be fined $10,000; the $10,000 fine may represent a collective judgment that the social cost of the unlawful act is, say $2,000 (supposing that the legislature in setting the penalty of $10,000 assumed that the chances of getting caught were 1 in 5). Not to violate the law would be withholding goods or services the society values at $12,000 in exchange for avoiding a $2,000 cost, a course of conduct for which, Engel points out, there is no clear-cut consensus. Engel, "An Approach to Corporate Social Responsibility," *Stanford L. Rev.,* 32 (1979):1.

4. The best and fullest discussion of this is in Engel, *ibid.*

5. This is one of the arguments relied on by Milton Friedman, in a well-publicized article, "The Social Responsibility of Business is to Increase Its Profits," *New York Times Magazine,* September 13, 1970.

6. Most significantly, while a true principal is free to discharge his agent at will, the shareholders are subject to a complex body of constraints on recalling the directors from office, between terms of election, without "cause."

7. For a general overview of these sorts of problems, see Jones, "Making and Keeping Promises," *Ethics* 76 (1966):287.

8. This, and some other of the comments that follow are treated in Stone, *Where the Law Ends* (New York: Harper & Row, 1975), chap. 11.

9. Some thoughtful reservations about managers making disclosures to the public, and perhaps even to lawmaking bodies, appear in Engel, note 3, *supra,* at 79–84.

10. See *Virginia State Board of Pharmacy* v. *Virginia Citizens Consumer Council* 425 U.S. 748 (1976), holding that commercial advertising, while not as protected from interference as other forms of speech, is not wholly outside the protection of the First Amendment, either.

11. The classic treatment of the development of law out of less authorita-

tive predecessors—folkways, customs, etc.—is W. G. Sumner, *Folkways* (Boston: Ginn, 1906).

12. See K. J. Arrow, *Social Choice and Individual Values*, 2d ed. (New Haven, Conn.: Yale University Press, 1963). For an analysis placing Arrow's work in the perspective of other contributions to social-choice theory, see A. K. Sen, *Collective Choice and Social Welfare* (San Francisco: Holden-Day, 1970), chap. 3.

13. See, generally, James M. Buchanan and Gordon Tullock, *The Calculus of Consent: Logical Foundations of Constitutional Democracy* (Ann Arbor: University of Michigan Press, 1962). In this context, one should consider also the so-called Paradox of Voting demonstrated by Nanson as early as 1862. See Sen, *Collective Choice and Social Welfare*, p. 38.

14. The more difficult question is whether any mechanism based upon some "looser" choice procedures, such as I advocate below in the text, can more suitably meet the requirements of Arrow *et al.* Surely rules of etiquette and express moral rules—what I call, below, R_1—are subject to the same infirmities. Rules of the sort that form the basis of my R_2 responsibility may be better suited to fill in some of the collective-choice-mechanism defects, but perhaps their vagueness simply serves to cloud comparable shortcomings.

15. See Christopher D. Stone, "The Place of Enterprise Liability in the Control of Corporate Conduct," *Yale L. J.*, 90 (1980): 1, 25–26.

16. It is important to remember, however, that when the law gets involved in people's lives, especially where severe criminal penalties are involved, there are moral and constitutional reasons to provide clear rules in the service of "fair warning" and the restricting of governmental abuse.

17. The quote is attributed to Shu Shiang, criticizing the codification of the criminal law on mental cauldrons on the view that "since all crimes cannot be prevented" their Confucian ancestors had "set up the barrier of righteousness (*i*) . . . [and] treated . . . according to just usage (*li*)," quoted in J. Needham, *Science and Civilization in China*, 2 (Cambridge: Cambridge University Press, 1956), 521.

18. The relationship between my R_1 and R_2 can be stated in various ways. Peter French, *The Scope of Morality* (Minneapolis: University of Minnesota Press, 1979), p. 102, distinguishes between moral judgments (close to my R_1) and moral principles, which Wittgenstein had denominated "hardened" moral judgments—"hardened" in the sense that, like "thou shalt not murder," no one in the community really regards them as open to R_2 re-analysis.

19. A good statement of reasons to doubt that moral codes of a sort appropriate to regulate ordinary human behavior can readily be transferred to the context of, e.g., corporate pollution, is to be found in R. N. McKean, "Economics of Trust, Altruism, and Corporate Responsibility," in *Altruism, Morality and Economic Theory*, ed. B. S. Phelps, (New York: Russell Sage Foundation, 1975).

20. See Stone, note 15, *supra*, at footnote 86 and accompanying text.

21. That is to say, over the years, many millions of dollars will be paid out in damages, year by year, beginning at some future date; but because an obligation to pay someone a dollar ten years in the future is less burdensome

than having to pay someone a dollar *now* (because the company can invest it in the interim), I follow the convention of financial cost-benefit analysis, such as a company is likely to engage in. Comparisons are made among alternative courses of conduct with different income effects over time by discounting the future earnings and losses to a net present value, i.e., value at the time of decision, supposing some rate of discount.

22. This is essentially the process I went through in supporting both the intelligibility, and the prudence, of fitting environmental objects such as lakes, rivers, and so on, into the legal system—in other words, giving them "rights"—in *Should Trees Have Standing? Towards Legal Rights for Natural Objects* (Los Altos, Calif.: William Kaufman, 1974; rev. ed., New York: Avon Books, 1975).

23. An expression of the view that ascriptions to corporate bodies are essentially unintelligible is found in John Ladd, "Morality and the Ideal of Rationality in Formal Organizations," *The Monist,* 54 (1970):488. Support of the contrary view—closer to that taken in the present article—can be found in Peter A. French, "The Corporation as a Moral Person," *American Philosophical Quarterly,* 16 (1979): 207; and in two selections in *Ethical Issues in Business: A Philosophical Approach,* ed. T. Donaldson and P. H. Werhane (Englewood Cliffs, N.J.: Prentice-Hall, 1979): Kenneth E. Goodpaster, "Morality and Organizations," and David T. Ozar, "The Moral Responsibility of Corporations."

24. For an interesting account of how informal company policies and managerial ethos can contribute to corporate misconduct, see John G. Fuller, *The Gentlemen Conspirators* (New York: Grove Press, 1962), which examines the roots of the widespread price-fixing in the electrical equipment industry that culminated in the well-publicized anti-trust trials of the early 1960s.

25. In some jurisdictions, even today a corporation itself cannot be indicted for manslaughter. Those working in the philosophical tradition may wish to give thought to the fact that in law, it is possible that the criminal intent of an agent may be neither a necessary nor a sufficient condition of finding criminal intent of the corporation. As one court has said

> The mere knowledge and intent of the agent . . . to steal would not be sufficient in and of itself to make the corporation guilty. While a corporation may be guilty of larceny, may be guilty of the intent to steal, the evidence must go further. . . . The intent must be the intent of the corporation, and not merely that of the agent. How this intent may be proved or in what cases becomes evident depends entirely upon the circumstances of each case.

People v. *Canadian Fur Trapper's Corp.,* 248 N.Y. 159, 161 N.E. 455 (1928).

The suggestion is that in speaking about the intent of an individual actor, and the intent of corporate actors, the law deals in two disparate (what Waismann called) "language strata." See Waismann, "Language Strata," in *Logic and Language,* ed. A. Flew (New York: Anchor Books, 1965), pp. 235–42, 244–47. The term "intent" is the same, there are obvious similarities in the rules for the usage, in neither usage does "intent" purport to be a mere description of physical events; yet, in each usage there are distinct procedures for verification, and so on.

26. See Stone, note 15, *supra* at 24–28.

27. See, for example, *U.S.* v. *Hilton Hotels Corp.*, 467 F.2d 1000 (9th Cir. 1972), upholding liability of hotel corporation under Sherman Anti-Trust Act notwithstanding jury's acquittal of hotel manager. See also *U.S.* v. *American Socialist Party*, 260 F.885 (D.C. S.D.N.Y. 1919) (American Socialist Society, a corporation, held criminally liable under the Espionage Act for willfully intending to obstruct enlistment based on publication and distribution of anti-war pamphlet, notwithstanding acquittal of the pamphlet's writer, the court supporting the jury's verdict by reference to corporate action—resolutions, committee reports, by-laws, etc.—as establishing the requisite corporate wrongful purpose).

10. Women in the Corporation: A Case Study about Justice

Catherine B. Cleary

For a long time I have been fascinated by the idea that although individuals assume a different role in their working as opposed to their personal lives, religious beliefs, if they mean anything, have to be a part of one's total life, of all of one's activities. Many corporate codes of conduct suggest as the final test that the individual consider how he would feel about explaining his proposed action to family members. IBM's Business Conduct Guidelines, for example, say:

> The next time you have an ethical dilemma, you might try this test. Ask yourself: If the full glare of examination by associates, friends, even family were to focus on your decision, would you remain comfortable with it? If you think you would, it probably is the right decision.

Discussions of the relationship of religious values to business decisions help individuals to think through and define for themselves their own principles and to anticipate ways in which they may be challenged. This, I believe, is the best insurance against ill-considered decisions made under pressure. Having said that, let me add that while I believe religious beliefs should influence the way a corporation conducts its business, I believe that a corporation is an economic institution and that although it is influenced by, responds to, and sometimes even anticipates social change and is regulated by political decisions, it should not become a political instrument.

The subject of our discussions involves organizations and individuals. I believe that corporations do indeed have a life of their own. Each company has its own history, its own style, its own goals; but it is also made up of people, and individuals have the power to shape as well as destroy a company's traditions and values.

There is great diversity among corporations in size, influence, ethical standards, and other attributes too numerous to mention. Some years ago in preparation for a speech I was to give at Smith College on business careers, I prepared a simple questionnaire which the college asked a small random sample of students to answer. The personal experiences of those students with business were heavily weighted toward part-time jobs they had had in small local retail establishments where they believed the owner exploited employees and ripped off customers. Their opinions of business, on the other hand, were based on their impressions of the life style in large corporations.

In my opinion most large publicly held corporations in this country today recognize that the corporation has an accountability beyond its accountability to stockholders for financial results. This was recognized by The Business Roundtable in its Statement on *The Role and Composition of the Board of Directors of the Large Publicly Owned Corporation,* in which it listed as one of the four major responsibilities of the board of directors "the consideration of significant social impacts of corporate activities and relatedly the consideration of views of substantial groups (other than shareowners), significantly affected by such activity."

The new word to describe these groups is "stakeholders," a term which recognizes that they have some claim on the corporation. In some cases the law has already defined the nature of those claims — for consumers, for example, or for neighbors affected by effluents from a plant — but because society's expectations are changing rapidly and industry's technological capabilities are growing, it is unlikely there will soon be a consensus on the standards of accountability to stakeholder groups. The process is further complicated by the activities of one-issue special-interest groups. Corporate managements must balance the interests of all stakeholders, including those not represented by activists.

High on the list of stakeholder groups are employees, and my purpose in this paper is to focus on women employees of the corporation, particularly in the context of the interface between work and family life. There is a tendency, arising perhaps from the development of the federal equal-employment-opportunity laws, to treat women and minorities as one group. Without in any way minimizing the needs of minority men, the thrust of this paper is that women have unique needs which must be addressed — by women themselves, by men, and by corporations. These issues involve fundamental questions of justice and human dignity, and they also involve difficult questions of the extent of personal as opposed to corporate responsibility. In addition, the family is one of the institutions on which the Judeo-Christian tradition is built.

Nowhere are the changes in society with which corporations must deal more striking than in the area of women in the work force. It is hard for me to believe the changes that have occurred in my adult life. When I entered law school in 1940, neither Harvard nor Georgetown (nor Notre Dame) Law School admitted women. There were six or seven women in my class at the University of Wisconsin Law School, by far the largest number in the history of the school. It was only after World War II that married women could work in financial institutions in Milwaukee. Prior to that time a woman who married lost her job. For most women at that time society dictated a choice of marriage or a career.

At the end of 1979 in the United States there were 44 million women in a labor force of 103.7 million. Over half of the women age 16 and over were working for pay, most of them working full time. The Bureau of Labor Statistics notes the dramatic increase in the participation rates of women in the labor force—from slightly above 30 percent in the late 1940s to more than 50 percent in the late 1970s—and cites among major influences on this increase "a lowering of the birth rate; increases in age at first marriage; a desire to maintain or increase the household's standard of living and the effect of inflation on a family's buying power; growth in those industries (particularly the service sector) and occupations which traditionally employ women; and, of course, the growing social acceptance of work for women."[1]

One of every seven families in the country is maintained by a woman who is divorced, separated, widowed, or has never married. Over one-half of the children in the country have working mothers.

About 80 percent of all employed women are in clerical, service, sales, factory, or plant jobs. Clerical jobs alone account for more than one-third. While women have made sizable percentage gains in managerial jobs, men hold 78 percent of managerial jobs. My informed guess is that the 22 percent women are concentrated in the lowest levels of management.

The full-time earnings of women are 60 percent of men's earnings, and this figure has remained relatively constant for many years. It is said that at the time of the Industrial Revolution female wages were consciously set at the 60 percent level because of women's lower subsistence requirements. In 1977 the median income of female college graduates, including those with advanced degrees, who worked full time, year round, was below the median income of male high-school dropouts. In 1977 fewer than 20 percent of men working full time, year round, earned under $10,000 a year. Over 66 percent of similarly situated women did.

The shocking differential in earnings between men and women is not due to any one simple cause. Women themselves — and the society in which they were raised and educated — must share the responsibility because of their failure to prepare realistically for the fact they would have to work and work over an extended period of time. How many parents and daughters realize that today the average married woman with children can expect to spend twenty-five years in the labor force?

Beyond women's own failure to prepare and to anticipate the length of their work lives, their earnings reflect the fact that they tend to be employed in low-paid, low-status jobs. Speaking of "stereotypically female jobs," it has been said:

> These occupations are characterized by lack of authority, vicarious rather than direct achievement, and low wages. Social conventions and pressures from male co-workers, particularly in blue-collar jobs, reinforce this concept of "women's place" in the world of work.[2]

Attention is now being focused on the relative worth of work traditionally done by women as compared to similar jobs done by men — equal pay for comparable work. It remains to be seen how strong a position will be taken by unions where women are at least as scarce in the top echelons as in corporate managements. Efforts to get women into nontraditional types of work are also important in terms of earnings potential as well as breaking the stereotype.

To expand long-term opportunities for women as leaders in corporations and in the business community, the focus must shift to women in management. The percentage of women students in business schools and particularly in M.B.A. programs is one indicator of the significant numbers of well-trained young women entering business today. There are in addition many older women seeking to use experience in other fields, including volunteer work, to gain entrance into management ranks.

The problems some of these older women face were illustrated in a report in the *New York Times* last fall about a woman who eventually went back to college and then secured a good management job:

> She grew up thinking a woman had only to marry a good man, and she could stay home and have children and never have to worry about the outside world again. So she never bothered to get a college degree, and when she married she left behind any thoughts of a career — forever, she thought. She settled down contentedly to having and raising eight children. Then her

husband died of cancer, and [her] life turned around. At 49 she had to take responsibility for supporting herself and providing for her children.

"It took me a long time to grow up," she said, "and I thank God I finally did." Accordingly, she is bringing up her daughters far differently from the way she was raised. "They all have degrees," she said. "You have to cover yourself in this world. If you're going to have a child, you have to make sure you can meet that commitment—to yourself as well as to the child."[3]

Let me make clear at the outset that I am not advocating that women who do not have to work for pay should or should not do so, although this story suggests the difficulty of assessing the need to work. In any event I believe deeply that women must have a choice. At the same time I believe that young women today have been slow to realize the implications of a commitment to a career—particularly when they attempt to combine it with marriage and a family. There are indications that they are becoming more aware of those implications and that is encouraging. While one might ask whether the rush to paid jobs represents a triumph of materialism, my own judgment is that it is a search for independence as well as for intellectual stimulus and the sense of accomplishment and personal growth that challenging work provides.

Obstacles

What stands in the way of women having opportunities to participate in the management of corporations?

There is a respectable body of professional opinion which holds that the difficulties women encounter in moving into management are due to the way they are brought up. Margaret Hennig and Anne Jardim in their book *The Managerial Woman* say that "women are much less likely to bring to the [management] setting the insights, understandings and skills which from boyhood men have acquired and developed among themselves—a mind-set learned, acculturated and socialized which gives men an immediate advantage as they move into management positions."[4] They cite a haunting incident of an interview with a business executive who persisted stubbornly in advocating the "vive la difference" philosophy until they asked him, "If you had known on the day that your daughter was born that starting at the age of twenty she would have to work continuously to survive would you have done anything differently with her than you have done up until now?" They recall that he "lowered his head for a moment and then looked up . . . , staring but not speaking. [They] had to ask him what he was thinking. He said, 'I don't *think*, I *feel* sick to my stomach. If she has to work, then I've done it all wrong.' "[5]

Carol Nagy Jacklin and Eleanor Emmons Maccoby have examined sex differences and their implications for management and have concluded that "only one sex difference might be related to management skills: aggression."[6] They go on to question to what extent aggression and concern for dominance are necessary or useful in management today.

At a conference sponsored by the Stanford Graduate School of Business in 1974, it was concluded that four major barriers hinder the entry of women into management: "(1) misconceptions about women's capabilities as managers; (2) inhospitable informal structures; (3) recruitment, hiring and promotion policies; and (4) perceived incompatibilities between career and family goals."[7]

Rosabeth Moss Kanter in *Men and Women of the Corporation* argues convincingly that behavior is the product of the corporate structure, and the implications of that thesis are, of course, that the structure and not people must be changed. She focuses on three particular aspects of structure—opportunity, power, and relative numbers of men and women.

Women are, as has been noted, heavily concentrated in low-level clerical jobs with little opportunity to advance or take initiative. Their self-image and their behavior reflect this lack of opportunity, Kanter believes, rather than an inherent female lack of motivation or work commitment.

Similarly, in a large corporation where there is heavy interdependence, power is necessary to get the job done. Again, women concentrated in low-level routine jobs do not have the opportunity to acquire power—through extraordinary activities or through alliances with superiors, peers, and subordinates. Kanter equates the preference of people for male bosses with the preference for a boss with power upward and outward, and she describes the type of critical, bossy, and controlling behavior often attributed to women as typical of the powerless.

Kanter and the Stanford Conference focus on some of the same factors. One of these is stereotypes. The Stanford report, as noted above, lists as a barrier biological-psychological misconceptions and socioeconomic misconceptions about women's abilities as managers. In the first category "the stereotype of the emotional female is a particularly potent myth." In the second, the myth of greater job turnover among women is a hindrance to their advancement. The Stanford report suggests that positive experiences will in time provide the answer to these myths.

Kanter, however, points out a more serious effect on women as a part of her theory that numbers have real consequences for performance. "This position as 'tokens' (representatives of their category rather than independent individuals) accounts for many of the difficulties such numerically scarce people face in fitting in, gaining peer acceptance, and behaving 'naturally.' "[8] When "tokens" become encapsulated in limited roles, they must constantly fight stereotypes in order to be seen as they are, in order for their managerial status to be recognized. Referring to the situation of the management women in a company she studied—a numerically rare number—Kanter says:

> In the office, they were often taken for secretaries; on sales trips on the road, especially when they traveled with a male colleague, they were often taken for wives or mistresses; with customers, they were first assumed to be temporarily substituting for a man who was the "real" salesperson; with a male peer at meetings, they were seen as the assistant; when entertaining customers, they were assumed to be the wife or date.[9]

Another aspect of role encapsulation, according to Kanter, is for certain jobs to become known as "women's slots." Recently the head of a major American corporation asked me why women resist being put in jobs "where being a woman is an advantage." We're fighting the stereotype, the limitation of our role.

Kanter also speaks of dominants fitting tokens into one of four stereotypical roles—mother, seductress, pet, and iron maiden—which in turn poses a difficult challenge to the tokens in terms of their own responses. How does the token establish her own identity and her own competence and maintain working relationships with the men in the organization? It is not possible to describe in a few words the dynamics of tokenism as Kanter sees them, but mention must be made of the pressure that visibility puts on a token's performance, as well as the need for the token to prove herself over and over again, in order to disprove the stereotype. Kanter refers to "the loneliness of the outsider, of the stranger who intrudes upon an alien culture and may become self-estranged in the process of assimilation."

Are these ethical, religious issues? I think so. For whom? For the corporation certainly in terms of setting its structures and policies and setting by management example acceptable standards of behavior. But these are issues too for individual men in the corporation. Their sensitivity and generosity are crucial, and my own career has been filled to overflowing with examples of that kind of generosity. In spite of that, I recognize the difficulty of what I am suggesting for men of my generation. Their experience with women in business has often been limited to secretaries.

The greatest resistance to the idea of any kind of social responsibility is at the middle-management level where these new demands must be fitted into a schedule which is already crowded with operating responsibilities. The new demands may at least initially slow down operations and thus interfere with economic performance. Middle managers may ignore these new demands unless compliance becomes a part of the job description, the performance evaluation, and the compensation package. If this is done, however, senior management must recognize the radical nature of what it is asking and must be prepared to train and support these men as they embark on this new course. The nature of that training and support will depend, of course, on how a given corporation diagnoses the sources of the problem. Hanging over the whole process and complicating it even further is the ever-present threat of reverse discrimination.

There is no question that inhospitable informal structures are a barrier to women coming into management. This is a very difficult barrier to surmount. Men sit together for lunch in the company cafeteria. They talk about football and baseball scores. They also talk about what went wrong that morning or the latest gossip about what's going on in the company. Men stop for a drink together to relax after work. As they relax, they review the day's events. Are women welcome? Is *one* woman welcome? Young men tell me that if a woman joins them, it is a different kind of conversation. Should the men welcome the women? Should the women want to join? If not, how do they become part of that informal structure? How do the men's wives and the women's husbands react to these sessions?

The peer relationships and information flow in the informal structures of a corporation are crucial to the manager's performance of his or her formal responsibilities. Acceptance of women in these structures cannot be mandated; it will depend heavily on individuals acting on their own initiative. Will this issue go away as younger men with mothers and sisters and wives who work move up? Kanter talks about the dominants heightening the barriers in response to the presence of a token. Dominants who feel secure in their economic role and masculinity can afford to be generous and helpful to the token, and beyond that the corporation can over time change that skewed group into one where males and females are more evenly balanced.

A related problem deals with mentors. It is increasingly recognized that a mentor is a tremendous asset to a young person in corporate management. I can identify at least three older men who played that role for me. There are very few women in upper management today to act as mentors for younger women, and many men are hesitant to assume that role for a woman, partly for fear of the relationship being misconstrued by others, but also, as Kanter points out, because mentors tend to select protégées in their own image. Again it takes imagination and generosity for older men to see the management possibilities in a young woman.

The sexual implications of women's presence in management cannot be overlooked. One of the early quandaries corporations faced was what to do about women in assignments involving travel, particularly travel with a male executive. Similar problems arise in management conferences at remote locations. I well remember the confusion my presence obviously provoked at a management conference of a company of which I was the first woman director.

Corporations can and probably must be sex-blind on these issues, and their successful resolution will be left to individual men and women. Women must at the beginning of their careers set their own personal standards, and my hope is that men in time will feel a similar responsibility. My own experience has been remarkably free of difficulties, but the literature suggests that a great deal of testing, of what might politely be called unprofessional behavior, continues, and women are faced with the burden of dealing with it.

The report of the Stanford Conference listed "perceived incompatibilities between career and family goals" as a barrier to the entry of women into management. Dealing with these incompatibilities — perceived or real — will in many instances be the responsibility of the woman and her husband, but corporations, employing more and more married women, are having to confront some of these issues. Corporations face a real dilemma in many ways because while women may hope for corporate policies adapted to their needs, they resent any assumption on the part of corporate management as to how they will handle personal responsibilities such as taking care of a sick child or asking a husband's approval of a business trip. One solution to this dilemma may result from similar questions being raised as to family demands on the husband and father.

In many large corporations frequent transfers from place to place have been an essential part of moving up the corporate ladder. Young people today — at least in some fields — see frequent job changes as the road to success, and often these changes involve relocation. What happens when both spouses work? A woman in a leading American corporation in the Middle West some years ago told about refusing a transfer to New York because her husband had at last been able to launch his own business successfully. The transfer was an essential step in an executive career path on which she was successfully launched. She reached her decision in the interests of her marriage, but she recognized it meant the end of her upward mobility. She also worried about the impact of her decision on other women in the company. Corporations are beginning to take a new look at the effect of transfers and also at their role in helping relocate a spouse. More and more young couples must make joint decisions on relocation.

It is too early to tell what a working wife will do to the career of a man in the management of a corporation where executive wives are expected to participate in numerous social functions and conventions, involving company personnel and customers. As more and more wives of chief executive officers become business or professional women, they will become less available as helpmates.

Probably the most difficult issue for a woman to resolve is the compatibility between a career and a family. One indication that this will continue as an important issue in the future was Betty Friedan's talk at the NOW-LDEF National Assembly on the Future of the Family in November 1979, signaling a new agenda for the women's movement which includes restructuring the institutions of home and work to minimize the conflicts between careers and children.[10] Here again many of the decisions must be made by husband and wife, mother and father, but increasingly the corporation is being asked to look at how its demands impact the family.

"The John Caron Story" in *Full Value* pointed out the danger of letting *excessive* time demands of a corporate job squeeze out time for wife and children.[11] For a woman with young children the *normal* time demands of a corporate job may create pressures—particularly if those time demands are set within a rigid unalterable schedule. Experiments to respond to this problem are under way. Some corporations have made available flexible working hours or flextime as well as part-time work. Some kinds of work can be done at home, and Alvin Toffler is suggesting that the home of the future may also become an electronic office. It is dangerous to generalize about these options because different businesses have different needs—customer service as compared to production, for example.

Flextime and part-time work have been viewed as helpful for mothers, but men are beginning to look at these options for fathers, too, as James A. Levine points out in his book, *Who Will Raise the Children?* This book, incidentally, dramatizes the effect of stereotypes when applied to men. Agencies specializing in the placement of women in part-time work have found it almost impossible to place men in part-time jobs, particularly if the reason they wish to reduce their working hours is to increase their participation in child rearing. A representative of one of the agencies is quoted:

> There's a stigma attached to a man who wants part-time work. It means he's not masculine, not aggressive. The attitude of society toward a man not gung-ho on his career is even less kind than that toward women who want part-time work. He's not only stuck in the low-end jobs, but even the low-end jobs don't want him because they don't understand why he wants to be there. . . .[12]

The problems of single parents operating within regular work schedules are great. The movie *Kramer vs. Kramer* shows a male single parent losing his job and gaining a reputation for unreliability as a result of his struggles to look out for his young son.

Child care is one possible answer to these problems. Some corporations have tried and failed, but experiments must be continued to find methods with satisfactory quality and costs. Concern for children touches the most fundamental religious beliefs, and yet our society has failed to come to grips with this issue. Its difficulty is perhaps illustrated by pointing out that in 1943 — 38 years ago — at the dedication of the Women's Rights Collection at Radcliffe College, Vera Micheles Dean said:

> We must make it possible, in practice, for women to combine a home and a career by expanding community facilities for child care, recreation and feeding; and create a social atmosphere in which women who work will feel no more guilty of neglecting their homes than do men who see nothing incompatible in being fathers and at the same time, lawyers, merchants, architects, statesmen, engineers, or poets.[13]

I am not at all sure that child care is a corporate responsibility. It is obvious that, for whatever reason, parents are too often not making adequate provision for it. It may be that only government can provide the solution, but in any case this is a by-product of the entry of women into the work force which must be dealt with.

If women drop out of the work force when their children are growing up, they encounter another barrier. In the hierarchical structure of the large corporation, success means moving up, and realistically any interruption in a career restricts that upward mobility. As long as there are substantial numbers of able people who work without interruption from 20 to 60, it will be a rare person who can get back on the ladder on a higher or even the same rung as he or she left it. Success can, however, be redefined by individuals, and indeed by the corporation if it chooses, to include other kinds of opportunity such as greater autonomy, growth, a sense of challenge, a chance to learn, as well as human relationships. And since the hierarchical pyramid narrows sharply at the top, a system which gives importance and interest to large numbers of jobs at lower levels has much to recommend it.

Conclusion

Alan Pifer devoted his 1976 report as President of the Carnegie Corporation to "Women Working: Toward a New Society." No brief reference can do justice to his thoughtful analysis of the implications of the working woman for American life. As an alternative to drifting along, he suggests "looking at the reality of the working woman as the opening wedge for broad social reform." In describing that future, he says:

> The new society would have the aim of greater occupational equality and freedom of choice for men and women in the work place. It would assume cooperation between men and women in the sharing of family responsibilities. It would entail better articulation than now exists between work and home life and between work and education. It would permit flexibilities in the amount of time an individual might allocate to education, work, family life, and leisure at any age during the course of a lifetime.
>
> Interrelated and interdependent, these goals, if they were achieved, would lead to a fundamental reordering of the values underlying American life—in which the objectives of greater choice for the individual and improved quality of life would for the first time be equated with our traditional concern for productivity.

In his conclusion, he describes this new society as "moral, pragmatic and humane."

> It would be moral because it would be founded on a belief that the worth and dignity of the individual and his or her right to be respected are more important than the claims of corporate struc-

tures or of the state. It would be pragmatic because it would release presently suppressed human abilities to the nation's creative and productive processes. It would be humane because it would have the flexibility to allow for the free expression of individual differences and would recognize that when these differences become disadvantages in the quest for job equality, as in the case of the female capacity for bearing children, society must make adjustments.

While I share many of the aspirations of both Kanter and Pifer, I would caution that their impact on economic efficiency remains to be tested, and my judgment is that the great virtues of our economic system — personal freedom and widespread economic independence — are dependent on that efficiency. The best hope for developing the kinds of structures Pifer and Kanter suggest rests with financially strong corporations competing successfully in the market. The resources, including management time, needed to experiment with this kind of change will only be available in a strong economy. Experiments now under way in industry give hope that corporations will take the initiative in dealing with the work/family-life issue in a variety of ways rather than letting the government step in to fill a vacuum.

The announcement of this symposium equates the influence of the modern corporation with that of the nation state. Political institutions reflect and are limited by the beliefs of the societies in which they exist, and the same thing is true of economic institutions. Even Milton Friedman, the advocate of the corporation as a pure economic institution existing solely to make profits, acknowledges that it must operate within the limits of "ethical custom." I believe the announcement overstates the influence of the corporation in defining the good life. The emergence of women's issues which many people believe was the significant social movement of the 1970s cannot be traced to the corporation in any major way.

Many young people today are giving careful consideration to the relative amount of time they are willing to give to their jobs and their families, and young men appear to be beginning to recognize that their wives' careers have equal priority with their own. To the extent these ideas are widely accepted by the kind of bright talented young people corporations want to employ, they will be reflected in the corporate structure.

This paper may have dwelt too much on specific details, but the purpose was to try to give reality to the issues surrounding the presence of women in the work force. It is increasingly apparent that what were first perceived as women's needs are in fact needs of men and women and families. Corporations which find ways to meet those needs have the potential of finding more productive, more satisfied employees in the process. This vision for the future, based on principles of justice and respect for human dignity, deserves to be pursued.

NOTES

1. Carol Boyd Leon and Philip L. Rones, "Employment and unemployment during 1979: an analysis," *Monthly Labor Review*, February 1980, p. 9.

2. *The Urban Institute Policy and Research Report* 9, no. 1 (Fall 1979): 2.

3. *The New York Times* National Recruitment Survey, October 14, 1979, p. 59.

4. Margaret Hennig and Anne Jardim, *The Managerial Woman* (New York: Pocket Books, 1978), p. 85.

5. *Ibid,* p. 235.

6. Carol Nagy Jacklin and Eleanor Emmons Maccoby, "Sex Differences and Their Implications for Management," in *Bringing Women into Management,* ed. Francine E. Gordon and Myra H. Strober (New York: McGraw Hill, 1975).

7. Gordon and Strober, *ibid.,* p. 158.

8. Rosabeth Moss Kanter, *Men and Women in the Corporation* (New York: Basic Books, 1977), p. 6.

9. *Ibid.,* p. 231.

10. See Betty Friedan, "Feminism Takes a New Turn," *New York Times Magazine,* November 18, 1979, p. 40.

11. Oliver F. Williams and John W. Houck, *Full Value* (New York: Harper & Row, 1978), chap. 13.

12. James A. Levine, *Who Will Raise the Children?* (Philadelphia: J. B. Lippincott, 1976), p. 68.

13. *Radcliffe Quarterly* March 1979, p. 26.

11. The Corporate Leader and the Ethical Resources of Religion: A Dialogue

James M. Gustafson and Elmer W. Johnson

The Emergence of Managerial Corporate Capitalism

ELMER JOHNSON

In my judgment, the development of modern managerial capitalism has given rise to important ethical concerns. As a result of two contemporaneous and interrelated evolutions over the last 100 years or so, one organizational and the other technological, most working members of our society earn their living today as employees of large-scale schemes of cooperation. These schemes of cooperation have vastly increased our economic productivity. This has come about through two chief means: an extensive differentiation of tasks, or specialization of labor; and a highly pyramidal, hierarchical structure of management. Relatively few people have been given the authority to direct and coordinate the work life of the masses of workers.

While such cooperative schemes of work life have been thrust upon us, we have nevertheless continued to spout the Western ideals of individualism: competition in the marketplace, private property, personal initiative, and so forth.[1] Let's call them the competitive virtues. We kneel in reverence before Adam Smith and John Stuart Mill, but we wonder increasingly whether the individualist tradition is adequate.

Yet, we cannot doubt the continued vitality of the competitive virtues in a new context: the intramural context of the large corporation. We have devised sophisticated bonus plans, stock-option plans, and other incentive systems that simulate the conditions of private managerial capitalism. We have supplemented pecuniary rewards with all sorts of ego-gratifying, recognition mechanisms. We continue to rely primarily on self-interest incentives to motivate our present and prospective corporate leaders to perform at peak levels of energy and dedication, and to ensure that the best candidates rise to the top. B. F. Skinner should congratulate us for this kind of behavioral engineering.[2]

Corporate Value Formation

Nevertheless, I have witnessed a mentality among some corporate managers that is sadly inadequate to the situation and which I believe is often traceable to our excessive reliance on self-interest. Let me explain. The top twenty or twenty-five positions in each of the 200 largest corporations are occupied mainly by persons between the ages of 50 and 65, and the very top positions by persons in their late fifties and above. Most of them are not persons of substantial means. They usually come into the top rungs of compensation only in the last five to ten years of their careers. Their opportunities for huge bonus compensation during those years usually depend on current results of operations. There is the temptation in many cases for the executive to make decisions that will make him and the corporation look very good in the short run (during the balance of his career). But this temptation can leave a shoddy legacy to his successors: a legacy of litigation, government investigations, and customer dissatisfaction. This can result in a long-term competitive disadvantage because of inattention to costly but necessary research and new product development.[3]

The top corporate executive is tempted in other ways to concentrate on immediate results. The very structure of our securities markets, which values instantaneous liquidity above all else, means that our corporate managers cannot make long-term decisions requiring short-term sacrifices of corporate profits. If they do, they risk a corporate takeover and loss of control overnight to a handful of professional arbitrageurs in New York City.

Let me add another unhappy phenomenon that I believe is partly traceable to excessive reliance on self-interest and inadequate attention to moral incentives. If, for the first twenty-five years of his career, a person is shaped primarily by self-interest incentives, it should not be surprising that we produce few corporate leaders who have an adequate vision of the long-term good of the corporation and its constituencies, much less any broader concept of the common good of society. The danger is that we tend to produce corporate leaders who, while being highly energetic and highly dedicated, are rather uninspiring and hardly deserving of the word leadership. Joseph Schumpeter once said that the corporate manager is anti-heroic and has no charisma; that his habits of life are not of the kind that develop personal fascination. He has been taught from Day One to keep his nose to the grindstone and his eye on current profits. Accordingly, says Schumpeter, outside the office the business executive is often unable to say "boo to a goose."[4]

The Manager's Fiduciary Responsibility to Stockholders

Almost 50 years ago, a famous exchange of law-review articles took place between two eminent professors of corporation law, E. Merrick Dodd, Jr., of Harvard and Adolph A. Berle, Jr., of Columbia.[5] Professor Dodd's article was entitled "For Whom are Corporate Managers Trustees?" In that 1932 *Harvard Law Review* article, Dodd argued that the time had long since arrived when the public demanded, and the courts were compelled to recognize, that corporate managers are trustees not only for stockholders but also for employees, customers, and perhaps other constituencies. He did not argue that managers should be required to act as fiduciaries for these other constituencies, but that they should be permitted to consider these other interests, and to do so without risking personal liability to stockholders. Professor Berle's prompt response, entitled "For Whom Corporate Managers are Trustees," was tough and to the point. He argued that our whole corporate law system was built on the cornerstone of the manager's fiduciary obligation to stockholders, and stockholders alone, and that until we were prepared to enunciate clear standards of fiduciary obligation to these other constituencies, it was irresponsible to propose that managers be permitted some vague and ambiguous latitude of discretion in making decisions based on socioeconomic considerations.

This mind-set of the corporate executive has been reinforced by the state laws of corporations which, throughout our history, have treated the corporate executive as a fiduciary solely for the stockholders. As long as directors and officers act in compliance with law and in accordance with good-faith determinations about the best interests of their stockholders, they understand that they will not incur personal liability and should not even be questioned as to whether they are acting in a socially responsible manner.

Yet the large corporation has evolved into a major social institution. It is composed of numerous employees who spend all their working time and much of their leisure time together and who accordingly develop a strong sense of community. Major decisions of the large corporation can have a very substantial impact on our lives and our environment.[6] Under these circumstances, isn't there a need for inspiring leadership in the large corporation? Is it not past the time when we should reexamine the values and institutional arrangements that sustained an earlier stage of capitalism? Can some new ethic of corporate leadership be developed that would be more appropriate to the modern situation?

Corporations and Stewardship

JAMES GUSTAFSON

I agree that it is time to examine the personal values and institutional conditions of capitalism. But before responding more specifically to your closing questions let me comment on your brief history of the development of corporate capitalism. In my judgment, the evolutionary, nonviolent emergence of corporate capitalism in the United States could not have occurred without the growth of labor unions and government regulation. Corporations and their managers did not voluntarily restrain their exploitative tendencies.

I am sure there were trustworthy, reliable, faithful persons who acknowledged their implicit obligations to communities, customers, and others, and who acted in a praiseworthy way in this regard. But such a person within a corporate structure surely has often had to subsume his or her personal morality to the requirements of the "office." As Reinhold Niebuhr taught many of us, corporate self-interest accumulates means of power that individuals no longer have (in the main), and the significance of individual choices within such structures is diminished.[7] I am reminded of Jonathan Edwards. The first chapter of his treatise on *Original Sin* is entitled, "The evidence of original sin from what appears in fact of the sinfulness of mankind." Persons and corporations have given evidence in fact of the necessity of regulation and coercion because they do not voluntarily assume a range of accountability for all the consequences of their activities. In the main, they are not faithful stewards.

By saying this, I do not denigrate the idea that corporate leaders can be educated in such a way as to accept more accountability in our society. Some improvement of moral education and moral development is in high order. And choices are made by individual persons, or by collections of persons, even when the means of action are institutionalized and magnified in power by corporations. But for all her admirable activities, Mother Teresa has not improved working conditions in industrialized Calcutta, weakened the caste system, or altered the vast discrepancy in distribution of wealth between the Birla family (one of the three families that control much of the Indian economy) and the rickshaw pullers on Swinhoe Street in Ballygunge.

To Form Their Moral Vision

Keeping in mind these Niebuhrian warnings as to moral man and immoral society, let me now respond to your questions by distinguishing two related problems. One is the criteria for the kind of managers that are desirable, and how such persons are educated, formed in their moral visions, sustained in them when institutional pressures against them are strong, and so forth. The second is the criteria for the organization of a corporation, or for that matter, any large-scale social organization which will extend the scope of its accountability, make possible the initiatives of responsible leadership, and restrain undesirable actions.

In considering the first problem, a number of questions need to be addressed. From the perspective of the history of Western moral thought, we are clearly involved in the concept of virtue. To introduce this concept might assist our discussion; it might also mislead us. We might better, I suppose, talk about "ego strengths" in Erikson's terms.[8] What virtues or elements of character are morally desirable in corporate leadership? Does the venerable list of cardinal virtues—justice, temperance, courage, prudence, or wisdom—cover the needs? Or do we want first to add or subtract from this list, and second to redefine these terms?

We know from our studies of Greek moral literature that the qualities of human excellence that were desired changed under different historic conditions. Are there present conditions which require different virtues from, let us say, an earlier period in our social and economic history? That is a second question. A third we can take right out of Plato's *Meno*: Can virtue be taught? Or does it come by nature? Or is it a gift of the gods? Obviously, it would be desirable to believe that it can be taught or formed in some way. Then we come to another question: how can it be taught? What are the necessary conditions for its formation?

The last question is worth pondering for a moment. We know that distinctive characters are best shaped by relatively closed communities with strong ideological or religious and moral beliefs. Such conditions do not today prevail for most persons. Also, there have to be limitations on access to conflicting ways of thinking, beliefs, and human values to secure the prospects for forming persons with certain virtues. The perils in this are evident: we only need to remember Plato's *Republic,* and countless visions since then.

There are also the affective aspects of lives: loyalties to certain persons, ideals, and beliefs, commitments to certain principles and values. Virtue is not knowledge without remainder.[9] So we must consider the conditions under which the desired commitments, loyalties, and so forth can be nourished. And, of course, who is to determine, insofar as determination can be made, which virtues are to be taught? Or, what persistent characteristics of action are to be instilled? Again, the perils in all this are evident.

A New Kind of Leadership

ELMER JOHNSON

I agree that we should consider the problems of virtue and character formation in the corporate leader before dealing with institutional conditions. Let me respond to your initial questions about morally desirable virtues or elements of character in corporate leadership. I will be so venturesome as to describe the kind of manager that I believe is necessary if large corporations are to function properly as the social institutions they have become.[10]

The candidate for corporate leadership, by the time he becomes a candidate, should have clearly satisfied a few important preconditions. These conditions begin with professional competence in the candidate's particular field of expertise, whether it be finance, law, engineering, marketing, or some other area.[11] He will have shown creativity and imagination in solving problems. Accordingly he will be a highly disciplined, slightly monastic, person. The self-indulgent hedonist is unlikely to develop great competence.

Second, he will have evidenced a pleasant disposition and a respect for others. He will be a team player. His competence will include peripheral vision in perceiving problems outside his area of expertise that call for the attention of others in the organization, a readiness to seek from and provide to others in the organization such assistance and cooperation as will serve the corporation's best interests. Without this kind of cooperation and team play in the large corporation, pooling of talent is wasted. Lone rangers have no place.

Third, he will have demonstrated maturity of judgment, not only in the solving of problems but also in the selection of key personnel, and in his dealings with other people within and outside the corporation. Maturity of judgment involves the rational capacity to see all the issues, to sort out the gut issues from the peripheral ones, the ones in need of prompt solution from those permitting or requiring a longer period for resolution, and so forth. As to qualities of moral character, I believe the essential ingredient is the capacity for empathy, the ability to put oneself in the place of those persons with whom one is dealing or those persons who will be affected by a decision. Many, if not most, of the people I know who have achieved a high degree of competence in their chosen areas have such ego problems, or are so insensitive to what is going on in the minds and hearts of other parties, that despite their competence they have no capacity for judgment in situations where the ability to foresee consequences counts for a great deal. After all, the most difficult part of foresight is that of anticipating likely actions on the part of other free agents who will be reacting to one's judgment. If one is so insensitive or so self-absorbed that he cannot put himself in the other person's position, then he will be quite a limited person.

Fourth, the potential corporate leader will be a productive person, in the sense of being well able to delegate responsibility and organize and carry out complex projects expeditiously and efficiently. Productivity is in large part a by-product of good judgment. The person who can promptly cut through to the central, immediate issues in confronting a problem has the ability to simplify. Moreover, the productive corporate or professional leader has the ability to restrict his time to matters of judgment and coordination. He knows how to stay out of the hair of his subordinates. He gives free rein to a trustworthy horse and yet exercises the necessary degree of oversight.

These four are the threshold criteria of corporate leadership. But of course, leadership means much more. The fifth criterion, then, is that the leader is an inspirer of others within the organization. He brings about solidarity and fellow-feeling among the key personnel. He assists younger executives in realizing their full potential. The leader has a vision of the common good of the organization. Not only has he devoted his efforts to articulating and working toward that common good, but it has become dramatically apparent to other members of the organization that his vision is a noble one, that there is a real passion in his commitment to this vision, and that he really cares for the members of the organization. The leader with this kind of vision and fidelity and caring has the fiber and strength that enable him to face up to tough problems and make decisions under pressure, to make constructive criticisms of young executives in a kindly manner, and to assist older executives in preparing the way (and making way) for the next generation of leadership.

Sixth, the corporate manager exhibits this same capacity for leadership in his dealings with the outside world. He builds bridges between the corporation and its various constituencies. His antennae are sharp and sensitive. As a result, his responses to outside criticism of his corporation or of large corporations in general, are not knee-jerk reactions. Rather, he is open to valid, constructive criticism, and his positions on corporate-social issues are thoughtful and well-reasoned. In his dealings with government officials he seeks to correlate the corporate purpose with the broader public interest and thereby reduce the adversary element of the business-government interface. He exudes a tone of magnanimity and surefootedness, and he inspires confidence. Only the leader of strong convictions, a person of vision and nobility, has great power to enhance the institutional strength and reputation of the corporation.

Having given you my litmus-paper test for identifying the ideal corporate leader, I confess I have no easy answers to the question of how such persons are developed. Undoubtedly, the leadership attributes I have described are largely "gifts of the gods," but these gifts come through family and religious nurture, excellent schooling, and on-the-job training with outstanding senior leaders. More specifically, however, what are the resources for educating or producing the leader of vision and high ethical caliber?

The Good and Effective Person

JAMES GUSTAFSON

The qualities you list would be prized in any profession. You have delineated the "good" person in terms of the "effective" person, and effective in many social roles and responsibilities.

It is interesting to note what your effective person is not. There is no reference to following the rules faithfully as they are given in manuals of procedure or in a table of organization. The faithful bureaucratic person would not make the grade. There is also no reference to the single-minded person who "with purity of heart" pursues one limited end or goal. Your effective person is no mechanic who spends energy primarily on putting the parts together according to a blueprint. In theological ethical literature the closest "type" that he or she comes to is H. Richard Niebuhr's responsive and responsible self.[12]

There are only a limited number of things that can be done to foster the development of your effective person. We can see how complex the task would be if we sort out five features of effectiveness, and assess what might be done about each.

1. Natural endowments, such as native intellectual capacities of a high order, are very important. Nothing can be done to overcome limits in this regard, though corporations might contribute to developing the size of the "pool" from which persons could be selected by affording naturally endowed persons the opportunities to develop.

2. Experiences certainly affect the development of the characteristics that are desirable. I have in mind early childhood experiences that affect the development of self-confidence, openness to others, curiosity to learn, and tendencies to trust or distrust others. These effects are not easily reversed or altered, even by forms of personal therapy. Yet these "ego strengths" are necessary "pre-conditions" at least to the virtues of effectiveness that you delineate.[13] They may be preconditions to moral virtues. Some persons have been unlucky in the genetic lottery, and/or in the lottery of family and community. Persons can, however, do some things to expose themselves to a wider range of persons, communities, institutions, and cultures; this might alter and elicit capacities formed by prior experience.

3. Habituation that results from conscious and consistent choices and actions over which individuals have some control. I refer to a number of things here: disciplined work habits, training of the mind by learning how to think effectively, developing moral character by adhering to certain moral principles and values, and choosing ends that are worthy and developing capacities to realize them. Good professional training in law, medicine, and other professions is a process not only of learning information, but also of habituating thought and patterns of conduct. Overdone, persons get into a rut, lose imagination, foreshorten vision, and lessen flexibility to respond innovatively. But in the absence of a process of habituation there is no professional or moral character to the agent. There is no base from which to be responsive.

4. Concepts, procedures of thinking, and other skills can be learned from relevant literature and tested in practice. The use of case-study methods in law and business schools is designed to do this; training in moral theology and ethics can also do this; But such training in schools is always presented from an observer's point of view, even when, in simulation, one is to act out the part of the agent. Practice adds

the sense of accountability for choices, and for their consequences. This is where senior professionals are important for younger persons; they can facilitate the development of these capacities by encouraging others to take responsibility, by critical analysis of their actions, and by constructive suggestions.

5. Mastery of relevant information is something that can be achieved by those who have the native capacity to learn, and have sufficient desire to achieve. But mastery of information does not of itself lead to sound judgment. We need something akin to wisdom.

All of these conditions are necessary for the effectiveness you describe. No one of them is sufficient. There are moral components which are involved in effectiveness. I want to stress that we can make choices about our ends, about those goals that are worthy of our commitment, about the components in a "good" life (morally good as well as good in other respects). These do not in themselves resolve dilemmas in specific circumstances, except in very critical situations, but they set perimeters of conduct and provide a sense of direction.[14]

Also, persons can develop systems of internal sanctions, or consciences. Commitments can be made to certain moral principles and values which are internalized by practice, and which provide some guidance to professional conduct. I am thinking not merely of commonplace matters, such as embezzling, but of more subtle matters as well.

But none of us is so professionally or morally effective that we do not need some patterns of accountability to others—to our institutions, to other individuals, to rules, and even to explicit (or at least implied) punishments and rewards. We all need to be "whipped and goaded like balky asses," to quote John Calvin on the instructive use of the law, even for the redeemed.

The Debate about Education in Virtue

ELMER JOHNSON

I can only underscore what has been said in reference to the elaborate means and difficult processes by which the potential corporate leader may approximate or attain the kinds of virtues and excellences we have in mind. It seems to me, as others have noted, that since the eighteenth century most moral philosophers and educators have directed their efforts largely toward attempting to find a substitute for virtue, or if not a substitute for virtue, certainly a substitute means of moral education in place of those envisioned by the Judeo-Christian tradition.

Let me cite just two examples, one from the eighteenth century and one from the twentieth. The idea in Rousseau's *Emile* (1762) is that with rational manipulation on the part of the mentor, any student can learn to manage his passions and sentiments out of enlightened self-interest. It is true that Rousseau sees the central importance of forming the capacity for compassion in his young student if he is to escape narrow self-interest and acquire a yearning for the common good, but Rousseau derives compassion even from self-interest.

It is interesting that as Emile comes into his late teens with all the potential turbulence of this time of life, Rousseau finds it necessary to articulate a natural theology or deism to carry on with the moral education of his student. But his theology has none of the fire and thunder of the Judeo-Christian vision, and his conception of God is ultimately a rather utilitarian one. Further, his theology does not envision any need for religious community.

My second example is Lawrence Kohlberg, the Harvard psychologist. In his 1968 lecture, "Education for Justice: A Modern Statement of the Platonic View," he reasserts "the Platonic faith in the power of the rational good" as the basis for his program of moral education.[15] His argument, briefly summarized, is that the name of virtue is justice, which in turn is a matter of equal and universal human rights; that virtue comes about by acquiring rational cognition of the good; and that this kind of knowledge can be imparted by the proper kind of teacher using the right methods. This teacher is one who is living the just life himself so that he is able to make his students uncomfortable about their own degree of goodness. He is able to lead them upward through a series of stages of moral growth.

Like Plato, Kohlberg perceives that the knowledge of the good is inside the child and that the goal of teaching is to draw out the capacity for virtue. While theology has no role to play in his program, he does place great emphasis on "full student participation in a school in which justice is a living matter." Though rarely attainable, his ideal school would be the self-contained little Republic "in which knowledge of the good is to be brought out through love and community."

Contrary to Rousseau and Kohlberg, the Judeo-Christian tradition, while holding out high hopes for the spiritual liberation and moral educability of the individual, nevertheless has a profound appreciation of the serious imperfections and limitations of man. It accordingly places great emphasis on the character-forming resources of religion, as well as on the law and other institutional mechanisms for holding people accountable and bringing about habitual dispositions in society.

In particular regard to the fiduciary, the person who is expected to act primarily in the interests of others and therefore to care for others, we are really talking about the combined virtues of compassion and fidelity. Rousseau to the contrary, I just do not find credible the idea that the rationally autonomous individual and potential corporate leader will acquire the virtues of compassion and fidelity by acting out of enlightened self-interest. Where there is no lively belief in God and his high purposes, where there is instead what you have elsewhere called an overweening aspiration for human self-sufficiency, the likely result, based on my observations, is not the true fiduciary, the person who feels for others and is faithful to his calling, but rather Michael Maccoby's corporate gamesman, who is "energized to compete not because he wants to build an empire, not for riches, but rather for fame, glory, the exhilaration of running his team and of gaining victories."[16]

Despite my reservations, I must say that I'm intrigued by Rousseau's need for a theology and Kohlberg's ideal of a quasi-religious community, which are two of the principal kinds of ethical resources offered by the Jewish and Christian religions. I'd be interested in your reactions to these aspects of Rousseau and Kohlberg's theories and how they compare to the character-forming resources of the Judeo-Christian vision.

The Resources of Religion in the Corporate World

JAMES GUSTAFSON

I generally agree with your remarks on modern moral philosophy. Your two examples of Rousseau and Kohlberg are very much in point. We do not have space here to critique these two authors or to go into their many differences. The groupings of various moderns for the secular equivalents of a theology and of the church are as you say, most intriguing. In the Judeo-Christian tradition, theology, religious community, and the life of personal faith or piety are of central importance when we come to talk of moral nurture. Let me make some extended comments in each of these three areas, and consider also how religious life might affect our persons, and thus in some ways qualify these virtues of effectiveness that you have lined out.

Churches as Communities of Moral Formation

I suspect that many persons of morally praiseworthy character in every profession would acknowledge the significance of religious communities as an important part of their moral nurture. Sometimes, that moral nurture has had trivial aspects to it, whether under Protestant, Roman Catholic, or Jewish auspices. But religious nurture often leads to at least a sense of moral seriousness and conscientiousness, and at its best instills strong moral commitments, high moral ideals, and good motives.[17]

Churches have been, and ought to be, communities of moral formation. But this is not always the case, for many reasons. One has to think carefully both about how morals are formed, and about what values and principles and ideals are to be fostered. Your effective person really exercises agency; a religious moral nurture around rigid rules would not fully prepare a person to be a responsive agent. Churches are failing as communities of moral nurture or formation, often as a result of social forces beyond their control. But I think they need to recover this aspect of their vocation. It is not an aspect that can be restricted to particular programs; it needs to penetrate education, preaching, worship, counseling, and other aspects of church life.

A second aspect of church life comes to mind: namely, the church as a community of moral discourse. Let us say that effective persons desire to think more clearly about moral aspects of their professional lives. Let us say that they are serious about their religious faith and beliefs. What churches provide the occasions in which they can think carefully about their faith and beliefs in relation to their professional responsibilities?

I would guess that most persons of professional effectiveness find little assistance from their churches in thinking about these things. Churches use professional persons—a banker, for instance, to handle parish finances—for their own institutional purposes; within limits this is correct. But do churches provide the intelligent leadership or the occasions for professional persons to become more morally effective, to see their ways through moral dilemmas in their work, to see possibilities for the improvement of society? Certainly the Protestant penchant to pronounce on the issues of the current newsweeklies does not carry either authority or assistance to professional persons. The authoritative teachings of the Roman Catholic church do carry some weight with many professionals. Some conditions have to be developed before churches can become communities of moral discourse, not the least being better recruitment and training of the clergy. Effective persons in other professions are seldom matched by equally effective persons in the clergy. A great deal needs to be done before congregations or other religious bodies can begin to fulfill this proper responsibility.[18]

Sin and Grace: The Theological Themes of Our Stories

Religious beliefs provide concepts and symbols by which we interpret ourselves, the circumstances of our actions, the larger ends or purposes of our actions, and the ordering of the importance of things in our lives and the world. Part of the authority that accrues to religious doctrines and symbols stems from their capacities to give insight into "how things really are," to the deeper realities of human life, to living in the world, and to the reality of the divine presence that orders and sustains life. Doctrines are not irrelevant to the professional world.

The easiest example to cite, in part because it was so effectively used by Reinhold Niebuhr[19] is the doctrine of sin. We need not be taught the doctrine; we simply can examine ourselves to see that it carries weight. I cannot develop all of its implications for interpreting life in the corporate world. There are grounds for becoming wary of the ways in which the intentions and ends of both persons and corporations are turned in on their own immediate self-interests. We realize that they are subject to overwhelming confidence in the rightness of their interests and their judgments. We know that there are objects of confidence for these persons and corporations that are misplaced, and that there is excessive confidence in some objects and defective confidence in other objects. We know that corporate interests must be restrained by countervailing institutions which represent other interests.

Sin as a concept or as a symbol has illuminative power to disclose human and institutional realities in which executives and professional persons live and work.

But there are other concepts and symbols. Certainly one aspect of grace is that it points to possibilities for creative action despite the limitations of reality; it points toward a degree of openness in institutions and events that offers opportunities for significant moral action. It provides a deep belief in the possibilities of rectifying many errors and their consequences, in possibilities of extending human activities for the sake of human well-being, socially and individually.

However, I would not argue that the same insights cannot be gained on other grounds; many a pagan has as sharp an eye for the effects of the human fault as does a Christian. But I do think there are religious resources that can be used with skill and persuasiveness to help the corporate leader grasp some of the deeper realities of his field of activity.

Theology provides a vision of a larger end of all human activity. It is one function of theological thinking to see particular events against a larger backdrop of events, to see the place and order of institutions like corporations, within a larger scheme of things. Institutions are not ends in themselves, but function in relation to each other to create conditions that ultimately serve human well-being. Institutions are, to be very theological, aspects of the divine governance of the world.

Another contribution of theology is its provision of examples of humanly, morally, and religiously effective persons. I am not so naïve as to say that Jesus provides a blueprint for the corporate executive. But loyalties to persons, to the stories of their lives, to the meanings that have developed around their lives, are important.

Notre Dame theologians have pursued this line of inquiry more than most theologians in North America.[20] This we know from *Full Value: Cases in Christian Business Ethics* (1978), by Father Williams and Professor Houck. Religious traditions provide, as these writers observe, a story, for example the Christian story, which informs our moral outlooks, creates our moral vision, sustains our moral loyalties, and nurtures our moral characters. This story also becomes the story of our lives. And stories are better than doctrines for this, since they impact on our affections and have the poignancy of detail which illuminates in a way that abstract doctrines cannot. Parables, narratives, or biographies can be more effective in shaping moral lives than the categorical imperative, a doctrine of God's will, an argument from a manual of moral theology, or from a responsum to the Jewish law.

Personal Faith and Piety

There are two aspects of these resources that I want to note briefly. One has been accented more by Protestantism than by Catholicism. It is the inner freedom that can be provided by a deep confidence in the goodness of the ultimate power that orders life. It is an inner liberation of the human spirit from the constant desire to be self-justifying, to be proving one's merits to oneself and to others. It is a kind of openness to be courageous, to take risks, to stand for what is right when consequences are painful. This resource of faith is grounded in the confidence that man's relationship to God is not won by human achievements. None of us embodies this in an ideal form; we continue to be plagued by anxieties of self-assessment, and we live in a world in which others are authorized to assess our achievements. But the possibility of a deeper confidence offered in religious faith can sustain the kind of responsiveness that effective persons seem to embody.

The second is the realization that religious life—worship, personal piety, and devotion—can do a great deal to deepen our commitments to moral ends, and sustain our visions and our courage. I refer to the affective aspect of religious and moral life that is underestimated by a view of morality which depends upon the exertion of will alone to adhere to principles. There are various aspects to piety: contrition, repentance, forgiveness, and the newness of possibilities that come from this; the lure of the vision of God in which gratitude for life and a sense of the divine governance sustains; and the moral seriousness of our professional lives when seen as our vocations in the service of God.

I have said only a little of what could be said about how we might encourage and sustain and develop the effectiveness that your last contribution set down so well, and only a little of what could be said about the resources of religion for persons. But we both recognize, to allude to a famous book by Reinhold Niebuhr,[21] that moral persons cannot change institutions and power structures on the basis of their motives and personal merits. We noted earlier the need to look at the institutional arrangements within corporations, professions, and society at large which establish structures of moral accountability. We recognize that some moral ends are realized only by institutional restraints, by the coercive as well as pedagogical functions of law, by peer assessment, and other such mechanisms.

I want you to say some things about this drawn from your own professional experience. But I want you to address not only the restraints that institutions need to develop against various moral evils, but also the institutional conditions that generate and sustain the kind of creative responsiveness that you describe. Only romantic idealists think that all we need in order to achieve a good society is to have good persons; neither of us belongs to that school. But only a deep cynic thinks that one creates a livable order of life only by coercion. Neither of us is a cynic. What institutional arrangements help both to restrain faults and sustain responsiveness?

Corporate Reform: A Prerequisite to Moral Leadership

ELMER JOHNSON

Listening to your comments on the importance of church as a community for moral formation, I cannot help feeling that the corporate leader has a special problem. Not only does he proceed with little if any help from the church, but as he rises to the top of the ladder, he divorces himself increasingly from those small communities within the organization itself that offer mutual nurturing. The top man or woman is a lonely person. I think we have somewhat more hierarchy than we need in most corporations. Perhaps the pyramidal structure of corporate management should be a little more trapezoidal, like that of a large, highly centralized law partnership. In some of the largest corporations, such as General Motors, I observe a healthy emphasis on group leadership. I mention this concern in passing and will now turn to the questions you have raised.

The Uses of Law

A major function of the law is that of coercion and restraint, but a very important side effect of this first use of the law is the schoolmaster or teaching aspect. Even top corporate executives, lawyers, accountants, and other professionals have grown in wisdom and character by experiencing directly or vicariously the prod and the whip of the law. As elevated standards of fiduciary conduct have come to be imposed by law and as we have seen the drama of individual executives and professionals brought before the bar of justice, and sometimes imprisoned for practices that had been condoned only a decade or two earlier, we become more conscious of the far-ranging effects of abuses of corporate power. Our consciences become sensitized to the need for higher standards of conduct.

The decade of the seventies was quite instructive in this regard, with all the corporate Watergates and the dramatic increase in imprisonments for white-collar crimes. I wonder how many executives and professionals have witnessed this scene saying, "There but for the grace of God go I," how many, feeling the sledgehammer of the law vicariously, have developed a heightened sense of responsibility.

Turning now from the coercive and schoolmaster function of the law, let me comment on a second religious insight, namely, the proposition that our institutions can be legally structured so as to perform a positive, enabling, liberating, channeling function. This second function of the law is based on a more hopeful view of the moral educability of the corporate leader. Both uses of the law are necessary as applied to our economic life, but the question is whether excessive reliance has not been placed on the first use of the law: the law as external restraint. As Alexander Solzhenitsyn said to the 1978 graduating class of Harvard College:

> A society based on the letter of the law and never reaching any higher fails to take advantage of the full range of human

possibilities. The letter of the law is too cold and formal to have a beneficial influence in society. Whenever the tissue of life is woven of legalistic relationships, this creates an atmosphere of spiritual mediocrity that paralyzes man's noblest impulses. . . . After a certain level of the problem has been reached, legalistic thinking induces paralysis: it prevents one from seeing the scale and the meaning of events.[22]

The idea behind the second use of the law is that the corporation itself should be structured in such a way that its own internal mechanisms can displace in large part the costly, stultifying bureaucratization and regulation of life resulting from overreliance on law as external restraint. The proponents of this second view sense that as the external restraints are multiplied to hedge the corporate manager in on all sides, we create a legalistic, even warlike, atmosphere, and the possibilities for true leadership are sadly diminished.

The Business Judgment Rule

Over the last six or seven years we have witnessed the widespread adoption by large corporations of measures of the second kind to which I am referring. These measures were adopted as a result of public pressures following the corporate Watergates. The New York Stock Exchange (NYSE) finally got on the bandwagon as a result of prodding from then Chairman Rod Hills of the Securities and Exchange Commission, who in turn was being prodded by the prospect of congressional adoption of the ill-considered ideas of Senator Metzenbaum and Ralph Nader.[23] What are these measures about which I am so pleased and hopeful? First, the NYSE requirement that each corporation have an audit committee of independent directors with important oversight responsibilities; second, the strongly urged NYSE suggestion that each corporation's board of directors be composed of a majority of nonemployees; third, the provision for a nominating committee of nonemployee directors whose job is to select nominees for election as directors.

I could name additional measures, but the purpose of all of them is to hold management accountable to high ethical standards without creating an adversary atmosphere. Yes, there is a healthy tension between the directors and the inside director-officers, but they also share a common function in overseeing the affairs of their corporation and working toward its, and society's, best interests. The corporate manager is reporting to superiors who sincerely want him to succeed.

Once we begin to develop this second approach to institutional arrangements, exciting possibilities come to mind. For example, with a truly independent majority of directors, the traditional "business-judgment rule" receives new life. This is the rule that says in effect that a court will not second-guess a board or committee of directors which has decided not to assert corporate rights of action, even against its own officers. This holds true if that board or committee was truly independent, if it acted in good faith, and if it acted with reasonable diligence.[24] The full and effective use of this rule would go far to reduce the adversary aspects of our business society.

I personally believe that a corporation which has adopted the various measures I have described should be granted access to the business-judgment rule, not merely in situations involving possible corporate claims against officers and directors, but also in those giving rise to possible rights on the part of consumers or some public interest, for example, on alleged product defects or environmental injury. A corporation having the appropriate self-governance mechanisms should, in such kinds of third-party actions, be able to initiate a business-judgment dismissal or summary judgment, if the corporate act in question was subjected to a prior special review by a committee of independent directors.

Obviously, a qualified corporation would not subject every significant corporate decision to formal committee review in order to maximize its access to the business-judgment defense. Such a policy would paralyze the company more effectively than the litigation it was intended to avoid. The kinds of major corporate decisions that boards deem appropriate for such prior review might include the timing and content of press releases reflecting board action likely to have a substantial impact on the market price of the corporation's stock, or the environmental or safety aspects of an important capital expansion, or new line of products. The committee's determination, provided it was made in good faith and with due care, could be a powerful tool in foreclosing claims that a product line or manufacturing process was negligently designed or that material information was inadequately or dilatorily disclosed. Such an expansion of the business-judgment rule for large corporations having the required self-governance mechanisms would be a powerful incentive toward more socially responsible forms of corporate leadership.

The business-judgment rule has other important applications. A favorite Wall Street game in recent years has been the forcible takeover. Corporate management never knows when it will read in the next day's *Wall Street Journal* that an offer for all its stock is being made by another large corporation for a price of twenty to forty percent over the current market value. In this atmosphere of managerial anxiety, more and more time of many corporate managements is concentrated on the design and implementation of antitakeover programs. These programs sometimes involve intensive acquisition efforts that create antitrust obstacles and exhaust the corporation's borrowing capacity. Corporations that are borrowed to the hilt are not attractive targets for the takeover artist. But even with all this diversion of management energies and the taking of corporate actions which are often unlikely to serve the long-term interests of the shareholders, employees, and customers, the takeover game continues.

When faced with an offer to buy out the stockholders at a premium price, the directors become highly nervous over the prospect of personal liability should they resist the offer. Sometimes the directors have reason to believe that after the aggressor has acquired control, it will promptly take action to liquidate certain of the target's divisions to pay off the borrowings it incurred to acquire control, at great cost in loss of jobs, irreparable damage to local communities, and so forth.

With the corporate reforms I have described, why shouldn't a committee of independent directors be able to reject a tender offer on grounds other than inadequacy of price—namely, on grounds of the socioeconomic effects on employees, customers, or communities served by the company? Control Data, McDonald's, and a number of other companies have recently adopted charter amendments, approved by their stockholders, that would permit their boards to take these considerations into account.[25]

Space does not permit me to talk about tax and other reforms that might encourage compensation packages providing strong incentives for corporate managers to concentrate on the long-term health of the corporation. But all these examples are by way of saying that in my judgment one of the more profound insights of the Judeo-Christian vision is the importance it attaches to institutional arrangements as *enabling conditions for responsible leadership.*[26]

Human Institutions and Divine Governance

JAMES GUSTAFSON

You indicated the need for constraints and the disciplinary function of "law," not only civil and criminal, but also rules and procedures of action which private institutions can create and sustain. This, in my judgment, is not only a "dike against sin," though it is that. It is also a way of ordering institutions which is more in accord with the "divine governance," or if that is too theological a term, in accordance with the necessary conditions for a humane society. Your suggestions, in a sense, align the institutions with those powers that are directed toward realizing a larger social and human good than narrow self-interest permits.

Your account suggests that corporations and corporate leaders undergo a process of change and development within a larger course of events. Out of your professional experience you have not given us a blueprint for the ideal corporation, which in turn we seek to actualize. Rather, you have shown that it is in and through events that moral requirements are developed and a moral consciousness is raised.

In this dialogue, we have not sketched out the basis for a major revolution in business society, but we have suggested possibilities for change and development that can be realized in the near future. On another occasion I would like to engage you in a dialogue to examine the possibilities of a more radical alteration in the institutional arrangements of capitalism over a longer time span. I have in mind, among other things, the historical development of our capital-formation system, from one that was dependent on the voluntary savings of the wealthy few to one that is now more dependent on the pension savings of the masses of workers, and the opportunity this development opens up for approximating a more equitable distribution of economic wealth and power and working in other ways as well toward a larger common good. Corporate leaders of the quality we have envisioned in this dialogue would be essential to this broader vision of a just society.

NOTES

1. Among the more insightful studies of both the individualist tradition in general and economic individualism in particular is Steven Lukes, *Individualism* (New York: Harper Torchbooks, 1973). Also see George C. Lodge, *The New American Ideology* (New York: Alfred A. Knopf, 1978); R. M. Unger, *Knowledge and Politics* (New York: Free Press, 1975); and C. B. Macpherson, *The Political Theory of Possessive Individualism* (New York: Oxford University Press, 1962).

2. See his *Walden Two* (New York: Macmillan, 1948).

3. See "The Reindustrialization of America," *Business Week: Special Issue* June 30, 1980, pp. 55–142.

4. *Capitalism, Socialism and Democracy,* 3d ed. (New York: Harper Colphon Books, 1950), pp. 137–38.

5. E. M. Dodd, Jr., "For Whom Are Corporate Managers Trustees?," 45 *Harv. L. Rev.* 1145 (1932); and A. A. Berle, Jr., "For Whom Corporate Managers Are Trustees," 45 *Harv. L. Rev.,* 1365 (1932).

6. In 1975, Christopher Stone, a professor of law at the University of Southern California, wrote a book on the subject of corporate governance entitled *Where the Law Ends* (New York: Harper & Row). Basically, he carried forward Dodd's argument of 48 years ago and proposed specific mandatory structural reforms designed to cause corporations to act "responsibly" toward consumers, communities, employees, and so forth. Like Dodd, he has been subjected to the Berle-type criticism for failing to enunciate anything but a vague "thoughtfulness" standard of responsibility to the corporation's other constituencies, and for avoiding the tough questions: exactly to whom and for what are corporate managers responsible?

For an excellent discussion by a moral philosopher of the necessity of nonlegal standards of managerial ethics supplementing the legal standards, see Alan H. Goldman, "Business Ethics: Profits, Utilities, and Moral Rights," *Philosophy and Public Affairs*, 9 (Spring 1980): 260. For a cautious, well-balanced consideration by a professor of law and business of the question whether the corporation can be governed in such a manner as to serve the stockholders while protecting social interests, see Walter Werner, "Management, Stock Market and Corporate Reform: Berle and Means Reconsidered," 77 *Col. L. Rev.,* 388 (1977): To the argument that the corporate manager cannot serve two or more masters, without loving the one and hating the other(s), my response is that the very essence of governing a political or social institution consists in looking to the common good and rising above the warfare of special interests, as Rousseau so clearly perceived in *The Social Contract* (1762).

7. Reinhold Niebuhr, *Moral Man and Immoral Society* (New York: Scribner's, 1932).

8. Erik Erickson, *Childhood and Society,* 2d ed. (New York: Norton, 1963).

9. Michael Maccoby, *The Gamesman: The New Corporate Leaders* (New York: Simon & Schuster, 1976), chap. 7.

10. My inspiration for the following few paragraphs of the text derives from my reading, ten years ago, the writings of Erik Erickson, particularly his theory of stages of character development. See, e.g., his *Childhood and Society,* 2d ed. (New York: Norton, 1963), and *Insight and Responsibility* (New York: Norton, 1964).

11. A few years ago I wrote out a series of tests or stages of development by which partners in our firm of 250 lawyers might be measured over the long-term for compensation purposes. As written, the earlier stages were foundational or prerequisite to the later stages. Together they end up describing my ideal of a top partner of a large law firm, which with a few modifications describes my ideal of a top executive of a large corporation: (1) professional competence; (2) personality and cooperation; (3) judgment; (4) productivity; (5) leadership; and (6) external representation.

12. H. Richard Niebuhr, *The Responsible Self* (New York: Harper & Row,

1963). See also James M. Gustafson and James T. Laney (eds.), *On Being Responsible* (New York: Harper & Row, 1968).

13. Erikson, *Childhood and Society.*

14. For further discussion in terms of Christian ethics, see James M. Gustafson, *Can Ethics Be Christian?* (Chicago: University of Chicago Press, 1975).

15. Published in *Moral Education,* ed. T. Sizer (Cambridge, Mass: Harvard University Press, 1970).

16. Maccoby, *The Gamesman,* p.100.

17. Cf. James M. Gustafson, *The Church As Moral Decision-Maker* (Boston: Pilgrim Press, 1970).

18. Cf. James M. Gustafson, *Treasure in Earthen Vessels: The Church as a Human Community* (Chicago: University of Chicago Press, 1976); also *Christ and the Moral Life* (Chicago: University of Chicago Press, 1976).

19. Cf. Reinhold Niebuhr, *The Nature and Destiny of Man,* 2 vols. (New York: Scribner's, 1964).

20. See, for example, John S. Dunne, *Time and Myth* (Notre Dame, Ind.: University of Notre Dame Press, 1973); David B. Burrell, C.S.C., and Stanley Hauerwas, "Self-Deception and Autobiography: Theological and Ethical Reflections on Spear's *Inside the Third Reich," Journal of Religious Ethics,* 2, no. 1 (1974), pp. 99–117; Stanley Hauerwas with Richard Bondi and David B. Burrell, C.S.C., *Truthfulness and Tragedy* (Notre Dame, Ind.: University of Notre Dame Press, 1977); Enda McDonagh, *Doing the Truth* (Notre Dame, Ind.: University of Notre Dame Press, 1979); and Oliver F. Williams, C.S.C., and John W. Houck, *Full Value: Cases in Christian Business Ethics* (San Francisco: Harper & Row, 1978).

21. Reinhold Niebuhr, *Moral Man.*

22. Alexander Solzhenitsyn, "A World Split Apart: The World Demands from Us a Spiritual Blaze," *Vital Speeches of the Day,* September 1, 1978, p. 678.

23. Senator Metzenbaum's Judiciary Subcommittee on Shareholder Rights held public hearings on corporate governance in 1977, leading to the senator's introduction, in April 1980, of a bill to require large corporations to have a majority of outside directors, to have independent audit and nominating committees, to have cumulative voting, and to be subject to other requirements. See S. 2567, 96th Cong., 2d. Sess. 126 Cong. Rec. 3751 (April 16, 1980). Ralph Nader has proposed similar federal requirements rather than leaving such matters to state law and the judgment of corporate leaders. See R. Nader, Introduction in *The Big Business Reader: Essays on Corporate America,* ed. Mark Green and Robert Massie, Jr. (New York: Pilgrim Press, 1980), and Jules Bernstein, *et al.*, "Conceptual Draft of Corporate Democracy Act" in *ibid.*, pp. 592–606.

24. See generally Elmer W. Johnson and Robert S. Osborne, "The Role of the Business Judgment Rule in a Litigious Society," *Val. U. L. Rev.,* 15 (Fall 1980); Comment, "The Business Judgment Rule: A Guide to Corporate Directors' Liability," *St. Louis U.L.J.,* 7 (1962): 151; Lewis, "The Business

Judgment Rule and Corporate Directors' Liability for Mismanagement,"
Baylor L. Rev., 22 (1970): 157; Arsht, "The Business Judgment Rule Revisited,"
Hofstra L. Rev., 8 (1980): 93. The role which I envision for independent
directors has close parallels with the function of administrative agencies of
government. Indeed, the judicial rhetoric for review of administrative decisions resembles the language employed with respect to the business-judgment
rule: administrative agencies are "presumably equipped or informed by experience to deal with a specialized field of knowledge," their "findings within
that field carry the authority of an expertise which courts do not possess and
therefore must respect." *Universal Camera Corp.* v. *NLRB,* 340 U.S. 474, 488
(1951). See *Securities and Exchange Commission* v. *Chenery* 318 U.S. 80, 88, 94
(1943). See generally Stewart, "The Reformation of American Administrative
Law," *Harv. L. Rev.,* 88 (1975): 1669.

25. Chairman Harold Williams of the SEC recently stated: "An effective
board of directors remains the institution best suited to weigh the oft-
conflicting factors that may influence a corporate response to such a situation."
Chairman Williams also emphasized the "special responsibilities for competence and objectivity" that the board faces in the takeover context and suggested that access to the business-judgment rule for decisions to oppose an
offer should be conditioned on satisfaction of these responsibilities. "Tender
Offers and the Corporate Director," Address by Chairman Williams, Current
Fed. Sec. L. Rep. (CCH) 82, 445, at 82,880 (Jan. 17, 1980). In *Panter* v. *Marshall
Field & Co.,* Current Fed. Sec. L. Rep. (CCH) 97,299, at 97,061 (N.D. Ill. 1980),
the Court upheld the business judgment of Marshall Field's board of directors
in rejecting a takeover proposal with these words: "Corporations in the kind of
business as important as that in which Marshall Field was engaged plan to exist
as on-going commercial or merchandising entities. Plaintiffs appear to believe
that large companies like Fields are developed for takeovers . . . Plaintiffs are
mistaken. . . ."

26. To those not sharing my normative concerns but who have a practical
interest in the survival of capitalism, I submit that my suggestions for new kinds
of institutional arrangements, if implemented, might just lead to a partial
restoration of the former flexibility and adaptability of our economic system. If
so, we could defy at least for a time, Schumpeter's gloomy response to the
question, "Can Capitalism Survive?" See T. Scitovsky, "Can Capitalism
Survive? — An Old Question in a New Setting," *Amer. Econ. Rev.,* 70 (1980): 1. As
the author correctly points out, Schumpeter's pessimism was based primarily on
sociological considerations. For Scitovsky the major threat to capitalism today
consists in the new rigidities arising out of society's preoccupation with social
legislation and the "liberals' excessive faith in capitalism and its ability to fly,
however much its wings are clipped." He offers the slim hope that a partial way
out may lie in recovering some of capitalism's lost flexibility through deregula-
tion and constitutional budget constraints.

12. Corporate Decision-Making and the Public Interest

Kirk O. Hanson*

The social and ethical performance of large American corporations is today of great interest to social activists, government officials, an increasingly larger percentage of the general public, and corporate executives themselves. Much is at stake: despite the election of Ronald Reagan and a new emphasis on "reasonable business regulation," corporations and corporate executives are still being asked to satisfy a broad range of social and economic objectives. The pressures for better corporate social performance will not weaken, and may paradoxically grow stronger as the public relies more heavily on voluntary accountability rather than on mandatory controls.

In this environment, corporate executives and their critics are examining closely the record of each firm in fulfilling social and economic expectations. One year ago I was asked by the Atlantic Richfield Company to examine their record of social concern and to write a critique for a "public-interest report" they planned to publish. ARCO is among a growing number of companies publishing such a social-performance report; the 1980 report is their third. Companies which publish such reports generally believe that examining their own performance aids the internal management of social-performance issues. The publication of a report available to the public is usually also designed to create an image of openness, candor, and responsibility, an asset in today's environment. ARCO's report, called *Participation III*, is unique in its inclusion of an outsider's critique.

In seeking to prepare a balanced and accurate assessment for Atlantic Richfield, I had to address several key questions about how corporations should manage their ethical and social performance. I want to share these questions and my tentative answers.

*An earlier version of this article was presented at the conference on Value Issues in Business, Millsaps College, Jackson, Mississippi.

Decision-Making Today

First, what role do "public-interest concerns" actually have in business decision-making today? What constraints are executives under today to make decisions that are sensitive to social and public impacts, to some definition of ethics or of the public interest?

It is clear that every business decision today is made within a web of influences which represent or try to represent the public interest. The most important influence is obviously the workings of the competitive market system. Relying on the expression of personal or consumer preference in the marketplace, the enterprise system allocates resources according to competitive forces, and reins in those business executives who try to flaunt its discipline. We have also supplemented that market system with a network of laws which seek to constrain or encourage corporate behavior in ways deemed important: state chartering laws and Security and Exchange Commission requirements protect the integrity of equity markets and the interests of investors; tax law and its incentives encourage some corporate decisions and discourage others (capital investment and employment incentives, for example, are based on our belief that these are in the public interest); federal, state, and even local regulatory laws address dozens of other public-interest objectives—from affirmative action to environmental control to occupational health to consumer protection. The conscientious businessperson spends a considerable amount of time simply keeping up with the public-interest constraints already in place.

I think we can point out even a few more pressures which influence business decisions today. In our system of free communication of ideas, it is not just formal law which influences business decisions, but also the informal pressures of public opinion, media scrutiny, and interest-group pressure. Business decisions are influenced by consumer and environmental-group advocacy, by public opinion about warranties or hunting lodges for entertaining politicians, and certainly by press scrutiny and the fear of disclosure. Business decisions are also often influenced by pressure from other executives. Business people may be pressured to take part in civic programs or contribute to charitable activities; businesses may also be pressured *not* to launch a major affirmative-action effort or support a politician in a way that might set a precedent for other area businesses.

Finally, I think business decisions are strongly influenced by the values and ethics of the decision-makers themselves. I believe it is impossible for personal values not to influence decisions. Each of us is more or less sympathetic to the demands of blacks seeking advancement in employment; more or less sympathetic to the desires of women (and men!) who want restructured work patterns so that they can handle both work and family responsibilities. Executives oftentimes value clean air as much as the environmental activist who comes to call on them. Executives have beliefs about the extent to which these concerns can and should be traded off against the profits of their business. Values and ethics cannot help but influence business decisions.

This brief review of the existing public-interest or ethical influences on business decision-making is a bit distressing. Executives typically find it easier to say that they follow the dictates of economics, that they simply try to make a profit. Yet it is clear from even a brief look that there are many influences — external and internal — that make that statement too simplistic.

Whose Values?

Second, if ethics or social values have a role in influencing corporate decisions, whose values should be considered and how much of an influence should they have?

I think this question has several answers. We are a representative democracy in America; through our legislative processes we establish the economic as well as the political system. We give various institutions, including business, roles to play in achieving our national objectives. Acting through our government, we have the power and right to assign any role we wish to business. A kind of social contract exists between the society and business, granting business decision-makers certain prerogatives and constraining them in certain ways. The contract is not unchanging, as we have seen in recent years. We may individually disagree with the role or prerogatives assigned to business at any point. It is our right as citizens to take part in the public-policy debate which produces that social contract. But it is also our duty as citizens to obey the laws and regulations which are in effect.

I argued earlier that it was inevitable that personal values and ethics influence business decisions. I now want to argue that this is not only inevitable but desirable. Laws have their costs and their limitations; we have witnessed some of the costs of the recent regulatory expansion. If we try to write a rule or regulation for every type of public-interest action we want from business, we risk stifling innovation, slowing productivity, and burying businesspeople under more paperwork than they can handle. What is the alternative? I would argue that we must rely on the responsible behavior and self-policing of the business community, on good corporate decision-making that is sensitive to the public interest and to ethical considerations.

Okay, you say, but what is the public interest and whose ethics are we talking about? Certainly President Reagan and Senator Kennedy have different views on what the public interest is. And there are individuals we have met in business or academic life whose ethics and values we abhor. Nonetheless, I would argue that we have no other alternative but to rely to a great extent on the ethical perspectives and values of business people. I would quickly add that business people must inform their own values with a great sensitivity to the ethical perspectives of others.

Whose values should a business executive use in making difficult business decisions? I would argue that there are three sources the executive ought to consult. His or her own values obviously are *central*. The executive who has not thought through for himself or herself some of the difficult trade-offs involved in managing a business is simply not a good executive. Second, because one's own perceptions are not infallible, any trade-off situation must be aired with one's colleagues. The dilemma must be discussed openly, gaining the perspectives which others in one's own organization can provide. Finally, we can get myopic in our own businesses about values and ethics. I remember doing consulting at a major bank where the top twelve executives had offices on one floor, arrayed around a central waiting room; the executives had coffee together at 10:15 promptly, went to lunch together in small groups to the company dining room, and frequently socialized together. I sat listening to the discussion over morning coffee, when events, people, and public-interest concerns were described in ways very different from the way in which I perceived them. The executives reinforced each others' views and went home satisfied that everyone believed as they did. At minimum, the responsible executive needs to consider outside perspectives on difficult decisions. That means sitting down face-to-face with community leaders concerned about mortgage-loan policies, consulting directly with black leaders trying to create minority job opportunities or economic-development opportunities. Nothing can substitute for that direct contact, for an executive's exposure to ethical perspectives from outside the organization.

How To Make Ethical Decisions

Third, how does a firm make decisions which are sensitive to ethics and the public interest? What are the practical day-to-day problems in making good decisions?

I want to make several practical suggestions. The *first* step is to understand what an ethical concern is, to know where ethical problems and considerations arise. I believe the best definition of an ethical concern is simply concern for how a business decision will affect some segment of a firm's public. Those influenced by a company's decisions include stockholders, employees, customers, suppliers, neighborhood residents, potential employees, and others who would like to do business with the company, other businesses, and the public at large. A decision to lay off 10 percent of a company's work force in a recession, for example, has strong ethical considerations. Why not cut everyone's salary 10 percent rather than lay off 10 percent? That might soften the impact on those who would have been laid off—the business manager has to weigh against that the impact on the 90 percent, the likelihood that the company can ever achieve full employment again, and the impact that the salary cut might have on the shareholders if it caused an exodus of the company's best employees. It is these trade offs between impacts on various constituencies which are the concern of ethics. These are the difficult decisions for which managers get paid so much.

If a supplier is substantially dependent for its livelihood on its business with your firm, what kind of advanced notice and assistance do you owe that supplier if you decide to terminate its contract? Ethics is concerned with how the firm treats its various constituencies; ethical norms are standards of fair treatment between the firm and its constituents. Does a firm owe its community certain types of charitable contributions, assistance in major civic initiatives, assistance in lobbying the state and federal government for needed aid? If a company opens a new plant in a rural area, does it owe that community some assistance in planning for local growth or financing new housing? If a company believes in equal employment, does that also mean the company should refrain from funding memberships for its executives in luncheon clubs and country clubs that have no black, Jewish, or female members? If it believes in equal employment, does that mean it owes women employees flexible work arrangements so that they can balance work and home responsibilities? These are all ethical questions which arise daily in executives' lives.

A distinguished corporate executive who has served also in government visited Stanford Business School and was asked what the similarities were between his top management experience in business and government. In both jobs, he reported, he was called on continually to make difficult trade offs between two or more stakeholders, or between a petitioner and a proper concept of the public interest. "I've concluded," he said, "that the manager is best described as a practicing ethicist."

A *second* step in making better decisions is to recognize that such decisions are not easy (as if executives need to be reminded of that!). Analysis of the broader impacts of potential decisions is every bit as important as financial analysis; the impact of a business decision on various constituents is not always easy to discern. We need to assign staff to study the ethical aspects of decisions and to study them ourselves, just as we study the financial implications or risks involved in a decision. I am convinced that most "unethical business practice" is due to bad analysis, not to malevolence. More typically, the executive didn't do his or her homework.

A *third* step is to consult with others in your organization and with those who are affected by a decision. This is difficult, embarrassing, often disruptive—but absolutely essential. A *New Yorker* cartoon portrayed an executive, about to stand up before the annual meeting for questions, saying to the assistant sitting next to him: "This is the part of capitalism I hate."

How To Implement Ethical Decisions

Fourth, how do you implement ethical decisions in an organization as large and complex as the typical modern American corporation?

All of the foregoing suggestions are reasonable for the individual decision an executive has to make. But companies make hundreds of such decisions every day. How do you so manage a company that all your managers, every day, will make good, consistent, and ethical decisions? The rest of my presentation focuses on nine aspects of a management system for improving the decisions companies make and for implementing decisions once they are made. It is this set of management techniques that should be followed by any company serious about its social and public-interest performance. It is these nine aspects I looked for when I audited the Atlantic Richfield Company.

The first and most important aspect is clearly *executive leadership*. American corporations are hierarchies. Policies get set at the top. No one in the company will consider ethical considerations important unless the top man or woman does. The following questions highlight steps the top executive should take. Does the chief executive talk deliberately about the need to consider the impact of business decisions on the firm's publics? Does the chief executive ask specific questions about such impacts when business decisions come before the management committee and the board? Does a chief executive ask the plant manager how community relations or the safety program are doing when he or she comes on an annual visit? Does the chief executive ask other senior executives about their attention to ethical concerns—to worker safety, to consumer affairs—when they are being reviewed for annual increases, bonuses, or promotions? Do promotions indicate to the organization that sensitivity to ethical concerns makes a difference?

Does the chief executive's personal life indicate his commitment to public-interest concerns—does he belong to an all-white country club; does he have business lunches in a club where women have to enter by the side door; does he know community leaders on a personal basis and work with them on important civic problems? Has the chief executive articulated his ethical and social concerns in an over-all statement of corporate philosophy that can become the basis for decision-making in the firm? Is that philosophy a part of the over-all strategy of the firm, of the firm's understanding of its total identity?

The second step in a management program is what can be called *environmental scanning*. Does the company really understand its own business and the ways in which its operations affect its many constituents? Does the company understand changing social and political pressures on the company? If you asked the management what types of performance, besides profitability and growth, society wants from the business, would they have an answer? Do they have some idea about the next laws that may be passed by the state legislature or Congress concerning their business? These give signals about public expectations of the firm. Do they have some idea about what the *next* issue is that community groups may bring to the company?

The third step is the integration of the corporate philosophy and the information gathered through environmental scanning into the company's ongoing *strategic planning process*. The vast growth of strategic planning in recent years has unfortunately encouraged a greater reliance on financial and mathematical models, and a neglect of the less quantifiable developments which may have a strong impact on the future of the company. Does the company know now how public-interest concerns and regulation affect its cost structure, its production processes, its product design, its distribution and retailing practices? What impact, for example, will toxic-substances control have on the firm? If public opinion or specific regulations changed, in what ways might the firm be vulnerable? Does management know? Does management have ideas about how to help address youth unemployment, urban blight, or the psychological or alcoholic problems of workers in ways that would cost the company little—or even pay a dividend?

The fourth step is *policy making and goal setting.* General exhortations from top executives to be ethical or to be sensitive to the public interest don't mean much. Only when those general concerns are embodied in specific policies, and further, in specific goals for each operating manager, will they get any serious attention. Adopting an affirmative-action policy helps, but only when each division has a numerical goal do things begin to happen. In what areas does the company have formal policies? And in what areas are there specific goals adopted annually, for the company and for each operating division?

The fifth step is fixing the *ultimate responsibility* for implementing social or public-interest concerns *with the operating structure* of the company and not with the staff side. Staff can provide important assistance to the line, but in the end, it is the operating manager who makes those difficult decisions where the interests of various constituencies get traded off. ("Yes, we have an affirmative-action program," says one executive, "and we hired an affirmative-action manager.") I always tend to become skeptical when the first thing an executive points to is his staff person in charge of pollution control, community affairs, or affirmative action.

The sixth step is the adoption of a *performance evaluation system* to reward managers who have met specific division-by-division goals with distinction. This is the second most important element in the management system I am describing. Executive leadership was the most important. If you don't reward and punish managers on their ability to address these public-interest concerns, on their ability to make good decisions trading off the interests of the firm's constituencies, then you give an unmistakable signal that these concerns take a back seat to the real business of the firm—profits and growth. Designing management evaluation systems which do this effectively is a very difficult job. It may be possible to measure occupational health and safety efforts by tracking injury rates, consumer satisfaction by tracking complaint letters, affirmative action by counting minority and female hires and promotions, but it is harder to evaluate community involvement, concern for employees' personal interests, and responsible dealings with suppliers.

The seventh step is the development of *innovative audit techniques* to provide executives with information as to how individual managers are performing and how the company as a whole is attending to public-interest concerns. Traditional reporting and audit systems may be useful in quantifiable areas like affirmative action, but not very useful in others. One of the most innovative techniques I have seen was in use at ARCO. In two areas, pollution control and occupational health/safety, ARCO has created special Audit Teams composed of line managers from various operating divisions. A team of about ten persons will spend a week at an ARCO facility examining in depth how pollution control or occupational safety is managed. A detailed audit manual has been developed which guides the team through a lengthy set of interviews and inspections. The written report is submitted to the facility manager and to the division executive, and the facility manager must make a written response in three weeks. Results have been excellent; audit team members, detailed to this task for a short time, learn a tremendous amount themselves about how to manage these concerns; and facility managers get good outside feedback on how to improve their operations. The teams create a heightened awareness throughout the company of the importance of pollution control and worker safety. Although other audit techniques can accomplish the same ends, this one is particularly valuable.

The eighth step is the development of good *support staff groups* in critical areas. Having belittled the staff groups earlier, I now want to give them their due. Though the primary responsibility for implementation must rest with the line organization, the help a staff group can give to the line is critical. Staff can conduct the environmental scanning; staff can serve as in-house consultants to help line managers improve their management of the social and ethical aspects of their business; staff can provide nonthreatening advice in times of crisis; staff can do ongoing research on the best ways to balance the many demands on the firm and the best management techniques for achieving company goals in public-interest areas.

The ninth and final step in the management system is a *top-level monitoring group* to track the company's public-interest or ethical performance. In most firms, the chief executive cannot hope to give adequate ongoing attention to how the company is managing these issues. In most companies I have studied, one of two techniques is used. Either a committee of top managers is appointed to oversee the complex task of balancing economic and public-interest concerns, or a special public-interest committee of the board of directors is given the same task. Such a group serves as a brainstorming committee to recommend new areas in which the company needs a policy or should initiate some programs. Such a committee also hears regular annual reports on company performance in selected areas—pollution, employment opportunity, safety, consumer complaints, marketing practices; or annual reports from each operating division on the range of public-interest concerns being managed. Such committees often sponsor or encourage the publication of an annual report such as ARCO's *Participation* or General Motors' equivalent, called the *Public Interest Report*.

Conclusion

We have discussed a rather detailed management system for addressing ethical or public-interest concerns. Why? Can't we rely on the ethical instincts of the managers we have hired? I would argue no. Every manager is influenced by complex pressures in the firm—its culture, the values expressed by the top executives, peer pressure. We have to get these influences running in one direction. And ethical issues are complex. They demand good analysis and careful decision-making. Our offhand instincts are often likely to be wrong. Finally, we are struggling with a widespread and traditional business ideology that leads many managers to assume that only short-run profitability can legitimately be considered in making business decisions. That is the surest prescription I can imagine for an ever-increasing regulatory burden and continued low repute for business in American life.

Atlantic Richfield has compiled an exceptional social-performance record, which can be attributed primarily to the enlightened and aggressive leadership of its chairman and its president. ARCO has been less effective in creating the implementation structure for continuing its good performance. As the current leadership departs from the company, ARCO's good performance will be subjected to considerable stress. Future leadership, no matter how enlightened and committed, will not have the influence wielded by the current leaders who built the company. Like most large American companies, Atlantic Richfield is entering a critical period in which the organizational structure or good corporate social performance must be strengthened. The challenge facing Atlantic Richfield is the challenge facing most large American companies. Enlightened corporate management can better satisfy both the economic and social expectations of American business and the same sensitivities which lead to good corporate social performance and usually result in improved productivity and profitability.

SELECTED BIBLIOGRAPHY ON MANAGEMENT AND ETHICS

Books

Beauchamp, Tom L., and Norman E. Bowie. *Ethical Theory and Business.* Englewood Cliffs, N.J.: Prentice-Hall, 1979. A collection of readings plus interpretive text and a few short cases.

Cavanagh, Gerald F. *American Business Values in Transition.* Englewood Cliffs, N.J.: Prentice-Hall, 1976. An excellent introduction to the values which have defined our business society and influenced life in our large corporate institutions. A new edition is due in 1982.

DeGeorge, Richard. *Business Ethics.* New York: Macmillan, 1981. A comprehensive and thoughtful analysis of the subject of business ethics. DeGeorge is a philosopher with an appreciation for management problems.

Donaldson, Thomas, and Patricia H. Werhane. *Ethical Issues in Business: A Philosophical Approach.* Englewood Cliffs, N.J.: Prentice-Hall, 1979. The second selection of readings which Prentice-Hall published in 1979 (see Beauchamp above). The readings are generally philosophical.

Silk, Leonard, and David Vogel. *Ethics and Profits: The Crisis of Confidence in American Business.* New York: Simon and Schuster, 1976. A very thoughtful analysis of the values of business leaders as reflected in their discussions at meetings of the Conference Board.

Steckmest, Francis, *et al. Corporate Performance: The Key to Public Trust.* New York: McGraw-Hill, 1982. This volume, by a working group of the Business Roundtable, presents the dimensions of corporate performance which have been of greatest concern to the public policy process and highlights ethical and responsive actions by selected corporations. Particularly useful.

Stone, Christopher D. *Where the Law Ends: The Social Control of Corporate Behavior.* New York: Harper & Row, 1975. A strong case for regulatory or voluntary measures to reform corporate organization and decision-making processes to improve ethical behavior.

Velasquez, Manuel. *Business Ethics: Concepts and Cases.* Englewood Cliffs, N.J.: Prentice-Hall, 1981. Velasquez, a philosopher with an M.B.A., has written the best blend of philosophical and managerial approaches to business ethics. The cases presented are very useful.

Williams, Oliver F., and John W. Houck. *Full Value: Cases in Christian Business Ethics.* New York: Harper & Row, 1978. An extensive treatment of business ethics from an explicitly religious perspective. Well-developed cases.

Wright, J. Patrick. *On a Clear Day You Can See General Motors.* Grosse Pointe, Mich.: Wright Enterprises, 1979. This book, which purports to be GM executive John DeLorean's look inside the automotive giant, is a fascinating study of internal corporate decision-making and how DeLorean believes moral man can make immoral decisions.

Articles

Andrews, Kenneth R. "Can the Best Corporations Be Made Moral?" *Harvard Business Review,* May–June 1973, pp. 57–64. Argues that only by careful structuring of corporate organization and incentives can corporations act ethically.

Business Week. "Corporate Culture: The Hard to Change Values That Spell Success or Failure," October 27, 1980, pp. 148–59. A thoughtful analysis of the importance of corporate culture and values to corporate operations.

Carr, Albert Z. "Is Bluffing Ethical?" *Harvard Business Review,* January-February 1968, pp. 143-50. A stimulating article that argues that anything goes in business.

Fendrock, John J. "Crisis in Conscious at Quasar," *Harvard Business Review,* March-April, 1968, pp. 112–20. A provocative case study of unethical action in a corporate bureaucracy.

Hanson, Kirk O. "Strategic Planning and Social Performance." In *Business and Society: Strategies for the '80's.* U.S. Department of Commerce, 1980. Presents suggestions for integrating social and ethical considerations into strategic planning.

Ross, Irwin. "How Lawless Are Big Companies?" *Fortune,* December 1, 1980, pp. 57–63. The best compilation of illegal corporate activity since 1970.

Waterman, Robert H., Jr., Thomas J. Peters, and Julien R. Phillips. "Structure Is Not Organization," *Business Horizons,* June 1980. Three McKinsey consultants present a way to analyze organizations that includes a look at corporate values and superordinate goals.

Corporate Codes of Conduct

Several hundred corporations have adopted codes of conduct during the past decade. Some codes are lengthy and cover detailed questions of corporate behavior; others are one page long and establish only general principles. Some cover the full range of corporate operations; others focus on one specific aspect, such as marketing infant formula in the developing world. The two codes I have found most representative and useful for study are those published by Bank of America and Caterpillar Tractor.

   1. BankAmerica Corporation. "BankAmerica Corporation Code of Corporate Conduct," San Francisco, May 1980.

   2. Caterpillar Tractor Company. "A Code of Worldwise Business Conduct," Peoria, Ill., September 1977.

Corporate Social Performance Reports

Approximately 100 corporations publish annual or biennial reports on their social performance. Some are public relations documents; others report candidly on successes and failures in affirmative action, environmental control, employee rights issues, community affairs, and corporate ethics. The two most complete reports are published by Atlantic Richfield Company and General Motors. The Atlantic Richfield Report includes the critique referred to in the preceding article.

1. Atlantic Richfield Company. *Participation III,* Los Angeles, 1980.
2. General Motors. *1981 Public Interest Report,* Detroit, 1981.

Contributors

JOHN C. BENNETT is presently at the Claremont School of Theology. He earned his degrees at Williams College, Oxford University, and Union Theological Seminary. He has taught at a number of theological schools and has served as dean of the faculty and later president of Union Theological Seminary, New York. He was president of the American Theological Society and co-editor of the journal *Christianity and Crisis*. He has published extensively in the field of religious social ethics, including the following volumes: *Social Salvation; Christian Realism; Christian Ethics and Social Policy; Christians and the State; Foreign Policy in Christian Perspective;* and *The Radical Imperative*.

CATHERINE B. CLEARY is the former president and chairperson of the board of directors of the First Wisconsin Trust Company, Milwaukee. She is a graduate of the University of Chicago and received her law degree from the University of Wisconsin. She has been consultant to several public and private organizations, and is currently a director of American Telephone and Telegraph Corporation, General Motors, Kraft, Inc., and Northwestern Mutual Life Insurance. She is a frequent lecturer at institutions of higher learning.

DENIS GOULET holds the William and Dorothy O'Neill chair in Education for Justice at the University of Notre Dame. He did his undergraduate and graduate studies at the Catholic University of America and received his doctorate in political science from the University of Sao Paulo, Brazil. He has worked as a factory hand in France and Spain and shared the life of two nomadic tribes in Algeria. He has filled visiting professorships at universities in France, Canada, and the United States, and has been engaged in worldwide research on value conflict in technology transfer at the Overseas Development Council, Washington, D.C. Besides articles, reviews, and monographs, he has published: *A New Moral*

Order: Development Ethics and Liberation Theology; The Cruel Choice: A New Concept in the Theory of Development; and *The Uncertain Promise: Value Conflicts in Technology Transfer.*

JAMES M. GUSTAFSON is University Professor in Theological Ethics, University of Chicago. He received his undergraduate degree from Northwestern University, his divinity degree from the University of Chicago, and his Ph.D. from Yale University. He was chairperson and professor in the department of religious studies at Yale University, twice a Guggenheim Fellow, and president of the American Society of Christian Ethics. In addition to numerous articles, monographs, and volumes, he has published: *Treasures in Earthen Vessels; The Church as Human Community; Theology and Christian Ethics; Protestant and Roman Catholic Ethics; The Church as Moral Decision-Maker; Christian Ethics and the Community; Christ and the Moral Life;* and *Can Ethics Be Christian?*

KIRK O. HANSON is a lecturer in business-government relations and management ethics at the Graduate School of Business, Stanford University. After receiving his A.B. degree in political science and M.B.A. from Stanford University, he took further studies at the Harvard Business School. He was a Rockefeller Fellow at the Yale Divinity School and was founder and president, for three years, of the National Affiliation of Concerned Business Students. He is consultant on political and social issues to major industrial and consumer goods organizations, including Atlantic Richfield Corporation and the Business Roundtable. Kirk Hanson has written several articles on corporate social and political management and is co-author of *Corporate Performance and Public Policy.*

JOHN W. HOUCK is professor of management at the University of Notre Dame. A former Ford and Danforth Fellow, he earned both a liberal arts and a J.D. degree from Notre Dame, an M.B.A. from the University of North Carolina at Chapel Hill, and a master of laws from Harvard. He has lectured and conducted workshops on the role of religious and humane values in business. In addition to articles and reviews, he has published: *Academic Freedom and the Catholic University; Outdoor Advertising: History and Regulation; A Matter of Dignity: Inquiries into the Humanization of Work;* and with Oliver F. Williams, C.S.C., *Full Value: Cases in Christian Business Ethics.*

KENNETH P. JAMESON is an associate professor of economics, University of Notre Dame, with a special interest in economic development theory and political economy. He earned his undergraduate degree at Stanford University and his doctorate at the University of Wisconsin. He has traveled extensively in Latin America while doing research. He has published two volumes: *U.S. Trade in the Sixties and Seventies: Continuity and Change,* and *Directions in Economic Development.*

ELMER W. JOHNSON is a partner in the Kirkland and Ellis law firm in Chicago. His undergraduate degree is from Yale University and his law degree from the University of Chicago. He specializes in the areas of banking, corporation, and securities law and was a lecturer in these subjects at the Law School, University of Chicago. In addition he has been a guest professor at Colorado College, a lecturer at Yale University, and in both the Divinity and Business Schools, University of Chicago. He has been a consultant to major multinational corporations in regard to their codes of conduct. He is a member of the executive committee, board of trustees, University of Chicago.

BURTON M. LEISER is professor of philosophy, with special interests in legal and social philosophy and ethics, at Drake University, where he has been chairperson of the department. He received his undergraduate degree from the University of Chicago, did graduate work at Yeshiva University, and received his Ph.D. from Brown University. His publications include: *Custom, Law, and Morality: Conflict and Continuity in Social Behavior* and *Liberty, Justice and Morals: Contemporary Value Conflicts.*

MICHAEL NOVAK is resident scholar at the American Enterprise Institute, Washington, D.C. He has received degrees from Stonehill College, the Gregorian, and Harvard University. He has been an advisor in national political campaigns and represented the United States at international conferences. Among his many books are: *A Theology for Radical Politics; Ascent of the Mountain, Flight of the Dove; Belief and Unbelief; The Experience of Nothingness; The Rise of the Unmeltable Ethnics; The Guns of Lattimer;* and *Toward a Theology of the Corporation.*

FATHER JAMES V. SCHALL is a member of the Society of Jesus and a professor of government at Georgetown University. He received his undergraduate degree from Gonzaga University, did graduate work at the University of Santa Clara, and received his Ph.D. from Georgetown University. He is a lecturer at the Gregorian, Rome. He is a frequent contributor to journals, and his books include: *American Society and Politics: Current Trends in Theology; Redeeming the Times; Human Dignity and Human Numbers;* and *The Praise of 'Sons of Bitches': On the Worship of God by Fallen Man.*

WILLIAM P. SEXTON is chairperson and associate professor of management at the University of Notre Dame. He did undergraduate and graduate work at Ohio State University, receiving an M.B.A. and a Ph.D. in administrative management. He has engaged in extensive consulting work, drawing on his industrial experience in personnel, labor relations, and manufacturing management, and has conducted seminars in leadership, group dynamics, and organizational development for both profit and not-for-profit firms. His publications include numerous articles and a book, *Organizational Theories.*

CHRISTOPHER D. STONE is Roy P. Crocker Professor of Law at the University of Southern California. He did his undergraduate work at Harvard University, received his law degree from Yale University, and was a fellow in law and economics at the University of Chicago. Besides articles in legal journals, he has published: *Law, Language, and Ethics; Should Trees Have Standing? Toward Legal Rights for Natural Objects;* and *Where the Law Ends: The Social Control of Corporate Behavior.*

EDWARD R. TRUBAC is chairperson and associate professor in the department of finance and business economics at the University of Notre Dame. After graduation from Manhattan College, he received his Ph.D. from Syracuse University. He has been director of the Master of Science in Administration program at Notre Dame, which focuses on the not-for-profit organizations and their management problems. Besides publishing in his field, he is consultant for financial forecasting and planning to U.S. and Canadian firms.

CHARLES K. WILBER is chairperson and professor of economics at the University of Notre Dame. After both undergraduate and graduate work at the University of Portland, he received his

Ph.D. from the University of Maryland. He has been a consultant about the humanities and economic analysis to various organizations. His publications in the field of political economy and development economics include the volumes: *The Soviet Model and Underdeveloped Countries; The Political Economy of Development and Underdevelopment;* and *Directions in Economic Development.*

FATHER OLIVER F. WILLIAMS is adjunct associate professor of management, University of Notre Dame, and a member of the Congregation of Holy Cross (C.S.C.). After undergraduate work in engineering and graduate studies in divinity at Notre Dame, he received his Ph.D. in theology from Vanderbilt University. He has been president of the Association for Professional Education for Ministry, director of the Master of Divinity program at Notre Dame, and research fellow at the Graduate School of Business Administration, Stanford University. He is a fellow of the Society for Values in Higher Education and of the Case Study Institute. In addition to articles and reviews, he coauthored with John W. Houck the volume, *Full Value: Cases in Christian Business Ethics.*

Index